The Good Common School

Good Common School Project Director

Richard Gray, Jr.

Report Authors

Joan First
John B. Kellogg
Cheryl A. Almeida
Richard Gray, Jr.

Special Thanks

Terry Heide
Nitza Hidalgo
Judy Carr Johnson
Lucia Gill
Noe Medina
John Willshire Carerra

NCAS Staff

Cynthia Coburn
Devon Davidson
Joan First
Armando Gaitan
Richard Gray, Jr.
Astrid Hiemer
Judy Carr Johnson
Vivian Wai-Fun Lee
Jan Peterson

Thanks for Assistance on Special Projects

J.B. Kellogg and Associates

Stan Kaplan
PCs at Your Command

Report Design

Mia Saunders

Production/Typesetting

Mia Saunders
Edda V. Sigurdardottir

Photo Credits

Cover, Title Page:
Kingmond Young
Chapter 1:
Designs for Change
Chapters 2, 3, 5:
David Grossman
Chapters 4, 6, 8:
Nita Winter
Chapter 7:
David Maung/
California Tomorrow

Printing

The Eusey Press

The Good Common School

Making the Vision Work for All Children

A Comprehensive Guide to Elementary School Restructuring from the National Coalition of Advocates for Students

Executive Co-Directors:
Joan First
Richard Gray, Jr.

October 1991

National Coalition of Advocates for Students
100 Boylston Street, Suite 737
Boston, MA 02116

To order, send $22.00 (price includes $4.00 shipping and handling).

The photographs contained in this report are for illustrative purposes only. There is no relationship between a particular child and the text. Although efforts have been made to use real-life situations in schools, all characters in the narrative section of each chapter are fictional.

The opinions expressed in this report are those of NCAS and do not necessarily reflect the views of funding sources. The authors assume full responsibility for any inaccuracies or errors that appear in the following pages.

Library of Congress Number: 91-062630

ISBN: 1-880002-00-0

Foreword

As individuals who shared the struggles that came with chairing the National Coalition of Advocates for Students during the period when this report was being prepared, it is a particular pleasure for us to describe the history of its development.

The National Coalition of Advocates for Students (NCAS) is a nationwide network of child advocacy organizations that work to improve access to quality public education for children of greatest need.

During the 1980s, NCAS completed two national projects. The first examined the status of at-risk students in U.S. public schools, reporting its findings in *Barriers to Excellence: Our Children at Risk.* The second was the first comprehensive national study of the encounter between recently immigrated children and families and the nation's public schools. Its conclusions are contained in *New Voices: Immigrant Students in U.S. Public Schools.* Data yielded by both projects were compelling, leaving no doubt that large numbers of U.S. and foreign-born students were denied quality schooling. Many were leaving school before graduation, or staying in school but failing to learn.

The Good Common School Project, which produced this book, was conceptualized by the NCAS Board of Directors and friends from the advocacy community who gathered at a Wingspread Conference hosted by the Johnson Foundation in the summer of 1987. At that time, NCAS member organizations were engaged in piecemeal efforts to transform schools in their own communities to make them more responsive to the most vulnerable students. Some gains had been made, but conference participants agreed these were inadequate, particularly when U.S. society was becoming increasingly characterized by economic stratification, a failing safety net of social programs, growing violence, and abuse of human and civil rights.

From this discouraging assessment sprang the thesis for the Good Common School Project—at once honest and optimistic: parents, advocates, and educators can work together to fundamentally restructure schools to serve all students well. Furthermore, only comprehensive, advocacy-driven efforts that define the role of parents in bold, new ways can result in schools that support the academic success of all students.

Before leaving the Wingspread conference, advocates identified ten universal school functions that must be carried out differently at the school level to achieve this goal: governance, admitting and placing students, developing curriculum, teaching children, assessing student progress, providing student support services, maintaining positive school climate, empowering teachers, and allocating resources.

Two separate strands of work were then undertaken by NCAS. First, national staff interviewed NCAS member organizations to document advocacy strategies that had successfully produced systemic changes to improve the educational lot of large numbers of students. Second, Education Policy Research, a Boston-based consulting firm, was retained to review research literature relevant to each of these ten critical functions. These reviews served as the basis for wide-ranging, heated discussions at several meetings of the NCAS Board of Directors. These discussions served several purposes: enriching staff and board understanding of the research; creating a common body of knowledge for NCAS member organizations; and producing consensus on many complex issues.

This manuscript is the result of a broadly-based process. The ten student entitlements on which this book turns were drafted by the twenty-four NCAS board members. In a process both fruitful and exhaustive, NCAS staff and consultants prepared draft chapters, which the NCAS board tirelessly read and revised. Descriptions of successful advocacy strategies and promising school-based practices drew on experiences of NCAS member organizations and public elementary schools around the country. Additionally, in late 1989 and early 1990, NCAS and its member organizations convened fourteen focus groups, allowing more than 200 parents, students, educators, policymakers, and community activists to participate in discussions of the Good Common School draft manuscript. Their comments provided a wealth of fresh insight.

These sometimes unwieldy processes had the redeeming virtue of infusing the experiences and perspectives of community-based advocates and parents into every paragraph of the document. *No positions on school restructuring expressed in this book are taken casually.* Each is rooted in the lessons learned by advocates working in many different communities.

Including those who testified at earlier NCAS public hearings that informed the Good Common School Project and those who participated in focus groups, hundreds of people have contributed to this book. Although we cannot thank them individually, we are deeply in their debt. The contributions of a few who reviewed draft material, provided encouragement, and shared their vast knowledge of public schooling must be singled out for special appreciation:

- **Vito Perrone,** Director of Teacher Education at Harvard University, who helped the authors to shape content on teaching and learning and teacher empowerment and who suffered with good humor the experience of seeing his thoughts woven into the fictionalized vignettes that open these chapters.
- **Harold Howe II,** Senior Lecturer at the Harvard Graduate School of Education, who co-chaired NCAS's Board of Inquiry Project at the start of the school reform movement and has been a constant source of wise advice to NCAS about improving public education.
- **Carole Ouimette,** Executive Director of The Network of Progressive Educators, and other members of the North Dakota Study Group, for deepening our understanding of how developmental appropriateness, curricular relevance, and teacher skill can converge to support the school success of young children.

We are energized by the fact that so many people who have contributed to this report share our unflagging belief that public elementary schools can and must be fundamentally restructured to help ensure a better future for our children and our society.

Aurelio Montemayor
Intercultural Development
and Research Association
San Antonio, TX
NCAS Chairperson,
1987–88

Laurie Olsen
California Tomorrow
San Francisco, CA
NCAS Chairperson,
1989–90

Lola Glover
Coalition for Quality Education
Toledo, OH
NCAS Chairperson,
1991–92

Acknowledgments

A number of philanthropic organizations supported the first phase of the NCAS Good Common School Project, including preparation of this report:

- **The Johnson Foundation,** Racine, WI, hosted a gathering of NCAS representatives and other child advocates at its Wingspread Conference Center where the notion of the Good Common School was conceived.
- **The Carnegie Corporation of New York, The Ford Foundation,** and **The Rockefeller Family Fund** generously supported project research, consensus building activities, and writing.
- **The John D. and Catherine T. MacArthur Foundation** provided a critical grant enabling NCAS to bring a preliminary draft of this book before a series of focus groups organized by NCAS member groups in communities across the U.S.
- **The John D. and Catherine T. MacArthur Foundation, The Aaron Diamond Foundation, The Abby Rockefeller Charitable Trust,** and **The Theodore Spencer Charitable Trust** supported preparation of the final manuscript.
- **The Lilly Endowment** made a unique contribution to the Good Common School Project by supporting NCAS's organizational health during 1990 and 1991 with grants for institutional renewal.

Funders who supported earlier NCAS work that has informed this book include: **The Andrew W. Mellon Foundation; The Hazen Foundation; American Baptist Churches, USA; The Atlantic Richfield Foundation; The New World Foundation;** and **The Southern Education Foundation.**

How to Read This Book

If schools are to be fundamentally restructured so that all children have access to quality educational experiences, all members of the school community must participate—parents, educators, advocates, community leaders, and policymakers. Teacher training institutions and researchers also have a vital role.

With this in mind, *The Good Common School: Making the Vision Work for All Children* provides easy access to information of particular interest to different groups and individuals who support advocacy-driven school reform.

The book is organized around ten vital student entitlements discussed within its eight chapters. Each chapter opens with a fictional vignette of an imaginary elementary school on its way to becoming the Good Common School—a school with the primary goal of providing educational excellence for all of its students. Step-by-step instructions or standards for achieving advocacy-driven school reform appear in boxes following these vignettes. The second section of each chapter supports the need for fundamental change by documenting the problems found within most public elementary schools.

Following the vignettes and problem statement sections, advocacy strategies in each chapter show how advocates work to reform schools in their own communities. These are followed by descriptions of promising school-based practices successfully implemented in real elementary schools. Finally, each chapter ends with a summary of education research relating to the chapter's topics.

There are many ways to read this book. For example:

- It can be a helpful resource for elementary school teachers and administrators seeking solutions to the worry-of-the-day, ranging from how to group children more fairly for instruction to how to organize a more effective staff development program.
- Some may wish to read only the first section of each chapter. If read sequentially, these vignettes offer a comprehensive description of the struggles of a fictional school community as it undergoes transformation from a traditional elementary school to the Good Common School.
- Other readers may wish to read the second section of each chapter to contrast the vision of the Good Common School with current policies and practices in most U.S. public elementary schools.
- Those who read the entire book will learn how advocacy groups and other community-based organizations make successful, positive contributions toward improving schools. They will also learn, through case studies of promising school practices, how some elementary schools are making significant progress toward attaining the Good Common School entitlements.

- All readers who believe that schools should use what is known about how to effectively educate children will find the research appendix at the close of each chapter of special interest.

Two previous NCAS publications, *Barriers to Excellence: Our Children at Risk* and *New Voices: Immigrant Students in U.S. Public Schools,* provide important additional contexts for those interested in bringing advocacy-driven reform to their communities.

Contents

The Good Common School

The Good Common School is an urban elementary school serving approximately 600 students in grades K through 6. Its racially and ethnically mixed student body is 19 percent Latino, 17 percent Anglo, 53 percent African American, and 11 percent Asian. There is also a sprinkling of Haitian students. The school has an African American female principal. Its faculty is 76 percent Anglo, 17 percent African American, and 7 percent Latino. Efforts are underway to make the composition of the faculty more closely reflect the ethnic and cultural diversity evident in the student body.

The Good Common School is governed by a local school council with a majority of parent members. The council includes six parents, two citizens, two teachers, and the principal. It is responsible for hiring and firing the principal, developing an annual school improvement plan, and making budget decisions that support implementation of the plan.

Believing that small schools work best, the teachers have organized three separate educational units called House One, House Two, and House Three to replace the single school of 600 pupils. Because of their desire to personalize and individualize the educational process, the teachers felt small schools would ensure that children would be well known, teachers would find it easier to work together, parents would feel more comfortable, and a stronger sense of community could be established.

Each of the three houses occupies a separate part of the building and has nine regular teachers, one of whom is the Teacher Leader, who teaches half-time. The teachers plan together, sharing a common philosophical perspective. In House One, teachers have agreed upon multi-age groupings, integrated learning without tight subject matter divisions, keeping teachers with the same children for at least two years, making use of some common themes to guide instruction, consciously promoting multiculturalism, celebrating differences, and working closely with parents.

In addition, enrichment and tutorial programs operate after school and during the summer. While separate from regular instruction, these programs are integral to the school's commitment to children and their families.

Introduction

For some, it may be a radical notion that schools should assign first priority to meeting the needs of their students. Those who dare to create such a vision of schooling must make a quantum leap forward, leaving their preconceptions behind and gathering new awareness as they go. Arriving at this new awareness requires a paradigm shift, letting go of old concepts of public schooling to conceive of a new, fairer reality.

The present state of the school restructuring movement is offered as evidence that it's not easy to let go of the past. After a decade of debate, most parents, advocates, and educators agree that schools must fundamentally change. Their conclusion is strongly and consistently supported by educational research. Still, transformation remains elusive.

NCAS invites you to park your preconceptions under the nearest tree, enliven your imagination, and step into a vision of the Good Common School where parents make important decisions, every child is a respected, successful learner, and teachers smile every day.

These profound changes spring from a single, central idea. At the Good Common School every decision, large or small, is measured against a single standard: *Will it help children?*

The educational success of all students in the Good Common School is protected by ten important entitlements, each rooted in a function that all schools already perform. The attainment of each entitlement does not necessarily mean schools must do more, but rather they must perform their ordinary functions differently.

Entitlement 1: Children are entitled to have parents, advocates, and concerned educators involved in all decisions affecting their education.

This commitment to inclusiveness holds potential for producing dramatic results. Many good things happen when parents are welcomed by schools as full partners in their children's education. At the Good Common School, parents hold a majority of seats on the local school council.

Children benefit when parents work with administrators and teachers to set policies about school staffing, resource allocation, and curriculum. Central office personnel are then freed to assume systemwide coordination, monitoring and oversight, and research and evaluation roles.

The Good Common School strives to answer the questions of parents through words and action. It values each family's hopes for its children and works to see these hopes attained. It speaks to parents in many special languages they understand—the language of caring, which takes into consideration the social and economic hardships some families must endure; the language of competency, which tries many ways of teaching a child before declaring failure; and the parent's own native language, which demonstrates inclusiveness.

When parents move comfortably through a school's physical and social structures, their contributions help to close large gaps between culture, language, and life experience. Positive school climate and the success of the instructional program are strongly supported. Along with genuine parent participation comes many benefits for students—improved attendance and academic achievement and more positive expectations and attitudes toward school. Children with the greatest needs reap the richest benefits.

Entitlement 2: Children are entitled to learn in an integrated, heterogeneous setting responsive to different learning styles and abilities.

Equal educational opportunity is a basic promise of U.S. public education. The Good Common School strives to keep this promise by holding every decision about the placement of an individual student to the single standard of student benefit.

Here, administrators attach a high value to ensuring equal access for all students. At the district level, all schools participate fully in school improvement efforts—all schools are on the road to becoming quality schools, replacing the more common pattern of superior schools and magnet programs intermingled with mediocre schools.

District policy ensures that all parents share equal access to the full range of choices the school system offers. Any selective admission process is designed to result in a school population that represents the entire community. Because communication is important, all parents receive complete information about available choices in the language that is spoken in their home.

The Good Common School ensures every child full access to the same body of knowledge. Children who are "different" are not prepared for less satisfying futures. The Good Common School does not sort its students; it groups children of differing needs, abilities, and interests together for instruction. It also acknowledges that heterogeneous grouping practices create greater complexities for teachers. As a result, teachers are provided with supports such as classroom aides, appropriate books and materials, and consulting or resource teachers. Teachers with specialized responsibilities—such as gym teachers—also use mixed age and ability grouping to minimize the number of pull-out activities on the school schedule.

Entitlement 3: Children are entitled to comprehensible, culturally supportive, and developmentally appropriate curriculum and teaching strategies.

At the Good Common School, fluency in a second language is prized, whether the second language is learned before or after English. Children whose families have a second language and culture are considered fortunate because they support the school's goal of multiple literacies in language and culture for every child. Because each child comes to school fluent in one language and then begins to learn another, limited proficiency in English is not viewed as a deficit, and English-language instruction is not regarded as remediation.

Most Good Common School students receive instruction in two languages using a two-way bilingual approach. When a small number of children speaking a particular first language makes separate instruction in English necessary, these children are instructed in their first language while learning English until they can move into the monolingual English classroom without ill effects on their academic achievement.

Multiculturalism is a primary goal. Because cultural differences are highly valued, students enjoy learning about how others live. Multicultural education enriches the life of every student and provides children with a strong foundation of skills to live successfully in a global community. Students understand economic and social power imbalances that limit the opportunities of many individuals and groups and consider how these imbalances can be corrected.

Entitlement 4: Children are entitled to access to a common body of knowledge and the opportunity to acquire higher-order skills.

Every teacher at the Good Common School shares a strong belief in and commitment to the academic success of every student.

The school curriculum is both powerful and rich with meaning. It is organized around central themes and concepts, providing multiple entry points so that children of differing abilities may participate. Teacher-made materials are encouraged and valued. The curriculum is at once complex and challenging, supporting the capacity of children to think more deeply. The role of the arts in enriching the lives of children and adults is acknowledged. Children are encouraged to apply all that they learn to their daily lives.

Classrooms are highly interactive. Teachers provide opportunities for children to work together in small group settings where they can inquire into subjects that interest them deeply. Children interact freely in the classroom, rather than through a formalized structure that provides "turns" for each child. The result is richer student interaction.

Group-centered learning processes support students as they develop basic and higher-order skills, including the capacity to analyze and evaluate their own learning and to challenge themselves and others. Such groups also provide chances for children to strengthen their social skills. Children develop individual skills and learn to work collectively toward common goals. Other strategies include cross-age tutoring, and peer tutoring.

Entitlement 5: Children are entitled to a broadly-based assessment of their academic progress and grading structures that enhance individual strengths and potential.

At the Good Common School, there is a prevailing assumption that every child has special talents and strengths, along with weaknesses. Human growth is understood to be an uneven, highly individualized process. When a child lags behind peers in a certain area of instruction, time and teacher ingenuity usually hold the solution. Teachers work to identify and build on individual strengths, using them to leverage growth in other areas so that each child can reach full potential.

Parents and educators have useful information gained through a variety of assessment strategies on which to base future instruction. They know that standardized tests do not provide information on which to base future instruction. No important educational decisions about a child or the curriculum are made solely on the basis of a standardized test score. A variety of approaches are used to assess and document a child's strengths and weaknesses, including student portfolios, performance tasks, student exhibitions, structured classroom observations, and conferences with parents.

Because the Good Common School Council understands that children progress at different rates, the school's grade structure provides opportunities for flexible, multi-age grouping. Mixed-age grouping guards against tracking and encourages teachers to work with each pupil as an individual.

Children who need more time to complete work now have that time without "flunking" a grade. This is a particular boon to limited-English-proficient and recently immigrated students. Because a single incident of grade retention increases the cost of educating a student through graduation by 8 percent, this grade structure is also economical. Best of all, no child is labelled as a failure, and no child is "pushed ahead" by skipping a grade.

Entitlement 6: Children are entitled to a broad range of support services that address individual needs.

The Good Common School has a well-developed guidance and counseling program. School counselors help teachers design classroom activities that strengthen students' academic, social, personal, and career development skills. They meet individually or in small groups with students referred by parents or teachers.

Counselors are an important source of information, support, and encouragement to parents and teachers. They establish strong linkages with community service providers to connect students and their families with a variety of services not available at the school.

Care is taken to provide counseling staff that speaks every language spoken by Good Common School students and families. If a family speaking yet a different language joins the school community, counselors ask immigrant community-based organizations to provide translators so that all students are ensured access to comprehensible support services.

Entitlement 7: Children are entitled to attend schools that are safe, attractive, and free from prejudice.

The Good Common School prides itself on being an inclusive, democratic community of children and adults. It seeks to become a special kind of community, quite different from the often exclusionary ethnic and racial neighborhoods that surround it.

At the Good Common School, diversity is the norm. Being "different" does not have a price tag attached. What's fair for one is considered fair for all. The principal treats other adults and children respectfully and expects each member of the community to respect each other's human dignity. Abusive treatment of others is not tolerated; there are clear consequences if it occurs, whether perpetrated by students or staff.

Entitlement 8: Children are entitled to attend school unless they pose a danger to other children or school staff.

The principal sets the tone regarding attendance at the Good Common School. She expresses to parents and students her view that children cannot learn if they do not attend school. As disciplinarian, she sets firm limits but won't suspend a student for a trivial offense, particularly an attendance offense. When a student frequently misses school, she asks a counselor to find the reason or she calls the parents herself to find out if the school can help.

The principal is committed to the preservation of a safe school environment. The discipline code, developed by a committee with broad community representation, spells out offenses in behavioral terms and relates specific offenses to specific consequences. The severity of punishment is appropriate to the severity of the student's misbehavior. It also states that students with drugs and weapons cannot stay at school. The code is enforced fairly and consistently. Students' due process rights are observed. Overall, disciplinary referrals and school suspensions are low. If a child is suspended, care is taken to uncover the underlying reasons for disruptive behavior.

In-school suspension programs are taught by certified personnel, allowing students to continue their regular classroom work for credit. The programs are characterized by a well-articulated flow of information between program staff, the regular classroom teacher, and the child's family.

Entitlement 9: Children are entitled to instruction by teachers who hold high expectations for all students and who are fully prepared to meet the challenges of diverse classrooms.

At the Good Common School, teachers are convinced that all students can learn. They no longer aim instruction toward a mythical "average" learner or declare students who don't fit the mold as "failures." Instead, teachers try a variety of teaching strategies until they discover one that best meets the child's needs.

Good Common School teachers permit students a fresh start each year, rather than pre-judging their capacity on the basis of previous years' reports, grades, or teacher conversations. They consciously seek out students who may need help but are not assertive enough to ask for it. All children are called on in the classroom and receive equal praise from teachers. Children's successes are celebrated, even the small ones.

Continued education for teachers is encouraged. Opportunities for teachers to come together to reflect on practice, share information, and engage in other team-building activities are provided.

Entitlement 10: Children are entitled to an equal educational opportunity supported by the provision of greater resources to schools serving students most vulnerable to school failure.

The Good Common School Council makes important decisions about how funds are spent. The principal helps the council by providing clearly arrayed materials for use by parents and advocates well in advance of public meetings. Program budgets relate expenditures to school improvement goals. Like all other public documents produced by the Good Common School, budget materials are provided to parents in a language they can understand.

A key tenet of the Good Common School's philosophy is that no child's school success should be limited by where he or she lives. Because the district that administers the Good Common School shares this view, it allocates funds to individual schools on the basis of students' particular needs. Some schools get extra funds because many students come from low-income families or have special educational needs that are expensive to meet.

This fair and common-sense approach to resource allocation is supported by state laws that have as their goal equalization of educational opportunity. They do not permit "reforms" that spread an even layer of extra resources over an uneven foundation. Instead, schools with large numbers of educationally vulnerable students receive extra funds. Equity is achieved by increasing funding for poor districts, rather than forcing wealthy districts to lower expenditures.

Advocacy-driven school reform is accomplished by parents, teachers, principals, students, and advocates providing vision, energy, talent, hard work, commitment, and tenacity in roughly equal proportions. When all sectors of the school community work together to attain the entitlements discussed above, every student is ensured the opportunity for school success.

If these pages have whetted your appetite for transformation, read on and follow the daily struggle of one elementary school as it strives to realize the vision of the Good Common School.

CRITERIA
RESPECT –
– willing to work
– Commands respect by Showing respect
– does or does not support staff, treat fairly
– Can/cannot mediate

Parent Participation

Children are entitled to have parents, advocates, and concerned educators involved in all decisions affecting their education.

A Vision of Parent Participation at the Good Common School

Ella and Harvey Davis sit in their dimly lit living room. Ella laughs uncontrollably. They are watching a rerun of an old Sally Fields movie— "Norma Rae." The film's heroine is a housewife turned activist union organizer. This personal transformation generates inevitable conflict with her family. When her long-suffering husband complains he doesn't have clean clothes, Norma Rae furiously dumps a basket of dirty laundry into the kitchen sink, pours in detergent, and opens the faucet wide. While a mountain of bubbles rises, she explodes in exasperation, "You want clean laundry? You got clean laundry!"

As Ella's laughter subsides, Harvey teases, "It takes one to know one. Since you started chairing the school council, things have sometimes gotten out of hand around here, too."

Chairing the council is more demanding than Ella expected. In their long marriage, she has never been more grateful for Harv's easy-going nature. Besides, she thinks, he is as angered as she by some of the things that have taken place at the school. Over the years, they have watched three of their own six kids and a host of neighborhood children turned off from learning.

Ella recalls the strong support she received from Harv and many of her neighbors when she ran for a seat on the Council last spring. When she was nominated, then elected for a three-year term as chairperson, she was pleased to have her leadership skills acknowledged and was slightly overwhelmed by the enormity of the task.

While raising six children, Ella sat on her share of school/parent advisory groups. She soon learned that parents usually don't have much power; paid professionals dominate decision-making. Ella is relieved that parents are the majority on this council. Some folks have reservations about parents having the most votes, but not Ella. In her mind, numbers aren't the real issue. The real issue is parity.

Ella knows—and others are learning—that although the council sets policies, principals and teachers run the school all day long, day in and day out. For professional educators, running a school is both a career and a full-time job. They needn't worry about staying well informed; they are automatically inside the information loop. And information is power.

For real negotiations to occur between the community and the school, a more equitable sharing of power is necessary. Even a very active parent spends relatively little time at the school—almost always after meeting the demands of his or her own employment. A parent's involvement with school is usually limited to the amount of time his or her child attends it. Having a majority of parents on the council is one way to offset this inherent power imbalance.

In addition to Ella, council membership includes five other parents, two community representatives, two teachers, and the principal. Ella knows educating children requires a strong partnership between parents and professional educators, and she works hard to build it. Because Ella deeply values a true partnership, she is determined that the shared decision-making of the council not play itself out as "anti-teacher." She knows this would sabotage the school's ability to support the academic success of its students.

She always perseveres until consensus can be reached at council meetings—even when the agenda is full and meetings run overtime. In fact, the council has agreed not to adjourn until all disagreements are settled. She is also very clear about the council's role. It sets policy. It hires the principal. It develops a plan that sets priorities for school improvement. It prepares and approves a budget supporting the school improvement plan.

The school's professional staff has a strong voice in helping to shape policy and is responsible for its implementation. A professional advisory committee works closely with elected teacher members of the council who carry staff views on various issues to council meetings. The professional advisory committee plays a large role in determining the content of curriculum and rethinking teaching methods.

Ella hasn't much patience with those who complain that professionals have lost power to parents. Rather, she argues, because so many more decisions are made at the local school level, there are more decision-making opportunities for everyone. This means a net gain in power for everybody at the school site. Only the central office loses power.

The Good Common School serves about 600 students. It is divided into three educational units. In one of these units, House One, teachers have gained a head start on school restructuring through participation in a school/university collaborative. As a result, they have accomplished considerable change. Now, the challenge is to move promising practices developed in House One into the other two instructional units.

House One teachers contribute time, energy, and leadership toward accomplishing this goal. For example, a teacher cluster from House One recently met with interested teachers from the other two units to share strategies for "hands-on" science instruction for middle elementary-grade students. A second House One cluster demonstrated whole-language teaching methods to teachers unfamiliar with them. The newly hired principal supported these efforts by finding funds to pay small stipends to all participating teachers.

In April of last year, the school principal took early retirement. Although he had administered the school for eight years, he had no experience working with a parent-majority council and little interest in learning to do so. After an exhaustive search, the council hired a new principal, Phyllis Walker, who views school restructuring as an opportunity to bring about positive change. As the result of recent reforms, all principals in the system, including Phyllis, are now on four-year contracts and their performance is evaluated by local school councils. This is a radical shift from the concept of lifetime tenure.

One of the first official acts of the new school council was to draft and approve a new mission statement for the school. Because this document expresses a commitment to establish a "good, common school that serves all its students well," the Council decided to change the school's name. Over time, the McDermott Elementary School has become the Good Common School in name, as well as in spirit.

When conflicts surface at council meetings, Ella works hard to find common ground. It helps that the entire council spent a Saturday early in the school year at a retreat where its members were trained in group dynamics, including conflict resolution. Ella's insistence that children's interests always come first and her respectful way of listening to everyone helped to smooth the rough spots.

As part of its work, the council develops an annual school improvement plan. The priority-setting process requires Ella to use all of her consensus-building skills. More than once, she has challenged silent council members by saying, "Look, I know you must have feelings about this. This is the time to express them. There are no mind-readers in this room. Even if you think somebody may not agree, please lay your cards on the table."

The current school improvement plan assigns a high priority to greater parent involvement in the social and academic life of the school. Because Ella understands the importance of early success to team-building and community organizing, she urged the council to also tackle some of the school's more concrete problems. For example, she named a council committee to address the warped boards in the gymnasium floor and the leak in the roof. By pressuring the maintenance department, the committee accomplished in a week what the former principal couldn't achieve in six months.

• • •

It is 4:30 on Wednesday afternoon. Eleven-year-old Billy McDowell, a Good Common School fifth grader, and his friend Brian, a middle school student, tire of games at the video arcade and drift across the mall to buy cheeseburgers, french fries, and soda. The two boys started this day of unexcused absence from school with $18.25 between them. Now, all that remains is the dollar bill, two quarters, a dime, and some pennies scattered on the formica table between them. It is an hour and a half past school dismissal time; dusk is beginning to darken an already drab February day. Anyone who wants to be home before dark should be on the way. Brian wants to catch the next cross-town bus.

Billy is not so sure. Things have been bad at home lately. His dad lost his job and started to come home late sometimes. Billy's mother is worried about Billy's father, about money, and about Billy's negative attitude toward school.

This morning at the video arcade, Billy told Brian he wanted to run away from home. Right now, he is tempted. But where do you go in a dark and impersonal city when you're eleven years old and only have $1.50?

• • •

Georgia McDowell, Billy's mother, stands in her underheated and minimally furnished apartment kitchen. It is 3:00 p.m. She jiggles a fussy two-year-old on one blue-jeaned hip as she rails into the telephone, "I want you to give a message to Billy McDowell right now. He's in Mrs. Stone's room. No, I can't wait until the class period ends. You tell him to come straight home from school. Last night, I had $15 in my purse; now it's gone. That was food money. I want to know what Billy had to do with this, and I want to know fast!" She slams down the receiver in frustration, dumps the baby unceremoniously into his playpen, and turns on the radio.

Celia Thornton, one of two clerks in the Good Common School office, looks at the dead telephone in her hand, then slams it down in exasperation. By Celia's lights, Georgia McDowell is a chronic pain in the neck—both rude and demanding. Celia stands, stretches, and decides she deserves a break. She digs in her sweater pocket, finds three quarters, and heads for the staff lounge. Mrs. McDowell can just cool her jets.

Sitting in her office, Principal Phyllis Walker reflects on how she has struggled to get a grip on her new job by talking a lot. And listening. She has maintained a steady dialogue with teachers, students, and parents. Her early conversations with staff played out in predictable ways. But it has been more difficult than she expected to communicate with community leaders and parents. Because she grew up in the largely African American neighborhood surrounding the school, she had expected to re-enter it easily. To her surprise, she quickly ran into skeptical—even hostile—attitudes toward the school. She has summarized these attitudes for Ella: "Sure lady, tell us more. We've heard it all before. Nothing really changes here."

Principal Walker finishes the last item in her "In" basket and glances at the clock on the wall. It is 5:25 p.m. Suddenly, she hears a ruckus. When she steps into the corridor she sees Sam, the custodian, hurrying toward the source of the noise. Outside the school's plate-glass front door is Georgia McDowell, pounding away for all she's worth. She clutches one snowsuited toddler under her free arm; a second stands crying at her side. Behind Mrs. McDowell, a small crowd of other mothers is gathering.

Sam opens the door and the tide of women surges toward Phyllis. Georgia McDowell is angry and scared. Her words tumble over each other as she describes to Phyllis her earlier conversation with Celia, her fruitless wait for Billy to come home, and her growing panic at his failure to arrive. The other women press forward. They live in Georgia's apartment building and have spent the past hour searching their neighborhood for Billy. One tells Phyllis that she spoke with a boy who saw Billy earlier in the day. Billy said he was thinking about running away, but first he was going to cut school and spend the day hanging out with a friend.

Phyllis disengages herself from the group of women in the outer office and goes to her desk. She dials the home telephone number of Helen Stone, Billy's teacher. A child answers the telephone, then leaves to get his mother. When Helen finally comes to the line, Phyllis asks her if Billy McDowell was in school today. Helen is clearly uncomfortable as she answers, "No." She adds that she forgot to turn in her list of absent students this morning. Phyllis curtly tells Helen to be in the principal's office at 7:30 tomorrow morning.

By this time, Hugh Stone has arrived home from work. He asks Helen what's up. She fills him in, adding, "I knew Billy was absent, but I didn't bother to write it up. Billy is a real nuisance. When I missed him, I just thought, 'This is my lucky day!'" Now she feels both worried and guilty.

Phyllis returns to Mrs. McDowell to report she has confirmed Billy's absence from school. Someone has evidently called Ella Davis, because she is now part of the group. One woman has taken Georgia's two toddlers aside and is reading a story to them. The others are telling "war stories" that express their continuing frustration with the school and its shortcomings.

One mother complains that her son got sour milk in the lunchroom again last week. Another recalls the time last year when several students—one of them her child—got sick after eating lunch at school and ended up in the emergency room. A third woman recalls the time a youngster left school early and accepted a ride with an adult who made sexual advances toward him. Frightened by the man's overtures, the child jumped from the moving car and was injured. Ella joins in, sharing a story about her own son who cut school for two days. She and Harv found out weeks later and were angry the school didn't notify them.

Phyllis is disturbed by all of these incidents, but her first priority is Billy. She takes his mother into her private office and is on the phone with the police when a telephone in the outer office rings. The caller is Georgia's next door neighbor who has stayed at the McDowell's apartment in case Billy should turn up. She reports that he has just come home.

Georgia McDowell seizes the telephone intending to scold Billy, but when she hears his voice she tells him that she loves him and will talk to him more when she gets home. Ella offers to drive Georgia and her children home and the little group leaves.

Phyllis asks the remaining mothers to stay for a few more minutes. She takes careful notes about their various complaints. At last she says, "Thank goodness Billy is safe. But the incidents you have described really disturb me. Clearly, we have a lot of problems to solve. I've learned more about this school in the last hour than in the past three months. If Ella and I call a community meeting for Thursday evening, can you come and help to turn out other parents?" Many heads nod in agreement.

• • •

The next day, Phyllis calls an emergency staff meeting during the morning teacher preparation period. Word travels fast. Teachers, sobered by the laxness that contributed to the crisis involving Billy, arrive expecting a lecture from Phyllis. She does not disappoint them.

She begins by noting that last night's emergency may appear to affect only one child and his family, but it is really symptomatic of a much larger problem. Billy symbolizes many "lost" kids at this school. Because these children are difficult to educate, they are at risk for becoming dropouts. It will take a lot to keep them in school and succeeding. Phyllis thinks one solution is an "early warning" dropout prevention system.

One of the most important components of this system must be a well-defined, scrupulously followed process for handling children who are chronically tardy or absent. Phyllis acknowledges the school is short of resources and says flat out that development of such a system means more work for everybody. Nevertheless, she expects everyone to participate.

She appoints three teachers to a faculty committee charged with responsibility for helping her to improve the absence reporting system and promises the rest of the teaching staff that this committee will make its first report at next week's faculty meeting. While she makes it clear a serious error was made in Billy's case, she doesn't publicly single out Helen Stone for criticism.

She concludes her remarks by reporting that Ella Davis plans personally to chair a new Parent Outreach Committee of the school council. Ella has asked Georgia McDowell to spearhead the committee's work in her own neighborhood. Helen Stone, Billy's teacher, groans audibly. Phyllis's response is curt. "I know you find Mrs. McDowell demanding and difficult, but you don't have to like the woman's style to work with her. Think about it. She got sixteen mothers involved in less than an hour yesterday. I'm impressed." The meeting is adjourned.

• • •

By noon, Phyllis has received calls from the incoming President of the NAACP branch, the Chairperson of the Latino Forum, and the Director of the Southeast Asian Coalition. All expressed their concern over the failure of the school to report Billy's absence to his family. All plan to attend the community meeting.

While driving home after school, Phyllis switches her car radio to WBLK. The station's manager, Don Pearson, is hosting a call-in talk show. The question of the day is: "HOW SAFE ARE OUR CHILDREN?" Between callers, Pearson urges concerned parents to attend a community meeting at the school on Thursday evening.

With this kind of build-up, Phyllis knows the meeting will be packed. She feels a bit overwhelmed by the swiftness and intensity with which events are unfolding. She is glad Ella knows community politics as the result of years of service on community boards and with local political campaigns. Technically, the school council will sponsor the meeting. However, Ella has asked Don Pearson to facilitate the meeting; several other community leaders plan to speak.

• • •

Tuesday evening is unseasonably warm. Wet, winter-bare branches glisten over street lamps as Ella and Phyllis drive down Broad Street toward the school. Although it is early, the school parking lot is half full of cars when they arrive. As Phyllis unlocks the front door, people troop towards the school. Ella is relieved that all members of the school council are present.

The cafeteria, which accommodates 200, fills quickly. Others file silently into the room to stand along the walls. Don Pearson calls the meeting to order. After he welcomes the crowd, he turns the meeting over to two other seasoned community leaders—Charles Sumpter, head of the local NAACP branch, and Eduardo Torres, chair of the Latino Forum.

Sumpter opens with a brief description of how indifference and error contributed to Billy's disappearance. He cites his organization's long struggle to gain educational equity for children of color and refers to his organization's files, bulging with examples of the school's failures.

Then Torres speaks, echoing Sumpter's assessment of the seriousness of the situation. He notes that Latino families and others for whom English is not a first language have additional problems with the school. Poor home/school communication is compounded by language problems. Pearson then asks Antonia Ramos and Steve Gray, respected long-time community residents and retired educators, to serve as recorders for the meeting.

The first speaker is Billy's father. Mr. McDowell describes the panic he and his wife experienced on the afternoon Billy failed to return home from school and tells the audience about his telephone call to the Area B Police Headquarters to report Billy missing. He concludes by describing the school staff's failure to report Billy's absence or attempt delivery of his wife's message to Billy. He demands those involved be replaced immediately. Antonia Ramos dutifully prints "Fire those responsible" in bold marker strokes on a sheet of newsprint taped to the wall.

When Mr. McDowell sits down, Ahmad Sanders takes the microphone. Although Sanders is one of the African American community's prickliest radicals, he has a decade-long record of consistent personal advocacy for better services for Black youth. He agrees that members of the school staff who are to blame should be fired or transferred, but he doesn't believe this will solve the problem.

Sanders quickly warms to his subject. The "problem" isn't just what happened to Billy. The "problem" has been around for a long, long time. The school's staff has never listened to parents or assumed responsibility for communicating with them. Parents only hear from the school when somebody wants to complain about a kid's behavior. He doubts the council can successfully close the gap between school and community. Since the council is *at* the school, he reasons, isn't it likely to be *of* the school, as well? Antonia writes "Close school/community gap" on the posted piece of newsprint.

María Gutierrez speaks next. "Will the meeting please stay focused on the child safety issue? What happened to Billy and his family is awful. Every parent in the room knows what his parents must have felt. But think about this: if Billy's mother had been a native Spanish speaker, he would probably still be lost!" Antonia writes "Need bilingual clerks," then motions to Steve Gray to relieve her as recorder.

The Executive Director of the Southeast Asian Coalition, takes the microphone long enough to say that children and families who speak Khmer, Laotian, Vietnamese, and other Southeast Asian languages also experience many language barriers at the school. It would help if clerks had a telephone list of bilingual persons in the community who could serve as emergency translators.

Donald Washington, an African American teacher who works in House One of the Good Common School, steps forward. Donald treads a thin line. He understands the anger expressed. He was furious when he first learned about the episode involving Billy, and he says so. He wonders aloud whether any of the parents present have specific ideas about how to pull the entire community together to keep their kids safe. Finally, he says he is glad to see so many fathers in the audience tonight—events at the school are not just women's business, although too often it turns out that way. He challenges the men present to remain involved.

When Donald finishes, Charles Sumpter suggests that everyone in the room participate in a brainstorming session. Anyone who has an idea about how to improve relationships between the school and families—and therefore improve the chances of keeping kids safe—should raise their hand. He will acknowledge speakers one after another and they can call out their ideas.

Steve Gray scrambles to capture the suggestions as they are called out:

- Don't give up! Parents and teachers can learn to communicate. If we think that it is hopeless, then it is hopeless.
- Develop a strong Parent Involvement Policy. Disseminate it to all parents in their first language.
- Provide translators at all parent meetings.
- Hold neighborhood meetings to solicit parent input into the annual school improvement plan.
- Take a lesson from the organizers of tonight's meeting. Enlist assistance of ethnic media in communicating with the broader community.
- Organize parents to go door to door talking with other parents and neighbors about activities at the school. Establish a parent telephone tree.
- Do a better job of publicizing events at the school that offer opportunities for parent participation. Send notices home in all languages spoken by school families.
- Use school-based activities as a chance to organize parents: set up parent information tables; ask parents to fill out surveys about policy issues; start a parent newsletter and disseminate it in all languages spoken by families that are members of the school community.
- Develop a pool of parents skilled to train other parents on various school-related subjects.
- Generate projects that offer opportunities for parents, children, and staff to participate. For example, gardens, cultural and historical collections, or an after-hours School Watch program designed to prevent vandalism.
- Improve the after-school program at the school. Show films. Put on a school play or organize a sporting event that allows broad participation.

Principal Walker also scrambles to take notes. After the final idea is shared, Steve Gray struggles to describe it on the bottom of his last sheet of newsprint. It is well past 10 o'clock. Eduardo Torres gavels the room to attention. Ella Davis asks for the microphone to make a statement on behalf of the Good Common School Council.

> *"On behalf of the Council, I want to publicly apologize to Billy McDowell and his family for the way they were let down. I also want you to know that those who contributed to the situation have been reprimanded. The clerk in question has been transferred to central office. She will be replaced by someone who is more effective, and who speaks Spanish.*
>
> *"I am not going to tell you things are all right, because things are not. But we are working on them. And we are making progress. It may not show yet, but Rome wasn't built in a day. You'll have to judge the changes the council makes on their own merits.*
>
> *"You've provided us with some very good ideas. Now it's our responsibility to put them to work. Most of you know that Phyllis Walker, the new principal, grew up in this neighborhood. We chose her because she is committed to our kids. Phyllis, would you like to say something?"*

Phyllis Walker moves to the microphone, where she stands shoulder to shoulder with Ella. She takes a deep breath as she looks out over the crowded room.

> *"I am new at this job, but I came here because I believe this community wants and deserves better educational programs for its children. My deepest wish is to join with you to bring this about. This meeting is a powerful first step. Most of you have no reason to expect me to succeed. But I am going to! All I ask is that, like the council, I be judged on the merit of my work."*

Both women take their seats. Charles Sumpter gavels the restless crowd to silence one last time. Then he says,

> *"It's very late. I just want to say this to Ella Davis. This community elected you folks to the council because we believe you can do the job. But there is a lot more at stake here than some council seats. Our kids are at stake. After this week, it's going to be very interesting to see what you do to improve safety at the school. Just remember, you're accountable to everyone in this room tonight and to many who aren't here, as well. We will all be watching. Good night, everyone."*

• • •

It is now Monday evening and the Good Common School Council is in session. Given last week's flap, it is not surprising that all members are present. Ella Davis has just finished summarizing the community meeting. She turns to Phyllis Walker to see if there is anything she wishes to add.

Phyllis's answer is direct, "All I can say is that I was extremely grateful to have Ella there with me. Otherwise, I would have been left—what's the phrase— 'twisting slowly in the wind.'" She then reports on her meeting with the faculty and the early work of the committee redesigning the absence reporting system.

Next, Phyllis presents a multi-point proposal she has developed, with advice from Ella, as a possible response to many of the concerns expressed at the community meeting. The proposal has two goals:

1. Better parent/school communication.
2. Stronger support services and improved student discipline.

Phyllis begins to flesh out the details. First, a Parent Outreach Network should be established with oversight by the committee chaired by Ella Davis. Many of the women who came to the school with Mrs. McDowell have agreed to participate. While the exact design of the Parent Outreach Network remains to be determined, its goal is to get parents talking with each other and with school staff about how to improve the school's service to the community.

Second, the council should create a School Security Committee to recruit parents to come to school to monitor the arrival and departure of students for a half-hour each morning and afternoon. Parents will be alert to any problems in the neighborhood as children arrive and leave. The presence of parents will be a constant reminder to staff that they must work more closely with the community.

Third, the council should approve funds to support a series of parent workshops to develop basic skills in team-building, group dynamics, conflict resolution, communications, and consensus-building. One important goal will be enhancing parent understanding of homework expectations. Ella has proposed an increased emphasis on recreational reading—specifically, that children be encouraged to carry books home from school that their parents will read to them for at least fifteen minutes each night.

Fourth, in response to long-standing requests from many parents, the school should offer GED, literacy, and English as a second language classes. In addition to providing an important service, these classes will regularly bring large numbers of parents into the school building.

Finally, Ella proposes establishing a special committee to help teachers and counselors resolve problems of children who are chronically tardy, absent, and truant. This will be the first step in the development of an "Early Watch" dropout prevention effort. Initial actions to improve school discipline will focus on making it clear to children and parents how students are expected to behave at school. Teachers will review the school code with all students and copies of the code will be distributed to all parents in appropriate languages. Phyllis will lead the effort to have all teachers enforce school rules more consistently.

Ella reminds the council that implementation of these proposals is sure to lead to yet other changes in teacher expectations and curriculum. She wryly notes, "We have already learned that when you jiggle one part of a school, the whole thing wiggles. We may find ourselves having to re-examine our school improvement goals, OK?"

A parent member of the council moves to approve the proposal as presented. Further, the parent suggests, all of the activities intended to help heal the split between the school and the community should be coordinated under the single umbrella of a **"KIDS FIRST"** campaign, complete with publicity—bumper stickers, lapel buttons, and public service radio advertisements. Her suggestion is greeted with a round of applause.

Ella beams as the council meeting comes to a close. **KIDS FIRST.** That says it all, in just two words.

CHARACTERISTICS OF QUALITY PARENT INVOLVEMENT PROGRAMS

- **Written policies** legitimize the importance of parent involvement and help frame the context for program activities by explicitly spelling out to participants what they are empowered to do. These policies give superintendents and principals leverage with central office, building, and classroom staff to ensure that parent involvement is central to the school program.
- **Administrative support** is provided through adequate funding from the school budget for program implementation and operation and supportive resources such as meeting space, computers, and copying facilities, and by designating school personnel to help carry out program efforts or events.
- **Training** for school staff and parents is carried out over time to develop partnering skills.
- **A partnership approach** is established with an emphasis on joint planning, goal setting, definition of roles, program assessment, development of instructional efforts, and setting of school standards. This is key to achieving a sense of ownership and pride in the program by all participants.
- **Two-way communication** is a central goal. This requires frequent contacts between school and home to allow parents to feel comfortable coming to school, sharing ideas, and voicing concerns. School staff must be helped to welcome parent input and fashion more relevant learning activities.
- **Networking** with other programs ensures sharing of information, resources, and technical expertise.
- **Program evaluation** at key stages, as well as at the conclusion of a cycle or phase, enables parents and staff to make program revisions on a continuous basis to ensure that activities strengthen the partnership.

Source: Williams & Chavkin (1989).

Problems with Parent Participation in U.S. Public Schools

Benefits and Present Limits of Parent Participation

Parents are a child's first and most important educators. Parents know their children's strengths and weaknesses. By helping educators provide each child with an appropriate educational experience, they can act as essential links between the classroom and the home to reinforce and animate learning.

Families and community organizations can provide crucial support to bridge gaps of language, culture, and life experience that can impede a child's education or cause misunderstanding and conflict in the classroom.

Decades of research lead to the inescapable conclusion that parents have a powerful impact on children's learning experience in school. Among the documented benefits of parent involvement are: gains in academic achievement; improved student behavior; lower absenteeism; more positive attitudes toward school; improved homework habits. Researchers also report more positive parent/child communications and greater parent/community support for schools.

Despite these clear benefits, researcher Joyce Epstein (in Brandt, 1989) has found that parent participation remains limited in most elementary public schools, with only one-fifth of all parents successfully involved with their children's schooling. While 2 to 5 percent of parents may present problems severe enough to interfere with successful teacher/parent partnerships, 75 percent of parents express a clear desire to become more involved.

Although parents may be encouraged to support school activities and events, they find it much harder to have real input into school decisions and operation. Even after a decade of school reform, active participation may be limited to making refreshments for a field trip, selling tickets for a school event, or applauding performances in a class play.

TYPES OF PARENT INVOLVEMENT

Joyce Epstein (in Brandt, 1989) has identified five major types of parent involvement in schools, each requiring varying levels of resources and support, and each resulting in different outcomes.

- **Parenting:** parents fulfilling their basic obligations to ensure children's health, safety, and development and to provide positive home conditions that support school learning and appropriate behavior.
- **Communicating:** schools fulfilling their basic obligations to communicate effectively with parents about school programs and children's progress.
- **Volunteering:** parents involved at school as volunteers, assisting teachers, administrators, and children, or attending school events or programs for their own training or education.
- **Learning at Home:** parents involved in learning activities at home, monitoring or assisting their children, often in coordination with classroom instruction.

- **Representing Other Parents:** parents participating in school governance and advocacy to assume decision-making roles through school organizations or advisory councils, to monitor schools through independent groups, or to work for school improvement at the school, district, or state level.

According to Epstein, each type of parent involvement is appropriate to particular circumstances; no single type can provide a comprehensive strategy for effective participation. To maximize parent involvement, schools must eliminate policies and practices that act as barriers and facilitate all five types of participation across a wide range of school and home circumstances.

BARRIERS TO PARENT INVOLVEMENT

With notable exceptions, many elementary school principals and teachers fail to consider parents as legitimate partners in their children's education. Instead, they may treat parents as intrusive amateurs who should defer to the more informed judgment of school staff. Low-income or minority parents are often viewed as apathetic or even hostile to their children's education and are seen by some educators as problems to be avoided or barriers to be overcome.

When school staff treat parents as problems, or as second-class citizens, parents may respond with apathy, alienation, and even hostility. This is particularly true when such treatment reinforces a parent's personal experience with public school. Unfortunately, alienation and hostility toward school act to reinforce staff perceptions of parent apathy and hostility, creating an ever-widening gap between parents and teachers.

Problems with Teacher Attitudes

During discussions in Timothy Rasinski's (1989) graduate-level education courses, teachers have revealed their general view of parents as pushy or overly aggressive, difficult to contact, resistant to their recommendations and, in some cases, intellectually or physically neglectful of their children. He also notes that while both educators and parents agree on the need for increased parent involvement, they disagree on its nature. Parents are interested in a wide variety of roles from tutoring to policy development. Most teachers and administrators view the role of parents in a traditional light—as primarily outside of the school's operation and curriculum.

Rasinski (1989) cites three major reasons why educators have difficulty implementing successful parent involvement programs, even when they understand the benefits. First, effective programs are complex, necessitating an accurate assessment of parental needs, detailed planning, strong leadership, and a high degree of cooperation and coordination. Teachers already overburdened with duties and responsibilities may find such a project daunting. Second, mutual mistrust may exist between teachers and parents, with teachers wary of parents checking up on them and parents feeling that teachers act as if only they know what is right for children. Finally, the failure of past programs may lead to the conclusion that parent participation doesn't really work and isn't worth the effort.

Perhaps most important of all, teachers and administrators may find it difficult to relinquish power to parents and community groups. In a highly bureaucratic structure, the exercise of even the most limited authority can become highly prized. Educators frustrated by their lack of influence are likely to be reluctant to turn over what little control they have in return for uncertain gains. Because schools provide few rewards to educators for greater parent/teacher communication, this pattern is hard to break.

Lack of Guidance and Training Programs

According to educator Polly Greenberg (1989), another key reason why educators are not more open to parent involvement lies in the failure of most teacher education institutions to offer the theory, practice, and guidance teachers need to enable them to work well with parents from all backgrounds and cultures. She notes that very few of the nation's 1200 teacher preparation institutions include an emphasis on parent involvement in their pre-service programs for elementary school teachers.

The importance of effective pre-service and in-service training is underlined by a 1987 study (Hoover-Dempsey, *et al.*, 1987) of more than 1000 elementary teachers in sixty-six schools in a mid-southern state. Of all the variables examined, the most potent predictor of successful parent involvement was teacher efficacy—a teacher's belief that he or she is effective in teaching and that the children they teach can learn. Teacher efficacy was found to be more important in encouraging parent participation than factors such as the school's economic profile, support from the principal, or average class size. The researchers speculated that confidence in one's teaching ability and security in the instructional programs allow teachers to collaborate comfortably with parents.

Attitudes Toward Low-Income Parents

Relationships between teachers and low-income parents can be particularly problematic. A survey of parents and educators conducted by researcher Don Davies (1988) in low-income communities in the U.S., England, and Portugal found that teachers and administrators tend to believe poor families do not have the interest or competence to be involved in their children's education. Only a few of the educators interviewed offered the view that school policies and practices might contribute to limited involvement on the part of low-income parents.

Other results from Davies' cross-national study further detail the strained attitudes that plague relations between teachers and low-income families:

- most low-income parents have little or no contact with schools; where communication does take place from schools, it is usually negative, focusing largely on a child's academic or behavioral problems;
- many low-income parents do not view themselves as competent to be successfully involved in their children's education;
- many teachers expect children from families that deviate from middle-class norms to have trouble in school; teachers often view low-income families as "deficient";
- many teachers and administrators believe that low-income parents and immigrant parents are particularly hard to reach because of personal characteristics or home and neighborhood conditions.

Davies also found that low-income parents in all three countries expressed a strong interest in their children's education, talked about the importance of schools, and wanted to be more involved at home or at school.

The myth of low-income or minority parent indifference toward their children's education is further challenged by a six-year study (Chavkin, 1989) of African American and Latino parents in six states. Ninety-five percent of those interviewed expressed a strong commitment to their children's education. Parents were ready to take a more active role by visiting schools, helping children at home, and assisting in school events. Parents were also interested in becoming involved in school decisions regarding student evaluation, classroom discipline, homework assignments, and setting behavioral rules.

Institutional Structures and Attitudes

Even when schools try to involve parents, institutional structures and attitudes can act to impede increased participation. An analysis of recent school/home initiatives (Rasinski, 1989) concludes that problems arise because: 1) schools fail to involve parents in conception, planning, or design, resulting in programs that may not address the realities of the home environment of all students; 2) schools and teachers direct parents rather than collaborate with them; consequently, parents feel little ownership and minimal commitment; and 3) programs are piecemeal; there is little continuity or coordination between grade levels or classrooms, presenting parents with a confusing mix of demands and suggestions about their children's education. The missing ingredient in many programs is active commitment and involvement from parents from the very beginning and throughout the process.

Tensions between families and schools are further exacerbated when school systems continue to assume that students live in traditional two-parent nuclear families where the father works and the mother stays home to keep the house and raise the children. Demographics indicate that such families are rare. Single-parent and two-working-parent households complicate the logistics of bringing schools and families together.

Importance for Limited-English-Proficient Children

Active parent participation is particularly important for limited-English-proficient children. Differences in culture, language, and life experience between students and teachers can be vast. In today's public elementary school, a middle-class, Anglo teacher might well be instructing a Vietnamese boy who has witnessed the torture or murder of family members in his homeland, or a young girl whose shattered family life has forced her to take on the full responsibility of caring for herself and others while still a child. Ignored or untended, these differences can undermine the effectiveness of instructional efforts and lead to chronic misunderstandings that frustrate teachers and alienate students and parents.

Parental Attitudes

Parents can also discourage effective partnerships with schools. By failing to endorse schooling at home or express respect for teachers and their profession, they instill negative attitudes within their children that undermine their education. Such attitudes are most likely to be expressed by adults who themselves had poor childhood experiences with schools.

Researcher David Seeley (1989) observes that parents can easily fall into the "delegation model," feeling they don't have to be involved with their child's education because the job has been delegated to schools, much the same way that the fire department is given the task of putting out fires.

SCHOOL GOVERNANCE

School governance encompasses decisions about staff selection, teacher assignment, quality of instructional materials, scope of the curriculum, assessment of student progress, and school mission and climate—vital decisions that have a direct and profound impact on a child's education.

In most public school systems, governance decisions are made by central office personnel. Many of the practical decisions that determine the effectiveness of a school are out of the control of school-based staff, parents, students, and others in the school's community.

Uniform policies on class schedules, student placement, and student assessment are often established and enforced by central office staff. Curriculum and student instruction may also be determined systemwide through the use of strict "scope and sequence" requirements for each grade and by selection of uniform textbooks and instructional materials. Individual schools are left with little discretion to address the differing needs and problems of their students.

Detailed budgetary decisions are generally made by the local school board, superintendent, or assistant superintendent. By the time money and other resources finally reach an individual school, the principal and teachers have limited say over how they can be used.

This highly centralized approach to school governance promotes rigid, impersonal schools. Variation or experimentation within a single school can be very difficult to initiate. Those who try are often discouraged. Parents seeking to influence school decisions must often deal with a distant, sometimes intimidating bureaucracy.

A school that isolates itself from parents and the community soon becomes overwhelmed by the pressing needs of its students and its inability to cope with the expectations of modern society.

SCHOOL-SITE MANAGEMENT

One of the popular elements of recent school reform is the move toward school-site management. Its basic strategy is to bring decision-making closer to those most directly affected—to decentralize power by locating authority over budgets, curriculum, and policy at the school building level and placing it in the hands of local principals, teachers, parents, and citizens.

A national survey of school executives conducted by researchers at the State University of New York (Heller, *et al.*, 1989) showed that some 25 percent of schools have instituted some form of school-based management during the 1980s; another 28 percent say programs are in the planning stages. An analysis of recent school system reform efforts indicates that about one-fifth of the programs have involved restructuring of school governance. To put this in perspective, 78 percent of school systems have instituted reform by increasing high school graduation requirements.

Naturally, the shape of school-site management varies greatly from community to community, with significant differences in the amount of power invested in school-site councils (or committees, or teams) and in the scope of their influence over school policy and operation. Some councils feature a majority of parent members; others have a majority of educators.

Challenges Facing School-Site Management

One study (Malen, *et al.,* 1990) of recent school-site management initiatives suggests the transition from centralized bureaucracies to more autonomous, democratic units is likely to present a variety of challenges.

- **Schools have deeply ingrained norms and well-established unwritten rules.** These norms dictate that district officials and administrators set policy, teachers deliver instruction, and parents provide support. As expressed by one school superintendent, "We are steeped in tradition and habit."
- **Schools rarely provide a full range of critical resources.** Councils often lack time, technical assistance, training, independent sources of information, funding, etc.
- **Site-based management plans are often ambiguous.** It can be difficult to determine what decision-making authority the site participants have actually been granted, leaving them uncertain of the scope of their formal power.
- **Parents are reluctant to challenge the professionals.** On councils composed of principals, teachers, and parents, the professional educators—principals and teachers—often set the agenda, manage the meeting, disperse the information, and control decision outcomes. Many parents are not ready to challenge this traditional dynamic.
- **Teachers do not exert meaningful influence.** Most school-site councils include the school principal, who often controls the meeting. Teachers tend to "accept the boss's opinion."
- **Council membership tends to be homogeneous.** Despite outreach efforts, council demographics may not reflect the school community's ethnic, racial, or cultural diversity.
- **Autonomy is limited.** The efforts of site councils are limited by state laws and regulations, existing contracts and agreements, and district policies and priorities.
- **Site-based management rarely results in major instructional reform.** Councils rarely have the skills or the resources to address subjects central to instructional programs, and where changes are proposed they are not often implemented.
- **School policy remains largely untouched.** Although participants are involved in schoolwide decision making, they rarely have influence over major policy.

Obstacles to School-Site Management

Researchers Karen Lindquist and John Mauriel (1989) observe a disparity between the theory and intentions of school-site management and its actual practice within schools and school systems. They identify three problem areas that have hampered effective implementation: 1) incongruence in the various definitions of what constitutes school-based management; 2) limited delegation of authority to individual schools; and 3) formidable requirements for time and skills on the part of parents and educators.

According to Robert Heller's (1989) survey of school executives, obstacles to school-site management from their vantage point include: labor contracts; state laws; school board policies; accreditation standards; inadequate resources to implement changes; fear of loss of power on the part of central office and school building personnel; and the difficulty of breaking with tradition.

Positive Responses to School-Site Management

Others are more optimistic about school-site management, concluding that it is premature to offer definitive findings. Instead, they urge adjustment and refinement of the model, recognizing the challenge of instituting fundamental change within school systems that are very set in their ways.

In Chicago, school reformers have approached school-site management by establishing school councils with a majority of parents on each eleven-member council—six parents, two community representatives, two teachers, and the school principal.

By granting parents a voting majority on matters such as hiring the school principal, developing school improvement strategies, and reviewing the school budget, Chicago reformers hope to resolve the imbalance of power inherent in most collaborations between professional educators and parents.

As school superintendent James Mitchell (1990) notes about the challenge of establishing successful school-site management: "Change can be difficult. To ask people to take part in a new process of shared decision-making is to ask them to form new relationships, to learn how to compromise and reach consensus, to team build and facilitate change. We needed three years... to see a lot of investment from our district."

Designs for Change: SCHOOLWATCH Campaign

During its 1986 annual planning meeting, Chicago's **Designs for Change** reviewed its SCHOOLWATCH campaign and concluded that only fundamental school restructuring would provide a foundation for improved educational outcomes in the city. As a result, Designs for Change altered the direction of SCHOOLWATCH to launch a campaign to restructure Chicago's public schools.

As part of its SCHOOLWATCH campaign, Designs for Change had organized parents since 1981 to work on school improvement. Believing that most of the city's active parents had either been coopted or limited to a few activities, Designs for Change concluded little had been done to draw out the untapped parent leadership that existed for every school. To help realize this potential, Designs for Change canvassed neighborhoods, gave presentations at churches and day care centers, and worked with community contacts established during previous projects and campaigns.

To identify effective policies and strategies, Designs for Change conducted comprehensive research on parent and citizen advocacy strategies and promising practices for school reform. As the restructuring campaign got under way, Designs for Change's research focused on issues of school decentralization, school-based management, and staff development in large urban districts across the country.

Restructuring Schools

As a result of its research and parent organizing, Designs for Change developed a clear understanding of the strong link between structural deficiencies inherent in public school governance and the lack of quality education provided at the school site.

A centralized, bureaucratic structure and the consistent failure of school authorities or officials to include parents or community members had resulted in a school governance system in which accountability was defined by directives from the central office rather than by the educational needs of students. The lack of authority at local schools to determine budgets and programs or to negotiate contracts with school staff provided little incentive for principals to exercise leadership or for staff to employ innovative educational techniques. On the contrary, school staff tended to restrict parent and community participation, viewing it as an impingement on their already limited authority. Parents avoided contact with the school, feeling their participation was neither wanted nor appreciated.

On the basis of its research, Designs for Change developed a restructuring strategy in which a significant measure of control over local schools would be placed in the hands of parents and concerned citizens serving on elected school-site councils. This proposed governance reform was designed to achieve: increased responsiveness and accountability to student needs; staff development tied to specific local school goals; greater parent participation in the learning process; and stronger principal leadership to ensure quality programs.

The CURE Coalition

Historically, coalition efforts have been an effective strategy for Designs for Change, providing a mechanism for putting pressure on decision-makers from different constituencies while mobilizing broad support. In the fall of 1986, Designs for Change joined a coalition called Chicagoans United to Reform Education (CURE), a collection of groups representing a wide range of communities in Chicago.

CURE was initially convened by Dr. Michael Bakalis, Dean of the School of Education at Loyola University and former Illinois State Superintendent of Instruction, with the purpose of discussing school restructuring. During CURE meetings, Designs for Change convinced the coalition to shift its focus from favoring a decentralizing plan that included sub-districts with elected school boards to a school-based governance approach, arguing that sub-districts in Chicago and elsewhere had proved too large to meet the needs of students at the local school level.

Outlining this vision, CURE released a position paper that called for shifting key decisions to a school council composed of parents, citizens, and teachers, replacing principal tenure with limited-year performance contracts, reducing the size and authority of the central adminstration, and creating more parent choice within the parameters of fair school admission procedures.

To unite the community around restructuring, CURE held a city-wide conference in the spring of 1987 attended by 400 parents, citizens, and educators from eighty schools. The coalition followed up the conference with a fall and winter campaign to draft school reform legislation to go before the state's General Assembly in the spring of 1988.

The Teachers' Strike

A teachers' strike in the fall of 1987 dramatically heightened demands for better schools. Bitterness generated by the strike caused silent parents to speak out and inspired divided communities to rally around the need for better schools. CURE gained support for its restructuring plan from groups with strong roots in the African American and Latino communities by capitalizing on the awareness and activism generated by the strike.

Unlike past teachers' strikes, the drive for school improvement continued even after the strike was resolved. Factors behind the steady momentum for school reform included constant pressure from CURE and other groups during and after the strike, the resolve of parents and community members, and the strong foundation for community action laid down by Harold Washington's mayoral campaign.

City Hall Opens Its Doors

Mayor Washington, expanding on his recently announced Education Summit, established the Parent Community Council composed of representatives from the school board, teachers' unions, the business community, community organizations, and education advocates.

The Washington administration's support of broader community involvement in Chicago's government paved the way for a more positive relationship between Designs for Change and City Hall. In fact, Designs for Change staff helped the mayor prepare his education positions, served on his transition team, and were appointed by him to the school board nominating committee.

A Partnership with Business

As the Education Summit progressed, a closer relationship developed between parents, advocates, and the city's business community. During the previous summer, a business group called Chicago United released a report citing the public schools' failure to implement its 1981 management recommendations. The report asserted that improvements in student achievement could take place only if schools, parents, and community and business organizations worked together within a newly organized school-based governance system. The business community's viewpoint was influenced by its own movement towards local plant-site management and other decentralization efforts.

Early in the Education Summit, members of the business community authorized a group of eight major business organizations—the Chicago Partnership—to develop and advocate a position on school reform. The position paper, similar to CURE's proposal, called for school-site management, reduced central administration, increased parent choice, and an oversight/monitoring authority with the power to remove school board members and withhold funds for failure to adhere to reform criteria. The oversight body became a top priority for the business community.

A newly formed coalition within the Education Summit—representing parents, community, advocacy organizations, and the business sector—met regularly to establish common positions. This coalition was able to win support for a number of amendments, bringing the Summit report closer to the positions held by CURE and the Chicago Partnership. This coalition ultimately became the Alliance for Better Chicago Schools.

The Drive for Legislation

Although the Education Summit had yet to decide whether to take its agenda to the state legislature or go through the school board, CURE was convinced that effective change would have to come through state law. In the past, direct negotiations with central office administrative staff and the Chicago Board of Education had proved ineffective.

In the fall of 1987, Designs for Change secured help from a legal and consulting firm called the Haymarket Group to begin the lengthy process of drafting legislation to satisfy the coalition's diverse membership.

After draft legislation was approved by CURE in February of 1988, legislative sponsors were secured to introduce the 144-page proposal in April of 1988. CURE's legislative proposal became crucial when an attempt to translate the Education Summit's final position into legislation was rejected by the Summit's membership.

Various other reform groups and individual legislators put forth proposals as well. But CURE pressed business groups and the Alliance for Better Chicago Schools' members to back its legislative proposal, including the oversight authority desired by the business community. Although the Alliance for Better Chicago Schools would not directly endorse the CURE proposal, it did endorse a detailed statement of similar legislative positions.

With aid from the Haymarket Group, CURE embarked on a determined grassroots organizing effort in all Chicago legislative districts, plus an appeal to legislators from outside of Chicago to restructure public schools to curb waste of state funds. CURE also secured support from the Latino community group, United Neighborhood Organization (UNO), significantly rounding out grassroots strength in almost every section of Chicago.

School reform supporters maintained a continuous presence at the state capitol during a six-week period early in the 1988 legislative session. Their efforts included weekly bus caravans of 50 to 150 parents, a petition campaign aimed at signing up 10,000 supporters for the CURE bill, and constant telephone calling and face-to-face visits in legislators' home districts. CURE also carried out a media campaign to educate the public, reshape the education debate, identify Designs for Change and CURE as expert resources, and apply pressure to the existing education system. The business community committed substantial resources to this phase of the campaign.

In an effort to achieve consensus, House Speaker Michael Madigan sponsored continued meetings of reform groups, school representatives, and union representatives to hammer out specific school reform legislation. During long hours of meeting in the Speaker's office, concepts were agreed upon, legislative language was drafted, and the specific wording of the bill was reviewed line by line. Because reformers had informed and pressured legislators, maintained a clear agenda, established informal lines of communication with legislators and staffs, and drafted legislation quickly, the speaker and many key legislative players were willing to support much of the coalition's agenda.

An important contribution was also made by the staff of the Chicago Panel on Public School Policy and Finance, who drafted language limiting central administrative power, shifting additional money to low-income schools, and establishing school-based budgeting.

As the bill was being drafted, the Republican legislative leadership and the governor indicated certain changes would ensure its passage with strong bipartisan support and the Governor's signature. While the Alliance for Better Chicago Schools did not view the requested changes as significant, they were offensive to the Chicago Teachers' Union, which pledged its support for the Democrats' reform legislation. The Democratic leadership pushed their version of the bill—the Chicago School Reform Act—through the House and the Senate in July of 1988 with less than a 60 percent majority. Under Illinois state law, this required the effective date to be delayed by a year.

Republican legislators attacked the Chicago School Reform Act a month after it was passed, citing several technical errors in the bill. Despite the Alliance for Better Chicago Schools' call for the commonly used practice of passing a "clean-up" bill to rectify technical error, Republican Governor James Thompson announced his intention to make major changes in the bill with his amendatory veto power.

Fearing no action would be taken on the bill and that it would die, the Alliance for Better Chicago Schools geared up with an intense grassroots lobbying campaign, a constant presence at the state capitol during the two-week veto session, position papers that analyzed key points at issue, and recommendations for specific legislative language. Additionally, the Alliance obtained endorsement of the bill by twenty-six nationally prominent educators. In the last days of the veto session, a compromise was reached. The bill passed the House and Senate and was signed by the governor in December of 1988, to go into effect in July of 1989.

For further information, please contact: Designs for Change, 220 South State Street, Suite 1900, Chicago, IL 60604-2163. Telephone (312) 922-0317.

Sterne Brunson School Development Program: Benton Harbor, Michigan

In 1981, Judge Douglas Hillman ordered the Benton Harbor Area School District in Benton Harbor, Michigan to adopt a School Development Program as part of a comprehensive desegregation plan. In the fall of 1982, the Benton Harbor School District implemented the program in a few pilot schools. By 1986, the model was adopted by all elementary schools.

Judge Hillman mandated implementation of the program as part of a remedy to improve the climate and academic conditions in schools. Eleven of sixteen elementary schools and all three inner-city high schools were classified as "high-need" schools on the basis of suspension and absenteeism rates, special education referral rates, and test results in mathematics and reading. At the time of the order, African Americans comprised 77 percent of the student population, up from 37 percent in 1966. By 1990, African American enrollment exceeded 90 percent. Benton Harbor was and has remained an economically depressed area where over half the students are eligible for the school's free or reduced-priced lunch program.

The model used for the court-ordered School Development Program, developed by Dr. James Comer, Professor of Child Psychiatry at the Yale University Medical School and Director of the Yale Child Study Center, is designed to build an active partnership between school staff and parents. It does so by creating a family-like environment within schools—one that emphasizes caring, social responsibility, and scholastic achievement. As Delores Gavin, coordinator for the School Development Program in Benton Harbor notes: "Parents are seen as an extension of the school community. In schools nothing is more important than the quality of the relationships among children, school staff, and parents. The model builds and fosters positive relationships. Children develop trust and learn more when they see parents and staff working hand-in-hand."

A key component of the model is a representative governance and management body in each school. In Benton Harbor this body—called the School Advisory Committee—is composed of teacher representatives selected by building teachers, parent representatives selected by the parent groups, the principal, and a representative member of the school support team. This governance and management body allows everyone with a stake in the school to have a voice in decision-making, leading to consensus planning, cooperative implementation, and a sense of ownership and trust between home and school.

The School Advisory Committee identifies problems and opportunities related to school climate, staff development, and the academic program. It develops a school improvement plan that details objectives in each area, strategies for meeting these objectives, and a process for monitoring and evaluating the plan. The committee prioritizes concerns, identifies and allocates resources, governs program implementation, and evaluates and modifies strategies and program elements.

The School Development Program provides important roles for parents in schools—work as classroom aides or as support staff, for example, in the library or main office. Classroom aides and other parent workers form the core of the parent group. They work along with other parents and with school staff to carry out and support all aspects of the school development program.

Parents also organize, run, and attend a number of school events designed to bring the school and community closer together. Such events are part of a carefully planned and coordinated yearly school calendar that helps to create a welcoming school setting.

Representative governance and management, extensive parent participation, and carefully planned school events interact to provide an environment that promotes learning and reduces behavior problems. This allows the School Support Team—a third critical component of the School Development Program—to concentrate on children with more serious difficulties. Through representation on the School Advisory Committee, the School Support Team assists parents and teachers to develop social and academic programs that address child development needs—especially their social and emotional needs.

To facilitate implementation of the model, Benton Harbor established an Urban Academy overseen by a Steering Committee that is the district level equivalent of the school-based School Advisory Committee. It is a representative governance and management body comprised of administrators, teachers, and parents. The Steering Committee reviews and analyzes school achievement and behavioral data. It sets policy, makes program decisions, sets program goals, and monitors implementation of the model at the school level. The committee looks for opportunities for program growth across the schools and also addresses common concerns.

The road to systemwide implementation of the model has not always been smooth. Many teachers were skeptical about having parents working in their classrooms and had difficulty seeing parents' strengths and building on them. Likewise, many parents harbored misunderstandings and mistrust of school staff members.

Because Steering Committee members were aware of the difficulties schools were experiencing in successfully involving parents, they established a systemwide policy and process to bring parents into the school in an atmosphere that was welcoming and free of hostility. But the principal's role was critical. Schools needed creative, innovative, and committed administrators to bring the two groups together.

When Joyce Johnson became principal of the Sterne Brunson School in 1984—an elementary school where over 95 percent of the children are African American and over 75 percent qualify for the free or reduced-priced lunch program—she was well aware of the problems experienced by some of the other elementary schools in their efforts to implement the School Development Model. As assistant principal of Hull Elementary School—one of the pilot schools—she also saw what a dramatic difference the program could make when it resulted in a successful partnership between parents and school staff. Johnson was determined to bring the model to the Sterne Brunson, but to implement it in a way that did not repeat the earlier mistakes of other schools.

The first obstacle she faced was convincing the Superintendent of Schools to allow the Sterne Brunson to become a School Development Model school for the upcoming school term. The Sterne Brunson was not slated as a second-round implementation school and the superintendent's first response was a resounding "No!" Convinced the model would make her school a better place for everyone, Johnson went directly to Dr. James Comer who was visiting the district and requested his support. She also attended a meeting of principals chosen to implement the model and persuasively presented her case. With the vocal support of the other principals, she finally received the "go ahead" from her superintendent.

Principal Johnson recognized that one of the errors made by earlier schools was an attempt to implement all components of the model at the same time when, in fact, the model required a step-by-step process. At the Sterne Brunson, the first year was spent developing the school improvement plan. Drawing on the school's Parent Teacher Organization (PTO), an already established and accepted body, Johnson asked the president of the PTO to sit on the School Advisory Committee and asked the PTO membership to elect two other representatives. Parent Rita Broadway, former president of the PTO and active in the school for nine years, emphasizes that parents had a strong and equal voice on the Committee from the beginning. Aware that parents may be anxious about speaking in front of school staff, Johnson actively sought out their opinions and encouraged parents to voice their concerns.

Johnson worked to convey to staff that the parents were not coming in to "take over" their classrooms. Likewise, she stressed that while staff should have high expectations of parents, they should not expect them to have the same skills as teachers. Social occasions were planned to allow parents and teachers to get to know one another and to reduce misunderstandings and mistrust between them. As Joyce points out: "Parents often shy away from schools because we, as professionals, make them feel little. We do not give them the message that they, as parents, have something to offer. At our school we try to find parents' strengths and build on them."

Through her words and actions, Johnson encouraged open communication among all members of the school community. She acknowledged and discussed the problems that other schools had experienced and that she wanted to avoid. An effort was made to build an open, accepting atmosphere that would allow anyone seeing a potential problem to feel comfortable about bringing it out in the open for discussion either at the School Advisory Committee meeting or individually with the principal or another staff member.

Teachers and parents were encouraged to work together in the classrooms, but the door was left open if either party felt that it was not a good match. A teacher who had gained the trust of parents and was highly respected by both parents and teachers was given the role of parent liaison. As parent Rita Broadway explains: "Parents are often anxious about what they say. They're afraid they'll mess up somewhere along the line or think they do not have a place speaking out." The parent liaison allows parents to present their concerns to someone they know and trust first, then the liaison and the parent together put the concerns before the School Advisory Committee.

Since the school began implementing the model, over 100 parents have participated in some capacity or other. The first year, 21 parents worked at the school on paid stipends, mostly in classrooms as teacher's aides. While the funding awarded to the school decreased each year, a number of parents stayed on in a volunteer capacity.

The school has reaped benefits from encouraging parents to have a valued role in the school and an active voice in how it is run. Large numbers of family members regularly attend school events. The school has an 85 to 90 percent attendance rate at parent/teacher conferences. Parents have consistently raised money for field trips and to pay for the badly needed renovations to the playground. A number of parents have left the parent-in-training program for full-time paid employment.

Because everyone has a voice—and therefore a sense of ownership—problems are solved through collective wisdom and there is strong support throughout the community for the school program. Equally important, children see that parents value the school. As parent Rita Broadway concludes: "The children often develop closer relationships with the parents. They trust you and see you as a familiar parent figure. Students who are real problems may just need a hug and to know that someone cares about them and is listening to them."

For further information, please contact: Ms. Joyce Johnson, Principal, Stern Brunson Elementary School, 1131 Columbus, Benton Harbor, MI 49022.

PROMISING PRACTICES

Literatura Infantil: Watsonville, California

A mother concludes: "Since I have no need to feel ashamed of speaking Spanish, I have become strong. Now I feel I can speak with the teachers about my children's education. I can tell them I want my children to know Spanish. I have gained courage."

Another father shares: "I discovered my children can write. I have discovered that by reading books one can find out many things. I have discovered I can read in Spanish about the history of this country and of other countries."

These two parents participated in an innovative children's literature project designed to help parents and children read and learn together. The program—Literatura Infantil—was developed jointly by Dr. Alma Flor Ada, a children's book author and director of the University of San Francisco's Department of Education's Multicultural Program; Dr. Paul Nava, director of Watsonville Migrant Education Program; and Alfonso Anaya, former director of the Bilingual Program of the Pajaro Valley School District in Watsonville, California.

The Pajaro Valley School District serves a mostly rural population of approximately 15,000 students. Half the children are Latino, over one-third are migrants, and one-third have limited proficiency in English. During 1985 and 1986, Dr. Flor Ada visited the children as part of a "Meet the Author" program which until that point had featured only English-speaking authors. Dr. Flor Ada read her stories, explained how a book is made, discussed what motivates an author to write, and talked about her decision to speak and write in Spanish. The children responded with great enthusiasm.

If the strategy works for children, why not for adults, wondered former Bilingual Program Director Alfonso Anaya as he struggled to find ways to increase the confidence and involvement of Spanish-speaking parents. He envisioned a program that would not only improve reading and writing skills, but also strengthen the relationship between parents and children and between home and school. His survey of parents revealed they were anxious to find learning materials and wanted to know how to teach their children at home.

Dr. Flor Ada collaborated with Alfonso Anaya, Dr. Paul Nava, and other school officials to design the program. The Bilingual Program agreed to fund the program for the first year. According to Dr. Flor Ada, two key beliefs drove program design: 1) the importance of parent involvement in children's education and 2) the need to help parents recover their sense of dignity and identity.

The program sought to convey to parents that they were their children's first and most crucial teachers—that they could influence their children's school achievement by teaching them at home regardless of their own educational experiences. To make instruction meaningful and relevant to the family's life experience and to increase self-esteem, all the books used and given to the families drew from Latino culture and were written in Spanish.

For the first meeting, invitations in Spanish were sent home from school with children inviting parents to meet a writer of children's books. Outreach efforts included communications to both mothers and fathers to convey that both parents had an important role to play in their children's education. To encourage parents to attend, transportation and child care were provided. Because many of the parents associated schools with failure—either their own or their children's—the group met in a roomy library rather than a classroom. The setting also surrounded the parents with books, reinforcing the message that books were important.

Nearly 100 parents attended the first meeting. Dr. Flor Ada had selected well-written and beautifully illustrated Spanish-language children's books to read to the parents. Books were chosen because of their quality and because of their relevance to the life experiences of the families. After explaining the purpose of the group and the importance and value of parents helping their children at home in their home language, Dr. Flor Ada read the books to the parents as they would read them to their children. A brief discussion of the books followed the reading. At the end, each parent was allowed to select one of the books to take home.

The project sought to strengthen family interactions and increase their skill and pride in the ability to read and write. With each book, parents received a list of questions to stimulate home discussions, related activities to try with their children, and a blank book to encourage their children to write their own stories. Parents reported reading aloud frequently to their children at home. Children brought home books from the school library. None of the parents had a library card at the beginning of the project. Nine months later, almost all reported visits to the library, often with their children. One father wrote a daily question on a blackboard for his children to answer in writing when they got home from school. The question and answer then formed the basis for a family discussion. At the parents' suggestion, their children's writings were compiled in a book.

Attendance at the monthly meetings remained high throughout the year—60 to 100 parents, many of whom were couples. At each of the sessions, parents met in small, teacher-facilitated groups to discuss the books they selected the previous month. Discussion focused on experiences of reading and writing as a family over the past month. Participating teachers were selected and trained for the program because of their history of strong involvement with parents. When the large group reconvened, some parents read their children's own stories. The opportunity to present their children's work to a large audience increased the self-esteem and confidence of the parents while helping to develop communication skills. New books were then presented, followed by small group discussions again facilitated by the teachers, including a critical analysis of the new stories as well as application to real-life situations. The facilitators reinforced the value of the parents as their children's teachers and the importance of the home language. All sessions were conducted in Spanish.

Although the project was very successful, the Bilingual Program could no longer provide funding after the first year. Lupe Soltero, a determined and committed teacher, continued the program on her own on a small scale with her student's parents for one year. She and others then wrote a proposal and were awarded a special grant to reinstitute the project on a large scale. It is now funded by the State Department's Office of Migrant Education and administered by Lucy Castano, Migrant Parent Coordinator for the Watsonville Migrant Program. The program involves parents from six different schools and is conducted bimonthly at three school sites. The parents are migrants with children from pre-school through third grade.

At each site, the program is conducted by a team of one or two teachers, a migrant parent, a psychologist, an aide, and a migrant work-study student. The aide and student provide child care during the sessions. Transportation is also provided. The parent education coordinator from the Migrant Program continues extensive outreach efforts to teach parents about the program and encourage them to attend the sessions. Supportive principals also assist in recruitment efforts.

The focus of the program has remained on reading and writing books together as a family. The format of the sessions remains basically the same. Parents are expected to read books with their children each month and to write or draw stories. Parents who are unable to read use picture books for storytelling. Team members encourage parents to write their family histories with their children. This way, family members learn to see their culture and the migrant experience as a source of pride and affirmation.

Part of each session is also dedicated to a discussion of parenting skills, especially increasing motivation and improving communication among family members. Team members use opportunities to model teaching strategies used in the classroom to help parents develop important teaching skills. Parents provide feedback at the end of each session on what they liked and why, what they would change, and what they wanted to learn more about. As a result of this feedback, additional workshops have been conducted on substance abuse, discipline, and other topics.

The program has seen many benefits. Self-esteem and pride in their culture has increased among family members. As their self confidence has increased, parents have taken a more active role in their children's education. They see themselves as important teachers and advocates for their children. A number have taken on leadership roles in their schools and community. Several petitioned the district school board for a meeting to discuss the academic future of their children and a number are active members of their school's Parent Advisory Committees. Parents have also given presentations on the program at regional and state migrant education conferences.

As Lupe Soltero, who remains a teacher in the program concludes: "Too often parents feel that because they do not speak English, they have nothing to offer to their children's education. We teach them this is not true—they have language, culture, heritage, and honorable work. We have seen children blossom as their parents begin to value themselves and see themselves as teachers of their children."

For further information, please contact: Dr. Paul Nava, Director, Watsonville Migrant Education, 440-B Arthur Road, Watsonville, CA 95076.

Current Research Relating to Topics Discussed in Chapter One

The Value of Parent Involvement

Active parent participation in schools in a variety of roles over an extended period of time can significantly enhance children's attendance, self-esteem, academic achievement, school behavior, and attitudes and expectations toward school **(Brandt, 1989; Chan, 1987; Chavkin, 1989; Comer, 1984; Epstein, 1984a, 1984c; Greenberg, 1989; Haynes, Comer, and Hamilton-Lee, 1989; Henderson, 1981, 1987; Henderson, *et al.*, 1986; Johnston and Slotnik, 1985; Leler, 1983; Lueder, 1989; Marockie and Jones, 1987; Rasinski and Fredericks, 1989; Tizard, Schofield, and Hewison, 1982; Wayson, 1984).**

Moreover, meaningful parent participation results in benefits to parents and their children that extend beyond the individual school. Parents develop increased self-confidence, have more positive attitudes toward schools and school staff, help gather support in the community for their schools, become more involved in other community activities, and enroll in other educational programs **(Becher, 1984; Chavkin, 1989; Comer, 1984; Cummins, 1986; Haynes, Comer, and Hamilton-Lee, 1989; Henderson, *et al.*, 1986).**

Assessments of programs that involve parents as decision-makers have been almost uniformly positive **(Chan, 1987; Comer, 1984; Henderson, 1987).** For students, these programs have improved academic achievement, reduced behavioral difficulties, increased attendance, and raised student expectations. Parents increased their leadership role in the school and worked collaboratively on common concerns.

Active parent involvement can also help bridge the gap between White middle-class school staff and low-income, limited-English-proficient, or minority children. Moreover, when educators engage low-income or minority parents as partners in their children's education, parents develop increased self-confidence and a sense of efficacy which is communicated to their children with positive academic results **(Chavkin, 1989; Comer, 1984; Cummins, 1986).** Additionally, attitudes and expectations of teachers toward students are changed through collaborative work with their parents **(Comer, 1984; Greenberg, 1989).**

Recent research indicates that parents' efforts to help their children learn have a greater impact on children's school success than the family's socioeconomic, educational, or racial/ethnic status. Children do well in school when their parents: express high expectations for school achievement and stress the value of schooling; conduct warm, nurturing, and frequent interactions with their children; demonstrate a strong sense of self-mastery and control over their lives; handle discipline issues in an authoritative rather than an authoritarian or permissive manner; conduct frequent discussions about school and provide positive reinforcement for schoolwork and other interests; establish regular routines and mealtimes; and encourage a purposeful use of time and space. **(Becher, 1984; Chavkin, 1989; Clark, 1983; Schiamberg and Chun, 1986).**

Parents have a strong desire to become involved in their children's education and are usually very supportive of efforts to engage them as partners in parent involvement initiatives **(Chavkin, 1989; Lindle, 1989b; Lueder, 1989).** In a survey of over 1,000 parents involved in various programs supported under Tennessee's statewide parent involvement initiative, 95 percent of parents reported they were more involved in their children's education, held more positive attitudes about their children's schools, were better able to help their children, and would recommend their particular program to other parents. Over 90 percent reported their children's achievement and overall attitude toward school improved, and over 80 percent saw an improvement in their children's behavior **(Lueder, 1989).**

Barriers to Parent Involvement

Although significant long-term benefits to several types of parent participation in the public schools are clearly documented, actual meaningful participation remains rare **(Davies, 1988; Foster, 1984; Fruchter, 1984; Greenberg, 1989; Lightfoot, 1981; Rasinski, 1989; Zeldin, 1990).** Researchers have identified five types of barriers to increased parent involvement: 1) logistics of organizing family life; 2) school/staff attitudes; 3) the cultural distance between school, staff, and families; 4) the organizational and legal structure of the schools; and 5) inadequate pre-service and in-service preparation for working with parents **(Comer, 1984; Cummins, 1986; Davies, 1988; Greenberg, 1989; Henderson, *et al.*, 1986; Ogbu, 1981; Rasinski, 1989; Rasinski and Fredericks, 1989; Williams, 1981; Zeldin, 1990).**

Because increasing numbers of children are living in one-parent or two-working-parent families, the logistics of organizing life to allow for significant parent participation in schools are more difficult. The competing demands of work and family can leave parents with little time to spend on school or their children's education **(Brandt, 1989; Epstein, 1984b; First, *et al.*, 1988; Fruchter, 1984; Henderson, 1987; Lindle, 1989a, 1989b).** Struggling with these competing priorities, some parents conclude that they do not need to be involved because the responsibility has been delegated to the schools **(Seeley, 1989).**

Researchers have identified a variety of school/staff attitudes that undermine parent participation, including: 1) the perception that parents as educational "amateurs" should defer to professionals in decisions regarding curriculum development, student instruction, and school governance; 2) a view of parents as pushy and overly aggressive, difficult to contact, and resistant to teachers' recommendations; 3) expectations by educators that children from families who deviate from standard middle-class norms will experience problems in school; 4) a willingness by teachers to blame the parents and families for the academic or behavioral problems of the students rather than considering parents as potential partners in efforts to address the problems; and 5) an emphasis by teachers and administrators on the problems of low-income families while ignoring their strengths **(Chavkin, 1989; Comer, 1984; Davies, 1988; Epstein, 1984c; Foster, 1984; Fruchter, 1984; Greenberg, 1989; Henderson, *et al.*, 1986; Lightfoot, 1981; Lindle, 1989b; Rasinski, 1989; Williams, 1981).**

Teachers and administrators often interpret low-income, limited-English-proficient, or minority parents' hostility to and withdrawal from the schools as indicating little interest in, or commitment to, their children's education. In fact, low-income or minority parents consistently express strong interest in their children's education, understand the value of schooling, and desire greater involvement in their children's education **(Brandt, 1989; Greenberg, 1989; Davies, 1988; First, *et al.*, 1988; Lightfoot, 1981; Olsen, 1988).** The results of a recent study completed by the Southwest Educational Development Laboratory **(Chavkin, 1989)** that surveyed 1,188 African American and Latino parents from six states clearly showed that parents, regardless of their ethnic background, are concerned about their children's education. Ninety-five percent of the parents surveyed expressed a strong commitment to their children's education. They were interested in supporting their children's schools in the more traditional ways through assisting at school events and helping their children at home, but they also wanted a voice in school decisions, such as how their children's progress is evaluated, and choice of classroom discipline methods.

Researchers have found that other factors lead to minority parent alienation from and confrontation with the schools, including: the attitudinal barriers listed above; differential treatment of low-income, limited-English-proficient, or minority students by the schools; and parents' own feelings of alienation and inadequacy stemming from their own difficult school experience **(Chavkin, 1989; Lightfoot, 1981; Lueder, 1989; Zeldin, 1990).** Staff accusations that parents lack interest in education act to enlarge barriers to effective home-school linkages. A cycle of mutual mistrust and misunderstanding develops between parents and teachers and acts as a deterrent to successful efforts to involve parents **(Chavkin, 1989; Greenberg, 1989; Lightfoot, 1981; Ogbu, 1981; Rasinski, 1989; Rasinski and Fredericks, 1989; Zeldin, 1990).**

The organization and structure of a school also limits the ability and desire of teachers and other school staff to establish effective home/school linkages. Teachers tend to be isolated in the classroom with little time and few incentives to establish lines of communication with parents. While individual teachers may excel at working with parents, they are seldom recognized for this skill or given support and encouragement to continue their efforts **(Chavkin, 1989; Greenberg, 1989; Henderson, *et al.*, 1986; Hoover-Dempsey, Bassler, and Brissie, 1987; Zeldin, 1990).** Many teachers come to see the classroom as their only opportunity to exercise uncompromising control and autonomy. As a result, parent intrusion into this domain comes to be seen as a threat to teacher control and professional competence **(Greenberg, 1989; Lipsky, 1980; Rasinski, 1989).**

School districts and individual schools will often have policies declaring the importance of shared responsibility and the value of parent participation but fail to allocate the staff time needed to meet the policy goals or to create the school structures required for collaborative efforts to occur **(Greenberg, 1989; Zeldin, 1990).** Other policy mandates often compete with and constrain efforts at shared decision-making and collaboration. These include a state's legal definition of instructional days and hours, a district's mandate for test score accountability, a district's requirements for curriculum, and provisions in the union contract **(Zeldin, 1990).**

Even when teachers and administrators strongly support the concept of parent involvement, they often receive little support or training to accomplish this. The vast majority of teacher education institutions fail to provide the amount of history, theory, practice, and guidance pre-service teachers need to enable them to work comfortably and extensively with all kinds of parents **(Greenberg, 1989). Chavkin and Williams (1988)** found that less than 4 percent of the teacher education programs in the southwestern region of the United States offered a course in parent involvement. Similarly, promoting parent involvement is not typically part of an administrator's training or experience, and they often find it difficult to provide the necessary leadership in this area **(Daresh, 1988, *cited in* Zeldin, 1990).**

The importance of strong pre-service and in-service training is underscored by the results of a study **(Hoover-Dempsey, Bassler, and Brissie, 1987)** that looked at the parent involvement efforts of over 1000 teachers in 66 elementary schools in a large mid-southern state. Teacher efficacy, defined as teachers' belief that they are effective in teaching, that the children they teach can learn, and that there is a body of professional knowledge available to them when they need assistance, was the most important factor associated with several types of parent involvement. It was a stronger predictor of parent involvement than several other school and staff characteristics including teacher degree level, grade level, and even school socio-economic status.

Research indicates that when schools do not work to involve parents, parent education and social class are strong determining factors in who does become involved. But when schools are committed to parent involvement and work hard to involve all parents, parent education and social class decrease or disappear as determining factors **(Brandt, 1989; Chavkin, 1989; Zeldin, 1990).**

Ineffective Programs

The failure of previous attempts to involve parents further discourages teachers from efforts to engage parents. Too often schools assume that programs designed to increase parent involvement fail because parents are unable or unwilling to participate, even though the effectiveness of the program was never evaluated. Recent analysis of home-school initiatives concludes that parent participation programs often fail because parents are not involved in the conceptualization, design, or implementation of such programs **(Chavkin, 1989; Rasinski, 1989; Rasinski and Fredericks, 1989).** Home-school programs are usually initiated and designed exclusively by the school and are very directive in nature. Under these conditions, programs frequently do not reflect the realities of the home situations of many children. Parents develop little ownership of them which leads to minimal commitment and eventual failure **(Greenberg, 1989; Rasinski, 1989).**

Alternative Practices

Simple but significant solutions can overcome logistical barriers to parent involvement. Transportation and child care can assist some parents. Flexibility in scheduling and location can increase access. A key to overcoming many logistical barriers is often simply to recognize them and to acknowledge a legitimate school interest in overcoming them **(Chan, 1987; Epstein, 1984d; Henderson, *et al.*, 1986).**

In examining schools with meaningful and well-developed parent participation, researchers have identified the following factors of their success: a school environment that welcomes parent participation, stresses two-way communication between home and school, and includes written policies that legitimize the importance of parent involvement; school leadership that is committed to involving parents and available to work with parents and teachers to increase parent participation; collegial and collaborative relations among staff and between staff and parents including a willingness to share leadership with parents; involvement of parents in all phases of planning and implementation; active and flexible outreach to parents that takes into account the many work and home demands parents face daily; numerous and wide-ranging opportunities for parent involvement in the schools and a commitment to maintaining parent involvement over the long term; district-level leadership that does not impede links between staff and parents; administrative support that includes funding and/or staff to carry out parent involvement efforts; on-going training available for staff and parents that focuses on developing partnering skills; and regular evaluation activities that enable staff and parents to make ongoing revisions to ensure that activities strengthen the partnership **(Brandt, 1989; Brooks and Sussman, 1990; Chan, 1987; Comer, 1984; Henderson, *et al.*, 1986; Hoover-Dempsey, Bassler, and Brissie, 1987; Johnston and Slotnik, 1985; Rasinski, 1989; Rasinski and Fredericks, 1989; Williams and Chavkin, 1989).**

Parent involvement initiatives work when parents are empowered partners in all phases of decision-making and have acquired substantial roles in the planning, design, and implementation of parent involvement programs **(Chavkin, 1989; Haynes, Comer, and Hamilton-Lee, 1989; Rasinski, 1989).** In effective partnerships, school staff recognize the invaluable knowledge and insight parents have about their children, their culture, and their community's views and values. Moreover, school staff realize that many parents will not readily offer their perspectives and thoughts, and they actively solicit parents' knowledge **(Chavkin, 1989; Rasinski, 1989).**

Developing and sustaining partnerships with parents requires schools to renegotiate essential relationships and roles and restructure organizational patterns. This type of change is a slow and incremental process. Schools need leadership, guidance, and time to allow these processes to work **(Brooks and Sussman, 1990; Zeldin, 1990).** When parents and teachers engage in an equal partnership characterized by mutual respect, they can develop joint accountability as they work toward the common goal of success for all children **(Greenberg, 1989; Lindle, 1989b; Rasinski, 1989; Seeley, 1989; Zeldin, 1990).**

School Governance

A major focus of current education reform efforts is on the restructuring of the governance system of schools. Across the country, school reform proposals include a recommendation that school districts shift significant decision-making authority over to the individual schools **(Cistone, Fernandez, and Tornillo, 1989; Lindquist and Mauriel, 1989; Malen, Ogawa and Kranz, 1990; Mitchell, 1990).** The intent is to strengthen school-site leadership and empower the people who are most closely involved with the daily operations of the school **(Cistone, *et al.*, 1989; Lindquist and Mauriel, 1989; Lomotey and Swanson, 1989).**

School-site management is essentially a form of decentralization. While school-site management plans vary, the general approach requires that the power and decisions formerly made by superintendents and school boards be delegated to the teachers, principals, parents, community members, and, where appropriate, to students of the local schools. This authority includes the power to make decisions in the central domains of budget, personnel, and program **(Lindquist and Mauriel, 1989; Malen, *et al.*, 1990; Marburger, 1985).**

A central component of school-site management is the formal structure (council, committee, team, board) that acts as the mechanism to implement school-site management. The goal is to delegate significant decision-making authority over the management of the school to a broad group of stakeholders **(Lindquist and Mauriel, 1989; Malen, *et al.*, 1990; Marburger, 1985).**

The promise of school-site management is based on the notion that giving representatives of school constituents an empowered voice in school decisions results in a feeling of ownership and commitment to the school by the constituents. The theory is that shared decision-making results in better decisions, higher-quality school-wide planning, and improvements in workplace conditions, which in turn lead to enhanced staff morale and motivation. Improvements and innovations in instruction are stimulated, and improvements in the achievement of students eventually follow **(Lindquist and Mauriel, 1989; Malen, *et al.*, 1990; Mitchell, 1990).**

The results of a nationwide survey of a representative sample of over 1,500 administrators suggest that there is widespread support for school-site management **(Heller, Woodworth, Jacobson, and Conway, 1989).** Eighty-seven percent of the administrators surveyed (96 percent of the principals and 80 percent of the superintendents) thought school decisions were best made at the building level. But administrators differed regarding who they thought should participate on school-site councils and what decisions the councils should have control over as a function of where they stood on the management ladder. Overall, 99 percent thought principals should participate on councils, and 97 percent supported teacher participation. Principals wanted to see principals, teachers, and parents sharing school decision-making. Sixty-two percent saw a role for the superintendent in the process, and 48 percent thought school board members should participate. In contrast, 65 percent of the superintendents supported school board member participation, and 82 percent envisioned a role for themselves in important school decisions.

While the vast majority of superintendents reported that they supported school-site management, they also indicated that they thought they should retain authority over budgets, hiring, staffing, and maintenance. They were willing to turn authority for textbooks and curriculum over to the school. On the other hand, principals want broad-based authority over decisions. They reported wanting authority over budget, staffing, hiring, purchases, maintenance, and curriculum **(Heller, *et al.*, 1989).**

Although survey results showed strong support for school-site management, albeit with different notions of what it entailed, they also revealed that implementation lags behind considerably. One-fourth of the administrators surveyed reported that school-site management was in effect in their schools, and 28 percent reported that it was in the planning stages. Who participated in the decision-making varied considerably. Principals (99 percent of the cases) and teachers (85 percent of the cases) were the only consistent players. Seventy-five percent of the schools got the superintendent involved and slightly more than half included school board, central office, and building staff members. Parents were included in the process in only 40 percent of the schools and community members in only 25 percent **(Heller, *et al.*, 1989).**

Barriers to School-Site Management

Lindquist and Mauriel (1989) posit that there is a disparity between the theory and goals of school-site management and the practice of school-site management as it is conducted at the school district's central office and school buildings. They hold that three general kinds of problems hinder the development and implementation of school-site management: 1) conceptual flaws in the notion of school-site management and inconsistency in the various definitions of school-site management employed; 2) a lack of motivation to delegate authority to schools; and 3) the formidable requirements of time and skill that the implementation of school-site management demands.

Recent research on the effectiveness of school-site management and the obstacles hampering its successful implementation provides strong support for Lindquist and Mauriel's position. Results of the survey reviewed above **(Heller, *et al.*, 1989)** point to the incongruence in the different concepts of school-site management held by the various stakeholders in the system. **Malen and others (1990)** also found that school-site management plans are often ambiguous, and the conceptual framework underlying them unclear. Moreover, the need to keep council decisions consistent with existing policies frequently acts to constrain site-management efforts **(Heller, *et al.*, 1989; Malen, *et al.*, 1990).**

Underlying the concept of school-site management is the belief that authority can be delegated from the school board to central administration to the school building to the site council. Not only is the process extremely complex, but its success requires the recasting of long-established organizational systems **(Lindquist and Mauriel, 1989)** which are, as one superintendent put it, "steeped in tradition and habit" **(Mitchell, 1990, p. 26).** Changing the line of command has proved one of the most difficult barriers facing the successful implementation of school-site management. Research completed by **Malen and others (1990)** revealed that school-site councils rarely address central policy issues. Moreover, council members typically described their involvement as "listening," "advising," "endorsing the decisions others have already made," or taking "rubber stamp" or "token" action **(Malen, *et al.*, 1990, p. 32).**

Members' roles are limited in large part because they tend to defer to traditional lines of authority. In the councils composed of teachers and principals analyzed by **Malen and others (1990),** teachers exerted little meaningful influence. Through a number of low-cost strategies, principals controlled the meetings and thereby the decision-making process. Teachers were reluctant to challenge this dynamic and tended to approve what the principal wanted. Not surprisingly, councils that included parents presented similar patterns.

Administrators surveyed by **Heller and others (1989)** also reported that central office staff were unwilling to let go of authority and feared loss of power. Superintendents were seen as blocking the path to school-based decision-making. Principals were faulted for lacking leadership and refusing to let go of control. Teachers were seen as unsupportive, resistant to accepting responsibility, and uninterested in change. Respondents pointed to the strong hold the past and tradition has on those who work in the schools. **Mitchell (1990)** reports similar findings.

As school-site council members struggle to forge new alliances and renegotiate old ones against the weight of habit and tradition, they find these time-consuming demands competing with numerous other responsibilities. Frustration, confusion, and anxiety can arise as participants work to redefine their roles, recognize the limits of their power, and confront fiscal constraints **(Lindquist and Mauriel, 1989; Little, 1984; Malen, *et al.*, 1990).** These struggles are exacerbated by union contracts, state laws, and school board policies which can all serve to limit the boundaries of school-site management plans **(Cistone, *et al.*, 1989; Heller, *et al.*, 1989; Lindquist and Mauriel, 1989; Malen, *et al.*, 1990; Mitchell, 1990; Zeldin, 1990).**

School-site management requires major changes in organizational structures, reallocation of power and resources, and renegotiation of the governance roles of the school board, central office, teachers' union, school staff, and community stakeholders **(Cistone, *et al.*, 1989; Lindquist and Mauriel, 1989).** The successful restructuring of the governance and authority framework of schools is dependent on process. Too often in the push for immediate changes and observable improvements the importance of process and time gets lost **(Zeldin, 1990).** Decentralizing authority and decision-making takes time and requires considerable resources. In general, schools have repeatedly failed to allocate the time, money, training, or logistical support required for the successful transfer to school-site management **(Cistone, *et al.*, 1989; Heller, *et al.*, 1989; Lindquist and Mauriel, 1989; Malen, *et al.*, 1990; Zeldin, 1990).**

Enabling Conditions for School-Site Management

For school-site management to reach its promise, the multiple and diverse obstacles that stand in its way must be confronted. While the research on school-site management is not extensive, findings to date suggest guidelines for addressing the barriers hindering its implementation.

Clarification of the roles and responsibilities of the members of the school-site council is required for councils to function effectively **(Jennings, 1989; Lindquist and Mauriel, 1989; Malen, *et al.*, 1990).** This clarification should specify exactly what authority is delegated to the council participants and how that authority is distributed. Moreover, the constraints placed on members' decision-making authority by union contracts, local, state, and federal policies and procedures, and/or accountability mechanisms have to be recognized and addressed **(Cistone, *et al.*, 1989; Malen, *et al.*, 1990).**

Schools must acknowledge that change is costly and takes time. Without the critical resources, school-site management will never fulfill its promise. School councils require extensive training, technical assistance, logistical support, and supplemental funds **(Cistone, *et al.*, 1989; Heller, *et al.*, 1989; Lindquist and Mauriel, 1989; Malen, *et al.*, 1990).**

Realigning power structures is a complex process. Sharing authority requires that some stakeholders lose power while others gain it. Tradition, norms, and the resistance to relinquishing power can nullify even the best laid school-site management plans **(Lindquist and Mauriel, 1989; Malen, *et al.*, 1990; Mitchell, 1990; Zeldin, 1990).** Training must directly confront concerns regarding entrenched power structures, traditions, and long-held norms. Such training should help administrators, teachers, parents, and other community members to redefine the roles they play in decision-making and build the skills required to carry out those roles **(Jennings, 1989; Lindquist and Mauriel, 1989; Malen, *et al.*, 1990; Zeldin, 1990).**

School-site management plans need to include provisions that require council membership to reflect the diversity of the community and include representatives of the various stakeholders in the community. Plans should also include strategies for recruiting participants with different backgrounds, perspectives, and orientations **(Malen, *et al.*, 1990).**

Research that has looked at successful school-site management efforts and other less comprehensive forms of shared decision-making point to the importance of a collaborative framework. The support of the superintendent and principal is critical for the successful implementation of school-site management **(Berman, 1984; Cistone, *et al.*, 1989; Heller, *et al.*, 1989; Lindquist and Mauriel, 1989; Mitchell, 1990).** In some cases, the support of the school board may also be key **(Cistone, *et al.*, 1989; Lindquist and Mauriel, 1989). Berman (1984),** in an extensive evaluation of California's statewide School Improvement Program, found that schools that had effective shared decision-making had a number of characteristics in common. These included: strong support for shared decision-making and collaboration from the principal and other school leadership; a strong sense of efficacy among the school staff; a willingness among the staff to go beyond the concerns of the classroom to address school-wide issues; collegial relationships among school staff; and a shared sense of purpose or vision among the various community stakeholders.

2

Student Admission and Placement

Children are entitled to learn in an integrated, heterogeneous setting responsive to different learning styles and abilities.

A Vision of Admission and Placement at the Good Common School

Joe García, who covers the education beat for the *Daily Ledger,* props his streaming umbrella in a corner and turns to survey the school board meeting room. Although tonight's meeting won't begin for fifteen minutes, parents are steadily filing in. Their numbers promise to fill the room. At front and left, a local television station is setting up lights. Several of Joe's colleagues are already seated in the press row, including reporters from WBLK, the local Black radio outlet, and *La Semana,* the Spanish-language tabloid where he cut his teeth as an education writer.

Joe guesses the larger-than-usual crowd and the interest from ethnic media outlets are stimulated by the equity issues on tonight's meeting agenda. Since Independent School District #4 set out to restructure itself a year or so ago, equity issues are raised more often than during the preceding phase of school reform when the pursuit of "excellence" for some outweighed a commitment to equal access for all.

There is one equity proposal on tonight's agenda. The board will vote on proposed modifications to the district's admission policies. Additionally, there will be an open microphone period to discuss student placement. After the meeting, Joe will return to the newsroom to write a piece covering the evening's meeting for tomorrow's early edition. He will also add notes from tonight's meeting to the computerized collection of information he is hoarding for a future series about equal educational outcomes for children of color.

Reverend Ben Washington, the school board's chairperson, is a respected leader in the city's African American community. Some have used the school board as a political stepping stone. Not the reverend. He joined the board six years ago, putting his sharp mind to work on the challenge of making schools more effective, especially for children of color. A year ago, he handily won a second term and ascended to the chair. Tonight, he moves quickly through housekeeping items, then asks Superintendent Jesse "Doc" Holloran to make some opening remarks about the evening's more substantial agenda items.

Doc begins by pointing out to the audience that decisions determining student admission and placement occur at two levels: the district level and the school-site level. He explains that district-level decisions determine which children have access to which schools, while school-level decisions determine how students are placed within programs and instructional groups inside the school building.

He observes that it is the school board's responsibility to create—and his own responsibility to implement—admission policies that ensure a student mix in each school that mirrors the racial, cultural, and linguistic diversity of the district as a whole. He then reviews the broadly-based, participatory process used during the past six months to develop student admission criteria, noting the process and the resulting criteria are systemwide, explicitly stated, easy to understand, and disseminated in comprehensible languages to all parents and community-based organizations.

Doc then explains in some detail how a computer-based system will be used to select an inclusive pool of applicants for each school, stressing the need to make admissions decisions centrally, not at individual schools. As Doc speaks, the margins of Joe's notebook fill up with a single word, absent-mindedly doodled inside pencilled squares and triangles: CHOICE. Staring at his notebook, Joe is momentarily startled to hear the word spoken by Doc, who says, "We value effective choice because it encourages greater engagement among parents, students, and school personnel. The point of choice in our district is not to get your child into the best school. Because we strive to make all of our schools equal in quality, choice turns on questions of program diversity."

Doc concludes with some comments on magnet schools. Remarking on the popularity of these programs in some communities, he reminds the board that its decision not to develop magnet schools was based on a commitment to avoid diverting resources from some schools to develop others as favored islands in a sea of mediocrity. Despite their popularity, he notes, magnet programs have not been rigorously evaluated.

At the end of Doc's remarks, Reverend Washington asks for comments on the policy proposal before the board. Three hands shoot up. First to the microphone is Ruth Jensen, who speaks on behalf of a group of J.B. Wilson Elementary School parents who want the Wilson School to become a basic skills academy/magnet school. She argues that such a school will provide parents with a sound alternative for their children and concludes by declaring that families who care enough about their children's education will find a way to transport them to school. Ms. Jensen's views draw a solid round of applause from a large delegation of Wilson parents.

The next speaker is Wilma Wentworth, the mother of three public school students and chairperson of CITYARTS. Ms. Wentworth speaks briefly about the importance of the arts in developing children's capacities to become well-rounded adults. She then reads a letter from CITYARTS proposing establishment of a school for the performing arts on the Wendell Phillips Middle School campus. As Ms. Wentworth returns to her seat, light applause is well distributed around the room. The CITYARTS proposal has some support in every sector of the community.

Ahmad Sanders approaches the microphone next. He is a fiery spokesman for the African American community and tonight he is in fine form as he vigorously opposes both magnet school proposals just raised and concludes, "Our children don't need 'academies' they can't even get to; they need to be able to go to a fine school that doesn't sort them into low-grade, know-nothing classes that set them up for failure or push them out of school!"

As Ahmad sits down, there is a sprinkling of applause from African American parents. Joe wonders if he is the only person in the room who has noticed Reverend Washington's barely suppressed smile as he calls the question on the proposed admission criteria. Apparently the Reverend has done his homework on the telephone with fellow board members; Joe can tell he isn't worried about whether the proposal will pass.

Sure enough, the new admissions criteria are approved by a board vote of four to one. The single "no" vote is cast by Henry Baker, who lives in the J.B. Wilson school service area. After the vote, Doc Holloran relaxes visibly, pleased the board has hung tough. Twenty minutes later, the meeting is adjourned and Joe makes his way to the front of the room where he speaks briefly with Doc about his views on homogeneous ability grouping. It is a perfunctory exchange and both know it. Joe is aware that Doc is pushing hard for detracking, and he needs a quote about the "next steps" toward equity.

• • •

Three weeks later, Joe García sits in the Good Common School cafeteria, observing a meeting of the Good Common School Council. Doc Holloran is building the rationale for a move toward heterogeneous grouping of students for instruction.

"Next Steps—Part Two," thinks Joe as he watches the faces of the school council's teacher members. Good Common School principal Phyllis Walker wears a pleasant but determined expression. She is obviously in on Doc's game plan—and persuaded by the research.

Tonight, members of the Professional Advisory Council have been invited to meet with the Good Common School Council. Ella Davis, who chairs the school council, is careful to provide an opportunity for members of both groups to share their reactions to the concept of detracking. She saves her own comments until last.

Jenny Milton, an elected school council member who teaches a first-grade class in House One, speaks in favor of mixed ability grouping. She knows the research on tracking forward and backward, having written her Master's thesis on the subject last year. She concludes by saying, "So, the bottom line is this—all students do just as well in mixed groups as in homogeneous groups, and 'at-risk' students demonstrate improved achievement." She speaks with conviction, knowing she may pay a price for her words in the teacher's lounge the next morning.

Tomás Torres, a parent member of the school council who chairs a community-based Latino organization, is brief and to the point. Low-expectation classes have too many Latino, Black, and Cambodian students. He wants to know why. Doesn't the school's mission statement include a strong equal opportunity clause? He doesn't see anything equal about children in accelerated classes getting more library time, more experienced teachers, and a more challenging curriculum.

Milagros Gómez, a fourth-grade teacher for the past six years and a member of the school's Professional Advisory Council, argues persuasively that it is "next to impossible" to teach a mixed group of students. Students who progress faster get bored. Slower learners impede the progress of the entire group or feel badly when they can't keep up. On the basis of her own classroom experience, she thinks the best thing is to get basic skills development well underway before confusing students with activities intended to develop higher-order thinking skills.

Clearly irritated by Milagros' comments, Tomás declares, "At that rate, some students might never get beyond basic skills!" He wants to say more but is gavelled into silence by the chair, who asks Rita DeMarco to speak.

Rita, a fifth-grade teacher and Professional Advisory Council member, is ambivalent. On one hand, she is not comfortable with mixed-ability grouping and has no experience teaching that way. On the other hand, most of her students will move on to middle school next year and she suspects those in "high" groups will continue in "high" groups, while those in "low" groups will remain in "low" groups—probably right on through high school.

Yatha Ngoc, a Cambodian bilingual aide who sits on the Professional Advisory Council, uses his time to offer a history lesson. He understands ability grouping and tracking were devised by U.S. public schools to "manage" the different learning needs of immigrant students at the turn of the century. He tells the council how teachers are revered in his homeland and how parents defer to their greater knowledge. In the U.S., however, he has learned he must speak up for his children. He feels a sense of kinship with earlier immigrants and sees no reason for history to repeat itself. He wants his sons to have a good life here, but knows they cannot be successful unless they are well educated. There is a moment of silence when he finishes, broken only by the sound of Joe García turning a page in his notebook.

Ella then asks for comments from parents in the audience. Rachael Fineberg speaks first. Her daughter, Shellie, is a fourth grader who experienced academic problems in second grade and spends part of each day in a program for learning disabled students. Rachael isn't happy with the fact that her daughter feels "different." She wishes her needs could be met in a regular classroom. She is not pleased with Shellie's academic progress in special education and doesn't think children should have to be labelled to get special services.

As Rachael speaks, Jenny walks to the blackboard and draws a horizontal line across its middle, writing "accelerated classes" to the far right and "classes for the educable mentally retarded" at the far left. She then divides the horizontal line with a vertical line, which she describes as the dividing line between regular and special education. She explains that children suffer from the effects of ability grouping and tracking inside special education as well as in regular education. In fact, she says, special education is a "track" that often lies below the lowest track in regular education because of the low expectations and simplified content.

Charles Watson, an African American father of three, speaks next. He spent the previous afternoon talking with Ruth Zeigler, who directs a local child advocacy organization. He is disturbed by national and local statistics about the overplacement of African American male students in classes for the educable mentally retarded. Unlike many Black elementary students, Charlie's two sons have escaped referral for special education evaluation. He is clear he wants it to stay that way. He will fight to see that John and Richard are educated "in the middle of the middle of the mainstream."

Genevieve Dover, another African American parent, speaks after Charles. Her daughter Lillian, now in third grade, has been in a "low" reading group since first grade. Genevieve says she can't see any future for Lillian except progression through a series of "low" groups. Lillian was upset when school opened and she found herself in a new grade but still reading with the same group of kids. "I just didn't know what to say to her," Genevieve recalls. "Sometimes I think there's not a thing in the world the matter with that child except that she is bored to death. I know Lillian would feel a lot better about herself in a mixed-ability group."

Wendall Wilson, who teaches physical education at the Good Common School and is a member of the Professional Advisory Council, says the school has done a good job teaching a lot of children. He has taught in this school system for seventeen years; throughout that time nobody ever questioned whether it was right or wrong to teach kids in ability groups. Practically speaking, it's the only way a teacher can function and it works almost as fairly for all students. He ends by saying, "If it isn't broke, don't fix it."

Charles Watson breaks the silence, addressing Wilson, "Wendall, you sound like you're stuck in a holding pattern waiting for retirement."

Ella Davis has listened patiently while everyone speaks. She now asks for a vote by the school council members, "Should the council establish a detracking policy?" The council members nod affirmatively. The policy has been approved by consensus.

Looking sympathetically at those who have spoken against the policy, Ella says softly, "Teaching is not an easy job. I know you all try hard to help children succeed. But most of what we've heard tonight doesn't support the assumptions about tracking that many teachers hold. Neither do the research findings. We need to make some changes. Change is always uncomfortable. We expect children to grow and change; as adults, we have to do the same."

She then asks Phyllis Walker to describe how mixed-ability groups would function. Phyllis moves to the chalkboard and begins to list with firm, bold strokes the key elements of a "detracked" school as identified by John Goodlad, Jeannie Oakes, and other researchers. She speaks as she writes, fleshing out the details.

- **A curriculum "rich with meaning"** organized around central themes or concepts rather than disconnected topics and skills, so that students of all ability levels can participate regardless of skill differences. Such a curriculum should be complex and challenging, requiring diverse tasks and allowing for multiple routes to success. It should emphasize critical thinking over basic skills. All students should have access to knowledge valued by society and be provided with opportunities to apply this knowledge to their lives.
- **An interactive classroom organization** emphasizing active rather than passive learning and generally relying more on cooperative learning in small groups than on competitive or individualistic learning activities.
- **Assessment of student progress** that supports learning by basing evaluation on what students have learned and on their personal improvement and development—not on how they compare to others. Assessment should avoid public comparisons of students' abilities or displays of grades and test scores.

Moving to a new section of chalkboard, Phyllis lists some alternative instructional strategies found effective with mixed-ability groups:

- accelerated learning;
- cooperative learning;
- cross-age tutoring;
- peer tutoring.

While the principal stands reading the list, Jenny Milton suddenly jumps up and strides to the chalkboard, wearing a smile a yard wide. She grabs a piece of chalk and writes in large letters:

REDEFINE BASIC SKILLS TO INCLUDE HIGHER-ORDER THINKING SKILLS!

Her audacity breaks the tension. Parents begin to talk to each other and to the teachers sitting among them. Wendall Wilson stands up and mutters something about going to the men's room. Joe García watches him leave and silently bets a day's pay that Wendall's departure is motivated more by anger than by the call of nature. No way to prove it, of course.

Tapping the gavel, the council chair promises adjournment in a couple of minutes. She asks Phyllis Walker and the faculty to prepare a written three-year timetable for detracking the Good Common School. The detracking plan should grant all elementary students access to teaching and curriculum advantages now offered to "advanced" students, phase out "advanced work" classes, and end practices that publicly label students by assigning them to separate programs or pull-out programs. She then asks Charles Watson to chair a parent committee to review the preliminary plan developed by the professional staff before it is shared with the full council. Genevieve Dover and Tomás Torres volunteer to serve on Charles' committee.

As Joe García puts his sport coat on, he notices that Doc Holloran has slipped out quietly. "Well," he muses, "it was a pretty productive evening. Doc got his 'next step.' Phyllis got support for making this a better school. The kids got a break. Wendall got an ulcer. And I got a great start on my equity series."

A MODEL SCHOOL ADMISSION POLICY

The primary goals of a school district's admission policy should be guaranteeing equal access for all children and achieving school populations that reflect the diversity of the entire community.

A model admission policy should:

- Ensure each school has a mixture of students that reflects the student composition of the whole district.
- Collaboratively establish criteria with assistance from an advisory committee composed of educators, parents, and appropriate members of the community.
- Be inclusive, not exclusive. Criteria should look beyond grades, test scores, and attendance records to appreciate the fact that young students come from very different backgrounds.
- For an elementary school, acknowledge that geographic proximity is an appropriate consideration, but must be subordinate to achieving the proper mix of students.
- Ensure that criteria are plainly worded, explicit, systemwide, and widely disseminated to parents and community-based organizations in a format and language they can understand.
- Provide that the selection of students for a given school be carried out centrally by a blind, computer-based system producing a pool of applicants with the desired mix of students (i.e., mixed achievement levels, majority and minority students, mixed income levels, etc.); once this pool is selected, spaces in a given school should be assigned by random selection if there are more students than seats available; selection should not take place at the local school level.
- Ensure that popular programs are available at all school sites to reduce competition for scarce space.
- Provide for a clear and fair appeals procedure that is widely disseminated to all parents in a format and language they can understand.

Source: Advocates for Children of New York (1985).

EFFECTIVE CHOICE

The aim of any choice program should be to achieve the highest quality for all schools, allowing choice programs to focus on variables that do not result in a differing quality of education according to where a child attends school.

Schools can have distinctive programs or facilities as long as all schools in the system are of high quality. High-status facilities or programs should be spread across the entire system. All schools in a district should be improved at equal rates.

The same range of choices must be made available to all parents and students. Admission criteria should not close off options for anyone. Choice options should be limited to selection among programs within a school or among schools in the same district, not among districts or between public and private schools.

An effective choice plan should include the following elements:

- A clear statement of goals that all schools in the district are expected to meet.
- Thorough information and counseling for parents in languages they can understand to help them select among the various programs available for their children.
- Admission procedures that are fair and equitable—not based on "first come, first served" or on past achievement or behavior of students.
- Support for all district schools to develop distinctive features, rather than simply concentrating resources on a few schools.
- Opportunities for principals and teachers to create programs.
- Transportation for all students within a reasonable geographic area.
- Procedures for ensuring a racial/ethnic/income balance that reflects the entire community.
- Oversight and modifications of the plan as necessary.
- Full funding; new programs require new money.

Adapted from: *Public Schools by Choice: Expanding Opportunities for Parents, Students, and Teachers, J. Nathan (1989), and Public High School, Private Admission, Advocates for Children of New York (1985).*

STEPS TO DETRACK SCHOOLS

Alternatives to tracking will be most effective if begun early. Kindergarten or first grade is a good place to start. Detracking of subsequent elementary grades can then proceed.

Where strong consensus for change exists, steps to detrack elementary schools might include the following:

- preparing all elementary schools in the district to offer all students the same teaching and curriculum offered to "advanced" students, such as smaller class size, continuity of teaching staff over several years, varied curriculum, access to library and other resources;
- phasing out all advanced-work classes;
- eliminating practices that publicly label students by assigning them to separate classes or pull-out programs;
- grouping children for instruction in heterogeneous clusters, employing instructional techniques such as team teaching, cooperative learning, interdisciplinary curriculum, and accelerated learning to ensure that all students are taught at grade level by the time they complete sixth grade.

Where greater resistance to detracking exists, gradual steps might include:

- designing lower tracks as vehicles to prepare students to enter higher tracks;
- reducing the number of tracks within certain subjects;
- cutting tracks out altogether in a few subjects or in certain grades;
- combining ability groups for instruction around specific skills and employing team teaching or multi-grading to encourage flexibility;
- employing after-school peer or adult tutoring to allow slower students to be mainstreamed into regular or more advanced classrooms;
- blurring the distinction between vocational and academic programs by introducing academic concepts into vocational study and hands-on, real-life activity into academic courses;
- maintaining racial, ethnic, and income balance in all classes at all levels.

Sources: Dentzer & Wheelock (1990); Oakes & Lipton (1990).

INTAKE/ASSESSMENT OF FOREIGN-BORN STUDENTS

To facilitate careful intake and assessment of foreign-born students, school districts should establish centralized centers to:

- orient parents to the U.S. educational system;
- assist with the enrollment process;
- assess the child's academic level both in English and the child's first language;
- assess the child's English-language proficiency;
- identify problems that may undercut the child's chance of school success;
- ensure access to needed physical and mental health services;
- track local demographic changes.

When schools fail to provide these services, foreign-born students are at greater risk of being placed at the wrong grade level or of being deprived of much needed English-language acquisition services.

Source: *New Voices: Immigrant Students in U.S. Public Schools.* NCAS (1988).

PROTECTING EDUCATIONAL ACCESS OF UNDOCUMENTED STUDENTS

The U.S. Supreme Court ruled in Plyler v. Doe *(1982) that undocumented children and young adults have the same right to attend public primary and secondary schools as do U.S. citizens and permanent residents. Public schools are prohibited from:*

- denying undocumented students admission to school on the basis of their undocumented status during initial enrollment or at any other time;
- treating undocumented students disparately on the basis of their undocumented status;

Public schools are also prohibited from:

- requiring students or parents to disclose or document their immigration status;
- making inquiries of students or parents that may expose their undocumented status;
- requiring social security numbers of all students, as this may expose the undocumented status of students or parents.

Additionally, public schools should:

- provide information about school matters to all parents in the language spoken in the home;
- establish an atmosphere that is open and welcoming to immigrant families; "front-line" personnel, such as secretaries, should be trained to understand the legal rights of immigrant children and families and gain cultural sensitivity;
- adopt policies that prevent intrusions upon, or harassment of, children within school buildings by immigration officials or any other agency officials seeking contact with immigrant students.

Adapted from: *Immigrant Students: Their Legal Right of Access to Public Schools.* NCAS (1989).

Problems with Admission and Placement in U.S. Public Schools

Admission to public school is played out on two levels—through district-level policy and procedures set by the school board that result in a systemwide student assignment plan, and through formal and informal decisions in schools that pick and choose among students applying to a particular school or school program.

At the district level, the primary goal of admission policy should be to achieve a demographic profile within each school that closely reflects the economic, cultural, and ethnic characteristics of the community at large. Within schools, all children should be guaranteed equal access to the full range of programs and resources.

Admission practices in many U.S. school systems, however, do not always ensure diverse student populations at all schools or support equal access for all students. Rather, these practices tend to exacerbate existing differences of economic class or cultural origin by granting a superior education to those already in the best position to negotiate the system—middle-class parents and their children—while placing many barriers between children of greatest need and opportunities for quality education.

The result is a national school system in which extra resources and the most capable teachers are granted to those who already have the greatest advantage. Those who might benefit the most—minority or low-income students in need of extra time and attention—are often relegated to the bottom of the system and prepared for inferior futures.

UNCLEAR, INCONSISTENT CRITERIA

In many school districts, admission criteria are poorly articulated, resulting in inconsistent application by administrators. Some school districts have no stated criteria at all. Differing state and district policies can determine where a child attends elementary school. Some children simply attend the school closest to their home; others receive school assignments intended to ensure racial integration and equal access to educational opportunity. In other communities, selective admission procedures control access to magnet or specialized schools.

Poor and Minority Families at a Disadvantage

When schools within a district are of uneven quality—often the case in large, urban school districts—the demand by parents and students for admission to "good" schools can be intense. Parents with education, time, superior information, and political connections are often effective advocates for their children's placement in better schools.

When school administrators and policymakers develop admission criteria without consulting all parents or groups in the community, this failure helps to isolate the school from many of the families it is supposed to serve, sending a blunt message that the needs and concerns of some families are not important. Further compounding the error, many school districts do not publicize their admission criteria by distributing clearly worded information to parents in languages they can understand.

In many districts, there is no mechanism by which parents can appeal their child's placement in school. Without recourse—and often without adequate explanation of the basis for the decision—parents of the most vulnerable students are especially likely to feel they have no choice but to accept the outcome, even if it means a significantly lower-quality school experience for their child.

Selective Admission Criteria

Some schools have selective admission requirements intended to nurture a particular student aptitude or meet a distinct educational need. An elementary school seeking so-called "gifted and talented" students, for example, will establish selection criteria claiming to identify such children. Similarly, a school emphasizing dramatic and performing arts or mathematics and science will attempt to select students with skills in these areas.

Selective admission criteria that determine which children gain access to enriched programs tend to favor those students with the best grades, the highest test scores, or the most reliable attendance records. Children placed at the greatest disadvantage by society find themselves excluded by a system that prizes the very qualities they may most need to develop.

Admission criteria are especially problematic for African American students. If criteria rely on subjective teacher judgment alone, discrimination may sometimes operate against a child. Placement problems may be worsened with reliance on standardized test scores, since African American students stand a greater chance of scoring lower on such tests.

Disadvantages of Selective Admission Requirements

While the aims of selective admission requirements may seem both well intentioned and logical, researchers (Advocates for Children, 1985; Moore and Davenport, 1988; 1989b) have identified several problems that counterbalance their possible value:

- Selective admission requirements often bear little relationship to their use; for example, standardized achievement tests used to select students for "advanced" programs emphasizing higher-order skills have been shown by research to measure those very skills poorly.
- Selection criteria—particularly standardized achievement tests—often discriminate on the basis of race, ethnicity, English-language proficiency, and socio-economic background, depriving many students of admission to high-prestige schools and sometimes increasing segregation of racial and language minority children.
- Selective admission practices divide students into "winners" and "losers," undermining the self-confidence and self-esteem of those unable to enter the superior school or program.
- When magnet and other enriched programs attract higher-achieving students from throughout the district, ordinary elementary schools are deprived of the presence of those students who can serve best as positive classroom role models to others.

MAGNET SCHOOLS

The origin of magnet schools can be traced to school desegregation efforts in the 1970s. In an effort to forestall court-ordered busing, many districts developed schools to attract students from all parts of the district on the basis of high quality, or academic specialization, or both. In theory, the racial and ethnic composition of the magnet school would better reflect the community at large, since all parents would seek access to these programs for their children.

Although magnet schools have been a less than completely satisfactory desegregation strategy, they have become a central element of many large school systems. While they are widely presented as an effective approach to school improvement, few magnet schools have been properly evaluated. Until such data are available, judgment should be suspended concerning their impact on school improvement.

One outcome of magnet schools is clear. It costs more—in actual dollars and staff—to establish and support a magnet school. The allocation of extra resources is most often at the expense of other schools in the district. Any improvement strategy that encourages uneven quality across a school system should be evaluated in light of the profoundly negative consequences to those children denied access to "good" schools.

Further inequity results when competition for admission to a magnet school becomes intense, favoring children with high academic performance or parents who are positioned to successfully manipulate the admission process.

PARENT CHOICE

There is unanimous agreement among researchers on the positive impact of parental involvement with a child's schooling. Numerous benefits flow to children, teachers, parents, and to the school itself. As a result, a high value is now attached to parent "choice" over many aspects of education as a means of increasing parental engagement with schools.

Generally, "choice" has come to mean broader curricula within a given school to allow an expanded selection of courses, or the option for parents to select among public schools within a given district or state. Proponents claim that if parents can choose among schools or school programs, competition will force schools to improve. Improved parent attitudes toward schools will further support children's academic success, the argument continues, and a measure of control will be transferred from the school bureaucracy to families and communities.

Rhetoric vs. Reality

Parental options to choose among schools within a district or a state may provide some students with a positive and superior educational experience. For many parents, however, the reality of "choice" is far different from the rhetoric. Some parents are well prepared by their education, experience, and access to information to make beneficial choices on behalf of their children. Other parents—especially those from groups already most disadvantaged by society—are left to "choose" between mediocre schools when lack of information, materials in appropriate languages, or assistance undermines their opportunities for selection. Their chances are further reduced when job requirements or income levels limit the time or transportation available to visit schools.

A two-year research study conducted by Designs for Change (Moore and Davenport, 1988; 1989b) of school choice programs in four large cities—New York, Chicago, Philadelphia, and Boston—concluded that choice programs can act to create a "new improved sorting machine," allowing schools to pick and choose among students. According to the report, the choice programs studied featured:

- complex admission procedures best understood by middle-class families with the skills and connections to make the system work for them;
- stated and unstated admission criteria that screen out students at risk for early school leaving, including previous courses taken, test scores, attendance records, conclusions reached in unstructured student interviews, and parents' willingness to do volunteer school work;
- aggressive recruitment at middle-class public and private schools in contrast to a single mailing of an information booklet to low-income schools;
- lack of services for handicapped or limited-English-proficient students, discouraging or barring their application.

The concept of choice has gained a great deal of momentum. It is attractive to many parents because it appears finally to deal them into the game in a meaningful way. It is attractive to many politicians and policymakers because it promises school improvement without investment of new dollars. It is attractive to those who are so angry with the public school system that they are ready to dismantle it.

While choice may hold some promise to engage parents more actively with schools, it should not be confused with comprehensive school reform—which is both more complex and more expensive.

ABILITY GROUPING AND TRACKING

Sorting and grouping children to provide them with varying levels of instruction is one of the most widespread practices of U.S. public schools. Ability grouping and tracking practices in most elementary schools grant some students access to a superior education while condemning others to a lower-quality experience, preparing different groups of children for vastly different educational and economic futures.

Most schools sort their students on the basis of "ability" into homogeneous instructional groups. Once a child is labelled as a low, average, or high achiever and grouped accordingly, teacher expectations are also adjusted. Such labels are more easily placed onto children than removed. Homogeneous grouping for instruction that begins in first grade may continue virtually unchallenged throughout the child's school experience, effectively defining future schooling and life chances in the world beyond school. One track can propel children toward college, while another track prepares children for low-paying, service-sector jobs.

Characteristics of Tracking Practices

The theory of homogeneous grouping is supported by the complex interaction of unchallenged assumptions about teaching, learning, and the purpose of schooling. It is further complicated by scheduling demands and the inflexible, bureaucratic nature of public schools. While it assumes different forms in different schools, researcher Jeannie Oakes (1986) has identified certain predictable characteristics of tracking systems:

- The intellectual performance of students is judged, and these judgments determine placements within particular groups.
- Classes and tracks are labelled according to the performance levels of the students in them (advanced, average, remedial) or according to students' post-secondary destinations (college, college-prep, vocational).
- Curriculum and instruction in various tracks are tailored to the perceived needs and abilities of the students assigned to them.
- The groups form a hierarchy with the most advanced tracks— and the students in them—on top.
- Students in various tracks or ability groups experience school in very different ways.

According to Oakes, the genesis of tracking can be traced to the beginning of this century when an enormous influx of immigrant children combined with the sudden expansion of U.S. industry to produce dramatic changes in the nation's education system. Established in the belief that racial and ethnic groups displayed innately different capacities for intellectual development, tracking was designed by educators to offer an "appropriate" education to groups of varying ability in preparation for entrance into the work force.

Erroneous Assumptions of Tracking

The original assumptions at the heart of tracking—natural inferiority of certain ethnic and racial groups, validity of rigid class stratification, schools as handmaidens to industry—have changed over the years. Building on the work of Jeannie Oakes, Ruth Mitchell, Associate Director at the Council for Basic Education, and Kati Haycock and M. Susana Navarro of the Achievement Council (1989) identify four erroneous assumptions that support tracking—assumptions that are strongly rebutted by current research.

Erroneous Assumption #1: Students of varying abilities learn best in homogeneous groups. Research shows that students assigned to middle or low tracks perform poorly in homogeneous groups, while high achievers do no better in homogeneous classes than in mixed-ability groups. Additionally, vocational training does not increase a student's chance of getting a better job. Therefore, with the use of heterogeneous groups, nobody loses, and the majority of children gain.

Erroneous Assumption #2: Students with lower abilities are protected from unfair competition when grouped with children of similar ability. Researchers note that tracking does not protect children. Rather, it exposes them to constant public humiliation by labelling them as "slow" or "dumb." Being in a low track can result in lower aspirations, a poor self-concept, and negative attitudes toward school. The real path of a low track may be right out the school door before graduation.

Erroneous Assumption #3: Assessment techniques used to assign students to tracks are fair and accurate. Researchers find that most tracking decisions are based on standardized tests, subjective teacher or counselor recommendations, or requests by parents or students. Research has effectively challenged both the fairness and accuracy of standardized tests, particularly for minority or low-income students. Subjective recommendations and parent or student requests should not qualify as criteria on which to make well-considered decisions concerning a child's educational future.

Erroneous Assumption #4: Homogeneous grouping makes teaching easier and more effective. In reality, homogeneous grouping does not provide teachers with truly homogeneous groups, just the dangerous illusion of homogeneity. Any group of twenty-five to thirty-five elementary school students will vary widely in terms of learning speed and style, interest level, or aptitude. When this reality is denied, the failure of instruction may be attributed to the child, rather than to the school or teacher.

Negative Effects of Tracking and Ability Grouping

Public schools claim to offer equal educational opportunity to all students. Tracking and ability grouping—one of the most pervasive and fundamental practices at all levels of schooling—operate in direct contradiction to this claim.

One study (Wuthrick, 1990) of elementary school children's experience in differing ability-group levels vividly displays the negative effects of homogeneous grouping. Among the findings: high-achieving reading groups often met for instruction earlier in the day when the children and teacher were most alert and eager; they met for a longer period of time as well. The teacher created a warm atmosphere by smiling more brightly, leaning toward the students, and looking into their eyes more often. Criticism was softer and more respectful; it was delivered in a friendly, gentle tone.

Instruction emphasized silent reading, allowing the group to progress at a more rapid pace. During oral sessions, the teacher stressed reading autonomy by not correcting each oral error, or by waiting until the end of a sentence before making a comment. Corrections focused on meaning rather than pronunciation. Comments were made in positive tones. The teacher's questions during group discussion focused on the meaning of the story, with comprehension as the goal. Questions from students were encouraged, but the lesson was clearly guided by the teacher.

The experience of the low-achieving group was quite different. The group met later in the day, for a shorter period, covering less material. Reading was generally done orally and in turns; it was slow, labored, and halting. In a misguided attempt to maintain interest, the teacher allowed anyone in the group to correct a reader's error by calling out the misread word, further slowing progress.

The teacher corrected readers in the low-achieving class three to five times more often, usually interrupting the reader at the point of the mistake rather than waiting for the end of a sentence. To keep the lesson going, the teacher quickly identified a difficult word instead of allowing the student to struggle with it.

During sessions with the low-achieving group, the teacher was likely to frown, glare, shake her head, or point her finger at a student. She tended to sit erect, leaning away from the children. A typical session might cover only one segment of a story, dragging out a single lesson for many days, making it tedious and fragmented. The low-achievers read silently only 30 percent of the time; half the session was spent in non-reading activities.

In interviews with children, low achievers said their level of performance was beyond their personal control. Their low level of achievement shaped their attitude toward reading—because they didn't read well, they avoided it when possible. As a result, once assigned to the low-achieving group, these children were very likely to remain there.

SPECIAL EDUCATION

The special education system, which advocates helped to create in the mid-1970s to ensure that no handicapped child would be deprived of access to a free and appropriate education, has helped to lower barriers to equal educational opportunity for millions of children.

Dangers of Misclassification

But the system also presents a unique set of school placement problems. On one hand, access to special education must be assured for all significantly handicapped children. On the other hand, too many children who are not handicapped—but who do learn or behave differently—are inappropriately diagnosed as handicapped and placed in special education programs. These children could be well served within a restructured regular education classroom and spared the additional burden of being labelled as handicapped.

Minority children who learn or behave differently, but who are not handicapped, are most likely to be misclassified and placed in programs intended to serve mildly handicapped students. Data from the Department of Education's Office for Civil Rights (NCAS, 1988) show that African American students are labelled as mentally retarded at more than twice the rate expected by their enrollment level.

Misclassification of children as handicapped is likely to occur when schools: 1) fail to provide a wide range of education options within the mainstream classroom to meet the needs of children with differing learning styles; 2) have a limited understanding of diverse cultural and linguistic backgrounds; and 3) employ inadequate student assessment techniques that focus on assigning labels rather than gaining information around which to develop useful education programs.

Many classroom teachers are not well prepared to deal comfortably with a child whose approach to learning deviates from a very narrowly defined range. These teachers tend to refer children who fall outside that range for special education consideration. After a child is referred, the evaluation and assessment processes used by many school systems encourages placement in special education. Too often, the question posed isn't "Is this child handicapped?" but "What is this child's handicap?"

The current classification system displays a number of other problems, including the need to formally put a label on a child— such as Learning Disabled (LD), Educable Mentally Retarded (EMR), or Seriously Emotionally Disturbed (SED)—before resources are available. Other problems cited by researchers include:

- use of labels based on deficits that are often irrelevant to instructional need;
- establishment of arbitrary categories that come to be accepted as real, preventing a more meaningful understanding of the child's needs;
- over-referral of students to special education, resulting in the use of complex and costly assessment procedures that deflect limited resources from determining educational needs and developing effective programs;
- over-reliance by regular educators on the special education system, resulting in resistance to modifying regular education programs to better meet the diverse needs of all children;
- failure to recognize the stigma attached to a label, including lower self-esteem for the child and reduced teacher expectations for the child's school success (Dentzer and Wheelock, 1990; Garter and Lipsky, 1987; Ysseldyke, *et al.*, 1982).

"Pull-Out" Programs

Special education programs often operate as "pull-out" programs where students leave the mainstream classroom for part of the day to participate in special activities, or as "substantially separate" programs where students are permanently assigned to separate classrooms, interacting with mainstream students only during activities such as physical education, music and art, homeroom, and lunch.

A study reported by the *Harvard Education Letter* (April, 1989) offered some disturbing observations on the quality and purpose behind "pull-out" programs. Examining remedial reading resource rooms in one large urban district and a nearby suburban district, researchers found substantial variation in the amount of time students spent in resource rooms, concluding that the variation was based more on school scheduling policies than on student need. When in the resource room, students spent a major portion of their time working independently at their seats, with little contact from teachers. Only one-quarter of their time was spent actually reading. In general, the resource rooms were not staffed by personnel with special training or expertise in reading.

While the negative impact of the special education label is assumed to be offset by the additional services the child receives, special education programs in many schools are characterized by low-quality services and low teacher expectations. As a result, children fall further and further behind their classmates and seldom have the opportunity to re-enter the mainstream.

GIFTED AND TALENTED PROGRAMS

At the top end of the continuum of school services are programs designed to serve children classified as gifted and talented. Not surprisingly, these programs are highly attractive to some parents and students, as well as administrators seeking the status they can bestow on a school or a district.

Admission standards for gifted and talented programs are arbitrary and inconsistent. Admission criteria are sometimes set by state or local policymakers to encompass a pre-set percentage of the school population. Access is often granted on the basis of standardized test scores claiming to measure intelligence or aptitude. If state or district policy sets a precise cut-off score on standardized tests, the student who makes that cut-off will be declared "gifted," while the student who scores one point lower will not.

An examination of federal government data on enrollment in gifted and talented programs (NCAS, 1988) raises serious questions of educational equity. At the national level, African American and Latino students are less than half as likely as their Anglo counterparts to be classified as gifted and talented. Until quality education can be guaranteed for all students, programs that expend extra resources on students who for one reason or another have been defined as gifted should be examined with the greatest care.

Locked In/Locked Out: Massachusetts Advocacy Center's School Tracking Campaign

For twenty years, the **Massachusetts Advocacy Center (MAC)** has addressed harmful educational practices that result in school exclusion and high dropout rates—practices with a differential impact on racial and ethnic minorities. Two essential themes can be found in all of MAC's work: all children can learn; and all children are entitled to a high-quality education. Unfortunately, most of MAC's work has been documenting the failure of the schools to live up to these assumptions and, in some cases, the refusal even to accept them.

One of the ways schools act to exclude students is through tracking and ability grouping. By foreclosing the opportunity for quality education and full development as early as first grade and, decisively, by the middle grades, the education of a great many children takes place within a framework of low expectations, presumed deficits, and the prediction of limited futures.

Reporting on Tracking and Ability Grouping

As a result of its continual confrontations with school tracking policies, MAC decided to prepare a report endorsing the elimination of tracking and ability grouping in Massachusetts public schools.

In addition to its direct program work with schools and parents, MAC had written a number of previous reports addressing the tracking issue. With advocacy experience and research from its earlier program work, MAC had a solid foundation to prepare its tracking report. Additionally, MAC was able to tap into a vast network of organizations with backgrounds in research and policy development, helping to augment the work of a staff skilled in information gathering and policy development.

Student Interviews

In retrospect, MAC believes that student interviews gave its tracking report a sense of urgency to lift it above mountains of other tracking research. In-depth discussions with a number of Boston public school students at the elementary, middle, and high school levels featured candid opinions about life in the classroom, why they attended school, and what they learned. The students were also asked to share perceptions and attitudes about class placement.

The general assumption is that children are unaware of the implications of being in a "slow" class. Many believe they simply accept their placement passively, assuming the school knows best. The MAC interviews documented how students are sensitive to the sorting that takes place around them and acutely aware of how difficult it is to escape the stigma of these labels once they have been applied. A telling comment was offered by one third grader. When asked about the difference between her class and the advanced class, she replied, "They're smarter, because they're taught more."

Although research alone could demonstrate that more learning takes place in advanced classes as the result of fewer students, more resources, and higher teacher expectations, MAC believed that quotes from children expressing how their educational development is stunted by what they are given in the classroom would cut directly to the heart of what the report was trying to illustrate: tracking and ability grouping limit children's potential.

Release of the Report

When the report—titled *Locked In/Locked Out*—was publicly released in the spring of 1990, MAC worked to distribute it to as many people as possible in grassroots community networks and governmental agencies and institutions.

MAC held meetings with local community groups to discuss the issues in the report and to plan possible collaborative activities. Copies of the report were sent directly to middle school principals, central office staff, every member of the Boston School Committee, people in the business community, and parent groups.

Because the media is a primary means of reaching the public, MAC does not wait until a publication is in its final form to contact the press. During preparation of the tracking report, MAC sent periodic memos to the press to keep them interested and to update them on the report's progress.

As a result of careful advance work, the tracking report drew a great deal of press attention, generating over 100 articles about the report and related issues. In addition to extensive local newspaper and television coverage, MAC's report was included in a week-long ABC News series hosted by anchor Peter Jennings that explored the status of public education.

In response to *Locked In/Locked Out,* the Massachusetts Department of Education soon released a position statement that incorporated many of MAC's recommendations on tracking. Similarly, the interim Boston Superintendent of Schools came out against tracking, and the Superintendent Search Committee adopted the MAC recommendations as part of their search requirements for a new school superintendent.

For further information, please contact: Massachusetts Advocacy Center, 95 Berkeley Street, Boston, MA 02116. Telephone (617) 357-8431.

PROMISING PRACTICES

Lacoste Elementary School: Chalmette, Louisiana

In 1987, Joy Connor was the special needs resource room teacher at Lacoste Elementary School in Chalmette, Louisiana—a predominately White middle-class suburb of New Orleans. The kindergarten through fifth grade school enrolled 700 children, 20 percent of whom received free or reduced-price lunches.

As a special needs teacher with fifteen years experience, Connor was concerned about her students' apparent lack of progress. Increased statewide curriculum and testing requirements seemed only to intensify their struggles. Trying successfully to meet the significant and varying individual needs of a number of children with learning difficulties in a limited period of time seemed an impossible task. She noted that placing children with minor behavior problems along with other children with similar problems caused them to feed off each other, increasing the negative behavior.

Frustrated and convinced there had to be a better way, she went to her supervisor with her concerns. Fortunately, he agreed and sent her to Temple University in Philadelphia to participate in a training program on the Adaptive Learning Environments Model (ALEM)—an educational approach designed to meet the diverse social and academic needs of students of varying achievement levels in regular classrooms. Underlying ALEM is the premise that students learn in different ways and require different kinds and varying rates of instruction.

Because individual differences are regarded as the norm rather than the exception, ALEM successfully combines several approaches including peer tutoring, multi-age groups, cooperative learning, individualized instruction, and self-esteem building.

With the enthusiastic support of principal Gwen Guillory, the school adapted the model to meet their local needs, calling their version "Rights Without Labels." The goal of the program is to serve children with special needs in a setting that does not isolate them from their peers. It seeks to address the low self-esteem frequently observed with special needs children. By placing them in a regular education classroom with their peers, the focus is on the children's strengths rather than their deficiencies. As Kathleen Warner, a fifth-grade teacher participating in the program, remarks: "We teach children to look for their own special gifts."

Under "Rights Without Labels," special education students are no longer pulled out of their regular education classroom to receive services, with the exception of those few students in need of a more restrictive placement. Children no longer spend part of their day in a resource room with a special education teacher but remain for the entire day with their peers in the mainstream classrooms. Children are assigned to second- through fifth-grade teachers who have agreed to participate in the program. The special education teacher works along with the regular classroom teachers to meet the children's needs.

To implement the program, Joy Connor worked with participating teachers every day during their reading period, dividing the remainder of her time between their language arts and math periods. Because all of the children progressed well in math during this first year, the teachers recommended she spend all her time assisting with reading and language arts instruction during the next year. In 1990, a second special education teacher was added to the staff when the school system moved fifth graders from the middle schools back to the elementary schools, increasing the Lacoste's population of special needs students. Presently, two special education teachers split their time between the reading and language arts periods of the participating teachers.

During reading and language arts, children spend approximately half their time receiving instruction with the whole class and half working individually with teachers in small groups. Each class at the Lacoste is comprised of students of varying achievement levels. Children are combined into small groups according to their skill levels and the academic objectives they are working on. When the class receives instruction together, the teachers team teach the lesson. During group time, two and sometimes three teachers rotate throughout the groups working with individual students.

When a teacher is not working directly with a group, the children are free to choose among a variety of centers or activities. But they also have an assignment to complete independently by the end of the week. If students fail to complete the assignment in the allotted time, they lose the privilege of choosing activities. Allowing children to schedule their own time teaches them to become responsible for their own learning.

Teachers work to create a climate of warmth and acceptance in their classrooms. As fifth-grade teacher Kathleen Warner comments: "Everyone in the classroom knows that if someone is being serious and offers a suggestion it's accepted. It is not 'you're wrong' but rather 'what might be a better solution or can you think out loud and tell me what you might do differently.'"

In all subject areas, learning activities are structured to encourage children to work together and help each other. Children are often paired to work on skills. Children with special needs in one subject serve as tutors for their peers in other subjects. In addition, older children frequently serve as peer tutors for younger children. In this manner, all children— including those with special needs—have an opportunity to be the "expert" and experience the reward of helping a peer succeed.

Children of differing abilities often work together cooperatively in small groups to complete projects. For example, under the direction of special education teacher Tammy Meyer, children from different classes were grouped by threes and each group was assigned a state. Each group had to prepare a weather forecast for their assigned state and explain how the weather affected the average citizen's life and work. Each group member was given an assigned role—weather expert, reporter, or citizen—and groups made presentations to the class. Children were assessed for their individual and group work.

Learning activities that may not have an end product are also often conducted in a group format. In Kathleen Warner's classroom, "Vocabulary Drill" takes the form of a tea party. Each "guest" receives cards with words they must use correctly during the course of the conversation. Children learn verbs by playing "Verb Charades" with each participant acting out their verb for the rest of the class to guess.

While participating teachers have remained committed for a second or third year, some were wary at first. Beverly Gordon, a second-grade teacher with special education training, acknowledges that she was concerned on one hand about sharing her class with another teacher and on the other about having assistance from the special education teachers for only a limited number of hours. But her firm belief that "the special education world and the regular education world need to meet and accept one another," coupled with her openness to change and willingness to take risks, led her to agree to participate. Her enthusiasm encouraged former student teacher Sheri Hanzo to become the newest member of the team.

Both Gordon and Warner have strong praise for the program but also point to a number conditions required to make it work. Classroom teachers have to be flexible. They have to be open to differences and trying new ideas and be willing to share their class with another teacher. Likewise, the special education teacher coming into the classroom must be flexible and sensitive to the concerns of the classroom teacher. She or he must be ready to work with the classroom teacher and become a part of the classroom. All the teachers need tolerance for high levels of noise but, as Warner remarks: "It doesn't take long for an observer to recognize the enthusiasm and excitement about learning."

Joy Connor notes: "There were a lot of small stumbling blocks that had to be negotiated." Removing some of the stumbling blocks required changing old patterns of behavior. For example, in the beginning Connor continued to keep the grades for all the special education students because special education and regular education had been thought of as separate for so long that it was difficult for her to let go of the notion of protecting her students. With time, all the teachers came to realize the children were all "just kids" who needed to master the same material but who required different teacher strategies and materials to do so.

Removing other blocks required developing strategies for team teaching in the classroom that everyone was comfortable with. Because the teachers did not share a common planning time, much of this work was completed before or after school and through experimentation in the classroom. The teachers' willingness to invest additional time attests to their commitment to the program. But they agree that a more structured support program, including a joint planning period and staff development activities, would have helped to ease the transition.

Funding remains a concern. While efforts to integrate special education and regular education students are occurring in the school, required changes in state and federal funding regulations have not followed. As Connor points out: "Funding follows labelling." If the school loses the funding for a full-time special education teacher because children leave or—more ironically—because the program works and fewer children are identified and labelled, it will become difficult if not impossible to maintain the model.

The experiences of children and teachers participating in the program have been very positive. All the special needs students have passed the tests required under Louisiana's Education Assessment Program, and behavioral problems have decreased. Equally important are dramatic changes in self-esteem and self-confidence. One child commented that the most important thing he had learned this year was "to like myself a whole lot more." Many of the children are not aware that they are special education students. Observers in classrooms would be hard-pressed to pick out the special education students. In fact, a visitor to Shirley Selsor's third-grade class inquired about the "gifted" child who answered all the questions. Selsor took great pleasure in reporting that the student was actually identified as having a severe language disorder.

Acceptance and friendships have developed that teachers feel would not have been possible without the program. One child with special needs was elected treasurer of the 4-H Club. Another was elected homeroom representative. In Kathleen Warner's classroom, a child with special needs has become the "protector" of a child who is gifted academically but has poor social skills. Children who are physically different have also been accepted as important members of the class.

Parent support for the program has also remained high. Some are lobbying for the middle school to create a similar program because they do not want their children placed back in a resource room. Although some parents of high-achieving children were initially concerned their children would be "held back" by the those with special needs, they now want their children placed in the program's classes. Having two or three teachers in the classroom simultaneously provides all students with challenging and enriching activities and parents realize that one of the best ways for children to master new material is by teaching it to other children.

The "Rights Without Labels" program at Lacoste has become a model for other schools in the area. Staff are conducting in-service training for teachers from other schools interested in implementing a similar program. Visiting teachers also observe the program in action in the classrooms. This may be the most valuable part of the training, as Kathleen Warner declares: "This is the best thing I have ever done. I am so excited to be involved in this because I can see the light going on in the children's eyes."

For further information, please contact: Joy Connor, Assistant Principal, Lacoste Elementary School, 1101 E. Judge Perez, Chalmette, LA.

PROMISING PRACTICES

Brooklyn New School: Brooklyn, New York

In the spring of 1986, a group of parents and teachers interested in providing an alternative education to all children from District 15 in Brooklyn, New York, began to meet and discuss turning their ideals into reality.

Both the parents and the teachers were concerned about a number of school practices, including a passive approach to learning, a curriculum that focused on developing skills in isolation rather than stressing how subject areas are interconnected, a policy of grouping students by a predetermined ability level that led too often to *de facto* racial, ethnic, and gender segregation, and a structure that excluded parents and teachers from the decision-making process.

The group wanted a school with a hands-on approach to learning that emphasized cooperation among students, a curriculum that organized subject areas around central themes, classrooms comprised of children of varying achievement levels, and a structure that allowed parents and teachers to collaborate on decisions. More importantly, they were committed to an integrated school that was equally accessible to all children and parents in the district.

The group spent the next twelve months visiting exemplary schools, refining the model for their New School, making efforts to reach out to parents, and lobbying School Board members for support. They videotaped classrooms that exemplified the type of school they envisioned and invited parents to screenings in neighborhood homes. Outreach efforts to parents included visits to day care centers and community agencies and handing out flyers at busy street corners. A study was conducted to examine the requirements to begin their school, and a detailed plan was completed. In the spring of 1987, with the recommendation of the Community Superintendent, the School Board approved the plan for the Brooklyn New School.

The New School still had to overcome a number of obstacles before it could open its doors in the fall of 1987. Because the school took a different approach to learning and was structured so that decision-making was a shared process among teachers and parents, administrators were critical and wary. The thorny question of who ultimately would be accountable was resolved by making the director of the school immediately accountable to the deputy superintendent of the district. The Brooklyn New School was "temporarily" housed in the unused 1894 annex of PS 27 in the Red Hook section of Brooklyn, but space remains a critical issue.

The New School also had to address concerns that it would siphon off resources from other schools in the district. Because the only other school open to all students in the district was for "gifted and talented" students, there was a misconception that the Brooklyn New School would also select students on the basis of specific admission requirements. The fact that New School students rode the same bus as those attending the "gifted and talented" school only exacerbated this belief. Parents and staff at the New School worked hard to overcome this misconception by educating parents about the school's admission policy.

Because founders of the Brooklyn New School want the school's population to reflect the ethnic composition of the district and want all children to have an equal opportunity to attend the school, there are no requirements for admission other than residency in the district. Children are admitted through a lottery system, including children of the parents who labored long and hard to make the school a reality.

Maintaining the proper ethnic balance is a top priority. The New School's lottery is structured to ensure that the school's population is balanced by sex and reflective of the ethnic composition of the district. The school is 35 percent Black, 35 percent Latino, and 30 percent other. Sex and ethnic balances are maintained by grade. Siblings of children selected through the lottery are guaranteed a place in their respective groups to maintain family integrity.

During the first year of operation, parents and staff noted that while the student population was ethnically balanced, it was not drawn equally from the various neighborhoods within the district. Consequently, they increased their outreach efforts to these neighborhoods, including visits to day care centers and community agencies and networking efforts by parents who were already part of the school. Loss of funding for a parent coordinator's position has hindered outreach, but staff and parents continue to address these concerns.

The first year the Brooklyn New School opened its doors, it had nearly as many children on its waiting list as were accepted. One of the school's goals is to maintain a school small enough for the director and teachers to know all the students. The intention is to create a caring, personalized learning environment for all students.

Staff at the Brooklyn New School work collaboratively. Because each teacher knows what themes or topics his or her colleagues are covering, they are able to integrate the curriculum from one grade to the next. Teachers share curriculum ideas along with their resources and materials. The school's curriculum is organized around central themes.

All classrooms are comprised of students of varying ability. Class structure varies across the grades. Presently, kindergarten, first-grade, and sixth-grade classes are single-grade classrooms. Second, third, fourth, and fifth are multi-graded, that is, they are comprised of children from more than one grade. The school combines second and third, and fourth and fifth graders in the same classrooms.

Teaching emphasizes the strengths each child brings to the classroom and an approach to learning that encourages children to work together cooperatively. Each winter every class works on a "peace" curriculum focused on the rights of people. Students study such topics as the civil rights movement, obstacles differently-abled people face, and issues surrounding homelessness.

Parents also have a central role at the Brooklyn New School. A Steering Committee comprised of parents and staff addresses many policy concerns and is central in handling any crisis. Membership on the committee is voluntary and open to all staff and parents, but a strong commitment and steady attendance are expected. All decisions are reached by consensus. During the first few years, the Steering Committee's time was generally focused on developing trusting relationships among staff and parents and managing crises. The school experienced serious difficulties with buses, security, space, and with continuing skepticism and hostility from traditional administrators. While the school has been successful in resolving its busing and security problems, the continuing space issues may threaten the school's survival.

The Steering Committee has now begun to reassess its role and is looking at ways to restructure itself to encourage further parent participation from different ethnic groups and geographic regions in the district. Curriculum and instructional decisions are collaboratively made, primarily by the staff, but the committee is reviewing how its members—and parents—can take a more active role in academic decisions. Recently, a screening committee comprised of parents and staff successfully participated in the selection process for a new director for the school.

Parents and staff at the Brooklyn New School are committed to maintaining an ethnically integrated school that provides a high-quality education to all children in a caring, personalized environment. In cooperation with the District Office, the school has assumed a year-long project of evaluation and assessment. This requires continued outreach efforts, collaboration among parents and staff, and the willingness to consider critically the processes and structures of the school. As Mary Ellen Bosch states: "It's exciting to be part of a school that is not static—one that asks critical, evaluative questions, keeps an open mind, and is not afraid to make changes."

For further information, please contact: Ms. Mary Ellen Bosch, Director, New School, Brooklyn, NY.

Current Research Related to Topics Discussed in Chapter Two

SCHOOL ADMISSION

Education advocates have raised several concerns regarding the recent growth of magnet schools and school choice systems. Because magnet schools are established as high-prestige schools, they fear that high-achieving students will be drained from other elementary schools, denying students the benefit of interacting with them and having them as role models **(Riddle and Stedman, 1989).** At the same time, by identifying students as "losers" (i.e., those unable to enroll in high-prestige schools) the district may undermine their self-esteem and self-confidence **(Advocates for Children of New York, 1985; Bamber, 1989; Moore and Davenport, 1988; Price and Stern, 1987).**

A study by education advocates revealed that choice plans can operate to deny the most needy students equal opportunity and segregate them into particular programs and schools. Choice plans encourage schools to cater to higher-achieving students by making the school's reputation a competitive weapon, by linking achievement rates with funding, and by allowing schools with high achievement rates to establish special programs **(Moore and Davenport, 1989a and 1989b).** Lower achievers are not only bad investments for a school's reputation, they also can more directly threaten a school's financial health. The cost of educating a special education student, for example, exceeds the state revenues that "follow" him or her to a school of choice **(Finch, 1989).**

In addition to functioning as new tracking mechanisms, choice plans may be "screens" for the dynamics of white flight or for economic agendas such as the consolidation of schools or diverting of resources from urban schools **(Bastian, 1989).**

Educators articulate concerns about the conceptual basis of choice systems. Some believe choice systems distract from the real problems facing American schools by creating an illusion of fairness and accountability **(Anderson, 1989).** In addition, the competition created by choice systems and touted by supporters as a stimulus to improvement can in fact be damaging, allowing some schools to corner resources while others languish **(Moore and Davenport, 1989).**

There is little evidence documenting the effectiveness of magnet schools as either improving student achievement or increasing parent choice **(Riddle and Stedman, 1989). Finch (1989)** contends that supporters of Minnesota's broad choice plan exaggerate the success of the program, which in fact has affected only a handful of high-achieving students. Finch also notes that the choices made by parents under Minnesota's plan have little to do with the quality of the school, and therefore could not be expected to drive efforts toward school improvement. In one instance, a school's raising of graduation requirements caused parents to switch their children to other schools. Most decisions by parents were based on the proximity of the school to the parents' home; a second major factor shaping choice was the quality of particular athletic programs **(Finch, 1989).**

Although some schools in systems experimenting with choice report significantly higher achievement differences between participating and non-participating students **(Bamber, 1989; Blank, 1984; Nathan, 1989),** this ignores the fact that students entering these programs already display much higher achievement and better behavior **(Moore and Davenport, 1988).** In contrast to claims of success with choice, a Designs for Change study revealed unacceptable levels of school failure, even in systems where choice had been in operation for fifteen years **(Moore and Davenport, 1989).**

Significant concerns have been raised regarding admissions criteria used by some schools to select students. Schools justify selective criteria as a means to identify students who can effectively participate in advanced programs. Yet the widespread use of standardized tests as admission criteria belies the validity of that justification. These tests measure only the most basic academic skills rather than the "higher-order" skills generally associated with advanced programs **(Bastian, *et al.*, 1985; Levin, 1987; McClellan, 1988; NAEYC, 1988).** Additionally, the tests measure current academic achievement rather than academic potential and have a history of discriminating against minority and low-income students **(Haney, 1984; Madaus and Pullin, 1987; Medina and Neill, 1988).**

Other admissions devices have also been identified as discriminatory. Admissions procedures can be cumbersomely bureaucratic or implicitly political, features that inhibit effective participation by lower-income and non-English-speaking parents and children. Researchers note that it is native-born, middle-class, more savvy parents who benefit from policies of "first come, first served" in choice systems **(Lezotte and Taylor, 1989; Riddle and Stedman 1989).** Recruitment activities actively target higher-achieving students at the expense of students in less prestigious classes or programs **(Finch, 1989; Moore and Davenport, 1989).** Some schools within a district may not offer services for SPED students or bilingual students, thus effectively eliminating the "choice" these students have in selecting a program **(Moore and Davenport, 1989).**

The use of subjective recommendations by teacher and counselor provides little benefit over standardized tests. Research indicates that teachers and counselors are likely to favor students with whom they can identify culturally and racially **(Gartner and Lipsky, 1987; Moore and Davenport, 1988).** Given the dominant composition of public school staff, this insures that White middle-class students are more likely to attend selective schools, and that ethnic and social segregation may evolve from choice plans over time **(Lezotte and Taylor, 1989).**

Magnet schools and school choice programs threaten to undercut efforts at schoolwide and systemwide school reform. New magnet schools tend to receive disproportionately high levels of funding and other resources from the school department. This comes, of course, at the expense of other schools in the system. The competitive dynamics of choice programs can function to deplete the resources or even bankrupt individual schools. **Finch (1989)** notes that the cost of running a school consumes a larger portion of per-pupil expenditures than does educating each child. Therefore, schools that are drained of enrollments (and per-pupil dollars) through competition from neighboring schools may not have the money to *operate* the school—much less to *innovate* within the school in order to attract more students **(Finch, 1989).** The financial inequities that can result from choice programs are illustrated by the St. Louis system, where magnet schools spend between 27 and 42 percent more than their general education counterparts **(Nathan, 1989).**

Students who are limited-English-proficient or who possess special needs may be required to attend a centralized program located at a particular school. Such requirements run the risk of creating increasingly segregated SPED and bilingual populations **(Landau, 1987).**

Tensions around the best approach for educating recently arrived immigrants also focus on segregation concerns. Some educators argue that time-limited programs at separate sites are more effective at providing recent immigrants with the educational, social, and emotional foundations they require to succeed in mainstream classrooms. Others point to the long history of deleterious effects for students of color from the segregation of schools or programs **(Chang, 1990).** Questions have also been raised about whether separate site full-day "newcomer" programs designed to service recently arrived immigrants meet the legal requirements of the nation's desegregation laws, even when these programs maintain a one-year time limit **(Chang, 1990).**

SCHOOL PLACEMENT PRACTICES

Schools claim to group students into different "tracks" representing varying academic needs or educational abilities. In reality, tracking does not help schools—especially urban schools—cope with increasing student diversity in achievement, preparedness, and language but, instead, serves to sort students by race, ethnicity, or class. Instead of providing a flexible strategy to serve students better, tracking operates as a rigid structure to categorize and separate them **(Children's Defense Fund, 1985; Green and Giffore, 1978; NCAS, 1988; Slavin, 1987a).** Instead of relying on a series of objective factors, tracking systems employ inaccurate, unreliable, and often biased methods **(Green and Giffore, 1978; Moore and Davenport, 1988; Oakes, 1985, 1986a).**

In many elementary schools, initial ability grouping for reading and mathematics occurs when children are only five or six years old **(Ann Arbor Task Force on Instructional Grouping, 1986; Goodlad, 1984; Moore and Davenport, 1988).** More extensive student sorting, usually based on those initial grouping decisions, is accomplished for all subjects when children are between eleven and thirteen **(Oakes, 1985; Orum, 1988).** Sorting children into special services such as SPED programs, "gifted" programs, and bilingual programs, along with dividing them within classrooms, is practiced early and vigorously. In Boston, approximately half of fourth graders have already experienced this sorting and labelling process to such an extent that it pulls them full-time or part-time from the mainstream **(Dentzer and Wheelock, 1990).**

Grouping decisions have long-term implications for students' school careers. Assignments to school at elementary and junior high school levels play a decisive role in determining whether students are subsequently eligible to attend prestigious high schools or participate in desirable high school tracks or programs **(Moore and Davenport, 1988; Rosenbaum, 1978).**

Minority, limited-English-proficient, or low-income students are consistently and dramatically overrepresented in low academic tracks. White and more affluent students are conversely overrepresented in advanced tracks **(Ann Arbor Task Force on Instructional Grouping, 1986; Children's Defense Fund, 1985; Green and Giffore, 1978; Dentzer and Wheelock, 1990, First, *et al.*, 1988; Oakes, 1985; Slavin, 1987a).** This racial and socioeconomic imbalance occurs regardless of whether student assignments are determined by placement tests, recommendations from teachers and counselors, or by student and parent choice. **(Oakes 1985, 1986a).**

Placement Mechanisms

Standardized achievement, aptitude, and IQ tests are the most common method of assessing student abilities. There is considerable evidence that these tests are fraught with social-class, cultural, and racial biases, and that they are flawed both in their construction and administration (see Chapter 4). Moreover, some standardized tests used for placement decisions are created for different purposes, making their use for placement decisions entirely inappropriate **(Kaufman, 1985; Shepard and Smith, 1988).** Test-makers have not provided evidence that standardized tests can predict a student's capacity to benefit from educational enrichment programs, bringing into question tests' role as gatekeepers for high-level tracks and "gifted" programs **(Dentzer and Wheelock, 1990).**

Teacher and counselor evaluations also play significant roles in student placement. While it is difficult to collect unequivocal data on the nature of teacher and counselor recommendations, evidence strongly suggests that school personnel are influenced by students' language, dress, and behavior **(Oakes 1985).** Teachers' judgments are also biased in favor of socially advantaged students and students demonstrating compliant behavior **(Ann Arbor Task Force on Instructional Grouping, 1986; Finley, 1984; Oakes, 1985).**

While all placement decisions—whether based on teacher and counselor evaluations or on other factors—generate disproportionately low placement of poor and minority youth, decisions on the basis of subjective recommendations by school personnel more often create racial and social imbalance than decisions based on test scores alone **(Dawson, 1987; Oakes 1985; Pink, 1984; Slavin, 1987a).** Strong motivation often figures more prominently in teachers' decisions than does superior ability **(Finley, 1984).** Teacher and counselor judgments may therefore result in disruptive students being funneled into lower tracks regardless of their achievement ability. In this way, schools fail to distinguish between students who are low-achievers because they lack skills and those who falter because of disruptive behavior or poor attendance **(Oakes 1985).**

Despite current emphasis on "parent choice," the roles of students and parents in making school admission and placement decisions remain quite limited. Parents—especially minority, low-income, or limited-English-proficient parents—often lack the information, skills, or experience to understand and take advantage of school options for their children **(Advocates for Children of New York, 1985; Moore and Davenport, 1988; Price and Stern, 1987).**

Impacts of Student Placement

There is strong and disturbing evidence that tracking undermines achievement of students at the bottom of the grouping structure **(Goodlad, 1984; Pink, 1984; Oakes, 1985, 1986a; Slavin, 1987a).** Both immediate and long-term damage results from classifying students as slow learners. By as early as fourth grade, students in high- or low-ability groups differ in overall scholastic achievement by the equivalent of four full grade levels **(Goodlad, 1984).** Another study reveals that students' IQ scores actually diminish following placement in a slow track **(Oakes, 1986a).** Students assigned to a low track fall progressively farther behind their high-track peers **(Pink, 1984; Oakes, 1986a).** Significantly, the differential in academic performance between high- or low-track students occurs independently of such factors as race, social class, and IQ **(Pink, 1984).**

Tracking systems damage long-term academic opportunities as well as short-term educational achievement **(Moore and Davenport, 1988; Rosenbaum, 1978).** By denying students equal access to information essential to social mobility, tracking places life-long limitations on their opportunities for achievement.

Tracking imposes obvious labels on students, sorting them into clearly defined groups as "successes" and "failures" **(Pink, 1984).** Students in low tracks come to perceive separation from their fast-track peers as representative of permanent and substantial differences between them and the more successful students **(Oakes 1985; Slavin, 1987a).** Lower-track students feel less involved, less in control, and more alienated from their school experience **(Oakes, 1985).**

Alienation and isolation expressed by lower-track students have a direct impact on behavior. These students withdraw and rebel more than their higher-track peers. They more often express a dislike of school, have higher delinquency and dropout rates **(Oakes, 1986a; Pink, 1984),** and blame themselves rather than school programs and personnel for the shortcomings of their school experience. Such attitudes are not surprising given the poor self-concepts possessed by low-track students **(Oakes, 1985, 1986a; Pink, 1984; Slavin, 1987a; Sorenson and Hallinan, 1986).** Poor self-concepts, behavior problems, and feelings of alienation and isolation contribute directly to limited aspirations and lower achievement **(Dentzer and Wheelock, 1990; Oakes 1985).**

Despite some inspiring counter-examples, teachers generally view low-track classes as unrewarding and undesirable, while coveting classes of upper-track students **(Finley, 1984; Slavin, 1987a).** As a result, tracking often leads to a clustering of the most creative and experienced teachers at the highest level of the ability hierarchy **(Finley, 1984; Oakes, 1985).**

Teacher expectations are substantially lower for students in low-track classes **(Anderson, *et al.*, 1985; Oakes, 1985, 1986a; Pink, 1984; Slavin, 1987a).** This is true for special education classes as well **(Gartner and Lipsky, 1987).** Teachers also articulate two distinct sets of academic and non-academic objectives for students in high and low tracks. For high-track students, teachers emphasize development of behaviors such as "critical thinking, independent work, active participation, self-discipline, and creativity." Teachers of low-track students, by contrast, emphasize students' abilities to cooperate, to work quietly, to be on time, to follow rules, and to fulfill expectations. Teachers are likely to view demonstrations of academic and social competence by low-track students as examples of insubordination **(Oakes, 1985).**

Generally, students in low-track classes are exposed only to rudimentary facts and computational and literacy skills associated with the simple features of everyday living. Instruction of lower-ability groups focuses on drill-and-practice and worksheets. These lower-order skills are also the focus of instruction in special education classes, to the exclusion of more profound modes of thought **(Gartner and Lipsky, 1987).** High-track students, on the other hand, are consistently given access to "high-status" knowledge—literature, concepts, and information associated with college and professional preparation. Higher-ability groups are often able to read "real" books and engage in discussions about what they have read **(Finley, 1984; Giffore, 1978; Oakes, 1985). Marjorie Wuthrick (1990)** reports that elementary reading groups within classrooms also reflect a division in the curriculum between high- and low-level groups. High-level groups spend more time on the content of their reading; low-level groups are subjected to tedious, fragmented lessons that focus less on content, more on phonics. This differential in curriculum makes it difficult for students to move to a higher ability level.

Teaching in tracking systems is informed by the misconception that "basic skills" must be mastered before higher-order thinking can be introduced. Lower-level students thus become locked at an early age into a "permanent state of remediation"—trapped in classes that emphasize rote learning to the exclusion of ideas and analytical skills. However, current thinking on learning holds not only that skill mastery is not requisite to learning more sophisticated material, but also that the early introduction of concepts and analysis can actually facilitate basic mastery **(Dentzer and Wheelock, 1990; Mitchell, Haycock, and Navarro, 1989).**

In Boston, the research of the Massachusetts Advocacy Center indicated that the benefits of guidance and support services may not be distributed equally to all groups. In interviews, higher-track students reported more, and more helpful, contacts with counselors than did lower-track students **(Dentzer and Wheelock, 1990).**

Low-track classes are more rigidly structured, with emphasis on strict deadlines, precise directions, and short in-class assignments or repetitive drills. There is very little interaction among students or even between students and teachers. Students are expected either to work quietly at their desks, listen to lectures, or respond to direct questioning **(Finley, 1984).** These differences are recognized both by researchers' observations and by the comments of students in high and low tracks **(Dentzer and Wheelock, 1990).** The quantity of time teachers spend on instruction is also more limited for lower-level groups. Low-track teachers spend more time disciplining their students than do teachers of high-track classes. Some spend more time on discipline than on teaching **(Oakes, 1985).**

Teacher behavior and the quality of instruction have been shown to differ markedly between high-level and low-level ability groups within classrooms. **Marjorie Wuthrick (1990)** reports that higher-level in-class reading groups in elementary grades meet for longer periods of time, are more likely to meet first, do more silent reading within the group, and are subject to softer criticisms than are lower-level groups. Teachers are more responsive, personable, and encouraging with higher-level readers, frequently smiling and making eye contact. Lower-level readers are subject to more frequent interruptions and corrections, frequent frowns and glances of alarm, and a less friendly and interactive teacher.

Finally, teachers of tracked classes at any level assume a greater level of homogeneity among specially grouped students than actually exists and conclude that individual differences are less important. Ironically, rather than encouraging teachers to respond to a broad range of student educational needs, tracking encourages teachers to ignore it **(Dawson, 1987; Oakes, 1985; Slavin, 1987a).**

Overplacement in Special Education

According to the U.S. Department of Education, the learning disabilities category of special education grew 125 percent between 1976 and 1982 **(Ysseldyke, *et al.*, 1983; *see also* Gartner and Lipsky, 1987; *Harvard Education Letter*, 1989).** Examining this rapid growth, researchers at the University of Minnesota found: 1) many non-handicapped students being declared eligible for special education services; 2) no defensible system for declaring students eligible for Learning Disabled services; and 3) no reliable psychometric differences between students labelled as learning disabled and those considered simply as low achievers **(Ysseldyke, *et al.*, 1982).** The most important decision in the process is when the classroom teacher chooses to refer a student for assessment. Once a student is referred, there is a high probability she will be placed in a special education program **(Ysseldyke, *et al.*, 1982; *Harvard Education Letter*, 1989; NCAS, 1985).** Once she is placed in special education, it will be much harder to get her out of an inappropriate program than it was to get her in one **(NCAS, 1985).**

Abundant research illustrates the inaccuracy and recklessness of special education placements. The inconsistency with which referrals and placements are carried out is noted by **Gartner and Lipsky (1987).** Referral rates vary among twenty-eight cities from 6 to 11 percent; placement rates range from 7.8 to 91.8 percent.

Moreover, special education placements appear to be both excessive and unjustifiable. Studies show that 80 percent of the general population could potentially be labelled as learning disabled based on one of the criteria used by schools. In one study, evaluators failed to distinguish between the records of students classified as learning disabled and those who had not been so classified. Other researchers could not find any differences between students classified as learning disabled and other low-achieving students on a variety of school-related measures. A Colorado report noted that more than half the special education students studied failed to meet valid statistical or clinical criteria for learning disorders **(Gartner and Lipsky, 1987).**

The dramatic inaccuracies in special education placements are further illustrated by the fact that students who behave in a way that deviates from an accepted classroom or cultural norm, or who are naughty, slow learners, often absent, or restless, are vulnerable to being mis-assigned to a special education program. Minority children and poor children are particularly likely to be the victims of a bad placement on the basis of behavioral considerations **(Gartner and Lipsky, 1987; NCAS, 1985).**

Bureaucratic factors also influence the degree and nature of special education placements. The number and type of programs as well as staff, space, schedule, and budget considerations have a significant impact on rates of referral and types of placement. The funding policies of the New York State Department of Education, for example, operated to reward school systems for placements in the most restrictive environments (as of 1987), a pull contrary to the dictates of the law **(Gartner and Lipsky, 1987).**

The increase in special education placements may be accompanied by an increase in the segregation of students classified as disabled. By 1987, 74 percent of the national special education population was enrolled in totally separate programs or pull-out programs **(Gartner and Lipsky, 1987).** This increase in segregation flies in the face of state and federal mandates to ensure that disabled children are educated in the "least restrictive environment" **(Landau, 1987; *Harvard Education Letter*, 1989).**

The intensifying segregation of special education students is alarming for several reasons. Researchers have demonstrated the negative effects of segregation of these students on their achievement and attitudes. The aggregate results of fifty studies revealed that special education students who were integrated into regular classrooms performed in the 80th percentile, whereas like students who remained segregated from their "normal" peers performed in the 50th percentile **(Gartner and Lipsky, 1987).** Mainstreamed children working with aides assigned to a regular classroom have demonstrated more on-task behavior and more independence than children who remain segregated **(Dentzer and Wheelock, 1990).**

Segregation of special education students is even more disturbing in light of its disproportionate impact on minority youth. According to the **Massachusetts Advocacy Center,** African American and Latino children in Boston are found in higher proportions in the most restrictive special education programs. White students, on the other hand, are heavily channeled into less severe special education programs. In Boston, where they make up only 25 percent of student enrollment, Whites comprise 70 percent of a group labelled "Bright Learning Disabled" **(Dentzer and Wheelock, 1990; Gartner and Lipsky, 1987).**

The National Association of School Psychologists (NASP) and the National Coalition of Advocates for Students (NCAS) issued a joint position statement titled *Advocacy for Appropriate Educational Services for All Children* **(1986)** that identified key problems with the special education system. A central concern was the inappropriate diagnosis and placement of students in special education because of "a lack of regular education options designed to meet the needs of children with diverse learning styles, a lack of understanding, at times, of diverse cultural and linguistic backgrounds, and inadequate measurement technologies that focus on labels for placement rather than providing information for program development". Other classification problems identified included: labels that are often irrelevant to instructional needs; arbitrarily defined categories based on deficit labels that come to be accepted as "real"; reduced expectations for children placed in special needs programs; and a decreased willingness on the part of regular education, at times bordering on abdication of responsibility, to modify curricula and programs in order to better meet the diverse needs of all children.

In their joint position statement, NASP and NCAS proposed the development and piloting of alternatives to the current categorical special education system. Alternative service delivery models would reduce the rigidity of the categorical system, and provide the necessary support services to children within general education, eliminating the need to classify children as handicapped in order to receive services while maintaining the protection offered by the federal special education law.

Continuing their advocacy for alternative service delivery models, NASP and NCAS, along with the National Association of Social Workers (NASW), issued a second position paper that advanced the concept of "Rights Without Labels" as a remedy to the classification and labelling problems of the current special education system. The Rights Without Labels guidelines presented in the joint statement are designed to encourage educators to serve children with special needs without labelling them or removing them from the regular classroom to the greatest degree possible. Programs in support of these aims should feature: pre-referral screening/intervention methods conducted by regular school personnel with support from special education specialists; curriculum-based assessment procedures that produce reliable and relevant measures of student performance; and a broadening of resources and skills within the regular classroom to maximize the option of serving students with special needs without removing them from the mainstream **(NASP, NASW, NCAS, 1987).**

Alternative Placement Practices

Researchers have examined a number of alternative practices to maintain ability grouping while avoiding the problems resulting from traditional tracking systems. These include "student regrouping" and "cross-grade ability grouping." Researchers have also examined ability groupings that are heterogenous rather than homogeneous **(Dawson, 1987; Johnson and Johnson, 1982; Slavin, 1987a, 1987b, 1987c).**

With student regrouping, students spend part of the day with other students representing a variety of abilities and part of the day with students representing a single ability level. Traditional "pull-out" remediation programs are examples of student regrouping.

Research indicates these programs fail to avoid many of the problems of traditional tracking systems. Students are still identified with high and low tracks, with the resulting impact on student and teacher attitudes and expectations. Moreover, in crucial subjects such as reading and mathematics, low-track students still suffer from limited, differentiated curricula. There are indications that frequent regrouping erodes a student's sense of identification with a specific group or teacher and is detrimental to growth and achievement **(Dawson, 1987; Slavin, 1987a).**

Cross-grade ability groups create homogenous ability groups that draw students from several grades for some subjects, while placing students in heterogenous ability groups within their own grades for other subjects. For example, a reading ability group could include third graders who are advanced readers, fourth graders who are average readers, and fifth graders who are poor readers. These groups are flexible and student assignment to a specific group might change during the year to reflect rapid or below average development. This approach is generally employed for mathematics and reading **(Dawson, 1987; Slavin, 1987a).**

Schools employing cross-grade ability groupings have had positive results. Because groups are less likely to be characterized as "high" or "low," differential student and teacher attitudes and expectations are less likely to develop. Moreover, the groupings encourage interactions between more and less advanced students—providing low-achieving students with academically successful role models. The presence of high- and low-achieving students also minimizes use of differential curricula and teaching styles **(Slavin, 1987a).**

Heterogenous ability grouping generally requires or encourages students to work together in small groups on specific academic tasks.

Peer learning replaces the traditional emphasis on individual student work with an emphasis on group work. Students work together, or on an associated set of sub-tasks, to produce a common product or master a common set of materials. Students within the group are encouraged to assist and support other members rather than rely solely on their own resources and abilities.

Cooperative learning, like peer learning, emphasizes group rather than individual work. These programs also employ cooperative rewards by rewarding students on the basis of a group product or the sum of the individual learning performances of the group. Group rewards may involve grades, but more often take the form of certificates, praise, and other types of recognition. Grades often continue to be based on individual performance **(Slavin, 1987b, 1987c).**

Heterogenous grouping practices in the context of peer learning or cooperative learning programs can be successful in improving student achievement and are at least as effective as traditionally structured classrooms **(Johnson, Johnson, and Stanne, 1986; Slavin, 1987b, 1987c).** Research indicates that cooperative learning programs are particularly good at improving minority student achievement **(Dentzer and Wheelock, 1990; Slavin, 1983).** Moreover, students in cooperative learning programs exhibit significantly greater achievement while developing important non-cognitive behaviors associated with greater motivation and achievement. In general, cooperative learning experiences promote positive interpersonal relationships and are beneficial in fostering both self-esteem and positive student attitudes toward schooling **(Dawson, 1987; Dentzer and Wheelock, 1990; Johnson and Johnson, 1982; Johnson, Johnson, and Stanne, 1986; Slavin, 1987, 1988).**

Group rewards associated with cooperative learning appear to provide an incentive for group members to help each other to achieve group success. Individual accountability, usually achieved by calculating group scores based on the sum of individual test scores, focuses the group on increasing the achievement of all its members. Group rewards and individual accountability encourage more able students to act as informal tutors to their less able peers, avoiding the need to separate students into different groups on the basis of academic abilities **(Slavin, 1987b, 1987c).**

3

Student Instruction

Children are entitled to comprehensible, culturally supportive, and developmentally appropriate curriculum and teaching strategies.

Children are entitled to access to a common body of knowledge and the opportunity to acquire higher-order skills.

A Vision of Student Instruction at the Good Common School

Long, low rays of afternoon sunlight slant through the windows of Ana Návarez's fourth/fifth-grade classroom to strike a row of hardy hanging plants—swedish ivy, philodendron, and trailing geranium. Below, dappled light plays on shallow boxes standing in a row upon the window sill; seedlings stretch toward the sun.

A folding table is positioned close enough to the window to catch the sun, but far enough away to escape drafts. It holds a row of glass aquariums. One, filled with water, houses a school of tropical fish—neon tetras. Henry, a box turtle, roams a terrarium. In a glass box, a trio of hamsters who have slept the day away in a deep pile of cedar shavings begin their nocturnal trek on a treadmill. On the far right, inside a glass-covered wooden box, Carlos-the-Snake lies darkly coiled upon a bed of bark chips.

Ana Návarez strives unsuccessfully for objectivity as she looks the room over one last time. Student work centers are tidy; so is her own desk. Both Ana and her students have worked hard today to make the classroom clean and neat. The special occasion that prompts this effort is a visit—due any minute—from the producer of a forthcoming nationally televised special on education.

The director of the teacher center at Ana's alma mater nominated House One of the Good Common School for inclusion in the telecast, especially suggesting Ana's classroom as an example of child-centered school reform. The school, Ana, and her students feel honored and hopeful, but today's meeting will be an important test of the pudding.

A van boldly displaying the network logo pulls into the schoolyard. Ana watches a man and a woman walk to the school entrance. The young woman is loaded down with lighting equipment. Ana recognizes the man as Ron Wellman, producer, director, and on-camera narrator for most of the network's education specials. Ana steps to the door of her classroom and waves to the visitors as they enter the school.

Introductions accomplished, Ana and Ron take kid-sized seats at a student workstation. The young woman, whose name is María, works to determine whether the classroom meets the technical requirements of a filming location. Ron is straightforward: "Dean Miller told me a bit about what is special about this school, but I always check things out first hand. I want to know why you think we should use your classroom as an example of how schools should be. I'm listening; persuade me."

Ana begins to describe her class this year as a heterogeneous group of fourth and fifth graders. Ron interrupts before Ana can complete her sentence, "You have two grades in this room? That sounds to me like a return to the one-room schoolhouse. How can you defend that?" Ana patiently explains that the one-room schools of yesteryear had eight grades in them; this has only two. She also acknowledges that some teachers prefer to work exclusively with younger or older children.

However, Ana thinks it is important for teachers to move steadily up and down grade and age levels as a means of maintaining a fresh, broad, developmental perspective on children's growth. In her eight years at the Good Common School, Ana has taught all of its grade levels. As a result she is confident she can provide individualized, developmentally appropriate attention to any child who is assigned to her.

Next, Ana warms to one of her favorite subjects—TIME. She knows time is an important element in children's learning and that it is unnecessary, even unwise, to rush all children through everything just because they are at a particular age. She stresses the importance of remembering that children learn at different rates and in different ways. She describes how she searches out each child's strengths and uses them as bridges to future learning.

Ron listens closely, making notes as she speaks. Encouraged that she has his full attention, Ana enlarges her subject to include the educational philosophy shared by Good Common School teachers:

> *"The most important thing we have in common is a developmental view of education. For example, we agree that children must be active learners. We want them to have a variety of experiences that range from the concrete to the abstract. We also believe curriculum content should be closely connected to children's real-life experiences.*
>
> *"Children aren't rushed into reading just because they are six, and aren't labelled as failures if they don't read at six. We know children's development during these early years is very uneven, even idiosyncratic. As a result, we work hard to ensure that children, regardless of their developmental levels, have considerable experience with success throughout the elementary school.*
>
> *"When a child experiences a significant failure at school, that failure paves the way for another one. We want to avoid that domino effect at all cost."*

Ron interrupts, "You're the third teacher I've talked with about this, but the only one to argue in favor of heterogeneous grouping for instruction. Why is that?" Ana walks purposefully to her desk and returns with an attendance book, running an index finger down a list of names.

> *"This year I have fourteen fifth graders who were with me last year as fourth graders and thirteen fourth graders who will stay with me through their fifth-grade year. Because I have an "experienced" group of students each year—children I know well and who know me well—I can establish a productive learning environment much more quickly at the beginning of the school year. And because this is a mixed-age group, I can also group children for instruction in ways that support every child's academic success."*

María joins Ana and Ron. The visitors listen as she continues, "In House One, we teach quite differently. For example, most teachers believe they can only teach in homogeneous age and ability groups. In House One, we've developed an appreciation for the benefits of younger and older, less- and more-skilled children working together.

> *"We do a lot here with cooperative learning," she continues. "In the beginning, it was the research findings that attracted our attention. Researchers find it a good way to enhance children's understanding, to extend learning to higher levels, and to foster children's leadership skills. Now we don't need research to tell us it works; we have seen the results with our own eyes. We are also committed to accelerated learning—that is, teaching all students the way gifted and talented students are taught—and cross-age tutoring—students teaching younger students."*

Ron shakes his head and says to Ana, "Twenty-seven kids, one teacher, a half-a-dozen subjects, and a short school day. I have just described a situation that will challenge any teacher—even one using traditional methods, which you have discarded. You refuse to ability group for instruction. You don't even seem to do all of the teaching yourself. What do you do about curriculum? Is it as disorganized as everything else sounds so far?"

At one level, Ana knows Wellman is deliberately baiting her, playing the devil's advocate. At another, she finds him irritating. She looks him straight in the eye.

> *"There is nothing disorganized about the curriculum, or any of the rest of it for that matter. In fact, the curriculum is organized around central themes and concepts so that all children can participate, regardless of their skill level. It is complex and it is challenging.*
>
> *"What happens here is the direct opposite of what happens in a back-to-the-basics classroom. There, tradition dictates that skills must come before knowledge and lower-order skills before higher-order skills. Here we don't expect "right-answer" thinking and we don't rely upon rote activities intended to develop skills.*
>
> *"In fact, we have redefined 'basic skills' to include a wider range of thinking skills. As a result, our students can discuss issues, defend their point of view in a debate, and engage in logical thinking. They can experiment. They can build models. They love to role play. Best of all, they can handle important concepts.*
>
> *"We don't believe in ability grouping and we don't believe in tracking. Both practices sort children out, preparing them for different adult futures. We refuse to offer some children cream while expecting others to settle for water!*

"Our goal is to provide each child access to a powerful curriculum, surrounded by real books, important questions, and content that is relevant to his or her life. 'Critical thinking' is in vogue right now, but it isn't really anything new to me. I have always worked to help children learn how to pose questions, consider alternative explanations, and make decisions. My students write frequently and also share their ideas orally. Our 'thinking' curriculum supports the fullest development of basic skills, while also going far beyond basic skills."

Ana describes how most special education services are delivered within the mainstream classroom. She notes that when children require special education services that must be delivered in separate settings, their time away from the regular classroom is minimized. This is important in the case of children of color, since they are especially vulnerable to special education misplacement.

While many schools don't consider such integration an element of multiculturalism, House One teachers view it as a basic ingredient. As they see it, multiculturalism is about building a society where social and economic justice exist for everyone. Keeping children of color in the mainstream, rather than sorting them out for special education programs from which they often never return, is the best insurance against present and future injustice.

Ana returns to an earlier subject—how time is used in the classroom:

"Rigid time schedules can keep children from completing work they can honor. For example, a good piece of writing can seldom be accomplished in fifteen-minute segments. Some of my students spend many uninterrupted hours on writing; it shows in the high-quality classroom books they produce and in the fact that they speak of themselves as authors. Painting a landscape may take several hours; completing a scientific or social studies research project may take several days.

"Because projects revolve around their own interests, my students work intensively on learning projects. I believe the two most important starting points for learning are children's interests and their personal strengths. When children are really interested, they are most likely to perform beyond conventional expectations. I want my students to reach high, to take risks, to extend themselves, to view their mis-steps and dead ends as natural elements in the learning process, not as mistakes for which they must feel shame.

"My students don't just know how to read and write; they are active readers and writers. They understand what it means to engage actively in science and history, constructing knowledge the way that scientists and historians do. I want these children to take what they learn with them into their lives beyond the school.

"I spend a lot of my time observing individual children to better understand their learning preferences, to learn how they interact with materials and with other students. I talk with them. I listen carefully. Knowing children means more than knowing their names. It means knowing their style and pace of learning, their interests, their understanding of a variety of subjects. Most importantly, it means establishing a relationship of trust and respect."

Ana describes how she uses careful record-keeping to support her commitment to knowing her students well. Every day she writes something about one-fifth of her students; by the end of each week, she has made special notes in her records about each child. She also asks children to account at the end of each day for their progress in all the learning areas: what they have done; what questions they have; what they understand or don't understand. Because of her record-keeping, Ana is able to describe to parents how their children are progressing. She can report on how children's interests are broadening, and how they are meeting their commitments.

"Fine," Ron acknowledges, "but you still haven't told me how you manage to be in two or three places at once. Do you have eyes in the back of your head?" Ana explains that she does not physically direct all of the learning in her classroom. As a consequence, she can move about the room working at various times with different children and groups of children. This way, she can respond more directly and sensitively to differing needs and interests.

Feeling the conversation has been awfully one-sided so far, Ana suggests they move around the classroom together so they can visit various learning centers—arts, library, technology, science, and what she laughingly calls "all of the rest." Ana is proud of the materials contained in her classroom. She believes that her students' learning is larger because a wide range of materials are within easy reach. A walk around the room reveals a lot about what she understands to be important, even though it only touches upon the highlights.

The first stop is the Arts Alcove. Unlike most fifth-grade classrooms, Ana's has four easels capable of accommodating a total of eight children. Brushes and a variety of paints—water and tempera—are close by. So are charcoal and chalk. A wide variety of other materials can be used for arts projects: colored paper of various sizes, shapes, and textures; vinyl tile; wood chips; wallpaper; yarn; glue; and magazines. Nearby shelves hold colorful ceramics completed by children during a visit by a local potter. The walls of the alcove are covered by student paintings produced during weekly sessions with another local artist.

Ana explains that she and her colleagues place great importance on the arts as a means of stimulating children's intellectual and social growth. They don't believe that arts call for a special talent—they make sure all children have arts opportunities. "Not having a strong arts program," Ana says emphatically, "ensures an uninspiring education."

The adjacent classroom library, a supplement to the main school library, is a particularly inviting environment. Centered by a bright rug on the floor that is surrounded by bookcases, it is really a room within a room. Here many books and magazines are fully accessible to the children. Ana picks up item after item. Some books are in English; others are in Spanish. All have been carefully examined to be sure that they are free of stereotypical racial, ethnic, and gender images and language. The collection covers a wide range of subjects and is responsive to the different reading levels of the students. There are also student-written books in English, Spanish, and Khmer.

Ana lingers to talk about the importance of "real texts" in the classroom, contrasting them to the textbooks, workbooks, and worksheets that fill so many school rooms. Realizing that she has lapsed into jargon, Ana explains to Ron that real texts are books with authors and points of view, acknowledged literature, diaries, newspapers, magazines, and primary accounts of events.

"For example," Ana reflects, "a real text is Walt Whitman's 'Leaves of Grass,' not a couple of paragraphs about Whitman's poetry. A videotape of the 1963 Civil Rights March in Washington and Martin Luther King's delivery of his 'I Have a Dream' speech is also real text. In contrast to workbooks and worksheets, real texts encourage students to develop an interpretation or make a leap of imagination. It is interpretation and imagination that stimulate intellectual growth among children."

As further evidence of the school's commitment to reading and language, a daily thirty-minute period is set aside for everyone in the building—students, teachers, administrators, office and maintenance personnel—to sit with a book and read. Ron and María exchange glances.

The Technology Center is nearby. Here are earphones attached to tape recorders so that six children can listen at one time. Here, too, are listening centers with informational and language tapes, stories that correspond to various books, interesting word puzzles, and various kinds of music. Tapes in the first languages of students play an important role in helping them to maintain those languages. Other tapes assist in their English acquisition.

The center also has four computers and one printer. The computers are used for classroom simulations, problem-solving exercises, skill development tasks, and word processing. Ana is proud that, by the end of the two years that each child spends with her, all are able to use the computer for several purposes and have functional, if rudimentary, keyboard skills.

Ana believes it is not enough to have a rich array of learning materials in the classroom. They must also be within reach; children must know how to use them all. In her classroom, children manage materials themselves. They mix paint and clean the brushes, operate tape recorders, filmstrip projectors and VCRs, as well as the computers. They also keep the reading, science, and other areas organized. Ana considers all of this as part of the process of helping children learn self-reliance and responsibility.

"And now, step right up to the Biggest Little Show on Earth," Ana clowns, suddenly feeling much more relaxed. For better or worse, her shot at winning national visibility for the Good Common School is just about over. Furthermore, here in the Science Area, Ana is among friends: Carlos-the-Snake undulates across the floor of his wooden box. The school of tetras tirelessly performs its underwater ballet. Three hamsters race steadily on the treadmill, nocturnal energy surging. Beyond the live things, shelves are lined with microscopes, magnets, prisms, pulleys, engines, plants, rocks, and a variety of books.

When Ron Wellman called to arrange this classroom visit, he asked for an hour; if all went well, he hinted, there might be a second visit. Ana knows that only ten minutes remains of today's time—maybe for all time.

Moving quickly to wrap up her comments, Ana notes that the environment in the community surrounding the school is rich in possibilities. She frequently arranges for small groups of children to visit various settings—museums, libraries, stores, businesses, different neighborhoods, government offices, childcare settings, and senior citizen centers—to enlarge their understandings of the world. The more children see, the more they have to talk about and learn about.

Noting the time, Ana smiles and says, "I hope this has been helpful. Let me see you to the door." María gathers up her light meters and jacket. Ron struggles into his parka and snaps his briefcase shut. They move into the corridor. Ron, still noncommittal in tone, remarks that the common spaces in House One are particuarly interesting and lively.

Ana explains that the House One faculty signed up as a group for an in-service course entitled "Literacy Environments." After that, the hallways became a lot more interesting. Now they are full of student art work, announcements about films, museum and library exhibits; work by students—their writing and painting, mathematics and science models, photographs of the life of the school, past and present, and representations of the community in which the school exists.

Every time Ana passes through these corridors, she is grateful for the progress made. She remembers all too well having once put up large photographs depicting Puerto Rican families and hearing a child say, "I didn't know it was Puerto Rico Day." Now every day is Puerto Rico Day and African American Day and Cambodian American Day. On every day, every child can find himself or herself represented in the hallways of the school.

At the door to the schoolyard, Ron Wellman faces Ana, turns his coat collar up for protection against the cold and grins broadly, setting aside his prickly attitude for the first time. "Ana, you have given us a lot to think about. Still, I have a lot of unanswered questions. Can you give us some more time next week? Tell us more? Show us more? Can I sit in on some of your classes? I'll call you." Ana catches the excitement in his voice and nods, "Yes."

Closing the door, Ana rests her forehead against it momentarily, then snaps upright. "Ohmygosh!" She has forgotten that Phyllis Walker is waiting in the principal's office, probably dying of curiosity. Suddenly bursting with energy, Ana dances down the empty corridor towards the office. As Phyllis sticks her head out of the office doorway, Ana sings out, "Hey, Lady! You aren't going to believe this. We may not be rich, but I do believe that fame is within our grasp..."

The following Thursday, Ron arrives mid-morning, alone. Ana's room is a beehive of activity and Ana mouths a greeting to him over the heads of the students who surround her, "Make yourself at home." He does. First he heads for the art corner, where he talks about paintings-in-progress with three students. Then, he tries his own hand at an easel.

Picture completed and hung to dry, he moves to the library center where he joins a small working group of students who are sorting through back issues of science magazines looking for pictures to illustrate a project on the greenhouse effect. For a time, he blends into the group, searching for photos, talking about what he finds, and entering into its mild horseplay.

Finally he stands, stretches, and moves to the table next to the window. When the bell sounds, he is gingerly nudging a heap of wood chips in search of sleeping hamsters. He straightens to find Ana at his side and says, "Good. Can we talk at lunch? I have a couple of specific questions to ask."

Seated in the teacher's lounge with trays, Ron pursues his first line of inquiry, "Just walking through that packed cafeteria, one is struck by the changing face of this city, and the nation as well. This school, like most schools in urban centers and many in smaller cities and towns, has a very diverse student population. Their faces are lovely; I can only guess at the personal experiences that have brought some of them to this country. Coping with this degree of diversity must be a real challenge. Talk to me about that."

Ana butters her roll and opens her milk carton before she begins to speak:

> *"Diversity is the greatest challenge that we face, day in and day out. Some teachers welcome it; others wish it would go away, for the sake of simplicity. For the most part, the teachers in my unit just say, 'The United States is like this now,' and get on about the business of teaching.*
>
> *"Increasingly, children arrive here with first languages other than English. We provide strong support for those languages. It is through these languages and the cultures surrounding them that children gain much of their social and linguistic competence and feelings of identity and self-worth. While all House One teachers recognize that children must become fluent in English, we are also determined that first languages shall not be denied, put aside, or forgotten.*

"In a truly multicultural environment, all languages are respected. There are several different approaches for supporting first languages in the Good Common School. In the primary grades, for example, where Spanish is the predominant non-English language, we have a two-way bilingual program involving Spanish-speaking and non-Spanish-speaking children. Instruction is in both Spanish and English.

"Right now, these two-way bilingual classrooms continue through the third grade, but there are plans to extend them through the entire elementary school. Our own experiences have convinced us this approach to bilingual instruction works far better than immersion English or separate bilingual programs, both of which we tried for several years.

"As children enter the fourth grade, English is the primary instructional language, though a portion of the teaching continues to be in Spanish. If a teacher with fourth-grade children is non-Spanish-speaking, a bilingual specialist comes to the room daily for ongoing support in Spanish. All non-Spanish-speaking teachers in the school are enrolled in Spanish language courses taught by one of the bilingual specialists.

"In addition to the two-way bilingual program, there are some more traditional bilingual and English Plus classrooms, mostly for children who enter the school in the intermediate grades or are speakers of low-incidence languages, such as Khmer. English Plus is English as a second language instruction supplemented with a variety of additional strategies. At this school, Khmer-speaking children benefit from regular help in the classroom provided by Khmer-speaking aides. They also get additional assistance from peer and parent volunteer mentors from the Cambodian community.

"A strong commitment to English Plus is important for several reasons. It provides immigrants and other LEP students with access to education in a language that they can understand while they learn English. It validates the child's own language and culture by providing role models and helps to connect the school with the child's community.

"Children in these programs receive some specialized language help for part of the day and are mainstreamed for a majority of the day with bilingual and English Plus specialists joining them in the mainstreamed classroom. We never drop support for children's first languages or stop encouraging English speakers to learn another language. Our goal is fully functioning bilingualism."

Ana stops in mid-sentence. "Ron, I have an idea. In a couple of weeks I have a mid-year parents' meeting. One of the things that we will be discussing is multicultural education. Would you like to film part of the discussion?"

Ron's interest sparks, although he cautions that filming any live event is a high-risk venture. It may yield useful footage; then again, it may not.

• • •

Within minutes after the dismissal bell sounds on the afternoon before Parents' Night, the network van is parked before the schoolhouse door. María, wearing jeans, boots and a warm sweater, is efficiently on the job. She moves back and forth between van and classroom, supervising the placement of lighting units, ferreting out electrical outlets, and using broad strips of metallic tape to secure cables to the floor so they will not trip entering parents.

Sara Stevens, whose son Sandy is one of Ana's "experienced" fifth graders, is busy putting out refreshments. A small table near the door holds flyers describing the school district's bilingual education programs, an overview of curriculum goals in multicultural education, and a stack of copies of the district's newly approved Human Rights Policy.

At 6:30 p.m. Ana has returned after flying home to change from her jeans to a bright blue wool dress. Within minutes María has hustled her into the teachers' lounge where Gene, the make-up man, is brushing powder from Ron Wellman's navy blue blazer. While Gene works on her, Ana's mind is focused upon other things.

Although it is snowing lightly outside, she is not worried about attendance. That's one of the other nice things about having "experienced" fifth-grade students; she also has quite a few equally "experienced" parents. In fact, two fifth-grade mothers telephoned the homes of two-thirds of her students last night. She called the rest herself, and knows at least twenty parents plan to attend.

By 7 p.m. she is back in the classroom. Savuth, the Khmer bilingual aide who will translate for Khmer-speaking parents, has arrived. Ana and Savuth tape a large, colorful sign to the classroom door. It says "Welcome" in three languages. Savuth and Ana are accustomed to working together. Because Spanish is her native language, Ana will do Spanish translations herself, then pause long enough for Savuth to summarize her words in Khmer.

The two post newsprint signs in English, Spanish, and Khmer describing the multicultural education program. They also tape samples of children's art work to the walls.

At 7:30 p.m. parents sit around medium-sized tables where their children ordinarily work. Savuth joins three Cambodian parents at one table. Latino parents are gathered at a second table, greeting each other in Spanish. English-speaking parents fill the remaining tables. All curiously watch the last-minute set-up activities of the television crews.

Following directions provided earlier by Ron Wellman, Ana stands immediately in front of her desk. Children's art work and poetry in different languages taped to the wall behind the desk provide a colorful backdrop. She welcomes parents in Spanish and English, then explains the presence of the film crew, pausing as Savuth translates to Khmer.

Ana begins by explaining to the gathered parents that she and other teachers respect the role of parents as children's first teachers. As such, they need to understand all aspects of what the school and their children's classrooms are about. Her comments are well received by the group, in part because she is in regular touch with these families by telephone calls, personal letters, or home visits.

Next Ana reviews the evening's agenda. She tells her guests that first she will describe efforts toward multiculturalism at the school. After that, there will be twenty minutes of discussion, followed by refreshments. The meeting will end at 8:30 p.m.

Ana opens her brief prepared presentation on multicultural education by telling the parents she has strong personal feelings about the subject. Her parents both came from Puerto Rico, so she understands how important it is for teachers to be respectful of children's parents and their cultural backgrounds.

> *"At this school, multiculturalism is a central theme. It is expressed in many ways. It is visible in the photos and banners in the hallways, in the diversity of books in the classrooms, in our conscious efforts toward inclusion, in the detracking that has been accomplished, in cooperative learning activities, and in the curriculum that reflects diversity of racial and ethnic perspectives."*

Ana is very serious as she explains how she is careful never to put children in a position where they must choose between the cultural, racial, or linguistic backgrounds of their parents and the school and its curriculum.

> *"Multiculturalism is about learning respect and appreciation for racial, cultural and linguistic diversity. It is about viewing differences as a matter for celebration. I pay close attention to the diverse lifestyles and cultures of my students.*
>
> *"We are really clear that multiculturalism is not just an orientation aimed at children of color. It is related to all children...the entire school...the full community...and the country. It is expected to benefit Anglo Americans as well as African Americans, Asians, and Latinos.*
>
> *"Multiculturalism also means helping children understand prejudice and the various ways discrimination limits the hopes and opportunities of many individuals and groups, helping them to become competent problem-solvers with particular skills in conflict resolution."*

Ana says she makes a conscious effort to help her students discuss matters of race, class, and ethnic difference more comfortably. "If they can't discuss such things here, where can they?" she asks. "I often raise with these children what it means for any person to feel excluded. If I didn't do this, I would be failing to deal with one of the most serious problems in this society."

She points to a poem by Noy Choy, a Cambodian student from the Boston area:

> *"I put this poem on the bulletin board because it's a particularly poignant example for children to discuss. I hope that you will all take time to read it before you leave.*
>
> *"A lot of my students understand what Noy Choy is writing about. They discuss what it means. I focus a lot on the personal backgrounds of the children. I do this by asking myself and the children: Who are the people who make up this school, this community, this nation? Why have they come here? What are their circumstances? What were the customs in their home lands? What customs have been retained?*
>
> *"Often students interview each other as well as people beyond the classroom. We talk about racial and cultural stereotypes and the harm they can do. This is all part of the curriculum here.*
>
> *"We teachers have been particularly conscious this year of the importance of how we describe children. We know, for example, that a language of judgment, built around various labels, only limits children's sense of self and ultimately their learning. As a result we focus in our descriptions of children on what's right about children, not what's wrong with them! This has helped us to have higher expectations for all the children we teach.*
>
> *"At this school, multiculturalism also means expressing appreciation for the various accomplishments of children. We applaud one another when a piece of work is well done, a good story is told, a creative response is given. We make it clear we care about each other.*
>
> *"Another way that caring is demonstrated is by our schoolwide focus on the biographies of individuals and groups who have struggled for justice in our country and the world. The lives of such Americans as Benjamin Rush, Harriet Beecher Stowe, Henry David Thoreau, Booker T. Washington, W.E.B. DuBois, Sojourner Truth, Susan B. Anthony, Dorothy Day, Eleanor Roosevelt, and Martin Luther King have been particularly inspiring. We also honor people in our own communities."*

Poem by Noy Choy

What is it like to be an outsider?
What is it like to sit in the class where everyone has blond hair and
you have black hair?
What is it like when the teacher says, "Whoever wasn't born here
raise your hand."
And you are the only one.
Then, when you raise your hand, everybody looks at you and makes fun
of you.
You have to live in somebody else's country to understand.

What is it like when the teacher treats you like you've been here
all your life?
What is it like when the teacher speaks too fast and you are the only one
who can't understand what he or she is saying, and you try to tell him
or her to slow down?
Then, when you do, everybody says, "If you don't understand, go to
a lower class or get lost."
You have to live in somebody else's country to understand.

What is it like when you are the opposite?
When you wear the clothes of your country and they think you are crazy
to wear these clothes and you think they are pretty.
You have to live in somebody else's country to understand.

What is it like when you try to talk and don't pronounce the words right?
They don't understand you.
Then they laugh at you but you don't know why they are laughing at you,
and you start to laugh with them. They say, "Are you crazy, laughing at
yourself? Go get lost, girl."
You have to live in somebody else's country without a language
to understand.

What is it like when you walk in the street and everybody turns around
to look at you and you don't know what they are looking at?
Then, when you find out, you want to hide your face but you don't know
where to hide because they are everywhere.
You have to live in somebody else's country to understand.

Source: Dentzer and Wheelock (1990, March).

Ana now invites questions and comments from parents on what they have heard or on any other subject. One after another, hands go up.

Chea Yem, a Cambodian father, expresses appreciation for the sensitivity that staff have shown for his son, who is recovering from war trauma. He tells the group that one morning his son and another Cambodian child were walking down a sidewalk towards the school when they glanced through the window of a house. They became very frightened, because they thought they saw a human body hanging inside.

When they arrived at the school, they told their teacher, who took them to the office to repeat their story to the principal.

The principal, in turn, called the area police station which sent an officer to the school. When he arrived a school counselor and the two boys accompanied the officer to the house in question. Everyone was relieved that the "body" turned out to be an old fur coat, hung by its hood. This Cambodian father is particularly grateful that teachers used the incident as an opening to talk with all children in his son's class about the hardships that his family had survived in their homeland.

Jennifer McBride, an African American mother, asks Ana how many students have been suspended during the past semester at the Good Common School and whether suspensions are equally spread over all cultural groups. She emphasizes that multicultural education should not focus just upon the customs and beliefs of various cultural groups, but should also teach children about the ways that some groups suffer because they are deprived of economic resources and power. She believes schools should put their money where their mouths are and give a priority to modeling fair behavior within their own walls.

Ana responds to her comments by fishing a copy of the semester's suspension report from her center desk drawer and printing the numbers of incidents, by race and ethnicity, on the chalkboard. She notes the numbers are very low overall and are proportional to the numbers of students in each cultural group at the school. This is a big improvement over the way things were two or three years ago.

She agrees with Mrs. McBride that suspending children from school for minor offenses can set off a negative chain reaction that may result in them getting discouraged and dropping out of school. Since children who get a good education are economically better off and have more social power as adults, implementing school discipline fairly is an important way to demonstrate commitment to the school as a multicultural environment.

Amaiza García speaks next. She says her son, Antonio, is working below level in reading and math. She believes this is because he recently transferred to this school from one in Puerto Rico, where his achievement was higher. She is certain that Antonio is not handicapped, but is fearful that he may be referred for special education placement.

Ana assures Mrs. García that she does not believe Antonio is handicapped either. She thinks he mostly needs extra time and more help from Spanish-speaking peer and adult tutors. She acknowledges the intersection of culture, language, and handicap is murky—a reason why some children get misplaced in special education.

Ana describes the school's building-level special education screening committee which has responsibility for developing regular education options for children who are struggling to keep up academically. She explains that when any child is referred for special education evaluation, the process cannot begin until parents give their permission. In the case of limited-English-proficient children, evaluations are carried out in the child's first language. Even this does not eliminate all problems. Tests that are simply translated to another language may fail to accurately assess the strengths and weaknesses of linguistically different students.

The meeting ends. Ana clears the refreshment table while the film crew knocks down their equipment and carries it to the van. Ron Wellman walks her to her car. He won't see the film until morning, but he is optimistic some good footage is in the can.

As he wipes a thin glaze of snow from her windshield with his gloved hand, he teases her about her adeptness at running meetings in both English and Spanish. Ana laughs and says her father once told her it is a good, marketable skill. "He said if I get tired of teaching, I can always get a job as a stewardess on a New York to San Juan flight."

FLEXIBLE TEACHING STYLES

Teaching strategies that respond effectively to a wide range of student needs—particularly those of low-income, minority, or limited-English-proficient students—are characterized by:

- genuine interaction between students and teachers;
- support for student-directed learning;
- encouragement of collaboration among students;
- integration of language skills with the entire curriculum;
- a focus on reasoning and problem-solving rather than simple recall of facts;
- stimulation of internal, rather than external, motivation.

In effective elementary classrooms, teachers use more varied teaching approaches. Although they employ lecture and seatwork, there is greater interaction between teachers and students, allowing teachers to monitor student progress, provide greater feedback, and make their lessons more responsive to individual needs.

Source: Cummins (1984)

QUALITY MULTICULTURAL CURRICULUM

Instructional strategies should be incorporated within a curriculum that embodies real and effective multi-ethnic studies. A multicultural curriculum should:

- describe histories, cultures, and languages as dynamic wholes;
- present events, issues, and concepts from the perspectives of diverse racial and ethic groups;
- examine the impact and contributions of various cultures on the United States;
- describe differences among cultures without judging them;
- focus on concepts of racism, class stratification, and victimization;
- emphasize the value of decision-making and citizen action.

Source: Banks (1987)

SUPPORTING SCHOOL SUCCESS

The Good Common School supports the development of children by promoting learning that is:

- **active:** hands-on learning rather than merely passive reception of teacher presentation;
- **experiential:** learning by doing, talking, and experimenting while drawing upon real objects and experiences;
- **meaningful:** capitalizing on children's varied interests;
- **exploratory:** inviting many possibilities instead of directing children to single, predetermined outcomes;
- **energetic:** honoring curiosity and delight as key sources of motivation;
- **appropriate:** keyed to a student's age and stage of development;
- **interactive:** cooperative and collaborative work, instead of competition;
- **process-oriented:** undertaking complex processes like reading and writing through appropriate steps and stages;
- **holistic and integrated:** not divided into skill fragments and "subskills;"
- **constructive:** encouraging creation and invention of tangible products;
- **conceptual:** involving movement toward higher-order thought processes and understanding;
- **rigorous:** stressing responsibility and initiative instead of dependency on the teacher.

Source: Chicago Project on Learning and Teaching (1989).

BUILDING HEALTHY FUTURES

In the Good Common School, teachers give attention to matters of physical and psychological health as part of the regular curricula. The elementary school years are a good time to begin healthy practices regarding diet, exercise, preventive care, and safety.

This is also an appropriate time to develop healthy attitudes toward drugs, alcohol, and tobacco, all of which are serious health problems in U.S. society. While there continues to be considerable controversy about sex education—called family life education in many communities—teachers in the Good Common School believe it is irresponsible not to give attention to this subject, particularly in view of the AIDS epidemic.

The following is a guide to developmentally appropriate information about HIV for elementary school students:

Grades K through 3

The primary goal is to allay children's fears of AIDS and to establish a foundation for more detailed discussion of sexuality and health at the sixth-grade level.

- Information about HIV should be included in the larger curriculum on body appreciation, wellness, sickness, friendships, assertiveness, family roles and different types of families.
- Children should be encouraged to feel positively about their bodies and to know their body parts and the difference between girls and boys. Teachers should answer their questions about how babies are developed and born.
- AIDS should be defined simply as a very serious disease that some adults and teenagers get. Students should be told that young children rarely get it and that they do not need to worry about playing with children whose parents have AIDS or with those few children who do have the disease.
- Children should be cautioned never to play with hypodermic syringes found on playgrounds or elsewhere and to avoid contact with other people's blood.
- Questions should be answered directly and simply; responses should be limited to questions asked.
- Children should be taught assertiveness about refusing unwanted touch by others, including family members.

Grades 4 and 5

It is appropriate to use the same approach as for grades K through 3 with an increased emphasis on:

- affirming that bodies have natural sexual feelings;
- helping children examine and affirm their own and their families' values.

Teachers of fourth and fifth graders should:

- continue providing basic information about human sexuality, helping children to understand puberty and the changes in their bodies;
- be prepared to answer questions about HIV and AIDS prevention.

Grades 6 and Above

The primary goal is to teach students to protect themselves and others from infection with HIV.

Source: For more information see *Criteria for Evaluating an AIDS Curriculum*, available from NCAS, 100 Boylston Street, Suite 737, Boston, MA 02116.

Problems with Student Instruction in U.S. Public Schools

Despite a decade of school reform rhetoric and policy changes, the reality of what occurs in the majority of public elementary school classrooms has changed little. While some students have benefited from a surge of attention and resources generated by the "excellence" movement, the needs of many students—particularly the most vulnerable—have been ignored or made more acute.

Lectures, seatwork, and quizzes continue to dominate teaching time in most schools. There is limited use of classroom demonstrations, student presentations, group activities, field trips, innovative audio-visual communication, computers, or the involvement of human resources from the broader community.

Although students benefit when schools make an effort to integrate their academic, emotional, social, and physical growth, most public school instruction tends to focus exclusively on the acquisition of basic academic skills. Elementary schools frequently fail to meet even the academic needs of large numbers of their students.

POOR-QUALITY INSTRUCTIONAL MATERIALS

Many elementary schools provide a narrow range of instructional materials, some of which are low in quality and of limited interest to students. The most notorious of these is the basal reader.

The Basal Reader System

According to educator Robert Peterson (1988), basal readers were first developed in the early 1900s as a means of offering public schools a reliable, "scientific" method of teaching a young child how to read. The essential claim was that any teacher could teach a child to read if the prescribed process was strictly followed.

As Peterson notes, the basal reader system features careful sequencing of simple words along with a high degree of repetition, followed by multiple-choice tests to measure progress. The design is predicated on the belief that reading is simply the acquisition of a sequence of skills for word identification and comprehension, in spite of more current research findings indicating that language development occurs as part of complex interactions between the learner and a wide range of environmental variables, including family, peers, and community.

A 1988 report on basal readers by the Commission on Reading of the National Council of Teachers of English underscored the entrenched faith teachers have in the established system. Noting that nearly 90 percent of all reading instruction relies on basal systems, at a cost of $300 million a year, the Commission stated, "So strong is the trust in basal technology that, when children fail to learn to read easily and well through basal instruction, the blame goes either to the teacher for not following the basal faithfully or to the children, as disabled learners."

Most of the "stories" in basal readers are unnatural, stilted devices designed to expose the child to words and sentence structure in a particular sequence with a great deal of repetition. Basals also feature highly simplified versions of classic stories that plunder the names of renowned storytellers while rendering their work unrecognizable.

In a critique of basal readers, Peterson (1988) contrasts translator Gerald McDermott's rendition of a well-known Japanese folk tale ("The Stonecutter") with the version offer by a popular basal reader. First, a selection from McDermott's translation:

> Tasuko was a lowly stonecutter. Each day the sound of his hammer and chisel rang out as he chipped away at the foot of the mountain. He hewed the blocks of stone that formed the great temples and palaces. He asked for nothing more than to work each day, and this pleased the spirit that lived in the mountains."

After fitting the story into the basal reader's proscribed vocabulary sequence, it is offered to children like this:

> Once there was a strong man. Each morning he went to the mountain. There he dug up stones. He broke them into pebbles with a large steel hammer. He carried the pebbles to the village where he sold them.

Amazingly, this version still bears the author's name.

Noting that "more vital decisions are made in American schools on the basis of the tests in the basal reader programs than on the basis of any other tests including the achievement tests," the Commission (1988) evaluates the basal tests as invalid and unreliable, stating "there is no evidence, in their design or in their apparent development, that they meet theoretical criteria for the type of testing they represent...the tests are...simply arbitrary sets of questions..."

Nevertheless, in thousands of elementary classrooms around the country, children's scores on basal reader tests continue to shape decisions about ability grouping, access to instructional programs, grade retention, and the effectiveness of teachers and schools. The Commission concludes, "...more than anything else, the basals are built around control: they control reading; they control language; they control learners; they control teachers."

Poor-Quality Textbooks

Poor quality is not limited to reading texts. An analysis of textbooks (DeSilva, 1986) reveals many elementary schools' texts are unclear and dull as a result of:

- readability formulas based on vocabulary and sentence length that produce artificial texts most children don't enjoy reading;
- a perception among publishers that schools will not buy books that are written well;
- avoidance of controversial topics as potential trouble for publishers;
- the desire to gain maximum sales by covering so many subjects that depth and accuracy are sacrificed.

Additionally, as noted by educator Lynne Cheney (1990), textbooks are usually chosen by committee, frequently without having been read. Instead of careful examination and consideration of quality and content, selection committees tend to rely on easily verifiable factors such as recent copyright dates, use of graphs and illustrations, or inclusion of a table of contents and an index—with each factor granted equal weight in the final decision, allowing inclusion of a glossary to be as important as accuracy of information.

Effects of School Rigidity

A teacher's ability to develop or use innovative materials in the classroom is further limited by rigid school organization and pressure to teach children so they perform well on standardized tests. In Texas, Cheney reports, there is a $50 fine for using unauthorized texts to teach reading. These problems are most pronounced in a school's lowest ability grouping or academic track where curriculum content is even less challenging or interesting and instructional material may be ineffective or non-existent.

INAPPROPRIATE CURRICULUM/ INFLEXIBLE TEACHING STYLES

Children grow physically, intellectually, and emotionally according to fairly universal and predictable sequences of human development, but the timing of individual development within this sequence varies enormously.

Young people develop rapidly. A child may change significantly within a single school year. Adding the cultural and language diversity present in today's classrooms, the challenge of matching curriculum and teaching styles to individual learning styles becomes even more complex.

A child's academic, emotional, social, and physical development are interrelated, but these elements do not progress at the same pace. Inflexible curricula and teaching strategies fail to acknowledge that some children require more time to master their lessons. When these varying rates of development are not recognized or respected, children are often denied the opportunity to reach their full potential.

The Myth of the "Average" Student

The dominant teaching style in public schools is based on the assumption that most children learn at an "average" pace, with others clustered at the high or low end of the spectrum. In reality, there is no "average" student. Each child displays a unique range of knowledge and abilities, exhibiting competence in some subjects while having trouble with others.

Teaching based on a mythical "average" student absolves educators from the sometimes difficult search for effective matches between varied teaching and learning styles, while undermining the self-esteem and sense of competence of those children whose learning styles demand more careful attention.

Students learn most effectively in circumstances that are personally or culturally familiar, but in many classrooms, lessons rarely acknowledge or build on the personal experiences and backgrounds of students. This is particularly problematic for low-income, minority, limited-English-proficient, or immigrant students who already face an institution dominated by a White, middle-class perspective.

Inappropriate Practices in Current Use

Examining curricula and teaching strategies in public elementary schools, the National Association for the Education of Young Children (1988) has documented numerous inappropriate practices, including:

- narrowly focused curriculum that stresses technical academic skills without recognizing that all aspects of a child's development are interrelated;
- preoccupation with how well a child conforms to group expectations, such as the ability to read at grade level or performance on standardized tests;
- expectations that all children will achieve the same level of academic skills at the same age and within the same time frame;
- division of the curriculum into separate, unrelated subjects with each assigned a carefully allotted period of time; primary emphasis is given to reading, then math, with social studies, science, and health covered only as time permits; art, music, and physical education are taught once a week;
- instructional strategies that are teacher-directed and that focus primarily on lecturing to the whole class, total class discussion, and worksheet exercises completed silently by children working individually at their desks;
- projects, learning centers, play, and outdoor time viewed as embellishments that are offered only if time permits or as a reward for good behavior;
- insufficient time to prepare enriching instructional activities because teachers use most of their planning time to prepare and correct worksheets or other seatwork;
- children expected, for the most part, to work silently and alone; they are rarely permitted to help each other and are penalized for talking; children are not allowed to participate in playful activity until all their work is done;
- instructional material primarily limited to required texts, workbooks, and pencils and paper;
- assignment of permanent desks which are rarely moved.

RIGID LEARNING ENVIRONMENTS

Learning styles—defined by David Hunt (1979) as the conditions under which a child learns best—differ widely among students. As noted by one study (Clary, 1989), researchers have identified key variables that contribute to an individual's learning style: environment; emotionality; sociological needs; physical characteristics; and psychological inclinations.

Within each of these five categories, a variety of elements contribute to the total learning experience. Environmental learning factors include sound, light, temperature, and room design. Emotional learning factors include motivation, persistence, responsibility, and structure. Sociological factors include the desire to work alone, in pairs, on a team, with peers, or with an authority figure. Physical factors include sensory input, food intake, time of day, and physical mobility. Psychological factors include brain hemispheric preferences, the need for inductive or deductive teaching, and the capacity for implusiveness or reflection.

Naturally, not all of these stimuli can be considered for each student. Time and resources simply are not available to provide a perfect learning environment for every child. But most public elementary schools fail even to make the most rudimentary adjustments to accommodate individual learning style, opting instead to rigidly impose a single, strict environment on all students.

For the most part, elementary classrooms remain quiet, motionless places where children work alone on standardized tasks at assigned desks, regardless of recent research that supports the need for varied, dynamic, interactive learning environments.

LIMITED ACCESS TO HIGHER–ORDER SKILLS

Many elementary schools continue to assume that mastery of basic skills must precede exploration of complex or challenging subject matter. As a result, students who learn at slower rates are sorted into ability group tracks characterized by dull materials that encourage children to disconnect from the learning process at an early age. Children in higher groups receive significantly greater opportunities to develop higher-order skills such as problem-solving, creative thinking, and critical reasoning.

All students need to develop conceptual, analytical, and critical thinking skills. For the most part, teachers overemphasize basic academic skills at the expense of higher-order skills and rely on inadequate or irrelevant materials that do little to enable students to go beyond the superficial acquisition of information to develop a deep understanding of underlying principles and concepts.

In a review of recent research, educator Andrew Porter (1989) noted two studies concluding that 70 to 75 percent of elementary school mathematics instruction focused on teaching basic skills—adding, subtracting, multiplying, and dividing. The remaining time was divided between developing conceptual understanding and problem-solving skills, primarily through story problems that often implied the operations needed to solve problems rather than explicitly reviewing the steps involved.

Porter's analysis of textbook content for fourth graders was no more encouraging: 65 to 80 percent of the exercises were devoted to skill practice, while 10 to 24 percent focused on conceptual understanding; only 6 to 13 percent offered problem-solving.

"Teaching for Exposure"

Another characteristic of elementary school instruction raised by Porter is referred to as "teaching for exposure"—that is, covering a large number of topics in a superficial manner. In one study of mathematics curriculum content, teachers devoted less than thirty minutes to more than 70 percent of the topics covered in a school year; less than 10 percent of the topics received two hours or more of attention. In a content analysis of fourth-grade textbooks, 70 to 80 percent of the topics were allotted twenty or fewer exercises.

Porter concludes that "teaching for exposure may communicate to students that knowing a very little about a lot of different things is more valuable than a deep understanding of a few key concepts."

Impact on Traditionally Underserved Students

One result of this imbalanced focus on basic skills is a continued significant learning gap between traditionally underserved students—such as minorities, limited-English-proficient, or low-income students—and the general student population, particularly in regard to higher-order skills. Because traditionally undeserved groups will make up an increasing proportion of the U.S. public school student population, the challenge to address their needs will continue to grow.

INADEQUATE BILINGUAL EDUCATION

The general aim of bilingual education is twofold: to help a child gain competence in English in order to allow full access to the school's curriculum and activities, and to provide instruction in the child's native language so the child can meet grade promotion and graduation requirements.

Bilingual education is a dynamic field. No one strategy has been found right for all situations. But while different approaches may be appropriate for varying circumstances, adopting some strategy is clearly better than offering none at all. In many school districts, no special services are available to limited-English-proficient (LEP) students. According to educator Herman LaFontaine (1987), up to two-thirds of the estimated 3.5 to 5.5 million LEP children enrolled in public schools are not receiving the language assistance they need to succeed in school.

Monolingualism Disguised as Bilingual Education

In schools where bilingual education is offered, it is too often characterized by minimal English as a Second Language programs that provide inadequate instruction taught by monolingual, English-speaking teachers using only English texts and materials. The primary focus of these programs is to teach children English as soon as possible to get them ready for instruction in English-only classrooms with the rest of the student body, most of whom have little or no exposure to any language other than English.

As noted by Harvard University researcher Catherine Snow and Kenji Hakuta of Yale University (1987): "Bilingual education in its present form may be one of the greatest misnomers of educational programs. What it fosters is monolingualism...The bottom line of all of these programs has been an almost single-minded interest in the extent and the efficiency of English proficiency development."

Effects of Premature Mainstreaming

Snow and Hakuta are also concerned that LEP children who are moved too quickly into a monolingual English classroom may be seen as "slow learners, as dyslexic, as learning disabled, or as just stupid by teachers who are unaware that their control of English is simply inadequate." They are joined by researcher Lily Wong-Filmore (1985) who finds "it takes some children six or seven years to master forms and uses of a new language... some never succeed."

Snow and Hakuta conclude: "Clearly, if we are going to mainstream non-English speakers prematurely, we must at least postpone diagnosing, classifying, or grouping them based on their performance in their second language."

Effects of Segregation

Substantially separate programs serving limited-English-proficient children often exacerbate student segregation. Because many schools do not educate limited-English-proficient or language-minority students effectively in the mainstream classroom, they act to isolate students from the racial and ethnic diversity of the entire school population.

When separate bilingual classrooms are necessary to avoid academic failure for limited-English-proficient students, these services must be available for students until they are able to re-enter the mainstream classroom with no reduction in the quality of their educational experience.

LACK OF MULTICULTURAL CURRICULUM

Although an increasingly diverse student population in U.S. public schools during the past decade has made the need for quality multicultural education more urgent, most schools and teacher training institutions have failed to grasp the importance of multicultural curricula and teaching strategies.

Because curricula in many schools remain geared to the experiences of students who come from White, middle-class households, they fall far short of reflecting the realities of the modern classroom. Not surprisingly, these curricula can fail to catch the interest of an increasing number of students who, for one reason or another, have different life experiences. In many schools, teachers must struggle on their own to obtain a broad range of high-quality teaching materials relevant to their students.

Inadequacy of Existing Multicultural Curricula

Multicultural curricula are altogether lacking in some schools. Where they do exist, advocates have observed that some are of pedestrian quality, holding little potential to provide students with the depth of insight about differing cultural backgrounds. In his analysis of dominant characteristics of multicultural studies, James A. Banks (1987) of the University of Washington finds that many multicultural curricula:

- focus on isolated aspects of histories and cultures;
- present events, issues, and concepts primarily from Anglocentric and mainstream perspectives;
- show development of the Americas primarily as the extension of European influence;
- trivialize histories and cultures;
- describe minority cultures as deprived or pathological;
- ignore or gloss over concepts such as racism, class stratification, powerlessness, and the victimization of ethnic and racial groups;
- focus sharply on assimilationist ideology while pluralist and radical ideologies are ignored or presented as undesirable;
- focus on lower-level knowledge, such as holidays, heroes, and the recall of factual information.

Common Misconceptions about Multicultural Education

After noting that intervention in early elementary grades is critical to effectively shape young children's basic racial and cultural attitudes, educator Patricia Ramsey (1982) highlights several misconceptions held by most public elementary schools about the nature of multicultural education.

- **Multicultural education tends to focus on information about other countries and cultures**—with an emphasis on names of countries, flags, foods, exports, and well-known people, young children are not offered any useful context to help them understand or interpret these facts; a focus on exotic differences can actually work against a greater understanding of other people and cultures by fostering a "we/they" view of the world;
- **Multicultural education is viewed as only relevant for classrooms with students who are members of minority cultural and racial groups**—most teachers fail to see that a multicultural curriculum is appropriate and necessary for all students regardless of their backgrounds; through television, movies, books, and magazines, minorities are constantly exposed to the details of middle-class, Anglo culture, yet members of the majority U.S. culture might grow well into adulthood with little or no exposure to other cultures;
- **Many educators feel there should be a unified set of goals and curricula for multicultural education**—because they cover the subject too generically, books and activities intended for multicultural education often fail to cover the cultures and backgrounds of all the children in the class; to be effective, goals and curricula will vary from class to class in order to fit the backgrounds, awareness levels, and attitudes of the children for whom they are intended;
- **Multicultural education is seen as a set of activities to be added on to the existing curriculum**—according to Ramsey, "multicultural education embodies a perspective rather than a curriculum." As such, she suggests, multicultural learning can occur throughout the school day, not just during set periods or lessons, and teachers should assess a child's multicultural skills in much the same way as they assess a child's social skills, emotional states, or cognitive abilities.

Current State of Multicultural Education

In his analysis of the condition of multicultural education in U.S. public schools, Bob Suzuki (1984) finds:

- schools are failing to meet the educational needs—either academic or social—of many racial and ethnic minorities, particularly those who are poor;
- biases in the sociocultural milieu of schools inculcate and reinforce prejudicial attitudes, adding to misunderstandings and conflicts between groups;
- while schools claim support of democratic values, their organizational structures and practices tend to promote values and behaviors antithetical to these ideals—for example, tracking systems that encourage competition rather than cooperation;
- schools often do not examine the explicit and implicit values they cannot avoid transmitting to their students and staff;
- while schools cannot operate independently of the prevalent culture, they still can play a significant role in the process of social change.

Benefits of Multicultural Education

Author Jaime Wurzel (1989) observes that "every culture creates a system of shared knowledge necessary for surviving as a group and facilitating communication among its members." He further contends that conflicts occur between cultural groups when their differing realities clash, an outcome he believes is inevitable to the human condition. One of the purposes of multicultural education, he concludes, is to manage and reduce such conflict.

Wurzel views multicultural education not merely as an instructional product but as a "continuous process involving: 1) reflection, learning, and the development of cultural self-awareness; 2) the acceptance of conflict for its educational potential; 3) the willingness to learn about one's own cultural reality from interaction with others; 4) the improvement of communications with people from other cultures; and 5) the recognition of the universality of multiculturalism."

Teachers must communicate essential knowledge about their own cultures and the cultures and customs of others in ways that prepare students to be caring and tolerant adults. All students benefit when schools and classrooms offer learning environments that are inviting to children from a wide variety of ethnic and economic backgrounds and social experiences.

California Tomorrow: Immigrant Student Project

In 1985, **California Tomorrow** began its Immigrant Student Project, a statewide effort to document the needs and experiences of foreign-born students in California public schools.

The project's genesis was California Tomorrow's belief that most schools fail to address the concerns of immigrants because immigrant families and communities lack access to the processes of politics and education. As a result, immigrants are less able to voice their perspectives or have them included at policy development and decision-making levels.

Advisory Panel

To aid with outreach and review the final report, California Tomorrow formed an advisory panel of individuals which launched the project in the right direction. The panel included education advocates, school administrators, policy analysts, and immigrant community leaders.

Among its duties, the advisory panel identified churches, health centers, and refugee resettlement organizations to be contacted during the project's data-gathering phase. To approach these organizations, California Tomorrow first offered the advisory panel's positions on immigrant student issues and then showed the groups how project information would be used, assuring its confidentiality. Examples of California Tomorrow's past reports and publications were also made available.

Public Hearings

Working with the National Coalition of Advocates for Students and some 200 community advocates, agency staff, researchers, and experts on immigrant student issues, California Tomorrow held two major public hearings on immigrant students' educational needs and school experiences—one in Los Angeles and one in San Francisco.

The hearings featured vivid and informed testimony by advocates, educators, parents, and students. A complete transcript of each day-long hearing was prepared to allow careful review of the procedings by those preparing the project's final report.

School Interviews

School district data were collected through structured interviews with school officials. Requests for information from larger school districts required formal application, involving a letter of request and completion of various school district forms. Smaller school districts were mailed a letter of introduction explaining the purpose of the project and the materials requested. To establish its credibility, California Tomorrow found it helpful to share examples of its previous reports and publications with school district leadership.

Drafting the Report

California Tomorrow called on several experts to review and analyze the large quantity of data accumulated by the project and to help outline sections of the draft report.

The initial draft, written by California Tomorrow staff, was sent to some ninety people for review and comment, including the project's advisory panel, people knowledgeable about state education issues, and California Tomorrow's board members. This allowed California Tomorrow staff to gain a broad perspective on its draft findings.

Disseminating the Report

In 1988, California Tomorrow published the project's final report, *Crossing the Schoolhouse Border,* documenting their findings concerning immigrant students in the state's public schools and listing recommendations for programmatic and policy changes. With data from some thirty-five school districts, representing a good cross-section of immigrant communities across the state, California Tomorrow offered an accurate and compelling description of the conditions and issues facing most young immigrants and their families.

During project interviews, students, educators, and parents revealed that most immigrant children had serious unaddressed needs and faced barriers of language, culture, health, and mental health that prevented their full participation in schools. Additionally, schools lacked the resources and direction to serve these students well and were, at times, unwilling to do anything considered "extra" for foreign-born children.

As part of its dissemination effort, California Tomorrow held workshops and presentations for legislators, school officials, teachers, and education professionals. California Tomorrow staff also attended various legislative hearings to offer testimony on the project's findings. To respond to the large demand for public presentations, California Tomorrow produced a videotape to supplement the written report.

Informing the Media

The purpose of the media campaign was to show that the needs of immigrant communities are inextricably connected to the needs of the entire state. In an effort to generate responsible and comprehensive news coverage, California Tomorrow staff selected a limited number of education writers on the basis of prior contact and respect for their work. These reporters were offered exclusive access to the report and a detailed briefing prior to its release. The result was a number of news stories that were both thoughtful and thorough.

The Next Stage: Turning to Teachers

Immediately following the release of *Crossing the Schoolhouse Border,* California Tomorrow's Immigrant Student Project embarked on an effort to identify and document promising practices and programs in immigrant education. This resulted in a second publication entitled *Bridges: Promising Programs for the Education of Immigrant Children,* intended as a tool for educators and community advocates to facilitate communication among those interested in shaping schools to better meet the needs of an increasingly diverse population.

The goal of this phase of the Immigrant Student Project was to provide new information and direction for teacher training and to support new professional development programs springing up in districts throughout California. In the face of a critical shortage of bilingual and specialty teachers, districts were struggling to transform the mainstream teaching force into staff able to work effectively with culturally and linguistically diverse students.

This new phase of the Immigrant Student Project set out to understand teaching in diverse classrooms through the eyes of the teachers themselves. California Tomorrow wanted project documents to present the work of effective teachers in their own words. Teachers themselves had to be actively involved in helping to make sense of the data and how to present it.

California Tomorrow utilized two main approaches for data collection: in-depth interviews with mainstream classroom teachers representing a range of grade levels, regional areas, and subject areas; and a three-day group process that included discussion of major issues raised in the interviews, reaction to the first cut at findings, and consideration of recommendations.

To select the teachers to be interviewed, project staff contacted school district staff development offices and asked them to nominate mainstream teachers in grades K through 12 who were developing new ways to bridge gaps of race, language, and culture to form a strong learning community in the classroom. Eighty teachers were nominated and screened by telephone interviews. California Tomorrow selected forty-five teachers for the study on the basis of the composition of their student populations, grade level and subject taught, and geographic diversity. Thirty-six of the teachers agreed to participate.

In-depth interviews were held at school-sites with all thirty-six teachers, focusing on the teachers' perspectives on teaching in diverse classrooms, discussing goals, intentions, and rationales for their approach to teaching, and gathering descriptions of classroom structure and curriculum. Teachers were also encouraged to reflect on their own development and the kind of training, development, and support that influenced them in creating effective multicultural classrooms.

Using transcripts, California Tomorrow analyzed the interviews, focusing on linkages and relationships between various components of curricula, pedagogy, and teacher development. Based on this analysis, a draft of the report's findings was prepared and circulated to participating teachers. They were given the opportunity to clarify their comments or indicate any portions they did not want to be used.

Seventeen of the teachers interviewed participated in a three-day round-table retreat in order to: respond to draft findings; solicit new material not fully explored in the interviews; clarify contradictions in the interviews; and design recommendations.

The teachers created several new sources of project data during the retreat, including personal maps of their professional development, and simulated demonstrations of specific classroom techniques. These discussions helped California Tomorrow understand the dimensions of the dialogue within the teaching profession about issues such as language support, school climate, and the politics of staff development.

While California Tomorrow's research focused on classrooms of mixed immigrant and native U.S.-born students, the project's implications are broader. The teachers' words point the direction for preparing all of California's children for the realities of the international society we have become.

For further information, please contact: California Tomorrow, Fort Mason Center, Building B, San Francisco, CA 94123-1380. Telephone (415) 441-7631.

La Escuela Fratney: Milwaukee, Wisconsin

The Fratney School, located in Riverwest—one of Milwaukee's few integrated neighborhoods—was slated to be razed in 1987. Its former staff and student body were to move in the spring of 1988 to a new school six blocks away that was to house a combined student population of able-bodied and differently-abled students. The prospect of an empty school building inspired a small group of local parents and teachers to discuss how the Fratney could become home to a school designed to capitalize on the unique features of the neighborhood.

Calling themselves "Neighbors for a New Fratney," the group developed a comprehensive proposal for an innovative school designed to be a model of multicultural, community-based, democratic education—La Escuela Fratney. As Bob Peterson, one of the school's founders, recalls: "Our goal was to establish a decent school that children want to attend in an integrated neighborhood, teaching children to be bilingual in Spanish and English, using cooperative and innovative methods, and governed by a council of parents and teachers."

The group proposed to build the school around the following elements and principles:

- a two-way bilingual program that treats the backgrounds of both Spanish- and English-speaking students as strengths and resources to be developed and shared;
- a multicultural curriculum with an explicitly anti-racist component that draws on the diverse school community;
- a view of subjects as interconnected and teachers and parents choose schoolwide themes around which the curriculum is organized;
- a whole-language approach to learning first and second languages that teaches children to acquire language through reading, writing, and listening for a purpose, instead of through isolated drills and skills exercises, allowing children to learn that language is for communication and accomplishment;
- a cooperative learning environment where children are taught to work together and to help each other;
- democratic discipline where limits are set but children have a voice in establishing the rules and the consequences and are expected to develop self-discipline;
- school-based management where a council of parents and staff members make all the major decisions for the school.

While Neighbors for a New Fratney were putting their vision on paper, school administrators were busy revising their plan to raze the building to convert the empty school building into an "Exemplary Teaching Center." At the Center, "master" teachers would provide staff development for struggling classroom teachers. Neighbors for a New Fratney argued that such a center could be established anywhere in the system, but their vision of a new Fratney could only happen at its present site.

In the face of the administration's resistance to their proposal, Neighbors for a New Fratney mobilized the community. They brought seventy-five supporters to a key school board meeting in February 1988 on the night of a driving sleet storm that closed down all the schools the next day. They succeeded in short-circuiting the administration's plans and won endorsement for their proposal. In addition, the school board directed the administration to cooperate with the group in establishing the school.

The group was aware that the political climate at that time aided their cause. The school board had recently gone on record in favor of school-based management. Members of the African American community were demanding an independent school district, charging among other things that the administration was incapable of responding to parents. It was difficult for board members to turn down a thorough community-based proposal that included school-site management as a key component.

Despite an explicit directive from the school board to assist the group, the school administration continued to place obstacles in their path. A one-page explanation of the philosophy and proposed structure of the school—designed to ensure the school would be staffed by educators supportive of their vision—was never distributed to prospective teachers. When Neighbors for a New Fratney called for a national search for an experienced bilingual principal, the administration refused and stalled before hiring anyone. A month before the doors of the school were to open, the administration finally hired a principal who was bilingual in English and German and had no urban experience.

Angered and determined, Neighbors for a New Fratney again mobilized the community and picketed school board meetings. Responding to community pressure, Milwaukee's newly hired superintendent, Dr. Robert S. Peterkin, rejected the central office's recommendation in favor of a more acceptable interim alternative principal and assured the group that a national search would occur the following year.

But the battle wasn't over. In July, the group was informed it had to order everything needed for the new school within two weeks if members wanted to have materials for the beginning of the school year. Despite the lack of help from the administration, they completed the difficult task. When they returned to the school in mid-August, however, they discovered the required renovations had only just begun, the building had never been cleaned from the previous spring, and—worst of all—none of the ordered materials and supplies had arrived. Calls to vendors revealed the orders had not been received. On further investigation, the group discovered the order forms had sat for a month in the purchasing division of the school department because the department did not have an authorization card with the deputy superintendent's signature.

Faced with the prospect of starting school in a few weeks without any materials or supplies and now stretched to their limit, the group stormed up to the central office. This time, however, they were greeted not with hostility but with full support from the new administration. The new superintendent's assistant, Dr. Deborah McGriff, heard them out and agreed to respond immediately. Finally, the group could direct their energy and attention to making their vision a reality at La Escuela Fratney.

Moving from the ideal to a working school is a massive undertaking. Since La Escuela Fratney opened its doors amid unfinished construction and unfilled book orders in September of 1988, staff and parents have grappled with the difficult challenge of organizing an entirely new school from the ground up. The initial struggle and the months of inaction and poor planning by the administration were acutely felt throughout the school's first year. Resources were limited and time was always in short supply. In retrospect, the staff questions whether attempting to implement all aspects of the program simultaneously might have demanded more than was realistic. But through commitment, determination, and sheer hard work, many of the innovative approaches envisioned for the New Fratney are now in place.

Now in its third year, La Escuela Fratney enrolled 350 pupils in kindergarten through fifth grade for the 1990 to 1991 school year, 26 percent of whom are African American, 60 percent Latino, 13 percent White, and 1 percent Asian. Over 75 percent of the children are eligible for the free or reduced-price lunch program. Approximately 30 percent of the students are Spanish-language dominant, but this varies according to the grade level. For example, the second grade has seen an influx of refugees and over half of the children are native Spanish speakers.

The school strives for a fifty-fifty balance of native English and Spanish speakers in each classroom. A major focus has been improving the school's two-way bilingual program. All classroom teachers at the Fratney are bilingual. The first year, every first- through fifth-grade teacher taught his or her students in Spanish and English, switching every other day. But the preponderance of English-dominant students created the tendency to spend more time teaching in English than Spanish.

As teachers struggled to meet the challenge of graduating truly biliterate students, their thinking was strongly influenced by consultation with Stella Morales, a teacher at PS 84 in New York City. Morales brought years of experience in bilingual education to the school along with a conviction that the success of two-way bilingual programs in this country required strict separation of the languages. Her message was persuasive. A "two-environment" model was expanded to all grade levels.

With the "two-environment" model, pairs of teachers are jointly responsible for fifty to sixty children. They share a common planning time to coordinate and integrate curriculum. Teachers do not duplicate lessons. As Rita Tenorio, a kindergarten teacher explains: "The 'two-way' model dispels the notion of bilingual education as a remedial or compensatory program. All students are learning a second language. Both languages are valued equally and all students receive instruction for significant amounts of time in each language. The focus of instruction is primarily academic; students are gaining knowledge in many subjects in two languages. Language is a vehicle for instruction, not simply an end in itself. I am not 'teaching Spanish' but rather teaching kindergarten 'in Spanish.'"

All teachers organize their curriculum around schoolwide themes. After learning during the first year that seven schoolwide themes were too much to cover in one year, the staff reduced the number to four. For the 1990 to 1991 school year the themes were: "We respect ourselves and our world; We send messages when we communicate; We can make a difference on planet earth; and We share stories of the world." To provide teachers and students with various avenues for study and to help them organize their work, each theme has three or four sub-themes. For example, "We communicate in many languages and in many ways" and "TV can be dangerous to our health" are sub-themes of "We send messages when we communicate."

Implementation of each theme begins with a brainstorming session among teachers and the support staff most involved with the students. The group generates a great number of ideas for ways to weave the various curriculum areas around the theme and sub-themes. Pairs of teachers then decide what ideas they want to implement and who will cover what content and in what language.

Becky Trayser, a fourth-grade teacher, repeats the brainstorming process with her students. The process takes the themes from complex abstract concepts to concrete topics and activities. It also serves to motivate students by giving them a voice in what and how they study. Because students learn best when they are interested in a subject, Becky follows their lead in deciding what topics and activities to focus on for the sub-themes. The class weaves together possible areas of study and project work within a sub-theme. Becky recalls her experience over the past two years: "The lessons learned included the need to directly teach cooperative skills throughout the year, the need to develop a sense of responsibility and self-reliance in students, and perhaps most importantly, the need to let go, as the teacher, of full responsibility for the curriculum as it becomes a cooperative venture with the students."

Writing is a cornerstone of the curriculum at the New Fratney. For each theme, children write in reaction to readings, to reflect on their own work, and on topics of their own choosing related to the theme. They may write short biographies, fictional stories, or opinion pieces. All students keep a personal journal and some classes have instituted dialogue journals between teachers and students. Children share their writings in authors' circles and edit each other's work.

In many classrooms, children regularly author and make books. Benefiting from the language-rich environment, students in Becky Trayser's classroom use peers as resources to create bilingual books. More elaborate student books with laminated covers are made in the Parent Teacher Resource Room. Books authored by children are among the most popular in the school library.

In all their writings, children are encouraged to draw on their own experiences. Each child's story—her history, family, ethnic, and linguistic heritage—is validated and celebrated. At Fratney, children's cultures are at the center of the curriculum. Culture is not "added" to the curriculum, it is the basis for it. The history and contribution of people of color are thoroughly integrated throughout the curriculum with an explicit emphasis on the negative consequences of racism and discrimination in our country's history.

The staff at Fratney strive to have the children know, analyze, and respect their own cultural roots, comprehend the historical nature of racial oppression, and grasp the potential of a multicultural, multilingual society. In order to ensure that multicultural and anti-racist teaching is central to the life of Fratney, schoolwide themes demand a discussion of the contributions and history of many cultures and analysis of the deleterious effects of prejudice and discrimination. For example, "People of all nationalities have worked for peace and justice" and "We need to overcome prejudice and racism" are sub-themes for the schoolwide theme of "We can make a difference on planet earth."

The Fratney School is governed by a school-site council comprised of five parents, nine teachers, one community representative, the principal, and a representative of the non-teaching staff. Six parent alternatives attend meetings to ensure a balance between staff and parents. The Council makes all non-staff, and non-physical plant budgetary decisions. They address issues of fund-raising, parent involvement, curriculum, and many other concerns.

Because the demands of governing the school are so extensive, a number of other committees have been created to address specific issues. For example, the Curriculum Committee, comprised mostly of parents, guided the schoolwide homework policy through five revisions, helped plan family day, made decisions on curriculum themes, and addressed a number of other curricular matters. While the committees hammer out details, their decisions are discussed and approved by the Council.

Staff and parents at the Fratney endeavor to meet the challenge of making their vision a reality. They struggle to find the time and energy to plan individually and collectively, to forge ahead and build on the successes they have wrought so far. The two-way bilingual model requires that each teacher meets the needs of up to sixty children. Organizing the curriculum around themes requires extensive groundwork, materials, and planning. Governance by council requires a commitment to a consensus process that is both labor-intensive and time consuming.

Sustaining the vision means years of hard labor, determination, and commitment. But as Becky Trayser concludes: "The ingredients for what happened at Fratney exist in many other communities. Teachers need to realize the power they can have collectively. Teachers struggle for respect as practitioners on the front lines. There has to be a fundamental change. Administrators and others need to realize that parents and teachers know what is best for children. But we have to empower ourselves. Power is not going to be handed to us. It is hard for school boards to say no to a group of committed teachers, parents, and community activists like we had for Fratney. We exist and are moving forward and experiencing success because we are a committed group of teachers and parents who share a vision."

For further information, please contact: Mr. Bob Peterson, Program Implementor, La Escuela Fratney, 3255 N. Fratney Street, Milwaukee, WI 53212.

Current Research Related to Topics Discussed in Chapter Three

Existing Approaches to Teaching

Elementary school classrooms are not generally thriving, dynamic, exciting places that instill a joy for learning. In the average elementary classroom, students spend most of their time listening to lectures, doing seatwork, or completing quizzes and tests **(Chicago Project on Learning and Teaching, 1989; Goodlad, 1984; National Research Council, 1989).**

Research has identified relatively typical instructional patterns in elementary school classrooms. While there are notable exceptions, teachers generally tend to lecture to either the whole class or small groups, followed by recitation and discussion, and then by individual seatwork. Acting out, role playing, dance, and the manipulation of materials are seldom used as supplementary or alternative methods of instruction **(Anderson, *et al.*, 1985; Goodlad, 1984; Porter, 1989)**. Typically, anywhere from 55 to 70 percent of class time is spent in individual seatwork **(Goodlad, 1984).**

In the average elementary classroom, interactions both among students and between students and teachers are seldom used to stimulate inquiry and foster learning. When group activities are conducted, students generally do not work together in cooperative and interactive ways, but instead work side-by-side on the same activity dictated by the teacher **(Goodlad, 1984)**. Classrooms remain passive learning environments with teacher/student interaction characterized by student's short responses to teachers' typically close-ended questions **(Goodlad, 1984; Schmidt, 1991; Suzuki, 1984)**. Teachers and students seldom engage in meaningful dialogue that requires higher-level analysis and critical evaluation.

In elementary classrooms, rote learning of basic skills is often emphasized rather than active, hands-on learning that focuses on application and conceptual understanding **(Bennett, 1986; Chicago Project on Learning and Teaching, 1989; Goodlad, 1984; National Association for the Education of Young Children, 1988; Porter, 1989)**. For example, two studies involving forty-one third-through fifth-grade teachers in at least seventeen different schools found that 70 to 75 percent of mathematics instruction was spent teaching basic skills—how to add, subtract, multiply, and divide—as opposed to development of conceptual understanding and the application of skills **(Porter, 1989)**.

Moreover, teachers covered a very large percentage of the topics for brief periods of time, engaging in a practice referred to as "teaching for exposure." Teachers in one of the studies, with one notable exception, devoted less than thirty minutes of instructional time to 70 percent or more of the mathematics topics they covered **(Porter, 1989)**. Other educators and researchers have also pointed to the problems of teaching for exposure **(Chicago Project on Learning and Teaching, 1989; Goodlad, 1984; Porter and Brophy, 1988; Sizer, 1984)**.

The National Association for the Education of Young Children (NAEYC, 1988) has documented the occurrence of similar inappropriate practices in elementary classrooms. These include: instructional strategies that are teacher-directed and focus primarily on lecturing to the whole class; worksheet exercises completed by children working individually at their desks; narrowly focused curricula that stress technical academic skills; the expectation that children, for the most part, will work silently and alone; and the view that projects, learning centers, play, and outdoor time are embellishments that are offered only if time permits or as rewards for good behavior.

Goodlad's work (1984) reveals that instructional problems in elementary education intensify as children progress through the grades. In the upper elementary grades as compared to the primary grades, teachers exhibit less variety in the use of instructional strategies. They have less interaction with students and have greater reliance on seatwork, and they make little use of group work.

Reading remains the dominant subject in elementary school, occupying one-third to one-half of the classroom day **(Porter and Brophy, 1988)**. Mathematics is a distant second, but is still a regularly scheduled subject each day **(Schwille, *et al.*, 1986).**

Other subjects, including science, social studies, and art, receive much less emphasis **(Anderson and Smith, 1987; Bennett, 1986; Porter and Brophy, 1988).** They are rarely taught on a daily basis. This pattern appears to reflect teacher knowledge and confidence in teaching these different subjects **(Anderson and Smith, 1987; Porter and Brophy, 1988).**

Inadequate Instructional Materials

Modern textbooks are widely perceived to be clumsy, unclear, dull, and lifeless. Their low quality stems from a number of factors: a perception among textbook publishers that "good writing is something other than what people who buy (school) books want" **(DeSilva, 1986);** continued use of "readability formulas"—mathematical equations based, among other things, on vocabulary and sentence length—which tend to produce books most children don't want to read; and efforts to expand potential market by avoiding controversial topics and "covering" so many subjects that depth and accuracy are often sacrificed **(Bennett, 1986; Cheney, 1990; DeSilva, 1986; Goodman, *et al.*, 1988; Peterson, 1988).**

Efforts to cram so much information into textbooks mean that often little attention is paid to context. Information is presented in a vacuum, unanchored to what came before and follows after **(Cheney, 1990; DeSilva, 1986).** As textbook analyst Harriet Tyson-Bernstein concludes, textbooks become "a dumping ground for facts" instead of tools for learning **(*cited in* Bennett, 1986, p. 62).**

A recent content analysis of commonly used fourth-grade textbooks found that 70 to 80 percent of the topics covered in the books were allotted twenty or fewer exercises. Moreover, 65 to 80 percent of the exercises focused on skill practice, while 10 to 24 percent were on conceptual understanding, and only 6 to 13 percent on problem-solving **(Porter, 1989).**

Basal readers, the most popular type of textbook, are particularly problematic. Based on outmoded teaching styles that contradict modern research, the sterile, unnatural text and revisions of traditional folk tales and classic fictional pieces undermine students' natural interests in reading **(Anderson, *et al.*, 1985; Cheney, 1990; Peterson, 1988).**

Basal reading systems teach reading as the learning of a sequence of skills for word identification and comprehension. Because developing word identification skills is considered the cornerstone of reading instruction, all basals use controlled vocabulary as a major sequencing element. In contrast, recent research indicates that reading is a constructive and interactive process focused on meaning **(Anderson, *et al.*, 1985; Chall and Snow, 1988; Goodman, *et al.*, 1988; Peterson, 1988).**

Low-quality textbooks continue to form the core of elementary class teaching as many school systems and governmental policies promote their use. Several states continue to mandate strict adherence to basal systems. Seventy-five to 90 percent of all reading instruction in elementary classrooms is based on the basal system **(Anderson, *et al.*, 1985; Peterson, 1988).**

Various school systems use the basal tests that accompany the readers as the basis for a variety of decisions about students, including promotion and ability-group placement. Some schools even use the results on basal reader tests to assess teachers' performances **(Peterson, 1988).**

Because increased emphasis on standardized test results has led many schools and school systems to "align" their curriculum with the test, there is considerable pressure for teachers to employ textbooks that can effectively teach skills associated with these tests **(Anderson, *et al.*, 1985; DeSilva, 1986; Medina and Neill, 1988; Peterson, 1988).**

Even when discretion regarding teaching materials exists in theory, that discretion can rarely be exercised by classroom teachers. Schoolwide or system decisions on textbooks are often made by a single school-based or central office administrator selecting from an approved list **(Corcoran, Walker, and White, 1988; McPike, 1987; Noblit, 1986).** The lists are usually drawn up by a textbook selection committee, which often selects books without the benefit of having read them **(Cheney, 1990; Peterson, 1988).** Selection committees tend to work from checklists that focus on the presence of easily verifiable factors rather than an in-depth analysis of quality **(Cheney, 1990; Peterson, 1988).** Where use of alternative materials is not formally prohibited, lack of resources may make it a practical impossibility.

Trends in Student Achievement

The effectiveness of any set of teaching strategies or curricular approaches must be judged by students' academic and social growth. Measuring student learning and development, particularly systematically and on a large scale, is fraught with difficulties. Currently, student assessment relies primarily on standardized tests. As discussed in Chapter 4, there are serious limitations to the information gathered by such tests.

Even with these limitations, however, test results reveal continuing deficiencies in student learning. **The National Assessment of Educational Progress (NAEP, 1985),** one of the most comprehensive of the assessment programs, provides valuable information on national trends and conditions in student learning. It has revealed student growth in basic reading and mathematics skills, but a decline in higher-order skills in both areas. Student writing competence has remained essentially stagnant for almost a decade and a half. Learning by students in science and social studies has declined dramatically over the last two decades.

Minority students and children attending schools in disadvantaged areas—both urban and rural—have generally improved their achievement since NAEP assessments were first conducted in the late 1960s and early 1970s. This improvement has been most marked in the areas of reading and mathematics **(NAEP, 1985).** Increases in minority achievement coupled with the overall trend toward declining achievement have helped closed the learning gap between minorities and the overall student population.

Increases in minority achievement, however, appear to be almost entirely attributable to improvement in basic skills. There has been virtually no improvement in higher-order reading and mathematics skills and the learning gap has not closed in these areas. Lack of growth in minority achievement in higher-order skills is of particular concern given the changing composition of public schools' student population. Already, minority enrollment levels in the nation's fifteen largest school systems range from 70 to 96 percent. By the year 2000, one out of three Americans will be non-White **(Hodgkinson, 1985).** Recent estimates place annual immigration into the United States at 100,000 to 300,000 individuals **(First, *et al.*, 1988).**

These trends document continuing challenges to learning, particularly in higher-order skills and among minority students, suggesting that current teaching strategies and curricular approaches have failed to meet students' academic needs.

Learning and Childhood Development

Some researchers and practitioners draw upon learning style and child development theories to suggest approaches and practices to address more effectively the needs of a diverse student population.

One of the basic premises of developmental theory is that all domains of development—physical, social, emotional, and cognitive—are integrated. Growth in one domain influences and, in turn, is influenced by the other domains **(Piaget and Inhelder, 1969; Cicchetti and Hesse, 1982).** According to this theory, teaching must integrate all four developmental areas **(NAEYC, 1988).**

As revealed by developmental theory and research, between the ages of approximately six and nine children's thought processes undergo a critical change. Children begin to develop the ability to think and solve problems mentally because they can manipulate objects symbolically. Although children at this age develop the ability to manipulate objects mentally they are not able to manipulate symbols mentally. Children use symbols, such as words and numbers, to represent objects and relations but still require real objects and relations as reference points **(NAEYC, 1988; Piaget and Inhelder, 1969).**

Based on these findings, developmentally appropriate curricula for young children in the primary grades should provide many materials for children to explore to expand their developing ability to manipulate objects mentally. Numerous opportunities for interaction and communication with other children and adults are also essential. Engaging in conservation strengthens children's abilities to communicate, express themselves, and reason. In addition, the content of the curriculum should be relevant, engaging, and meaningful to the children **(NAEYC, 1988).**

A major task for young children, according to developmental research, is developing a sense of competence **(Damon, 1983; NAEYC, 1988).** Young children continually assess their ability to successfully meet the social and academic demands of the school setting. When children are pressured to acquire skills beyond their capabilities and are pushed to succeed too early at complex tasks—such as reading—their motivation to learn as well as their self-esteem is frequently impaired. Children with low self-esteem and a limited sense of competence often have continued difficulty reaching their academic potential at school **(Dweck, 1986; Dweck and Elliott, 1983).**

In developmentally appropriate classrooms, teachers recognize that each child has a unique personality and individual family background, and best demonstrates his or her abilities through familiar cultural forms. Recognition of individual differences necessitates the use of a variety of teaching methods and materials. Developmentally appropriate classrooms are flexible about when and how children will acquire certain skills and abilities, and they employ a wide variety of teaching methods and materials **(Kamii, 1985; NAEYC, 1988).**

Learning style theory holds that students learn in identifiably different ways. **Hunt (1979)** defines learning style as "the educational conditions under which a student learns best, particularly in terms of the structure provided." Accordingly, effective teaching requires the use of different teaching methods that match different learning styles, an approach that has been found to improve student learning **(Carbo, 1987; Dunn, 1987; Dunn, *et al.*, 1989; Weinberg, 1983, *cited in* Hilgersom-Volk, 1987).** At the same time, research indicates that children who succeed in school academically are able to use several different learning styles. Thus, the effective use of learning styles theory in the elementary classroom requires a balance. Efforts to match teaching styles with student learning styles must be complemented by efforts to teach students to learn in a variety of styles **(Hilgersom-Volk, 1987; Lober, 1989).**

Research has identified learning styles that vary along a number of dimensions, including: environmental—how children work in varying sound, light, and temperature conditions; emotional—how children's emotions, motivations, and willingness to conform affect their abilities to learn; sociological—how well students work alone, in pairs, or in groups; physical—which of the five senses provides the best intake of information for children; and psychological—how children process information, for example, global thinking as opposed to analytical thinking **(Clary, 1989; Dunn, *et al.*, 1989; Hilgersom-Volk, 1987).**

Research in the use of learning styles has shown that when teaching strategies complement children's learning styles, students demonstrate higher test scores, improved attitudes toward school and learning, and fewer disciplinary problems **(Dunn, *et al.*, 1989; Hilgersom-Volk, 1987).** For example, teaching strategies in reading usually demand strongly analytic/auditory reading styles, while poor readers are predominantly global, tactile, and kinesthetic learners. When teaching practices are varied to accommodate their styles, poor readers, even those who have experienced years of low achievement, demonstrate significant progress **(Carbo, 1987).**

The different diagnostic instruments used to measure learning styles have limitations. Because learning style inventories generally rely on self-reporting, such reporting may be inaccurate. Learning style profiles of students may also change over time. In addition, while patterns of cultural interaction may influence learning preferences, learning styles are not culturally based. There are as many within-group as between-group differences in learning styles among cultural groups. Even within families, the parents, their offspring, and the siblings tend to be more different from than similar to each other **(Dunn, *et al.*, 1989).** Thus, determinations of learning styles cannot be viewed as permanent. Profiles of learning styles are most effectively employed as a tool for selecting teaching strategies, rather than as a mechanism for rigidly categorizing students **(Hilgersom-Volk, 1987; Stice and Dunn, 1985).**

Successful strategies to address varied learning styles require considerable teacher training and a commitment by school leadership to meet diverse students' needs. The ultimate focus of responding effectively to various learning styles is the perception that children are unique individuals. Many teachers have difficulty applying this focus because they cling to the "average child" concept, leading them to view their students as groups of similar classmates. An approach geared to varied learning styles does not seek to change the student, but to change teaching practice to meet the unique needs of the student.

Effective Classroom Teaching

Researchers have identified three basic factors that distinguish between academically effective and ineffective classrooms: 1) teachers' classroom presentations; 2) their classroom management; and 3) their expectations and use of praise **(Brophy, 1986, 1987; Brophy and Good, 1986; Teddlie, Kirby, and Springfield, 1989.)**

Rather than relying solely on lecture or seatwork, effective teaching employs a variety of techniques, including demonstrations, small group activity, peer tutoring, and individual work. Teaching is presented in short, manageable steps, both to reduce confusion and frustration and to maximize student opportunities for success. At the same time, lessons are designed to provide constant academic challenges to individual students. Finally, effective teaching demands a great deal of teacher interaction with students, particularly in providing feedback on student work and reteaching when necessary. Effective teachers reteach concepts using different strategies and approaches until students demonstrate mastery **(Bain, *et al.*, 1989; Brophy, 1986, 1987; Brophy and Good, 1986; Murphy, Weil, and McGreal, 1986; Pearson and Doyle, 1987; Porter and Brophy, 1988; Teddlie, Kirby, and Stringfield, 1989).**

The key to effective classroom management is not so much in knowing how to respond to problems when they occur as knowing how to prevent problems from occurring in the first place by appropriately arranging the physical environment, establishing and reinforcing rules, continually monitoring the entire class, effectively pacing students, and providing clarity regarding how students can get help when they need it. High task-engagement rates attained through successful classroom management are among the most powerful correlates of learning **(Brophy, 1986; Everston, *et al.*, 1983; Good and Brophy, 1987; Strother, 1985; Teddlie, Kirby, and Stringfield, 1989).**

Effective teaching depends not only on greater interactions between teachers and students, but on interactions based on a different set of teacher perceptions and expectations. Effective teachers not only have a high expectation for all students, they build on the self-confidence and high expectations young children bring with them into the classroom **(Bain, *et al.*, 1989; Good, 1987; Good and Brophy, 1987; Teddlie, Kirby, and Stringfield, 1989).**

Effective teachers use praise sparingly rather than effusively and focus it on specific rather than global behavior. Praise addresses the content of the accomplishments and not the recipient themselves. The statement of praise identifies the specific accomplishment, attributes the success to ability and effort, and implies that similar achievements are attainable in the future. Inappropriately excessive praise is often intrusive, may embarrass the recipient, and distracts the class from the lesson at hand **(Brophy, 1986; Good, 1987).**

Effective teachers appear to recognize the importance of parents as their children's first and foremost teachers. In one study **(Bain, *et al.*, 1989),** 95 percent of the teachers identified as effective used a number of strategies to involve parents in their children's education. Teacher efficacy is also strongly associated with parent involvement. That is, teachers who believe that they are effective in teaching and that the children they teach can learn, tend to promote and facilitate the involvement of their students' parents **(Hoover-Dempsey, Bassler, and Brissie, 1987).**

Content Areas and Higher-Order Skills

Recent research in mathematics and science instruction suggests that successful teaching does not involve infusing information into a vacuum but rather, inducing changes in students' existing concepts and perceptions. Effective instruction connects new learning to prior knowledge, both by taking advantage of correct information as a base for new knowledge and by addressing and confronting misinformation and misconceptions to make sure that they do not persist.

To implement this instructional approach, teachers need solid knowledge of the content to be taught, the required strategies for teaching it, and an understanding of the perceptions and misconceptions their students bring with them into the classroom **(Bonnstetter, 1989; Brophy, 1987; Chicago Project on Learning and Teaching, 1989; Porter and Brophy, 1988).**

Research in reading instruction has revealed strategies for integrating reading comprehension across the content areas and for promoting the development of higher-order skills such as problem-solving, critical thinking, and reasoning. This research indicates that students often need to be taught the strategies or thought processes involved in complex reasoning **(Knight, Waxman, and Padron, 1989; Pearson and Dole, 1987).**

This instruction requires that teachers implement several instructional practices, including: demonstration and modeling of the strategies required for learning to comprehend or problem-solve; guided practice to help the student learn to use the strategies over time; independent practice of the strategies with teacher feedback; and independent application of the strategies to new learning situations, particularly content area work **(Chall and Snow, 1988; McTighe and Lyman, 1988; Murphy, Weil, and McGreal, 1987; Pearson and Dole, 1987).**

This explicit comprehension instruction appears to benefit low-achieving students in particular. Such students may need to learn the comprehension strategies that high-achieving students use more intuitively. In one study, poor readers in an experimental group performed as well as high-level readers in a control group despite a three-year grade difference in average reading scores **(Brown and Palincsar, 1985).** Brown and Palincsar also found that small groups of poor readers given direct comprehension instruction improved their daily comprehension test scores from below 40 to over 75 percent correct.

Meeting the Needs of Students of Color

Some needs of students of color can be met through approaches that address individual differences. But recent research suggests minority students may resist full engagement in academic pursuits for a number of reasons. **Fordham and Ogbu (1986)** hold that this has its origins in the historical subordination in economic, political, and social domains of racial and ethnic minority groups to the dominant White culture. Almost in self-defense, minority groups seek a collective identity both to strengthen themselves and to protect themselves against "encroachments" by the dominant White culture.

In establishing this group identity, minorities develop behaviors and activities related to areas in which it was long held that only Whites could succeed and in which minorities traditionally were not given the opportunity to succeed or were not rewarded if they succeeded. Many minority students see the public schools as just such an area and fear that full engagement in school will lead to acceptance of a White, middle-class collective identity in exchange for rejection of their own. Consequently, many students from subordinated minority groups either do not fully engage in or fail to persevere with academic activities **(Fordham, 1988; Fordham and Ogbu, 1986).**

Howard and Hammonds (1986) also suggest another reason why some minority students might resist full engagement in academic pursuits. They point out that minority children are constantly exposed to "rumors of their inferiority" and, as a result, develop poor concepts of themselves as academic achievers. Minority students may consciously or unconsciously avoid engaging in academic activities for fear of verifying the "terrible myth" of their inferiority. **Vecoli (1987; *cited in* First, *et al.*, 1988)** reaches similar conclusions regarding immigrant children.

Teaching strategies designed to respond to the needs of minority students must take these perceptions into account. **Cummins (1986)**, for example, suggests that effective teaching for many minority students should be highly interactive and characterized by: genuine dialogue between students and teachers; support for student-directed rather than teacher-controlled learning; student collaboration; integration of language use and development with curriculum content, rather than in isolation from other subjects; focus on cognitive skills rather than the recall of facts; and tasks which stimulate internal, rather than external, motivation.

Recent research **(Banks, 1988; *Harvard Education Letter*, 1988; Neisser, 1986; Reyhner and García, 1989)** has found that patterns of interactive learning behaviors differ in White middle-class and poor minority families. White middle-class families are more likely to emphasize story-reading and a form of questioning that requires children to exercise their memories, to reflect on experience, and to give complete descriptions and tell complete stories. Poor minority families are more likely to use analogies or metaphors and storytelling. The different patterns of interacting provide White middle-class children with a significant advantage in school over poor minority children— not because the minority behaviors are inferior, but because schools generally reflect and employ White middle-class perspectives and approaches **(Banks, 1988; Comer, 1984; Cummins, 1986).**

Children from culturally different homes often experience serious cultural discontinuity between home and school **(Comer, 1984; Phillips, 1988; Reyhner and García; 1989; Suzuki, 1984).** The students experience a language and culture at home that differs significantly from the language and culture of the school. This creates grave conflict for them and may require that they give up their home culture in order to achieve in school **(Phillips, 1988; Reyhner and García, 1989).** Children of recent immigrant families may suffer the most from this discontinuity **(First, *et al.*, 1988; Suzuki, 1984).**

This cultural discontinuity is exacerbated because teachers often fail to recognize the cultural and linguistic strengths of children from ethnically different backgrounds, but instead view them as deficits or problems to overcome **(Comer, 1984; *Harvard Education Letter*, 1988; Reyhner and García, 1989).** Teachers need to use their cultural knowledge about children in their care to build bridges between the home and school environment. With this approach teachers can increase the points of access for all students to meet achievement goals **(Comer, 1984; *Harvard Education Letter*, 1988; Phillips, 1988).**

Implementing these teaching strategies requires teachers to have a strong belief in their ability to teach, high expectations that all children can learn, and a willingness to accept responsibility for student failure. Teachers must examine their own cultural backgrounds, experiences, and attitudes to see how they might affect their expectations of children of differing cultural backgrounds. Equally important, teachers must be aware of how easily culturally determined behavior can be misinterpreted and lead to unnecessary conflict in the classroom **(Banks, 1988; Baptiste, 1987; First, *et al.*, 1988; Olsen, 1988).**

Multicultural Education

Education that is multicultural promotes an understanding of the complexity of the American experience and the ways that the nation's various groups have interacted and influenced each other. It acknowledges and discusses the history and contributions of various ethnic groups to the development and maintenance of economic, political, and social institutions. Multicultural education addresses social structural inequality by helping students better understand the causes of oppression, prejudice, and ethnocentrism and provides them with the tools to begin to challenge this inequality and promote cultural diversity **(Banks, 1987; Baptiste, 1986; Phillips, 1988; Sleeter and Grant, 1987; Suzuki, 1984).**

Clearly, multicultural education is a critical strategy to combat internalization of negative stereotypes by students of color because it affirms the intrinsic value of all cultures and provides them with educational content that is personally meaningful and has some relationship to their lives. But one often cited and erroneous assumption is that multicultural education is only relevant in classrooms with students who represent different groups **(Banks, 1987; McLean, 1990; Ramsey, 1982; Suzuki, 1984; Viadero, 1990).**

Traditionally education in the United States has been dominated by an Anglocentric perspective **(Banks, 1987; Banks, 1988; Montero-Sieburth, 1989; Ramsey, 1982; Reyhner and García, 1989; Suzuki, 1984).** Children usually learn about the history and development of the United States through the eyes of the dominant European group. When different ethnic groups are discussed, it is through their interactions with the dominant group **(Banks, 1987).** Students from culturally different ethnic groups seldom encounter educational content that is personally meaningful and has some relationship to their lives **(Banks, 1987; McLean, 1990; Ramsey, 1982; Reyhner and García, 1989).**

A central factor affecting children's understanding of other groups is how differently they perceive groups to be from their own **(Ramsey, 1982).** Teaching that focuses on contrasts and differences tends to accentuate the "we/they" polarity and can serve to foster separateness and reinforce negative cultural stereotypes **(Ramsey, 1982; Wurzel, 1989).** The additive approach to multicultural education implemented most often by schools tends to result in this type of teaching.

The additive approach misconceives of multicultural education as "a set of activities added on to the existing curriculum" **(Ramsey, 1982; p. 16).** This introduction into the curriculum of fragmented ethnic content, such as ethnic heroes, holidays, and foods, implicitly conveys that ethnic minority groups are not an integral part of mainstream society **(Banks, 1987; Viadero, 1990).** Banks holds that this superficial teaching of ethnic content can do more harm than good—"this kind of teaching about ethnic cultures often perpetuates misconceptions and stereotypes about ethnic cultures and leads well-meaning but misinformed teachers to believe that they have integrated their curricula with ethnic content and helped their students to understand ethnic groups better" (p. 533).

Instead of helping children to understand the history and contributions of various ethnic groups to the development of this country and the interrelatedness among groups, the additive approach tends to result in an emphasis on cultural differences and the presentation of cultural content outside of a meaningful context **(Banks, 1987; McLean, 1990; Phillips, 1988; Ramsey, 1982; Viadero, 1990; Wurzel, 1989).** Most of what is taught is depersonalized. People and their systems of belief are taught in a context devoid of emotion. Students do not get the opportunity to discuss and understand the complex values and emotions that are inherent in belonging to a particular culture **(Suzuki, 1984; Wurzel, 1989).** Nor do they come to see that all groups share in common this struggle of self and other identification.

According to **Banks (1987),** most multicultural education is characterized by: focus on isolated aspects and trivialization of the history and cultures of ethnic groups; presentation of events, concepts, and issues primarily from an Anglocentric perspective; description of ethnic cultures as deprived or pathological; scant attention to the concepts of institutional racism, class stratification, and powerlessness; domination of the assimilationist ideology; emphasis on the mastery of knowledge and cognitive outcomes.

In contrast to an "add-on," multicultural education is more appropriately viewed as a perspective that permeates the structures and practices of the school **(Banks, 1987, Phillips, 1988; Ramsey, 1982; Suzuki, 1984; Wurzel, 1989).** The goal of multicultural education is not to teach children about different countries or groups but to help them understand that there are many equally valid life-styles, languages, and points of view. Multicultural education should provide children with a conceptual framework for understanding the experiences and perspectives of all groups, including the causes and consequences of oppression, prejudice, and discrimination **(Banks, 1987; Cushner and Trifonovitch, 1989; Ramsey, 1982; Suzuki, 1984).**

Banks (1987) has defined effective multicultural education as encompassing the following characteristics: describes histories and cultures holistically; describes cultures as dynamic wholes and processes of change; presents events, issues, and concepts from the perspectives of diverse racial and ethnic groups; presents information on the origin and impact of various cultures on the United States; describes the differences among cultures while emphasizing that they are all normal; focuses on concepts such as institutional racism, class stratification, powerlessness, and victimization; and emphasizes decision making and citizen action.

Suzuki (1984) has identified a number of goals of multicultural education for students that are compatible with Banks's characteristics. For example, Suzuki holds that students should develop positive feelings, attitudes, and perceptions toward their own and other ethnic groups; acquire knowledge, understanding, and appreciation of the experiences and contributions of ethnically diverse groups to American society; understand the nature of pluralism and interethnic conflicts, including the basic causes of racism, sexism, and poverty; and develop the skills and commitment to begin to address these pressing social issues.

While multicultural curricula should embody certain defining characteristics and goals, the specific objectives emphasized and curriculum content will vary from classroom to classroom depending on the racial, cultural, and socioeconomic backgrounds of the students, their experience with other groups, and their attitudes toward their own and other groups **(Ramsey, 1982; Phillips, 1988; Suzuki, 1984).** For example, children from low-status groups often need to build respect and appreciation for their cultures. In contrast, children from high-status groups need a more realistic view on the relative value of their own cultures **(Ramsey, 1982).**

The successful implementation of multicultural education requires a process of cultural self-awareness for teachers. Teachers need to carefully examine and come to understand their own cultural backgrounds, their relationships within the larger society, and their beliefs and attitudes toward other ethnic groups **(McLean, 1990; Ramsey, 1982; Suzuki, 1984; Wurzel, 1989).** Because educational practices are "inextricably bound up with the teacher's personal and cultural beliefs" **(McLean,** p. 202**),** it is critical that teachers recognize their own prejudices and attitudes and how these strongly affect student self-esteem, motivation, and achievement. Like the students in their charge, they must also develop an understanding and appreciation for the history and contributions of diverse ethnic groups and the basic causes of race and class inequality **(Banks, 1987; Phillips, 1988; Suzuki, 1984).** Because teachers work within a power structure, they require the support and guidance of administrators to effectively implement multicultural education **(Sleeter and Grant, 1987).**

Several researchers and educators provide guiding principles or strategies for the implementation of multicultural education **(Phillips, 1988; Ramsey, 1982; Suzuki, 1984; Wurzel, 1989).** While there is considerable overlap, Suzuki's recommendations appear to be the most extensive. He proposes that the implementation of multicultural education be guided by the following principles: start "where people are at," that is, begin by dealing with individuals' own ethnic backgrounds first; help de-center people by using their ethnic backgrounds as a cross-cultural bridge and thereby help depolarize interethnic conflict; integrate multicultural concepts and content across all the curriculum; be affective as well as cognitive; use teaching approaches and materials that are relevant to students' sociocultural backgrounds to increase their achievement in all areas; deal with the social and historical realities of society, the causes of oppression and inequality, and ways to address and eventually eliminate these problems; produce changes not only in the content of curriculum but also in teaching practices and the social structure of the classroom; understand that the most important influences on students' motivation and performance may be the care, concern, and sensitivity shown to them; increase the involvement of parents and use other multicultural resources found in the community; recognize that it is a long-term process that will take a minimum of five years to produce any significant results **(Suzuki,** p. 309**).**

Suzuki (1984) and others **(Montero-Sieburth, 1989; Phillips, 1988)** argue that while schools cannot operate independently of the dominant culture, they can still play a significant role in social change. Multicultural education offers the promise of broadening all children's awareness and appreciation of the complexity of the human experience as well as its common themes, a belief in the inherent equality of all groups, and a commitment to work to make this a reality.

The Need for Quality Bilingual Education

One of the larger ironies in U.S. public education is that while the acquisition of a second language and cross-cultural communication skills are extolled as highly desirable, bilingual education generally has met with resistance and negative criticism **(Arvizu and Saravia-Shore, 1990; Twentieth Century Fund Task Force, 1983).** Critics fail to recognize that the goals of foreign-language education, second-language education, and bilingual education are compatible. All three develop second-language skills and cross-cultural competencies among students **(Arvizu and Saravia-Shore, 1990; First, *et al.*, 1988; Snow and Hakuta, 1987).**

Minority-language students in bilingual programs bring a language other than English into the classroom. In contrast, students studying a "foreign" language are for the most part English monolinguals. It is a telling contradiction that the study of a foreign language is usually viewed as enrichment for English monolingual students while minority language students who speak that same "foreign" language and learn English as a second language are viewed as needing remedial education **(Arvizu and Saravia-Shore, 1990).** For the language-minority student, their language is often seen as a liability to be overcome as quickly as possible rather than a strength to build on for instruction **(Cummins, 1986; *Harvard Education Letter*, 1988; Reyhner and García, 1989).**

The goal of bilingual education is twofold. It seeks to have language-minority children achieve competence in English and it strives to enable them to meet grade promotion and graduation requirements by providing instruction in their native languages **(First, *et al.*, 1988).** Yet an estimated two-thirds of the 3.5 to 5.5 million limited-English-proficient (LEP) students enrolled in public schools are not receiving the language assistance they require to succeed in the classroom **(LaFontaine, 1987).** While a number of school districts argue that providing bilingual education is impractical or impossible, a U.S. Government Accounting Office report estimated that only 22 to 26 percent of LEP students are in schools where bilingual education is truly impractical due to very small numbers of children in a given language group **(U.S. Government Accounting Office, 1987).**

Even when schools provide bilingual education it is often of poor quality and/or focuses to a large degree on English proficiency development **(First, *et al.*, 1988).** As educators and researchers **Snow and Hakuta (1987)** point out, "Bilingual education in its present form may be one of the greatest misnomers of educational programs. What it fosters is monolingualism; bilingual education programs are efficient revolving doors between home-language monolingualism and English monolingualism. The bottom line of all these [bilingual] programs has been an almost single-minded interest in the extent and the efficiency of English proficiency development."

Snow and Hakuta (1987) hold that the "costs of monolingualism" are borne by both society and individual. Educational costs result because teachers, school time, and school dollars end up allocated for foreign-language training of monolingual students. Yet, the resultant fluency and linguistic competence of foreign-language students is much lower than those who have learned the language at home. Economic costs result from a loss in competitiveness due to the low number of Americans competent in languages other than English. Moreover, it takes much more effort, time, commitment, and hard work to learn a second language in high school than it does to maintain a language already learned at home. Evidence also exists that children proficient in two languages are better able to perform well on tasks that require cognitive and linguistic flexibility **(Snow and Hakuta, 1987).**

There are a number of different programs designed to teach limited-English-proficient students. These include Structured Immersion, English as a Second Language (ESL), Sheltered English, Transitional Bilingual Education, Two-Way Bilingual Education, and Maintenance Bilingual Education Programs (*see* **First, *et al.*, 1988,** for a description of each). Recent research indicates that high-quality programs, that is, programs that conform to model descriptions of their characteristics, effectively educate limited-English-proficient students **(Krashen and Biber, 1988, *cited in* Reyhner and García, 1989; Schmidt, 1991).** A study completed by the U.S. Department of Education followed 2,000 Spanish-speaking elementary school students with limited English skills through three types of model bilingual programs—programs that immersed children in English, changed to mostly English over four years, and those that eased more slowly into English over six years. Findings revealed that children in all three types of programs achieved at a rate equivalent to the general student population, and had higher achievement than other at-risk students. Moreover, significant amounts of instruction in their native language did not impede children's ability to master English **(Schmidt, 1991).**

The results also suggest that programs that favor heavy instruction in the native language may be the most effective over the long run. By the end of sixth grade, students enrolled in late-exit programs (i.e., eased into instruction in English over six years) appeared to be gaining in math, English-language, and English-reading skills faster than the general student population. In contrast, students in early-exit programs appeared to be losing ground in these areas as compared to the general student population **(Schmidt, 1991).**

Likewise, **Krashen and Biber (1988, *cited in* Reyhner and García, 1989)** identified effective bilingual programs in California. They found that successful bilingual programs were characterized by: high-quality subject matter teaching in children's native language; development of literacy in the native language; and comprehensive English as a Second Language instruction with Sheltered English instruction in the content areas. **LaFontaine (1987)** has also identified the components of quality bilingual education programs to include the following: clearly articulated goals; identification and comprehensive assessment of students; appropriately designed programs that address the unique needs of the particular students; qualified and well-trained staff who are provided a well-designed and continuing program of in-service training; appropriate instructional materials; parental and community involvement, and an ongoing strong evaluation and research component.

One danger of substantially separate programs serving limited-English-proficient children is that they can exacerbate student segregation. When bilingual programs are separated from the life of the school community, they can act to isolate their students from the entire school population **(Dentzer and Wheelock, 1990; First, *et al.*, 1988)**. Limited-English-proficient children often experience prejudice and discrimination, and their teachers frequently do not share the same status as teachers in monolingual classrooms **(Dentzer and Wheelock, 1990; First, *et al.*, 1988).** Two-Way Bilingual Programs have not only proved to be effective (for example, see the description of the Hernandez School in **Dentzer and Wheelock, 1990,** or La Escuela Fratney in Chapter 3 of this report), they also successfully address these concerns. The two-way bilingual approach teaches language-minority and language-majority students side by side in the same classroom. The two native languages of the students in the classroom are used alternatively for instruction. In contrast to the remediation approach, two-way bilingual programs view children's native language skills as a strength and a resource to be shared with the other children **(Dentzer and Wheelock, 1990).**

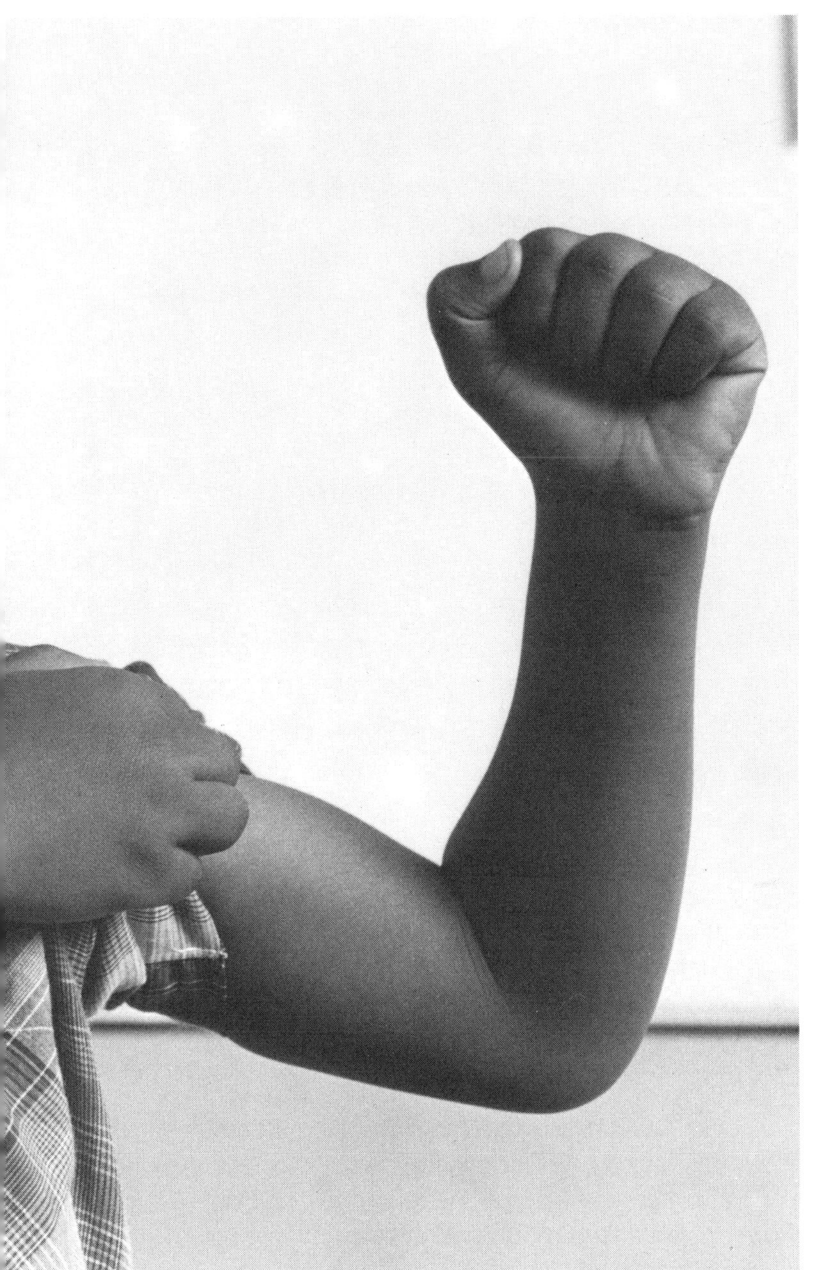

4

Enhancing Individual Potential

Children are entitled to a broadly-based assessment of their academic progress, and grading structures that enhance individual strengths and potential.

A Vision of Student Assessment and Grade Structure at the Good Common School

Jean Larson, a second-grade teacher in House Two of the Good Common School for the past five years, walks the aisles of her classroom as a test monitor must. Twenty-four young heads bend intently over test sheets; twenty-four young hands grip #2 pencils. And—she's willing to bet—half that many young stomachs are tight with anxiety, despite her careful instructions, despite group-taught relaxation lessons, and despite the fact that she knows she is a good teacher.

She does not administer standardized achievement tests to her students out of any love for large-scale, multiple-choice testing. She administers them because the school district insists. She dislikes test days, has little faith that the test measures what she has taught or what her students have learned, and dreads the reactions of students who score poorly—and of their parents, as well.

She dislikes the political ways test scores are used in her school district. Last year, it was obvious that a prize principalship went to the applicant whose previous school had the highest standardized test scores. She knows that these tests yield little diagnostic information useful in planning how to instruct students better.

After administering the tests, she always finds herself filled with feelings of frustration and helplessness. On every test day, she is tempted to ask the Good Common School Council to request a waiver from the school district, allowing the school to replace standardized tests with alternative assessments of student progress. But she has never yielded to the temptation.

Jean knows she is a good teacher, but she doesn't consider herself a leader. Backing her car out of the school parking lot, she remembers the quiet courage of Rosa Parks, and thinks wryly, "This girl's soul is weary too."

As she enters her kitchen, the telephone is ringing. It's the mother of one of her students, anxious about her daughter's progress. When the call is finished, Jean picks up the phone again and dials the number of Ella Davis, who chairs the Good Common School Council. She asks for a place on the agenda of next week's meeting. Permission is quickly granted, as Jean knew it would be. Now the wheels are turning; she can't retreat.

She has two important tasks to accomplish quickly. She must develop a brief position paper based on research to back up her presentation and she must build support among teachers and parents. She doesn't expect many teachers to disagree with her. She knows most of her colleagues share her frustration over standardized tests.

She suspects Phyllis Walker, the new principal, is sympathetic but still susceptible to the influences of central office politics. She knows parents will vary in their responses. Some believe test scores are an accurate indication of how well their children are progressing. Others don't. Even among parents who support the testing program, there is ambivalence; too many youngsters don't sleep the night before test day.

• • •

Jean goes to school early the following morning to tell the principal she has taken action. The conversation goes better than she expects. First, Principal Walker reveals that some principals and central office administrators are already critical of the massive changes that have occurred at the Good Common School under her administration. Then she says, "Go for it. The tiger already has so many stripes, one more won't matter." So far, so good.

Next, Jean goes to the teacher's lounge to spend the remaining minutes before first bell buttonholing other teachers. Two of her colleagues are drinking coffee. One responds positively. The other shakes her head and says, "Hey, I just get paid for doing my job. I am not a fan of these tests, but I'm not going to make waves." Jean then heads for her classroom, mentally noting she must call a few parents tonight—including some of those who sit on the school council—to explain her concerns.

During lunch hour, she calls the Boston College Center for the Study of Testing, Evaluation, and Educational Policy and the offices of FAIRTEST—a national organization based in Cambridge, Massachusetts that advocates broadly-based assessment in public schools—to ask for resource materials describing alternatives. Both organizations promise to put information in the mail.

• • •

By the time the council meeting arrives, the memorandum is drafted, and Jean is firmly convinced she is doing the right thing. Faculty support is strong; conversations with parent members of the council have been encouraging.

Jean opens her presentation by stating firmly that she favors accountability, but she opposes both the pressures associated with testing and the tendency toward "high-stakes" testing, explaining the latter involves making important decisions about children's futures solely on the basis of standardized test scores.

She names a few such decisions that affect students: grade promotion, graduation from high school, assignments to remedial classes, assignment to "gifted" programs. Then she gives examples of how "high-stakes" testing affects teachers when merit pay, certification, or recertification ride on a single score. She explains her view that high-stakes testing is really "automatic" decision-making deliberately designed to eliminate the input of educators.

Jean next talks about how she and other teachers often feel pressure to "teach to the test"—and how, when they yield to that pressure, parts of the curriculum that deserve in-depth attention only receive it once-over-lightly.

Aware her audience is interested, she scores some additional points. Students may actually possess skills or knowledge measured by the test but may—for many reasons—be unable to demonstrate that knowledge on test day. She notes that students have a legal right to receive instruction in skills and knowledge covered on tests prior to being tested.

She proposes a variety of authentic assessment alternatives, including student portfolios, student performance tasks, student projects, structured classroom observations, and curriculum-based assessment.

Next, she hands out copies of a resolution for consideration by the council. The resolution:

- Asks the superintendent for a waiver from large-scale testing of students and seeks approval of a proposal to test only a random sample of Good Common School students to provide the school district with a measure of the school's quality; these scores will not be entered in individual student records.
- Requests formation of a teacher/parent committee to develop alternative assessment strategies.
- Seeks participation of counselors and parents in the assessment of each child's progress.
- Asks for replacement of simplistic letter grades with written descriptions of progress prepared by a child's teacher.

After some discussion, the council approves the second and third points, tables the fourth point for later consideration, and agrees to send the first point to the superintendent of schools.

• • •

The next day, Phyllis Walker hand-carries the first recommendation to the superintendent's office. The superintendent, in turn, presents the request to the school board at its next meeting with a recommendation that it be approved on a one-year pilot basis, effective for the next school year.

At the meeting, two members of the school board are worried the waiver will poke a hole in the district's accountability plan and generate criticism from parents. Several Good Common School parents in the audience speak in support of the proposal. The superintendent notes that increasing numbers of educators are becoming critical of large-scale, multiple-choice testing programs; one state, North Carolina, no longer funds testing of primary school students.

After that, Reverend Washington moves for approval of the proposal. His motion is quickly seconded and the waiver is approved by the school board with a vote of three to two. Reverend Washington asks the Good Common School Council's Assessment Committee to report back to the board on the outcome of its search for assessment alternatives.

For the remainder of the current school year, Good Common School students must still take standardized tests. However, the school council is considering a policy that no decision about a child's placement be made on the basis of a single test score. Next fall, experimentation with assessment alternatives will begin and standardized tests will be used solely as one rough measure of the quality of the Good Common School's instructional program.

The school board meeting adjourns at 10:30 p.m. Jean Larson is bone-tired, but her soul feels fine. She is already thinking about another school practice she dislikes: forcing children to repeat grades.

• • •

The superintendent, who closely follows educational research, does not favor holding students back. In fact, every fall he presents research findings to principals showing that:

- children make progress during the year they repeat a grade, but not as much as similar children who are not retained;
- use of transitional grades or tracking on the basis of readiness tests is no more effective than retention.

Although the retention rate at the Good Common School is significantly lower than that of other district elementary schools, it is still high enough to concern the school council— especially since the majority of children who repeat grades are students of color or are limited-English-proficient.

As the council discusses grade retention at its next meeting, one mother in the audience asks to be recognized. When council chair Ella Davis gives her the floor, the woman rises to speak eloquently of her son's experience with retention:

> *"The day he brought that yellow slip of paper home I was devastated. So was he. He came home for lunch and cried. He felt like a failure at school. I felt like a failure as a mother.*
>
> *"I didn't know that making children repeat grades is something schools do to cope with their own failures. I took it personally and my son took it personally. All over this city children and parents are taking it personally— while the school system does business as usual."*

Another mother in the audience also raises her hand and is recognized. She stands and says she thinks it is just "good common sense" to have a student repeat a year if he is having difficulty.

The principal then reviews the district's promotion policy and gives each member of the council a copy. She notes how research indicates that a single grade retention increases a student's chance of leaving school before graduation by 40 percent, while a second retention increases it by 90 percent (Mann, 1986).

Next, Principal Walker passes out a memorandum summarizing suggestions from researchers to lower retention rates (Smith and Shepard 1987):

- replace inflexible grade structures with classes that encompass a wide range of developmental levels and learning styles, allowing children to progress at their own pace;
- use a variety of instructional practices that consider natural variations in children's achievement, ability, linguistic competence, and background;
- provide services to enhance school success and minimize school failure, such as tutoring, summer school, learning laboratories, guidance services, parent education, and individualized instruction;
- provide enrichment and remediation in the regular classrooms as students proceed through grades;

After considerable discussion of these suggestions, Ella Davis asks the principal and the school faculty to draft a set of specific recommendations for changes in grouping practices, curriculum, and support services that could be implemented during the coming school year, and to set target goals to lower the school's future retention rates.

Finally, the council chair asks the principal to prepare statistical data at the end of each school year on the number and kinds of children by race, gender, and ethnicity who are retained in grade at the Good Common School. This information will be translated into the necessary languages and distributed to all parents who have children attending the school.

The discussion winds down. Phyllis Walker writes herself a reminder to take care of one last matter. She must ask the Pupil Personnel Services Director to generate a set of labels coded by families' first languages from the district-wide computerized data base. Last year, the Central Office produced parent information about the district's testing program, had it translated into several languages, then delivered stacks of these materials in all languages to each school. In some schools, chaos resulted when teachers who didn't know the home language of their students sent Laotian translations to Khmer-speaking families.

At the Good Common School, consciousness levels have risen a good deal. Still, there is no need to risk repeating that disrespectful and embarrassing blunder. As the meeting adjourns, Phyllis wonders how she would have responded as a young parent if she received a communication from her child's school written in Vietnamese. She might have wondered if it was a message from outer space. In those days, communities weren't nearly as diverse.

STRATEGIES FOR LOWERING RETENTION RATES

- Promote an understanding that children do not develop in even stages according to a set internal timetable.
- Provide training to ensure that teachers have skills to employ alternative methods of assessment, instruction, grouping, and classroom management to work successfully with highly diverse student groups.
- Establish high expectations for all children.
- Establish flexible standards of competence in early grades.
- Provide enrichment and remediation as students proceed through grades—in the regular classroom to the maximum extent possible.
- Use a variety of curricula and instructional practices that consider natural variations in achievement, ability, linguistic competence, and background.
- Provide services to enhance school success and minimize school failure, such as tutoring, summer school, learning laboratories, guidance services, parent education, and individualized instruction.
- Support teachers as they strive to resist sorting, labeling, tracking, and retention.
- Form teacher support teams to assist regular classroom teachers to meet students' differing needs.
- Adopt the assumption that promotion is preferable to retention.

Source: Smith and Shepard (1987); Dentzer and Wheelock (1990).

WHY STANDARDIZED TESTS FAIL LEP STUDENTS

Standardized tests are particularly inappropriate when assessing the academic progress of children for whom English is not a first language. Children not fluent in English are likely to score poorly on standardized tests for several reasons.

- Many schools fail to instruct limited-English-proficient (LEP) students in their native language while they are learning English.
- Many schools terminate English language acquisition and related support services before students have acquired academic command of their new language.
- Standardized tests contain inherent cultural biases.
- LEP students may lack test-taking skills and many experience intensified anxieties during test taking.

Source: First, *et al.*, (1988).

IMPROVING ASSESSMENT OF STUDENT PROGRESS

The best schools do not rely on data generated by standardized, multiple-choice tests to assess student progress. Instead, they use a variety of assessment strategies to:

- gather information about individual children in order to plan future lessons;
- document each child's progress toward mastery of specified educational goals during the school year;
- evaluate each child's achievement of appropriate goals.

When teachers use a variety of assessment strategies to verify a child's progress, there is a high level of accountability. Among such strategies are:

- **Teachers' observations and notes.** Teachers combine information gained from basic evaluative activities, such as focused observations of children's classroom behavior and activities, along with examples of student's work, such as writing, records of books the student has read, and how well she comprehends and uses the information the books contain.
- **Student portfolios.** These collections contain progressive samples of a student's work, such as successive drafts of a paper he has written. Parents can look at these materials for themselves and compare the teacher's evaluation with their own. This offers important protection against teacher bias.
- **Checklists and inventories.** These simple record-keeping techniques help teachers maintain a clear focus on the progress of an individual child. They should not be used in isolation.
- **Tests with open-ended questions.** These tests help teachers by showing how students think and use knowledge in different subject areas. They are often teacher-made.
- **Products.** A picture drawn in art class is a product. So is a paper based on historical research. Products offer a concrete demonstration of student progress.

These assessment techniques provide teachers and parents with useful information on which to base educational decisions about individual students. Multiple-choice tests can be one part of an overall assessment program when they are administered to a sample of students and are not administered at every grade.

Adapted from *Grades 1 and 2: Assessment in Communication Skills & Mathematics*, by North Carolina Department of Public Instruction; and *Standardized Tests and Our Children: A Guide to Testing Reform*, by FAIRTEST, the National Center for Fair and Open Testing.

CRITERIA FOR EVALUATION OF STUDENT ASSESSMENT SYSTEMS

The National Forum on Assessment offers the following guidelines for evaluating existing and proposed assessment systems at any level of education.

1. **Before assessment procedures and exercises are developed, educational standards should specify what students should know and be able to do.** For assessment information to be valid and useful, assessment must be based on a consensus definition of what students are expected to learn and perform at various developmental stages. Such standards should address important abilities, such as problem solving, rather than discrete pieces of information or isolated skills. Standards should be determined through open discussion among experts, educators, parents, policymakers, and others, including those concerned with the relationship between school learning and life outside of school.

2. **The primary purpose of assessment should be to assist both educators and policymakers to improve instruction and advance student learning.** Students, educators, parents, policymakers, and others have different needs for assessment and different uses for assessment information. For example, teachers, students, and parents may want information on individual achievement, while policymakers and the public may want information for accountability purposes. In all cases, the system should provide not just numbers or ratings, but useful information on particular abilities. All purposes and uses of assessment should be beneficial to students; assessment that cannot be shown to be beneficial should not be used at all.

3. **Assessment standards, tasks, procedures, and uses should be fair to all students.** Because individual assessment results often affect both students' present situation and future opportunities, the assessment system, the standards on which it is based, and all of its parts must treat students equitably. Assessment tasks and procedures must be sensitive to cultural, racial, class, and gender differences, or disabilities, and must not penalize any groups. To ensure fairness, students should have multiple opportunities to meet standards in different ways. No student's fate should depend upon a single test score. Assessment information should be used fairly. It should be accompanied by information about access to the curriculum and about opportunities to meet the standards. Students should not be held responsible for inequities in the system.

4. **The assessment exercises or tasks should be valid and appropriate representations of the standards students are expected to achieve.** A sound assessment system provides information about the full range of knowledge and abilities considered valuable and important for students to learn. Multiple-choice tests, the most common type of assessment, are inadequate to measure many of the most important educational outcomes and do not allow for diversity in learning styles or culture. More appropriate tools include student portfolios, open-ended questions, and extended reading and writing experiences which include rough drafts and revisions, individual and group projects, and exhibitions.

5. **Assessment results should be reported in the context of other relevant information.** Information about student performance should be one part of a system of multiple indicators of the quality of education. Multiple indicators permit educators and policymakers to examine the relationship among *context factors* (such as the type of community, socioeconomic status of students, and school climate), *resources* (such as expenditures per student, physical plant, staffing, and money for materials and equipment), *programs and processes* (such as curriculum, instructional methods, class size, and grouping), and *outcomes* (such as student performance, dropout rates, employment, and further education).

6. **Teachers should be involved in designing and using the assessment system.** For an assessment system to help improve learning outcomes, teachers must fully understand its purposes and procedures and must be committed to, and use, the standards on which it is based. Teachers should participate in the design, administration, scoring, and use of assessment tasks and exercises.

7. **Assessment procedures and results should be understandable.** Assessment information should be understandable to those who need it—students, teachers, parents, policymakers, and the general public. At present, test results are often reported in technical terms that are confusing and misleading. They should be reported, instead, in terms of educational standards.

8. **The assessment system should be subject to continuous review and improvement.** Large-scale, complex systems are rarely perfect. Even well-designed systems must be modified to adapt to changing conditions. Plans for the assessment system should provide for a continuing review process in which all concerned participate.

Source: National Forum on Assessment (1991).

Problems with Student Assessment and Grade Structure in U.S. Public Schools

STUDENT ASSESSMENT

One of the most problematic results of recent school reform is an increased reliance on inflexible measures of student academic achievement. The drive for accountability has further rigidified public schools at precisely the time when shifting student demographics require greater flexibility.

Children perceived as "different" by virtue of their race, language, culture, or economic class are not well served by narrow assessment methods that heighten existing inequities while providing very little information actually useful for improving individual instruction.

Assumptions of Assessment Techniques

Researcher Dennis Wolf (1989) suggests some basic underlying assumptions that shape assessment techniques currently used by most public schools.

- Achievement matters most—even to the exclusion of development.
- The full range of intuition and knowledge isn't what counts in school—only a student's performance on the slice of skills that appears on tests.
- Assessment comes from without. It is not a student's personal responsibility.
- First draft work is good enough.

As noted by researcher Lorrie Shepard (1989), assessment techniques that serve the growing obsession with competitively ranking schools and school systems are likely to be large-scale, formal, objective, time-efficient, cost-efficient, widely applicable, and centrally processed. In order for the results to be useful to policymakers, they must also be highly simplified. These demands are nicely filled by standardized tests.

Standardized Testing

Researchers Noe Medina and Monty Neill (1988, 1990) observe that public schools in the United States administer an estimated 100 million standardized tests to more than forty million students each year—an average of more than two and one-half tests per student.

The number of states that mandate standardized testing has increased greatly in recent years. By 1987, twenty-four states required students to pass a standardized test before graduating from high school, twelve states used standardized tests to determine grade promotion, and forty-two states used standardized tests for student assessment.

Standardized tests are now widely employed to make critical decisions in early elementary school grades. A survey conducted by M. Therese Gnezda and Rosemary Bolig (1989) reports that thirty states employ readiness testing prior to kindergarten, and finds use of readiness tests prior to first grade in forty-three states. As a result, more and more five- and six-year-old children are being denied the opportunity to enter or attend school with their age-mates.

"High-Stakes" Testing

Researchers George Madaus and Diana Pullin (1987) warn of the perils of "high-stakes" testing—the reliance on standardized tests to make important decisions such as school admission, grade promotion, assignment to remedial classes or "gifted" programs, graduation from school, allocation of funding, or certification of teachers or schools.

High-stakes testing usually begins when a state board of education or the legislature mandates a testing program for implementation by the state Department of Education—often as the result of demands for increased accountability or tougher school standards. Because of understaffing, many state education departments must contract with an independent vendor to create, validate, score, and report test results. Generally, this contract goes to the lowest bidder.

Testing Companies

Madaus (in Brandt, 1989) notes that two types of testing companies have come into existence over the years—established, main-line businesses that publish and market their own tests, and smaller companies that build customized tests for their clients. These smaller companies have captured a large share of the lucrative state-level market, even though many states lack the personnel or training to properly evaluate the technical adequacy of test contractors.

The type of test most often used is a traditional norm- or curriculum-referenced test. Nevertheless, school districts simply set a cut-off score and assume the test is valid for use in any context. The pressure to come up with test scores—particularly higher scores—has become great, while there is little political incentive to properly evaluate the tests or their impacts.

Reliability, Validity, Norms, and Bias

The development and selection of standardized tests is driven more by concerns of cost and ease of use than by quality and accuracy. The American Educational Research Association (1985) has joined other national organizations to urge those who develop and use standardized tests to consider issues of 1) reliability, 2) validity, 3) norming, and 4) bias, but many test developers address these issues in either a cursory or inadequate manner.

1. **Test reliability** assesses the degree to which a test provides a consistent measure. In demonstrating reliability, test publishers generally examine consistency among different forms or subsections of a test. They rarely inform potential test buyers about variations in individual test scores from one administration of the test to the next.

2. **Test validity** assesses how well a test measures what it claims to measure and what can be accurately inferred from its measurement. Efforts to demonstrate test validity often rely on review of test items by a panel of experts or a comparison of test results with results from other standardized tests. Because validity relates to the particular use of a test, not simply to the test itself, a test can have high validity for one purpose and low validity for others. Test publishers and purchasers often ignore or fail to understand this and assume or imply that tests are equally valid for all purposes.

3. **Establishing test norms** to effectively gauge student scores has become controversial in recent years. Because test norms are often based on populations considerably different from those being tested, some norms are so inaccurate and out-of-date that they artificially inflate test scores, leading to the ludicrous impression that most children are performing above average.

4. **Tests can be biased** because they are designed by and for White, middle- to upper-class individuals and rarely offer an accurate measure of academic skills and abilities of minority, low-income, or limited-English-proficient students. Instead, such tests actually measure divergence from White, middle- and upper-class language, cultural experiences, and learning style.

The Evidence Against Standardized Testing

While proponents base increased reliance on standardized tests on claims of improved educational accountability, evidence continues to mount that such tests: employ faulty assumptions about how children learn; fail to provide parents, students, and teachers with useful diagnostic information; and are racially, ethnically, and economically biased.

Standardized tests operate on the assumption that human intelligence is essentially one-dimensional and that learning patterns are consistent among different individuals. This simplistic view of thinking and learning is contradicted by established theories of intelligence and child development which conclude that children develop at their own pace, following individual paths to learning, problem-solving, and thinking.

Because standardized tests focus on a limited range of basic academic skills, their increasing importance distorts student instruction. "Teaching to the test" has narrowed curricula in many classrooms, a phenomenon intensified by textbook publishers who shape book content to prepare students for standardized tests—a trend that has not made the learning experience more interesting to students. It is ironic that many efforts intended to promote "higher-order" skills—such as decision-making, problem-solving, and comprehension—have also mandated the use of standardized tests that measure little beyond basic academic skills.

The National Association for the Education of Young Children (NAEYC, 1988) notes that multiple-choice, true/false, and fill-in-the-blank questions generally test basic reading, writing, or mathematics skills in an artificial manner. Even though current research supports an approach to reading instruction that integrates oral language, writing, reading, and spelling in a meaningful context that emphasizes comprehension, standardized tests view reading simply as word recognition and phonics.

NAEYC also observes that, while current theories of math instruction focus on use of first-hand experiences that allow a child to construct a concept of numbers, standardized tests continue to define math skills as knowledge of numerals. Test results reveal little about the ability to read and comprehend, to write and communicate ideas effectively, or to compute and use computations to solve real-world problems.

In most high-stakes testing programs, a single test score—called a cut-score—is used as a point at which automatic decisions are made about students, ignoring the fact that most skills, knowledge, or competencies are continuous in nature. George Madaus (in Brandt, 1989) observes that the use of cut-scores makes each question a "mini-test" in itself, because a single wrong answer or faulty, ambiguous, or miskeyed item can be the difference between passing or failing the test.

Standardized tests offer one single opportunity for students to display the skills or knowledge they possess. For many reasons— personal, health, problems at home, test anxiety, lack of test-taking skills—a child may be unable to demonstrate these skills or knowledge when taking the test.

Danger of Reliance on Test Scores

While many seem persuaded that standardized test scores are accurate indicators of academic achievement, simplistic interpretations of test scores as a tool for educational accountability fail to consider a dark truth. There are two ways to "raise" student test scores. Children can learn more, or the composition of the testing pool can be altered. Low-achieving students, who may get lower test scores, can be removed from the testing pool by labelling them as handicapped and placing them in separate special education classes, by transferring them between elementary schools, or by pushing them out of school by "counseling" them to leave before graduation.

Readiness Testing

The most disturbing trend in recent years is the increased use of standardized tests to delay a child's enrollment in kindergarten, to retain young students in a second year of kindergarten, or to place children in "extra-year" programs such as junior kindergartens, developmental first grades, or "transition" classes. A survey by researcher Tom Schultz (1989) revealed that forty states report the use of developmental kindergartens or transitional first grades in some school systems.

Faulty Assumptions of Readiness Testing

Barbara Willer and Sue Bredekamp (1990) of the National Association for the Education of Young Children view the increase in readiness testing as a means of "gatekeeping" rather than as an earnest effort to determine children's needs as a basis for effective intervention and provision of services. They suggest a series of faulty assumptions that act to exclude children who fail to demonstrate certain skills in a certain way:

- **Learning only occurs in school.** Although parents are children's first teachers—providing rich, experiential bases for language, social, emotional, physical, and cognitive development—current conditions in the U.S. work against children being prepared for formal school experience; more young children are in poverty than members of any other age group; children start life ready to learn, but the lives they live enhance or restrict their potential.
- **Readiness is a specific condition inherent within every child.** In fact, readiness is multidimensional, including social skills, physical development, cognitive abilities, and emotional adjustment; tremendous individual differences exist; gatekeeping definitions of readiness are based primarily on a single dimension such as knowledge of numbers and letters.

- **Readiness can be easily measured.** Researchers agree that no reliable and valid measure of readiness is available.
- **Readiness is more a function of time; some children need more time than others.** Outdated theories of child development view growth as a function of maturation; development is now viewed as an interaction between what goes on inside a child's head and their experience with people and objects; rather than waiting for it to occur, adults have to play an active role by structuring an environment that challenges the child's construction of new knowledge.
- **Children are ready to learn when they can sit still and listen to the teacher.** Children learn through active manipulation of materials and experiences; when forced to sit still, not talk, and circle the correct answer, they learn: 1) not to work cooperatively with peers; 2) there is only one right answer; and 3) learning takes place to pass a test, not for the sake of learning.
- **Children who aren't ready don't belong in school.** The very traits that are used to label children as "unready" are often those best developed in school; the concept of "readiness" assumes it is the child's task to meet demands of school, rather than the school's job to be ready for the child.

GRADE STRUCTURE

Public elementary schools are generally organized around a rigid set of sequential grade levels, beginning with kindergarten and—depending on the school system—continuing through grades 4, 5, 6, or 8.

Although students are expected to remain in each grade for a single school year, they are allowed to proceed to the next grade only upon demonstrating competence in knowledge and skills deemed appropriate to that grade level. Students who fail to demonstrate the necessary competence are not promoted and are generally required to repeat the grade until competency can be demonstrated.

Grade Retention

Because the practice of requiring children to repeat grades has always been viewed as a state or local issue, there is no reliable longitudinal data available on national retention rates in public schools. After reviewing available state and local data, researchers Mary Lee Smith and Lorrie Sheppard (1987) estimate an overall retention rate of 15 to 19 percent, placing U.S. public schools on a par with those of countries like Haiti or Sierra Leone. By contrast, Japan has a 1 percent rate of grade retention.

What the Research Shows

In a 1989 survey of forty urban school districts, Joseph Gastright (1989) found that:

- Eighty percent of schools reported a formal promotion/retention policy.
- Only 15 percent of schools reported their policy was required by state law.
- Schools reported that their promotion/retention judgments were based on teacher decisions (85 percent), state-mandated tests (73 percent), local district tests (55 percent), and student attendance (50 percent), as well as a variety of other factors.
- Mean grade-level retention rates ranged from a high of 22 percent at ninth grade to a low of 4.3 percent at fifth grade; retention rates varied widely across school systems at every grade level and by socioeconomic status.
- Promotion/retention policies were determined largely by local school systems, accounting for the great deal of variation in guidelines and accounting procedures; 40 percent of the school systems did not even report retention data.

For elementary schools, the survey found that:

- The highest mean retention rate was for first grade (9.7 percent)—significantly higher than other elementary grades; this rate was even higher for children with the lowest socioeconomic status (12.4 percent).
- The lowest retention rate for elementary grades was for students in fourth grade with the highest socioeconomic status (1.8 percent).
- In general, retention rates for children with the lowest socioeconomic status were at least twice the rate of those with the highest socio-economic status.
- Retention rates tended to decline steadily from first to sixth grade.

Perhaps the most important conclusion of research on grade retention is that it simply does not help children learn. Although children make progress during the year they repeat a grade, they do not progress as well as similar children who are allowed to advance to the next grade level. Research also shows that the use of pre-kindergarten or pre-first-grade transitional classes on the basis of readiness tests are no more effective than retention.

Harmful Effects of Grade Retention

According to research, grade retention not only fails to help children, it has harmful effects. Those who are retained suffer poorer self-concepts, have more problems with social adjustment, and express more negative attitudes towards school. Students retained in grade become more likely to be retained again and to experience disciplinary and academic problems.

Research also shows a strong connection between grade retention and dropping out of school. A student who is retained once faces a 40 percent increase in the likelihood of dropping out. If retained twice, that likelihood increases by 90 percent (Mann, 1986). For those students already at high risk for dropping out, the experience of grade retention makes it almost certain they will leave school before graduating.

Critics of grade retention raise other issues, as well. As noted earlier, standardized tests used for retention decisions are rarely reliable or valid for this use. The cycle of testing and retention prevents teachers from using responsive, age-appropriate teaching methods with young children. The marked difference in retention rates experienced by male and minority students combined with families' differing capacity to provide high-quality pre-school services for their children raises serious equity concerns.

No matter how carefully grade retention is handled by educators and parents, children understand they are being taken from their age-mates because of some failure. According to a survey of school children conducted by Byrnes and Yamamoto (1986), next to blindness and death of a parent, grade retention is rated as most stressful.

Smith and Sheppard (1987) observe that grade retention also has a substantial financial impact. A single incident of retention in grade increases the cost of educating a student until graduation by 8 percent. When multiplied by the vast number of students who are held back each year, the cost totals billions of dollars nationwide—money that could fund considerable school improvement.

Reasons for the Practice of Grade Retention

Despite the overwhelming evidence against it, grade retention continues to be widely practiced at every grade level through the United States. Smith and Sheppard (1987) have identified some key issues that help explain why this discredited practice maintains its tenacious hold:

- **Teacher beliefs.** Much of what teachers know about the research is cited by test manufacturers and publishers, who offer highly selective or incorrect information; a teacher's classroom experience may appear to support retention, as the child who is retained often makes gains in achievement during the repeated year—but the teacher never has a chance to compare this with the achievement gains of those who are promoted; many teachers believe retention has no costs or risks; many believe retention in an early grade prevents retention in later grades when the stigma is even greater.
- **Childhood development beliefs.** Many hold the outmoded view that childhood development unfolds in a series of strict stages, governed by an internal timetable—thus, parents and teachers can do little for a child to make her ready for school, and altering instruction, supplying remedial help, tutoring, or personal guidance are not helpful.
- **Schoolwork in kindergarten.** What was once the curriculum of first grade—learning readiness—is now the purpose of kindergarten: the curriculum of kindergarten is now pre-school. This reflects a new, narrow purpose of schooling—literacy and numeracy, and while this may be a successful definition for some students, it has resulted in increased retention in early grades for others—when the curriculum is considered correct, the child who fails to keep pace is labelled as a failure.
- **Parental pressure.** Some parents are eager to give their child every competitive advantage; they instruct them at home, enroll them in instructional pre-school programs, then pressure kindergarten teachers to step up the pace. Children without home training in numbers or literacy are at an early disadvantage and may become candidates for retention. Some parents hold their children in pre-school or at home for a year to have them enter kindergarten at the oldest age in the class to give them an advantage. Children whose parents must work or who can't afford pre-school are unlikely to be able to perform at the same level and will be at greater risk for retention.

Atlantic Center for Research in Education: Campaign to Eliminate Testing

The campaign to end the use of norm-referenced standardized testing in the first and second grades of North Carolina's public schools began when the state's General Assembly voted in 1983 to use the California Achievement Test in early grades.

The **Atlantic Center for Research in Education (ACRE)** opposed the use of this test because of its low reliability and validity for young children, and its failure to provide useful instructional information to teachers. Additionally, the tests resulted in narrowed, test-driven curricula and pressured school staff to spend a disproportionate amount of instructional time testing rather than teaching their students.

According to ACRE staff, repealing the testing mandate was "as much a state of mind as any set of techniques." Working to eliminate testing required a strong conviction that these tests were ineffective and destructive to students, particularly young children. Because testing enjoyed strong popular support, including the governor and the State Superintendent of Public Instruction, ACRE knew it was in for a long battle.

Monitoring the Testing Environment

ACRE began by gathering research on testing and collecting information and support from testing experts. In addition, ACRE monitored meetings of the State Board of Education and the North Carolina Testing Commission—the organization responsible for the state's standardized testing programs.

The decision to monitor these meetings helped to shape ACRE's strategy in a number of ways. When discussion of the California Achievement Test appeared on the commission's agenda, ACRE was ready to provide an alternative viewpoint. Discussions and presentations in these meetings enabled ACRE to understand political and administrative attitudes toward testing, allowing them to locate the most vulnerable point of attack. This specialized knowledge led ACRE to focus on first and second grades, since people seemed reluctant to label children at an early age.

While the state's General Assembly was in session, ACRE monitored relevant committee meetings to better understand the workings of the assembly and the positions of individual legislators. From its past legislative activities, ACRE was able to gain support from a small group—spanning the political spectrum— within the assembly. However, development of a strong legislative movement was frustrated by the governor's strong support for standardized testing.

Finding a Strong Ally

ACRE found a firm ally in the North Carolina Association for the Education of Young Children (NCAEYC), composed of professors, teachers, and day care providers concerned with the quality of services for children from infancy to eight years of age. The ACRE staff had worked previously with NCAEYC and knew them to be a highly effective policy and lobbying organization. When ACRE staff formally presented their ideas to NCAEYC, both organizations discovered shared views about the use of standardized testing in early grades.

The two groups complemented each other. ACRE had experience with lobbying and cutting through the bureaucratic maze of the State Department of Public Instruction. NCAEYC had 1,700 dues-paying members with vast knowledge about testing, facilitating letter-writing campaigns, and telephone trees. In addition, ACRE held workshops, published articles in its newsletter, and created the Parent and Citizen Test Review Commission to champion the cause of opposing standardized testing.

A Move to Legislative Action

In 1987, NCAEYC persuaded a state legislator to introduce a bill to stop standardized testing of first and second graders. By this time, the governor was less interested in testing, and the legislature was beginning to hear complaints about the amount of classroom time devoted to testing and the stress it was causing to young children.

ACRE's organizing efforts produced a small group of dedicated teachers willing to lobby the state assembly in conjunction with the testimony of NCAEYC teachers presented to legislative committees. To quote an ACRE staff member, "Few things are more persuasive than having someone who looks like your first-grade teacher tell you what to do." The telephone tree and letter-writing campaigns, along with other organizing and lobbying efforts, resulted in unanimous passage of the anti-testing bill by the state senate.

Members of ACRE and NCAEYC attended all meetings of the House Education Committee, finding the bill stalled when opposition surfaced from the state superintendent and the former governor. Political pressure had caused the committee chair to dramatically slow down the bill's movement through the committee process.

ACRE and NCAEYC reported the stalled bill to three supportive state senators from the Appropriations Committee. While it was impossible for these legislators to get the bill out of the House Education Committee, they were able to attach an amendment to the overall education budget that removed $150,000 in funding for testing and transferred it to the Division of Instructional Services with the expressed condition it be used to produce developmentally appropriate, individualized assessment instruments for first and second graders. By continuing their telephone and letter-writing campaigns, ACRE and NCAEYC helped to enact a further provision in the spring of 1988 to eliminate the testing requirement.

What Made It Work

The greatest strength of this campaign was the combined effort of two organizations with a shared vision of eliminating standardized tests from the lives of young students. One group offered a sizable membership with education knowledge and experience. The other offered a politically experienced staff.

Six years is a long time to sustain a volunteer group as it faces off against the vast capacities of a state bureaucracy and national testing companies. This campaign, like many grassroots efforts, suffered from a lack of time and money. Due to lack of resources, the campaign had limited success with generating parent support. But it was able to maintain an astonishingly persistent group of volunteers who became increasingly skilled in lobbying and communicating.

For further information, please contact: Atlantic Center for Research in Education, P.O. Box 1068, Durham, NC 27702. Telephone (919) 688-6464.

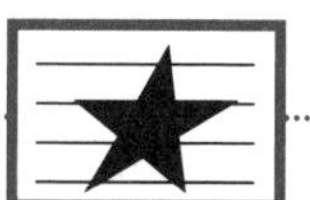

PROMISING PRACTICES

North Carolina Elementary Schools: Grades 1 and 2

In the summer of 1988, the Mathematics Section and Communication Skills Section of the North Carolina Department of Public Instruction received the mandate to develop alternative assessments for grades 1 and 2 in lieu of the California Achievement Test.

Prior to passage of the assessment reform legislation, staff at the Communication Skills Section were concerned that standardized testing was driving the curriculum. They feared that teachers, pressured to increase test scores, were teaching isolated test skills rather than developing integrated reading, writing, and oral language abilities. Over the preceding year, they had designed an alternative assessment for use with first and second graders to assess communication skills. Their draft assessment instrument had been sent to over 300 teachers for feedback and recommendations.

While staff from the Mathematics Section had not developed an assessment tool, they too were concerned that teachers were teaching mathematics as a set of separate discrete skills instead of a series of interrelated concepts. When they received the directive from the State Board of Education, they were in the midst of a mathematics leadership skills seminar attended by more than 300 teachers from across the state identified as leaders in mathematics instruction. Workshop sessions were modified to include extensive discussion on the design of the assessment instrument. Teachers' input was used to design alternative mathematics assessment techniques.

Developers of the alternative assessment program wanted to "affect instruction through assessment," according to Jeanne Joyner, Elementary Consultant with the Mathematics Section of the North Carolina Department of Public Instruction. Her counterpart at the Communication Skills Section, Cindi Heuts concurs: "We wanted to put the focus of assessment back where it should be—improving instruction. Educators must become keen observers of children by looking at their accomplishments and mistakes as part of the developmental process. It's not that children have failed but that they have not yet reached that level of understanding."

The assessment program is designed to gather information about individual children in order to plan future lessons, to document each child's progress toward specified goals during the year, and to evaluate each child's achievement of those goals. In both communication skills and mathematics, assessment evaluates development in several content areas. For communications skills, these include oral language, orientation to print, reading strategies, listening and silent reading comprehension, and unassisted writing. The seven content areas for mathematics, based on recommendations of the National Council of Teachers of Mathematics, include numeration, geometry, classification and patterning, measurement, problem-solving and mathematical thinking, understanding and using data, and computation.

Evaluation of a student's progress and understanding in any of the content areas is based on information from a number of sources gathered over a period of time. Responses to questions, demonstrations with materials, products and displays, samples of written work, and informal observations all provide teachers with information for completing student profiles.

Summaries made two or three times a year on the assessment profiles are to reflect multiple sources of information. The profiles are not designed to be used as check-off sheets but rather as a synthesis of anecdotal records kept by the teacher on each child. Because teachers verify children's progress through a number of methods, a high level of accountability is possible.

According to the developers, the assessment program is more appropriate for young children than standardized tests because it evaluates children's understanding through what they are able to do, as well as what they are able to explain and to write. Teachers use activities and manipulative materials as part of the evaluation. The assessment acknowledges children's early abilities to solve problems, identify patterns, and see relationships by validating other demonstrations of these capacities in addition to pencil and paper examples. The assessment assists teachers in planning appropriate experiences for individual children and identifies their progress toward curriculum goals, as well as their achievement of them.

The assessment program was piloted at eight elementary schools across the state during the 1988 to 1989 school year. In September, teachers at the pilot schools attended two days of intensive training on the assessment program. In November, a full-day follow-up session of all pilot teachers took place to address teacher concerns, share ideas, and develop and revise strategies for implementation. Teachers met again for two days in January to continue to share their ideas, experiences, and recommendations, but also to celebrate their successes. Throughout the year, state and regional staff maintained contact with teachers piloting the program in order to respond to concerns, give suggestions, and hear teachers' recommendations for revisions of the assessment tools. In the spring, videotapes were made of teachers and students engaged in assessment activities for use in the more extensive statewide training.

In the summer of 1989, the State Department of Instruction began statewide training for the assessment program. Because schools are not mandated to use the new assessment techniques—the legislation prohibited the use of state money by local school districts to purchase standardized achievement tests for first and second graders but mandated only the development of alternative assessments, not their implementation—staff can only invite school systems to participate. They encourage local school systems to select one "lead" teacher for every twenty first- and second-grade teachers to send to the statewide training—an intensive week-long summer institute conducted by a state team. The training team works with the lead teachers, who in turn conduct local training sessions using videos and other materials prepared by the state team.

Training for lead teachers focuses on the philosophy and purpose of the assessment program. Teachers examine the first- and second-grade curriculum, discuss issues and concerns related to mathematics and communication skills for young children, and work with manipulative materials and activity-oriented lessons.

The training also focuses on the specific staff development sessions lead teachers are responsible for conducting in their own school systems. Participating teachers receive classroom sets of profiles and guidebooks for teachers that review the philosophy, discuss record-keeping, and detail strategies for using the assessment program. Brochures are also provided to distribute to parents early in the school year. In addition, each school system receives a videotape for training that is also suitable for parents' nights and community awareness programs.

During the year, regional consultants in each of North Carolina's eight education regions are available for staff development. They provide support to teachers, locate appropriate materials, bring in speakers and observe in classrooms. In addition, local school systems are encouraged to sponsor and facilitate sharing and discussion sessions for participating teachers every four to six weeks. Early informal surveys indicate that the most successful implementation of the assessment is occurring where administrative support is the strongest. This support includes purchase of appropriate materials, special training sessions for school staff, parent nights, and monthly teacher sharing sessions.

Carol Midgett, a second-grade teacher at Southport Elementary School, has "tremendous support from the principal" for the assessment program. Located in rural working-class Southport, the school hosts over 800 children in kindergarten through fifth grade. Because the school was one of the eight that originally piloted the assessment program, Midgett attended the pilot trainings, the statewide week-long trainings, and has conducted staff development sessions for local teachers.

Assessment has become an integral part of Carol Midgett's teaching day. As she puts it: "I seize every opportunity for teaching moments and assessment moments from the minute I walk into the classroom until I leave for the day." She finds she has become more attuned to what her children know, what they are learning, and what they need to know and has become a "better observer of kids, the activities they engage in, and the meaning of these activities."

Portfolios of her children's work and her observations provide accurate and useful records of when children demonstrate knowledge of a concept as well as the depth of their understanding. Through the math journal each child keeps, Midgett has often discovered that children understand concepts she did not realize they had grasped or they fail to grasp others she thought they understood.

A writing folder allows children to visualize their progress from the beginning of the year to the end. At the close of the year, she takes representative samples of work and binds them in a book for each child, to reaffirm their growth and achievement over the year. She also finds the portfolios "a tremendous value" in demonstrating children's progress to their parents. "They reaffirm parents' beliefs that their children are learning and picture it in a very convincing way."

To date, the State Department of Instruction has trained teachers to use the assessment program in 106 of the 134 school districts in the state. Close to 1,000 lead teachers have been trained in either the communication skills or mathematics assessments. However, the degree of implementation of the assessment program has varied from school district to school district, ranging from a few first- and second-grade teachers in scattered schools to all the first- and second-grade teachers in every elementary school in a system. Because school systems are not mandated to use the assessment instrument, it is up to individual districts to make decisions regarding use and implementation.

State staff have discovered that the largest obstacle teachers need to overcome is continuing to view assessment as something they do at the end of an activity rather than as part of ongoing observations and documentation. As Cindi Heuts points out: "They need to fight the temptation to see assessment as something they do at the end of six weeks."

State staff have also learned that some administrators have concerns about accountability. They question how they can evaluate teachers who use the assessment program since it does not provide hard statistics as compared to standardized tests. State staff stress this assessment process has more accountability than most tests—teachers must keep observation records and samples of children's work to document their progress and achievement.

For further information, please contact: Ms. Jeanne Joyner or Ms. Cindi Heuts, Department of Public Instruction, 116 West Edenton Street, Raleigh, NC 27603.

PROMISING PRACTICES

Graham Parks School: Cambridge, Massachusetts

At the Graham Parks School, kindergarten through eighth-grade classrooms are structured to celebrate and promote diversity. As Principal Len Solo states: "We believe that diversity is the best starting point for learning."

The 400 children enrolled at the school reflect a diverse student population. Fifty-three percent of the children are of color, 23 percent of whom are recent immigrants from Haiti. Sixty percent of the children come from working-class or poor families. Because the school has gained a reputation among parents for success with learning-disabled students, 35 percent of its student population has special learning needs.

All the classrooms at the Graham Parks School, with the exception of kindergarten, are comprised of children from more than one grade. The school has experimented with several different classroom structures over the years but has settled on one that combines two grades in each classroom with no overlap among classrooms. Children are placed in a first/second, third/fourth, fifth/sixth, or seventh/eighth classroom. They remain with the same teacher for two years.

In the past, classrooms were structured for overlap between grades; for example, one class was a second/third while another was a third/fourth, to help meet the diverse needs of students. While this structure offered optimum flexibility for placing students, it created difficulties for freeing teachers to meet for joint planning times, staff development, and support. In the end, the staff chose to give up some of the flexibility in return for consistency in staff support and development as a team.

Teachers form teams based on their classroom structure. For example, all the kindergarten and first/second classroom teachers form a team, all the third/fourth teachers form a team, and so forth. First/second, third/fourth, and fifth/sixth teams meet once a week after school. Seventh/eighth teachers meet three times a week during the school day. The school is presently examining ways to replicate the seventh/eighth team structure at the lower levels. During team meetings, teachers discuss instructional approaches, discuss and develop curriculum, share materials and ideas, and address any individual student concerns teachers may bring before the team.

A complex process that involves staff members as well as parents is used to place students in classrooms. The appropriate "sending" teacher team, the special needs and bilingual teachers, the staff developer, parent coordinator, and principal review all students moving into the next grade cluster. Using corkboards and visual aids (for example, different color index cards to signify various ethnic backgrounds) they create groups of students that are balanced by race, sex, academic achievement, socioeconomic status, and special education and bilingual status. According to Principal Solo, the goal is to "create groups that mirror each other as much as possible." The staff then pulls teachers names out of a hat to match each group with a particular teacher. The school also solicits feedback from parents on what class they would like their children placed in based on their learning needs and friendship groups.

After the initial grouping decisions are completed, the staff reviews them with the appropriate "receiving" teachers and two additional parents. At this point, parent requests and teacher concerns are taken into consideration. However, maintaining the balance among the classrooms is a top priority. Children are only moved if the change does not affect the overall balance. Letters are then sent home to parents sharing placement decisions.

A grievance process is available to parents who are not satisfied with their child's classroom placement. A grievance committee comprised of the principal, the staff developer, the parent coordinator, and two other parents hears parent concerns. According to Principal Solo, on the average, the committee hears ten grievances a year of which half are usually granted.

Judy Richards, a third/fourth-grade teacher, espouses an "approach to teaching and learning that embodies democratic values and seeks pluralism." According to Richards, teachers must address the status of each child in the classroom, including validating and respecting their culture. They must also recognize that children learn in a number of different ways.

Linda Fobes, a first/second-grade teacher, points out that all teachers have a group of students with a wide range of abilities, regardless of classroom structure. The teacher's role is to access each child's strengths and needs and develop and draw on strategies, resources, and materials to facilitate each child's progress.

In Richards's and Fobes's classes, children are active participants and take considerable responsibility for their own and their peers' learning. Fobes begins the year by exploring which themes or topic areas students most want to learn about. After they make decisions about topics, she develops charts with various subject areas they plan to cover over the year. Then they decide on activities and lessons for the various subject areas.

For example, because many of the children were interested in learning about dinosaurs, this was a topic studied for a couple of months. For mathematics, the children measured dinosaurs. They also made dinosaur cookies. As a class, they collaborated on building a dinosaur skeleton out of cardboard with each child responsible for different bones. In addition, they made dinosaur eggs to study dinosaurs' reproductive process. For language arts, they each produced dictionaries on dinosaurs. In another collaborative class project, the children made a Big Book (an oversized book children can read together) on dinosaurs entitled *Dinomites*. Each child had to make up or "discover" a dinosaur, give it a name, and provide two interesting facts. Once the book was completed, the class read it to fifth/sixth graders.

In Judy Richards's classroom, the curriculum is also theme-driven. For example, a unit on "Changes" covered base changes in number systems for mathematics and verb changes in both English and Haitian Creole for language arts. In science, changes studied included chemical changes, the growth cycle, and the birth and death cycle. The children also read folk-tales and studied historical changes and character and plot changes.

The children in Richards's classroom often teach each other. As Richards puts it: "There are twenty-six teachers and twenty-six learners in my classroom." She has developed a mechanism for her students to let her know if they are grasping a concept; if children understand a concept, they signal with a "thumbs up" sign; if they don't, the signal is "thumbs down." Judy believes teachers too often repeat the same auditory approach—"saying it once, saying it again, and saying it yet again louder." Instead, Richards has the "thumbs up" students "repackage" or use a different approach to explain the concept to the "thumbs down" students. In this way, students have the responsibility for teaching their peers, who are more likely to grasp the concept because it is presented in a number of different ways. The students become involved in their own education and get excited about their capacity to learn.

Children teaching children and working together cooperatively in a variety of small groups is a thread that runs through all classrooms at Graham Parks. Children often tutor peers who are having difficulty and collaborate on whole-class or small-group projects. Because the curriculum focuses on themes and content rather than skills alone, all the students work together regardless of individual skill level. For example, in Linda Fobes's class, groups of children worked together to construct Native American villages. Each group decided what tribe to study and developed and assigned the various tasks they had to complete to successfully construct the village.

Teachers strive to create an atmosphere where children recognize that each of their peers has important and valuable knowledge to offer the group. Differences are recognized but never seen as deficits. Diversity and different cultural contributions are recognized and celebrated throughout the curriculum. As Judy Richards states: "It is essential to make all children's words, all children's heritages part of the curriculum."

A unit on "Islands" in Linda Fobes's class allows children to spend considerable time studying the history and culture of Haiti. When covering the topic of "Space," as with all topics, they study the contributions to space explorations by scientists and others from various cultures. Judy Richards uses the folklore of her students to present mathematics problems.

While meeting the diverse academic needs of students in multi-graded classes requires considerable skill, both Judy Richards and Linda Fobes agree that this is not the biggest challenge they face. Rather, it is the differences in social/emotional development among the children. Peer tutoring and cooperative group activities allow children to take on leadership roles and help their less mature peers. In addition, both teachers recruit parents to assist in their classrooms, providing an extra pair of hands in the classroom and allowing parents to take on an important role in their children's education. Discrepancies between home and school culture are reduced, parents and teachers acquire a better understanding of each other, and children see that their parents value their education.

The ability to develop strong, rich relationships with parents is one benefit of having children stay with the same teacher for two years. Parents and teachers are more invested in knowing each other because they share their children's lives for an extended period. Having children for two years also means that teachers can better understand and plan for the needs of half of their students before the beginning of the next school year. Moreover, because the older children have already developed a trusting relationship with the teacher and understand the routines and structures of the classroom, they become leaders—or as Judy Richards says "disseminators of the classroom culture"—and can help younger children to adjust successfully to their new classroom.

Linda Fobes has developed activities to promote the leadership role of her second-year students. At the end of each year, her upcoming first graders visit her classroom and meet her present first graders. Children choose buddies and before the year is over, the older children write welcoming letters to their buddies. Linda sends the children's letters in August with her cover letter telling the children to look for something special in their cubby on the first day of school. The children arrive at their first day in their new classroom knowing they have a special surprise in their cubby along with an older buddy to show them around. For the first few weeks of school, the older children are responsible for helping their buddies during lunch, recess, at the end of the day, and at any time during the day if they are having difficulty finding materials or with the general routines of the classroom. Buddies also help each other with lessons and activities.

With up to six or seven grade levels in some multi-graded classrooms, academic ability range can be very wide. Linda Fobes's first/second classroom has children working on pre-reading skills while others read at a sixth-grade level. Because children remain with the same teacher for two years, grade retention is an infrequent practice at the Graham Parks School. According to Principal Len Solo, only two or three children are retained each year, and retention is very rare beyond first grade. A full review of the child by a team of staff members with parent input is completed before any decision is made to retain a child.

Successfully teaching multigraded classes requires careful planning and organization. Among other things, the curriculum must be planned for two-year cycles because children stay with the same teacher for two years. Adding to this difficulty is the fact that the majority of commercial curricula still focus on specific subject areas and skill development. At the Graham Parks, teachers are not boxed in by a standard curriculum they must follow and complete. They are empowered to develop their own curriculum within school and city guidelines.

The team structure becomes critical in facilitating this process. Teachers share resources, materials, and ideas. They develop curriculum together and problem-solve together to address any difficulties a team member may be experiencing in his or her classroom. Ongoing communication, support, and mutual respect help teachers to build confidence and encourage them to become risk-takers in their classrooms. As Linda Fobes concludes: "The most important thing is the support we get from each other. Here one always feels that there is more to do, that whatever you are doing you can do it better. We are able to communicate with each other and have a lot of respect for each other. People go into each other's rooms. There is an openness and willingness to share that you do not find in many schools. All too often in many schools teachers go in their classrooms and close the door."

For further information, please contact: Mr. Len Solo, Principal, Graham Parks School, Upton Street, Cambridge, MA 02139.

Current Research Related to Topics Discussed in Chapter Four

STUDENT ASSESSMENT

Increased Use of Standardized Tests

Public schools in the United States administer an estimated 100 million standardized tests to their more than 40 million students annually—an average of more than two and one-half tests per student **(Medina and Neill, 1990).** The volume of testing has been increasing by 10 to 20 percent annually over the past forty years **(Haney and Madaus, 1989).**

Between 1985 and 1987: the number of states requiring students to pass a standardized test to graduate from high school increased from fifteen to twenty-four; the number of states using standardized tests to determine grade promotion increased from eight to twelve; and the number of states using standardized tests as part of a state student assessment program increased from thirty-seven to forty-two **(Medina and Neill, 1990).**

In many public schools, standardized tests are the primary or sole criteria for making a number of decisions affecting students, teachers, and schools. Standardized tests determine: student assignment to special education or remedial programs; admission to gifted and talented or accelerated programs; grade promotions; and high school graduation **(FairTest, 1990; Medina and Neill, 1990).**

Problems with Standardized Tests

Compelling evidence undermines claims by test developers that standardized tests are scientifically developed instruments which simply, objectively, and reliably measure student achievement, abilities, or skills.

When test publishers claim that standardized tests are "reliable," they generally mean tests are internally consistent or that different forms of the same test produce consistent results. They generally do not mean that tests demonstrate consistency in results over time ***(see reviews of the California Achievement Test, the Comprehensive Tests of Basic Skills, the Iowa Tests of Basic Skills, the Metropolitan Achievement Test, the SRA Achievement Test, and the Gesell Preschool Test, in* Mitchell, 1985*)*.** The reliability of some widely-used standardized tests—such as the Gesell School Readiness Test—is remarkably low. On the Gesell test "a child measured to be four and one-half years old developmentally and unready for school could very likely be five and fully ready" **(Shepard and Smith, 1988).**

Test publishers should determine a test's validity by whether it measures what it claims to measure, how well it measures it, and what can be inferred from that measurement **(Anastasi, 1988).** In fact, efforts to validate standardized tests are generally limited to asking subject-area experts to make qualitative judgments **(Madaus and Pullin, 1987; *reviews of various tests in* Mitchell, 1985).**

Moreover, test validity can only be determined in a specific context of how test results will be used **(Anastasi, 1988; Madaus and Pullin, 1987).** Information and conclusions regarding validity in one context are often not relevant to other contexts. Too often, test publishers and schools ignore this and assume or imply that a "validated" test is appropriate for use in any context **(FairTest, 1990; Madaus and Pullin, 1987).** In addition, testmakers and testgivers assume, often erroneously, that students have had exposure to the material on the test **(Oakes and Lipton, 1990).**

Researchers have identified several characteristics of standardized tests that result in bias against minority or low-income students. These characteristics reflect the White middle- to upper-class focus of such tests in use of language, cultural perspective, and "ways of learning and problem-solving." Test results are therefore as much a measure of race, ethnicity, or income as they are of achievement, ability, or skill **(FairTest, 1990; Hoover, *et al.*, 1987; Loewen, 1980; Oakes and Lipton, 1990; Taylor and Lee, 1987; Williams, 1979).**

Educators, researchers, and the public generally assume that standardized tests are administered under relatively uniform conditions. **Anastasi (1988)** emphasizes the importance of such a controlled setting: "Even apparently minor aspects of the testing situation may appreciably alter performance...In general, children are more susceptible to the examiner and situational influences than are adults; in the examination of pre-school children, the role of the examiner is especially crucial."

Recent research demonstrates that tests are administered in far from "standard" conditions, particularly to young children: "The actual context [of test administration] often includes confusion, anxiety, behavioral resistance, negative attitudes toward testing on the part of staff and students, lack of properly trained test examiners, developmentally or educationally immature children, and other institutional problems that are endemic to many schools" **(Wodtke, *et al.*, 1985).**

When constructing a standardized test, test developers assume that intelligence is one-dimensional and levels of intelligence are distributed within the population according to a statistical bell curve. They also assume that learning and the development of intelligence is fairly consistent among all individuals. Thus, test questions have only one "right" answer and ignore the process used by children to arrive at their answers **(FairTest, 1990; Oakes and Lipton, 1990; Soo Hoo, 1989).** Individuals who deviate from the average answer and problem-solving process are either exceptional or deficient **(Gill and Levidow, 1987; Gould, 1981).**

These assumptions contradict much of what researchers and theorists have discovered about human intelligence and child development. Child language research, for example, demonstrates that "some children develop the use of pronouns before the development of an extensive noun vocabulary. For others, the reverse pattern of development occurs." Neither is considered to reflect a learning disorder or disability, just variations in development patterns **(Meier, 1983; National Association for the Education of Young Children (NAEYC), 1988; Taylor and Lee, 1987).**

Researchers into human intelligence have observed that knowledge, learning, and thinking have multiple facets, and that a high level of development in one area does not necessarily indicate a high level of development in others **(Gardner, 1985).** Unitary test scores and linear scaling of scores ignore this complexity and provide a deceptive picture of individual achievement, ability, or skills.

Problems also arise when test publishers use national test score averages ("norms") as reference points for interpreting student performance. These norms are developed by administering the test to a group which, in theory, represents the national student population. Some widely used tests were "normed" on small, unrepresentative populations **(Kaufman, 1985; Mitchell, 1985; Tittle, 1978).** Moreover, when norms are not regularly updated, they result in the absurd situation—dubbed the "Lake Woebegone Syndrome"—where most students score above average on the tests **(Cannell, 1987; Koretz, 1988).**

Impact of Standardized Tests

The current emphasis on standardized tests threatens to undermine educational diversity by forcing schools and teachers to focus on quantifiable skills at the expense of less easily quantifiable academic and non-academic abilities, particularly for young children. As the **National Association for the Education of Young Children (1988)** recently noted: "Many of the important skills that children need to acquire in early childhood—self-esteem, social competence, desire to learn, self-discipline—are not easily measured by standardized tests. As a result, social, emotional, moral and physical development, and learning are virtually ignored or given minor importance in schools with mandated testing programs."

Standardized tests generally focus on basic skills rather than critical thinking, reasoning, or problem-solving. They emphasize the quick recognition of isolated facts, not the more profound integration of information and generation of ideas. Several studies have demonstrated that teaching strategies effective in raising scores on tests for lower-level cognitive skills conflict with strategies to develop complex cognitive learning, problem-solving, and creativity **(Bastian, *et al.*, 1985; Levin, 1987; McClellan, 1988; NAEYC, 1988).** As Linda Darling-Hammond of the Rand Corporation concluded: "It's testing for the TV generation—superficial and passive. We don't ask if students can synthesize information, solve problems or think independently. We measure what they can recognize" **(Fiske, 1988).**

Teachers find that certain aspects of student development and performance, critical to their own evaluations of student growth, are not adequately (if at all) assessed by standardized measures. These elements include attitude, ability to self-correct, willingness to take risks, process of writing, ability to organize information, ability to present an argument, and willingness to take initiative **(FairTest, 1990; Oakes and Lipton, 1990; Shepard, 1989; Soo Hoo, 1989).**

In addition, students asked how they gauge their progress in school cited teacher feedback and the quality of their classroom work—not tests—as the most meaningful measures of their growth. Parents also see information other than that measured by standardized tests as most important in making an assessment of a child's progress. These findings suggest the need for alternative kinds of assessment based on teacher evaluation and portfolios of student work **(Soo Hoo, 1989).**

The educational price paid for allowing tests to dictate the curriculum can be high. Julia R. Palmer, Executive Director of the American Reading Council (1987), recently wrote: "[T]he major barrier to teaching reading in a common-sense and pleasurable way is the nationally normed standardized second-grade reading test." Ms. Palmer explains that test questions force teachers and students to focus on "reading readiness" exercises and workbooks in early grades rather than on reading. Many students become disenchanted with reading because they rarely get a chance actually to do it or they never read anything of real interest to them **(Palmer, 1987; Guthrie, 1988).**

Likewise, the "overwhelming testimony of practitioners" holds that standardized tests inhibit the teaching of writing **(Haney and Madaus, 1989).** Other research confirms that curriculum is shaped—and warped—by the prevalence of standardized testing. Elementary teachers reported cutting back on time for science and social studies in order to focus on math skills that would be tested **(Shepard, 1989).** What's more, tests bind curricula to an emphasis on lower-level skills. Although evidence shows that basic skills can be effectively taught in the context of more conceptual learning **(Carpenter, 1988, *cited in* Shepard 1989; Levin 1987),** many teachers simply teach the precise content of the tests, ignoring underlying concepts and often sticking to the rigid formats used to frame test questions **(Oakes and Lipton, 1990; Shepard, 1989).**

Dennie Palmer Wolf (1989) contends that current assessments not only fail to promote but actually prohibit students from becoming thoughtful critics of their own work. The message of tests is that what matters is a "slice of skills" addressed by the test; that on-the-spot work is sufficient; and that achievement takes priority over development. Along with other critics of standardized tests, Wolf advocates adoption of assessments based on students' work and growth over a period of time. A portfolio, or "longitudinal collection," of students' work would serve not only to give a full and accurate representation of their abilities and development, but also to expand the students' own understanding of the learning process.

Just as curriculum has been narrowed, so too have textbooks. A recent report by the Council for Basic Education concludes that "instead of designing a book from the standpoint of its subject or its capacity to capture the children's imagination, editors are increasingly organizing elementary reading series around the content and time of standardized tests...As a result, much of what is in the textbooks is incomprehensible" **(Goodman, *et al.*, 1988; Tyson-Bernstein, 1988).**

GRADE STRUCTURE

Traditionally, students progressed through a sequence of year-long grades from kindergarten to grade 12 and were promoted from one grade to the next on the basis of class grades. Grades were determined by a number of factors, including student classroom and homework activities, teacher observation of student classroom efforts, and student performance on teacher-developed tests. For some students, grades were also affected by immaturity and misconduct, previous retentions, and tardiness and absenteeism **(Safer, 1986a; Shepard and Smith, 1986, 1988).**

In recent years, many schools have supplemented or replaced class grades with standardized achievement tests. Increased reliance on these standardized tests is directly related to increased public focus on school accountability and the mastery of basic skills.

Grade Retention

Although increased use of standardized tests has not reduced a teacher's discretion to retain students, it has limited their ability to promote them. As a result, these policies have been accompanied by dramatic increases in non-promotion of students **(Baenen, 1988; Holmes and Matthews, 1984; Medway, 1985; Schultz, 1989).** Increases in initial retentions are likely to lead to sharp increases in multiple retentions and eventually to more school dropouts **(Hess, 1986; Hess, *et al.*, 1987; Massachusetts Advocacy Center, 1988; Safer, 1986b; Smith and Shepard, 1987).**

The assumption behind using tests for non-promotion is that success in the next grade will require knowledge of a particular proportion of items covered by the test, and that schools are capable of pinpointing what this percentage is. On some tests, a difference of two or three responses can move a child into the next grade level or keep her a grade level behind **(Oakes and Lipton, 1990).**

Certain students are retained more often: racial and ethnic minorities; children from low-income families or of less-educated parents; language-minority and limited-English-proficient children; handicapped children; children from the south; young males; and children who are small for their age **(Illinois Fair Schools Coalition, 1985; Medway, 1985; Shepard and Smith, 1986; Smith and Shepard, 1987; Walker and Madhere, 1987).**

Some schools have sought to reduce retention rates by preventing children from entering school until they are "ready." This has involved raising school entrance age requirements and using readiness testing for kindergarten students. Seven states mandate readiness testing before kindergarten, thirty states have some communities that do this; six states require tests before first grade, forty-three states have some communities that do this. These tests have been ineffective in achieving sustained higher performance among students **(Schultz, 1989).**

For several reasons, these strategies are generally unsuccessful: statistical differences in achievement between the youngest and oldest students are small and disappear entirely by the third grade **(Shepard and Smith, 1985, 1986).** Teachers are more likely to recommend retention for a younger child than an older peer even where both have identical achievement levels; raising the school entrance age simply creates a different group of "youngest" children **(Shephard and Smith, 1986, 1988);** readiness tests are among the least valid or reliable of all standardized achievement tests—for example, the widely-used Gesell School Readiness Test fails to meet American Psychological Association standards for validity, reliability, or normative information **(Kaufman, 1985; Shephard and Smith, 1985, 1986),** and it is extremely difficult to establish a standard testing environment for young children, further undermining the already low validity and reliability of readiness tests **(Kaufman, 1985; Shepard and Smith, 1986).**

A second year of kindergarten in the form of pre-kindergarten classes, repeating kindergarten, or attending pre-first-grade classes have been proposed by some educators to help reduce grade retention. Such programs are in operation in communities in forty states **(Schultz, 1989).** But these approaches do not produce student achievement gains. Children placed in such programs achieve at the same rate as equally at-risk children who have not had the extra year. Children in two-year kindergarten programs develop lower self-esteem and slightly more negative attitudes toward school **(Shepard and Smith, 1985; Smith and Shepard, 1987).**

Standards for non-promotion in the early grades are inconsistent and subjective. In California during the school year 1985–1986, district-level retention rates ranged from 0 to 50 percent **(Schultz, 1989).**

Impact of Grade Retention

Non-promotion remains enormously popular in the United States **(Baenen, 1988; Byrnes and Yamamoto, 1986; Gallup, 1986).** To justify the use of non-promotion, many teachers and parents rely on their personal experience as they cite examples of students whose achievement levels were improved due to grade retention **(Shepard and Smith, 1988).**

Research demonstrates that retaining students not only fails to help them catch up with peers and succeed in school, it actually contributes to academic failure and behavioral difficulties. Studies comparing academic gains by retained students with gains by academically comparable students who were promoted found that retained students do not benefit academically regardless of grade level or student achievement level **(Baenen, 1988; Gampert and Opperman, 1988; Hess, 1987; Holmes and Matthews, 1984; Illinois Fair Schools Coalition, 1985; Labaree, 1984; Medway, 1985; Oakes and Lipton, 1990; Safer, 1986; Shepard and Smith, 1988; Smith and Shepard, 1987; Walker and Madhere, 1987).**

Students who have been retained, even the youngest students, consistently suffer poorer self-concepts, have more problems of social adjustment, and express more negative attitudes toward school at the end of the period of retention than do similar students who are promoted **(Holmes and Matthews, 1984; Illinois Fair Schools Coalition, 1985; Shepard and Smith, 1988; Walker and Madhere, 1987).** Children fear retention, citing it third on their list of anxieties, following blindness and death of a parent **(Byrnes and Yamamoto, 1984).**

Some schools have sought to reduce problems created by student non-promotion by linking grade retention to remediation programs. Proponents of retention with remediation claim it allows schools to identify and serve children who are failing academically before they fall further behind. Although students in such programs do make significant achievement gains, those gains are no greater than progress made by comparable students not retained in grade, and social and behavioral problems associated with retention are not alleviated **(Gampert and Opperman, 1988; Illinois Fair Schools Coalition, 1985; Labaree, 1984).**

Grade retention is enormously expensive. The cost of educating a student until graduation after only one retention increases by 8 percent—an amount that runs into billions of dollars nationwide **(Smith and Shepard, 1987).** A report on the Austin Independent School District's promotion policy concluded that the added cost for Austin's 4,118 retainees was $9,081,100. The Illinois Fair Schools Coalition (1985) estimated that the state was spending between $392 million and $436 million on retentions. These concrete costs, of course, do not include the incalculable costs to society of school failure and increased numbers of students leaving school without diplomas.

Characteristics of Low Retention Schools

Schools with low retention rates feature teachers and administrators committed to implementing practices that respond to a wide range of individual differences. In addition, these schools are characterized by: strong teacher efficacy and high expectations that all children can learn; flexible standards of student competence; reduced pressure on teachers for student accountability based primarily or solely on achievement test scores; a variety of services to enhance learning—summer school, guidance and counselor services, tutoring, parent education, and individualized instruction; a variety of curricula and instructional practices that consider the natural range in achievement, ability, linguistic competence, and background among the students **(Shepard and Smith, 1988; Smith and Shepard, 1987).**

Alternative Grade Structures

Alternative grade structures generally rely on student groupings involving several grade levels or ages of students. Thus, a single class could encompass children ages five through eight or those enrolled in grades K through 2. The succeeding class could encompass children aged seven through ten or those enrolled in grades 3 and 4.

Recognizing that individuals develop at different rates, children in multi-age classes are allowed to progress through curricula at their own rate and are grouped with older and younger peers as appropriate. Children move from one class to the next class based upon both age and level of development. Retention, in the traditional sense, does not occur in multi-age classes because at least half of the students are expected to remain in the class at the end of each school year rather than be promoted to the next set of grade levels. Because teachers have a second or third year with students, they feel less pressure to retain them if they have not yet achieved a determined set of skills.

Studies of multi-age classrooms have found no consistent or significant effects on academic achievement **(Pratt, 1986; Veenman, Lem, and Winkelmolen, 1985).** However, students in multi-age classes do exhibit better self-concepts, improved attitudes toward school, and a general improvement in social abilities. Children demonstrate more nurturance and cooperation and less aggression and competitiveness than children in age-segregated classes. Moreover, few socially isolated children are found in multi-age classes, in part because younger children are particularly effective at reducing the isolation of withdrawn older children **(French, *et al.*, 1986; Pratt, 1986).**

5

Student Support Services

Children are entitled to a broad range of support services that address individual needs.

A Vision of Student Support Services at the Good Common School

The Good Common School's struggle to guarantee educational entitlements to its students has generated a homegrown slogan:

"DON'T DO MORE. DO DIFFERENTLY."

The words are oddly comforting to a stressed principal, a hard-working teaching staff, and a group of parents who do double time, working in the daytime and often coming to evening meetings at the school. Doing "differently" seems possible; doing "more" doesn't.

But now, the slogan is about to be challenged. The main topic of discussion at the next school council meeting is every child's right to receive a broad range of support services that address individual needs in a language the student can understand.

Principal Phyllis Walker searches her files for information about elementary guidance programs to share with council members. She doesn't find much. Nor does her file of back issues of the district's monthly newsletter on school restructuring contain anything useful. She isn't surprised; the school reform movement has pretty much ignored the subject of student support services.

In desperation, Phyllis calls the head of the Guidance and Counseling Department of the state university, who faxes to her sections of *Children Achieving Potential,* a report of the National Conference of State Legislatures and the American Association for Counseling and Development (Glosoff and Koprowicz, 1990). She is relieved when it arrives. She knows from experience that the school council will want a standard against which to measure the existing program, as well as ideas to strengthen it.

Using highlights from the report and her own dozen years of experience as a teacher and a principal, Phyllis prepares a memorandum describing how a comprehensive, high-quality elementary school guidance program should look.

As the school council meeting opens, a group of parents report on their study of the social needs of children attending the Good Common School. The Guidance Committee is very broadly based. Its membership represents all racial and ethnic groups in the school's student body. The committee has been at work for several months, gathering information about students' social and psychological needs and parental perceptions of how well they are being met.

The Guidance Committee's report, based on interviews with a cross-section of parents and students, describes the struggles of many families as they face a wide range of problems: unemployment, poor housing, drug and other substance abuse, domestic violence, serious health problems including AIDS and malnutrition, crime and violence, a shortage of child care, stress associated with cultural adaptation, and other mental health issues.

Following discussion of the report, Council Chair Ella Davis asks the school counselor to comment. Roberta Rodríguez's remarks substantiate the committee's findings. Roberta—the only professional guidance counselor on the school's staff—describes how her days are spent counseling individual students and completing tedious paperwork. Closing on a note of frustration, she acknowledges that students are still waiting to see her when the daily dismissal bell rings.

Listening to her words, two members of the Guidance Committee exchange knowing looks. Their interviews with parents have already made it clear that even students seriously in need of guidance services often fail to get them. The parents do not blame Roberta. She has been at the school for several years. Parents know she is competent, caring, and hard working. It is simply unrealistic to expect one counselor to meet the needs of 600-plus students, especially when many of them come from families struggling with difficult economic and social issues.

As Roberta finishes, the principal passes around copies of a memorandum describing an effective elementary guidance program. The room falls silent, as the breadth of the gap between the ideal and the existing levels of services becomes clear.

It is quickly apparent that restructuring the Good Common School's approach to guidance services will require both "doing more" and "doing differently." Funds must be identified to support salaries for at least one more professional counselor and for bilingual counseling aides. Parent volunteers must be recruited and trained. A new role must be defined for Roberta. Teachers will have to do more.

Jessica Wilson, a first-grade teacher in the audience, listens with her head in her hands, overwhelmed. When she is granted the floor by Ella Davis, she declares, "Teachers are already doing too much, every day of our lives. Why does the school expect us to do it all? Let's face it, a lot of families are letting their kids down. Too many kids are already seriously damaged by the time they start school. How can we be expected to rescue them all?"

Before she can finish, a father in the audience jumps up. He does not wait to be recognized by the chair. His anger is visible.

> *"Look, lady, you're jumping to a lot of conclusions. Almost all the parents I know are struggling to do the best they can. People care about their kids—but they're stretched to the breaking point. Some parents have been unemployed for months. Too many of the jobs that are available don't pay a living wage. We used to talk about a "safety net" of social programs. Now budget cuts have poked big holes in the so-called safety net—which never did provide much safety for poor people, anyway."*
>
> *"I am here to tell you this—you may not want to do more; you may not like to do more. But you need to get busy for the simple reason that schools are where our kids are. And our kids are important!"*

When he sits down, there is a long moment of silence. Jessica Wilson sighs, but says nothing. Ella Davis breaks the silence, "Thank you, sir. That was a powerful statement of why we have to move ahead. If there are no objections from the council, I'll ask the Guidance Committee to continue to work with Phyllis Walker and Roberta Rodríguez to develop a plan for reorganizing our guidance program. I urge you to pay especially close attention to what parents and community leaders have to say."

Roberta listens carefully. For years, she has wished that more attention would be paid to the social aspects of children's needs. She wonders why—now that change is imminent—she feels so defensive.

• • •

Three months later, a new plan for the delivery of guidance services is submitted to the school council. The guidance program's new mission statement is couched in language from the National Conference of State Legislatures and the American Association of Counseling and Development (Glosoff and Koprowicz, 1990): "To provide a planned program of guidance and counseling services based on...developmental needs and to help all children achieve their greatest academic, social, and personal potential."

Strategies for restructuring the guidance program parallel NCSL/AACD standards. For example:

- Counselors will spend less time attempting to change the behavior of individual students and more time improving the learning environment for all students.
- Early identification of problems and intervention at the early childhood level will be stressed.
- Most guidance activity will occur with small groups of students.
- Counselors will assign a high priority to providing parent education and facilitating parent involvement.
- The counselor's role as a facilitator for change will be expanded.
- The guidance program will be an integral part of the school program.

(Adapted from *Study of Exemplary Guidance Programs in Elementary Schools,* Solomon, *et al.*, Brooklyn, NY, 1988.)

After these strategies have been reviewed by the council, another is added to ensure that children and families from all language groups have access to services in their first language:

- The composition of professional and paraprofessional staff and volunteers will include at least one individual who speaks each language represented in the student body.

With regard to the new goal, Ella notes the school must make a special point to draw upon the language and cultural resources available from community-based organizations that serve various ethnic groups. Ella then asks Phyllis Walker to include an article in Spanish and Khmer describing the proposed changes in the next edition of the school's newsletter.

• • •

It is now late September of the next school year. Considerable progress has been made in the implementation of the new guidance plan. One new Spanish/-English bilingual school counselor and two additional bilingual counselor aides—one speaking Spanish and English and one speaking Khmer and English—are on the job. The Khmer-speaking aide works three mornings each week. Several volunteer counselor aides have been trained. The front office has taken on some of Roberta's paper work. Even with these changes, the Good Common School still falls short of its goal of a counselor/student ratio of 1:250.

Roberta Rodríguez directs an expanded Guidance Department. Under her strong leadership, and with consistent support from the principal, school staff are developing a new commitment to identify and resolve the underlying causes of problems that undercut children's school success.

Roberta's days are varied. In addition to supervising guidance staff, she helps teachers develop and implement developmentally appropriate preventative guidance activities in their classrooms. She works to get more parents involved, assists with student assessment, trains and oversees peer counselors, and makes referrals to community agencies.

Youngsters with problems likely to affect their academic achievement are still referred by teachers and parents for individual counseling. Among these problems are classroom misbehavior, separation anxiety, difficulty with peers, conflict with teachers, poor school attendance, low self-esteem, parental unemployment, homelessness, parental neglect or abuse, and loss of a parent through death, separation, or divorce.

There is no shortage of serious problems. One wintry Wednesday morning, the two guidance counselors encounter these challenging situations:

- Eight-year-old Katanga K. suddenly begins to pound fiercely on another child's back during recess. The second child slips on a patch of ice, falls, and cuts her forehead. She is taken to a hospital emergency room. During the counseling session, Katanga says her father has been out of work for a long time. Tomorrow, the family has to move out of their apartment. They have no place to go.
- Juan L., a quiet ten-year-old from a large family, is withdrawn and unresponsive in class. This morning he is found alone and crying in the music room. During counseling, Juan reveals that his oldest brother is very ill with AIDS. Juan says he is afraid other children will shun him if they find out about it.

- Julia T., a second grader, returns to school after several days of unexplained absence. When the counselor calls her home to find out the reason, there is no answer. During counseling, Julia explains she and her mother are living temporarily at a shelter for battered women because her mother was beaten up by her boyfriend. Julia is very anxious and wonders where she will live when she leaves the shelter.
- A counselor discovers Tommy M. , a sixth grader, showing a friend some white powder in a small plastic bag that he quickly hides when he sees an adult coming. Tommy says he doesn't know what the substance is; his older brother borrowed his jacket last night. Maybe the powder belongs to him?

When appropriate, children who have similar problems are organized into small counseling groups. One criterion for placing a child in a small guidance group is whether he or she is likely to benefit from the group experience. Participants in small guidance groups usually share a common concern, as well. Guidance groups typically meet for forty-five minutes once or twice each week. So far, the Good Common School has conducted successful groups for children struggling to cope with the effects of abuse, homelessness, and divorce.

Additionally, the school has subcontracted with community-based organizations with Cambodian and Central American constituencies to provide translations, facilitate involvement of foreign-born children in extracurricular activities at school, and help counselors organize and run peer support groups for students recently arrived from war-torn countries.

Bicultural staff members sometimes work directly with individual teachers to increase their understanding of children's first cultures. One good outcome has been an increasing number of teachers who regularly pair new foreign-born students with U.S.-born students for orientation, peer counseling, and peer tutoring.

Working together, teachers and counselors provide structured guidance activities to entire classrooms of students. The counselor helps the teacher plan in-class work and locate appropriate resource materials. Teachers are then able to engage students in structured learning activities that focus on issues such as stress, career options, alcohol and drug abuse, and divorce.

The Good Common School's commitment to support each student's achievement of full potential does not mean all necessary services must be provided at school; it does mean the school knows how to make accurate referrals to community agencies. Pupils with serious psychological problems, or those from homes with severe family problems, are referred to community-based human service agencies for long-term treatment. Two such agencies have been offered space at the school so services are delivered more conveniently to students and parents.

Since the overhaul of the guidance program, Roberta has become expert at negotiating the interface between school and community. She spends more time networking, trying to keep communications open between the school and community agencies. Agency personnel appreciate her efforts to avoid duplication. They also appreciate her generosity in returning professional favors by offering meeting space at the school, by volunteering to serve on committees, or pitching in to help out at special events.

Because parents are strongly supportive of the Good Common School Guidance Program, it is not surprising that counselors are staunchly committed to strengthening the home/school link by:

- convincing teachers to hold parent conferences at community locations more comfortable and convenient to parents than the school—sometimes important meetings are held twice so all parents can attend with equal convenience;
- writing articles for the school newsletter describing activities parents can use at home to support their child's school success;
- encouraging parents to participate in a variety of school advisory roles;
- reducing language barriers by engaging bilingual aides or volunteers from community-based immigrant organizations to act as translators.

(Adapted from *Study of Exemplary Guidance Programs in Elementary Schools*, Solomon, *et al.*, Brooklyn, NY, 1988)

Since the Good Common School staff agrees that counselors are in the best position to "see the big picture," the guidance staff takes turns chairing meetings of the school's Student Support Team—a forum where information useful in addressing individual problems is collected and discussed. By including staff familiar with both academic and social service needs, the Student Support Team reflects a wide variety of approaches and perspectives.

Counseling staff and volunteers play important roles in supporting the Good Common School's development into a democratic, multicultural community. They work steadily to promote improved understanding among different racial and ethnic groups; they search for new ways to destroy stereotypes; they keep a sharp eye out for school policies and practices that undermine the school success of the most vulnerable students. Parents view counselors as friendly liaison workers who reach across cultural lines to communicate with all segments of the community.

YOU KNOW IT'S A GOOD GUIDANCE PROGRAM WHEN...

- **Counselors are supportive of all teachers.** Guidance is available to everybody, and staff doesn't hesitate to seek out counselors at any time of the day.
- **Counselors get around to all corners of the school.** They make themselves visible and available to staff and parents. The least likely place to find the counselor is in the guidance office.
- **Counselors don't wait for teachers to initiate requests for help.** They know the at-risk pupils and anticipate their problems. Teachers feel counselors are aware and concerned about their students.
- **Counselors approach teachers in a non-threatening way.** They view teachers as peers and avoid being perceived as an "expert" or "supervisor."
- **Counselors always take some kind of action.** They achieve closure on their cases. They never leave a teacher or parent "hanging," even if action is only a short note assuring a further response.
- **Counselors are willing to experiment.** They use a variety of guidance approaches, such as visualizations, stress reduction exercises, etc.
- **Counselors often manage to avoid the red tape.** They know red tape can interfere with the job of helping children.
- **Counselors and teachers have mutual respect for each other as human beings and professionals.** This fosters open communication and a sharing relationship.
- **Counselors are knowledgeable about the surrounding community.** They reach out to agencies and organizations and invite shared responsibility for helping children.
- **Counselors act as facilitators.** They identify and define needs and problems, assembling resources and coordinating the individual and collective efforts of many people to get the job done.

Adapted from *Study of Exemplary Guidance Programs in Elementary Schools*, Solomon, *et al.* (Brooklyn, NY, 1988).

TEN IDEAL GUIDANCE PRACTICES

1. Guidance in elementary schools stresses early identification of learning barriers and provides appropriate strategies to negate or minimize these barriers.
2. The guidance program includes individual counseling, small group guidance, and whole class guidance lessons in which pupils explore and share their individual and collective concerns.
3. Involvement of parents is considered an essential ingredient of a successful guidance program.
4. Counselor time is wisely utilized on activities that contribute most to the achievement of the counselor's objectives.
5. A school guidance committee enhances the development and implementation of the guidance program.
6. The counselor functions as a consultant in a role that offers unmistakable direct benefits to administrators, teachers, other school personnel and—indirectly—to children.
7. A successful guidance program often reflects the counselor's ability to intervene as a facilitator of change, creating conditions that enhance the growth of children.
8. An essential role of the guidance counselor is to establish an effective relationship with community-based agencies and organizations to provide a variety of programs and services to individual pupils and their families.
9. The school's guidance goals are clearly defined and communicated to all school staff.
10. Well-designed evaluations are conducted to demonstrate the effectiveness of guidance in the school.

Adapted from *Study of Exemplary Guidance Programs in Elementary Schools,* Solomon, *et al.* (Brooklyn, NY, 1988).

LINKING SCHOOLS AND COMMUNITIES

Barriers that Inhibit Collaborations

- competitiveness and cynicism about the benefits of sharing;
- lack of shared leadership;
- inflexibility in scheduling and procedures;
- lack of mutual understanding between schools and community agencies;
- time constraints;
- lack of an open and inclusive participation ethic;
- prescribing actions for the partnership instead of allowing players to shape their own decisions over time.

Recommendations for Establishing Successful Collaborations

- keep channels of communication open between schools and agencies;
- learn how the various partners in the collaboration operate, what their needs are, and what they perceive their roles to be;
- be clear on the goals of the collaboration and the role each agency is to play in achieving these goals;
- follow through on commitments to hold meetings, perform tasks, or deliver services;
- pay attention to details such as recording and disseminating minutes of meetings;
- involve staff at all levels of the various agencies in joint planning and implementation.

Source: Melville and Blank, 1991; Robinson and Mastny, 1989.

A SUPPORT SERVICES CHECKLIST FOR SCHOOLS SERVING IMMIGRANT STUDENTS

___ Are language and other barriers to participation eliminated so that all parents can be involved in the development of school-based guidance plans?

___ Are bilingual/bicultural counselors/counselor aides provided to ensure that foreign-born children have sympathetic intermediaries at the school?

___ Are peer discussion and support groups available to students who experienced trauma in war-torn homelands or during their journey to the U.S.?

___ Are culturally comfortable in-school and extracurricular clubs available to foreign-born students?

___ Does the school regularly reach out to staff of immigrant self-help organizations involved in helping newly arrived families bridge cultures and plan for children's future in school and beyond?

___ Does the school forge linkages with community-based service providers and immigrant self-help organizations to ensure that mental health services are available to immigrant children and families?

___ Does the school contract with immigrant self-help organizations to provide a range of appropriate support services?

Adapted from First, *et al.* (1988); Olsen, L. (1988).

Problems with Student Support Services in U.S. Public Schools

As we enter the 1990s, children in the United States are faced with an almost insurmountable array of societal problems—particularly poor children, children of color, and those who are limited-English-proficient, culturally different, recently immigrated, or handicapped. At the same time, traditional sources of support for children are severely overburdened. Families are often fragmented and experiencing severe economic and social stress.

Many public programs designed to provide a safety net in the areas of nutrition, health, daycare, and child safety have failed to keep pace with children's growing needs. Between 1979 and 1986, more than half of the increase in poverty experienced by families with children was caused by reductions in government benefit programs such as Social Security, Aid to Families with Dependent Children, food stamps, subsidized housing, and Medicaid (Chafel, 1990).

Private sector attempts to close the gap between need and available assistance to families, such as those made by non-profit community-based organizations and churches, are increasingly stretched beyond their capacity.

PROBLEMS FACING TODAY'S STUDENTS

The plethora of problems facing many students and their families can appear overwhelming to public school staff. For many teens, pregnancy interrupts or abruptly ends formal schooling. Participation in drug or gang cultures spawns crime and violence in communities already burdened by economic struggle. For many school children, shortages of housing, food, clothing, and health care are a daily reality. AIDS and other diseases present the greatest threat to life and health in communities that are most sorely pressed.

A look at some current statistics—compiled by the Children's Defense Fund (1987, 1988, 1990)—provides a startling picture of the challenges young people now face—problems that cut across race, economic class, and geographic location.

- About half of U.S. teens are sexually active by the time they leave high school.
- More than half a million teens give birth each year; the teen birth rate in the U.S. is twice that of any Western nation.
- Each year 400,000 teenagers have abortions.
- Each year 2.5 million teens contract a sexually transmitted disease—about one teenager in every six.
- Adolescent AIDS cases increased by 40 percent between 1987 and 1989.
- Almost 75 percent of school-aged youth report having experimented with drugs; one in fifteen adolescents has tried cocaine; 1.2 percent of high school seniors report heroin use; the U.S. has the highest rate of teenage drug use of any industrialized nation.

- In a 1987 survey, about one-quarter of eighth-grade students and more than one-third of tenth-grade students reported having had five or more alcoholic drinks on a single occasion during the previous two weeks.
- The number of children living with a divorced mother more than doubled between 1970 and 1986; 2,989 children see their parents divorced each day.
- Almost one-third of all children are considered "latch key kids," with no parental or adult supervision or companionship until the end of the working day.
- An estimated 1.5 million children are homeless in the U.S.
- More than 9 million children have no health care. Twice as many have never visited a dentist.
- Fewer than half of all pre-school children are immunized against preventable diseases.
- Twelve million children, one in five, live in poverty—an astounding 43 percent of African American children and 38 percent of Latino children.
- An estimated 2.2 million children were reported abused or neglected in 1986; the average age was seven years.
- Every day, six teenagers commit suicide; 1,000 young people attempt suicide each day.

These concerns are not limited to low-income students or children of color. Two-thirds of children who are abused or neglected are White. Two-thirds of pregnant teens are White, do not live in the inner city, and are not poor.

Multiple Risk Factors

As reported by policy analyst Lisbeth Schorr (1988), researchers from a variety of countries conducting studies of young people over many years have reached similar conclusions:

- It takes more than a single risk factor to produce a damaging outcome for a child.
- The presence of more than one risk factor at the same time for a child dramatically compounds the damage of each separate risk factor.
- Damage is most likely to occur when a child's physical vulnerabilities interact with risk factors generated by an unsupportive environment.
- Damage is most likely to occur when the negative elements of a child's home, school, or community environment combine with other risk factors to multiply the effects.

To further sharpen the policy perspective, Schorr offers three related observations: 1) risk factors leading to later damage occur more frequently among children in families that are poor; 2) the plight of children bearing these risks is not just individual and personal, it requires a societal response; 3) the knowledge to help these children is already available.

The implications are clear. First, children's chances for school success can be improved with the elimination of some risk factors, even if others still remain. Second, the children who now receive the least and worst society has to offer are the ones who will benefit most from intervention efforts.

Despite the clear benefits that even limited support can provide and the fact that effective intervention strategies have been clearly defined, most elementary schools do not provide the range of support services required to help students succeed academically or mediate environmental effects that can cause physical and emotional damage.

Too many school personnel seem to conclude that the most vulnerable children are "damaged goods" by the time they arrive at school, and accordingly lower their educational expectations for these students. In some public schools, staff members actively reject the responsibility to address problems that lie outside of a narrowly defined school mission, proclaiming instead that "schools just can't do it all."

BARRIERS TO SUPPORT SERVICE DELIVERY

The delivery of student support services in public schools can be hampered by an array of obstacles, as identified by NCAS (1990) in cooperation with six national organizations representing student support professionals:

- failure to include the commitment to high-quality support services as part of the school's mission statement;
- lack of administrative leadership at the school site coupled with inadequate central office leadership;
- lack of clear standards and ineffective monitoring of quality;
- insufficient funding resulting in heavy caseloads and assignment of support service personnel to multiple school sites;
- inadequate training or continuing education for school staff;
- inadequate collaboration and coordination with community-based organizations;
- lack of coordination between various federal, state, and local programs, resulting in complex reporting requirements.

As a result of limited resources and blurred professional roles, individualized support services may be available only to students with the most glaring needs, in spite of the fact that nearly all children and adolescents experience periodic non-academic problems that can threaten their chances for school success.

Poorly Defined Professional Roles

Support service personnel often find themselves carrying out functions related to school administration such as scheduling, monitoring student attendance, proctoring tests, chaperoning student activities, or assisting with college and financial aid applications. A recent study (*Harvard Education Letter,* 1988) by the U.S. Department of Education reported that school guidance directors spend one-sixth of their time on such activities. The resulting paperwork can be overwhelming, drastically reducing the time available to counsel students on either a group or individual basis.

Circumstances that define a child's daily experiences should also shape the elementary school counselor's responsibilities and approaches, but this frequently is not the case. Many elementary schools do not have guidance programs, despite the fact that their students and families struggle to survive the effects of drug and alcohol abuse, unplanned pregnancies, domestic and social violence, and child neglect and abuse.

In affluent communities, unique pressures exist when children suffer from "hurried childhoods" as parents urge precocious learning and social achievements. Pressure to succeed in elementary school may be tied to parental demands for subsequent academic achievement. A recent survey reported in the *Harvard Education Letter* (1988) found that 40 percent of guidance counselors in upper-income schools devote more than half their time to college-related issues. In low-income communities, less than 6 percent of counselors' efforts focused on college admission.

High Counselor/Student Ratios

As of 1989 (Glosoff and Koprowicz, 1990), only twelve states mandated counselors in elementary schools. In the absence of state mandates, staffing levels for these positions are highly uneven. Some districts have all but eliminated counselors, while others make them a high priority.

There are differing views on what constitutes an effective counselor/student ratio. The guidance and counseling profession itself suggests a ratio of 1:250. Advocates for students facing multiple risk factors maintain that a ratio of 1:50 is needed to address these children's pressing needs.

According to a study of student counseling commissioned by the College Board (Commission on Pre-college Guidance and Counseling, 1986), the average ratio is about 1:350, with some districts reporting ratios of 1:600 or greater as the norm. Staffing levels can also vary widely among districts within the same school system. An examination of thirty-two elementary school districts in New York state revealed ratios that ranged from a low of 1:626 to a high of 1:10,504. Only six districts displayed ratios lower than 1:1000. Five districts, serving a total of almost 65,000 children, had no elementary school counselors at all.

Schools with large enrollments of immigrant students find they must stretch their capacities to meet complex and urgent needs as newly arrived children struggle to adjust to a new culture and language, sometimes experiencing loneliness, depression, grief, academic difficulties, and hopeful dreams that turn into despair. Schools rarely have enough bilingual counselors to cope with the diversity of language and culture now presented in most U.S. gateway cities.

In schools where no staff positions are provided for counselors, classroom teachers often act—formally or informally—as primary providers of social services, even though they often lack the training, resources, or support to fulfill such a role successfully.

Lack of Integration and Coordination of Services

Each student's unique background, experiences at home, in school, and in the community, and the resources available outside of school shape particular needs for guidance and other support. Although these needs vary considerably by individual, most schools are not organized to respond adequately to growing student diversity. When different needs are presented by a single student, schools rarely have the capacity to mount an integrated response.

A guide to linking schools and communities published by Rutgers University (Robinson and Mastny, 1989) delineates factors that inhibit effective collaboration, including:

- competitiveness;
- inflexibility in scheduling meetings and activities;
- dominating rather than sharing leadership, which discourages group decision-making;
- lack of understanding about how schools and community agencies operate;
- hidden agendas for personal advancement;
- pressure to "push things through" without allowing adequate time for discussion and to work through conflicts;
- preferring to do things alone rather than having to negotiate with others;
- closed participation—only a selected few invited to take part in decision-making.

All children suffer when there is poor coordination between school-based and community-based support services. Among those who suffer the most are children from families with language and cultural differences. Immigrant community organizations, for example, have a unique capacity to function as essential bridges between schools and newly arrived families— but they are rarely granted the opportunity to do so.

Lack of Parental Involvement

Despite copious research on the positive impact of parental involvement in helping a school's efforts to secure both short-term and long-term academic and social progress for students, most schools do little to reach out to parents to inform them about available services or the status of individual students. The *Harvard Education Letter* (1988) reports on one survey of guidance directors which found that only 10 percent of counselors conferred with even a third of their students' families.

POSITIVE IMPACT OF STUDENT SUPPORT SERVICES

Counseling in Elementary Schools

Much research is now available documenting the positive impacts of elementary school counseling on young children's capacity to cope with the complex challenges they face.

Among the findings of various studies cited in one review of research (Glosoff and Koprowicz, 1990) are:

- A study of 117 underachieving fourth graders showed significant differences in class rank in favor of the counseled students by the time the students were high school seniors.
- The U.S. Department of Education discovered 47 percent fewer dropouts and 50 percent fewer failures in schools with adequate counselor/ student ratios.
- Fourth- through sixth-grade students referred to small group counseling by teachers for exhibiting hostile and aggressive behavior scored significantly lower on measures of aggression and hostility than a control group at the conclusion of the intervention.
- Weekly group guidance sessions provided to sixty elementary students identified to be at high risk of dropping out resulted in significant improvement in attendance, attitude toward school, and self-esteem.
- Evaluations of elementary school guidance centers in San Diego showed a reduction of 80 to 90 percent in suspensions and referrals to the principal.

Comprehensive Pre-school Programs

As the result of thoughtful and well-documented early experiments, as reviewed by author Lisbeth Schorr (1988), the profound value of comprehensive pre-school programs has been established for decades, particularly for children disadvantaged by society. Pioneering efforts that remain benchmarks are the Early Training Project, the Perry Pre-school Program, and the IDS Harlem Project. By following the course of participants into adulthood, researchers documented remarkable results.

Participants in the Early Training Project finished high school at a rate one-third higher than a control group and were one-sixth as likely to be referred to special education. In the Perry Pre-school Program, participants, by the age of nineteen, were twice as likely to be employed, attending college, or receiving further training. Their high school graduation rate was one-third higher, their arrest rate was 40 percent lower, and their teen pregnancy rate was 42 percent lower. By the time participants in the IDS Harlem Project reached twenty-one years of age—compared to a control group—twice as many were employed, one-third more had graduated from high school or had obtained equivalency diplomas, and one-third more had gone on to college or vocational training.

These dramatic outcomes result from high-quality programs that consider and respect young children's broad range of needs. To be effective, Schorr notes, a pre-school program should:

- provide intellectual stimulation with books, the spoken word, play, and interchange of ideas;
- offer nurturance, approval, and responsiveness;
- include health, nutrition, and social services;
- involve, collaborate with, and support parents;
- be staffed by competent adults with a staff/child ratio that allows each child to get the personal attention he or she needs to thrive.

Until all children have access to quality comprehensive pre-school programs, the human and financial costs of failing to help young children develop and grow to their fullest potential will continue to plague U.S. schools.

Advocates for Children of New York: Educating Homeless Children

In 1986, as in other years, **Advocates for Children of New York (AFC)** handled over 2,500 cases. This large volume enabled them to identify a clear relationship between the treatment of children in temporary housing and the education system. Many homeless children were not attending school or were placed in segregated, transitional classes that stigmatized them while failing to address their needs for specialized education services.

To decide how best to educate children in temporary shelters, AFC convened a series of meetings with advocates for the homeless. By assembling as many people as possible with knowledge about issues related to homelessness, AFC hoped to quell possible "turf" issues among these groups. Information from these meetings and from AFC's research and case work provided the framework for a proposal to the New York City School Chancellor. The proposal noted the following elements as essential to meet the needs of students in temporary housing:

- A system to identify the students to be served, determine their needs, and monitor their educational outcomes.
- Specific policies and standards to address each student's living circumstances and education needs, based on two assumptions:
  1) students should attend the schools to which they had been assigned before they became homeless, subject to student/parent options;
  2) students should be integrated into the school as quickly as possible without being segregated into separate classes or programs.
- A central administrator to establish a planning process and ensure that all students had equal access to the full range of services offered.

Media Strategy

Before approaching the chancellor's office with its proposal, AFC mounted a media campaign to expose school conditions faced by homeless families. Reporters and camera crews were taken to hotels and temporary shelters in the middle of the day to witness children out of school, in the streets, living in terrible conditions.

AFC believes the media attention was effective because it forced the chancellor to deal with their proposal at a high level, rather than through normal bureaucratic channels.

Building Support

With the mood set by the media coverage, AFC approached the chancellor's office with its proposal. As the result of formal and informal communications between the chancellor's office and AFC, it was clear the chancellor: agreed there were problems with school policies and practices; believed these problems were not the fault of the children themselves; feared a possible lawsuit for their treatment of homeless youth; and was aware of general public sympathy for the children's plight.

AFC then met with each school superintendent to attempt to get an endorsement of their plan, arguing that it was in school officials' best interests to support a proposal that would result in money and resources to deal with a pressing problem. AFC also met with community representatives to gain their support.

Earmarking Funds

After assessing the size and needs of the homeless population, AFC realized substantial funding would be required.

AFC secured funding for their proposal by successfully lobbying the chancellor's office and City Hall to include their program in the mayor's budget. An important element of the lobbying effort involved getting school staff to endorse the concept that more money was necessary to meet the needs of these students.

To raise the necessary funds, AFC proposed a per capita tax increase of $667 per year, with the revenue earmarked to support children in temporary housing. With this money, schools would be more willing to accept these students and would be better equipped to address the students' needs. By agreement with City Hall, the money would be used for school supplies, after-school programs, breakfast programs, and establishing a data bank to trace students' educational progress.

Staff Development

As a result of previous advocacy work with homeless families, AFC staff knew that school personnel would need professional training to help them deal more effectively with these children.

After talking with various organizations offering sensitivity training, AFC Executive Director Norma Rollins decided to work with Mount Sinai Hospital, which had provided this type of training for their own staff. Subsequently, a program was designed to help school staff identify their feelings and overcome biases and misconceptions about homeless children.

AFC's Proposal Is Accepted

The AFC plan was given an unexpected boost when one school district in Queens moved to exclude two large temporary shelters from its schools. When AFC filed a grievance against the district, there was no regulation or policy in place to guide the chancellor. This pushed the chancellor's office to accept the AFC plan—perhaps more quickly than it might have in other circumstances.

A full-time staff person was assigned by the chancellor's office to oversee the AFC program. It soon became apparent, however, that implementation was too complex to be handled by a single person. In fact, the staff person assigned to the program resigned after six months, largely due to an inability to handle the task's political dimensions.

The program has since been decentralized, with day-to-day operations carried out at the community level. Monitoring and coordinating responsibilities remain with the chancellor's staff in the central office.

As part of the program, a study was completed on the homeless student population, analyzing objective data on their educational progress and offering interviews with students in which they expressed their views on their treatment by schools.

For further information, please contact: Advocates for Children of New York, 24-16 Bridge Plaza South, Long Island City, NY 11101-4620. Telephone (718) 729-8866.

PROMISING PRACTICES

Sulphur Springs Elementary School: Tampa, Florida

When Principal Stephanie Moffitt arrived in 1984 at this pre-kindergarten to sixth-grade school of close to 800 students—95 percent of whom were eligible for free or reduced-price lunch—she found a school building that was uninviting to both children and staff.

Students fought frequently and brought weapons into the school. Staff arrived in the morning to find empty alcohol bottles, needles, and other drug paraphernalia in the schoolyard. During the day, people with questionable purposes would cut through the schoolyard, bang on windows, or try to enter the school.

Principal Moffitt realized her first order of business was to create a warm, safe, and calm learning environment—an environment that welcomed students and staff, encouraged them to learn together, and conveyed the message that school was an important place. She recognized that children—particularly those disadvantaged by society—required an array of support services to enable them to engage in meaningful learning activity. Children who are hungry, cold, angry, sad, or frightened do not learn well. As Principal Moffitt emphasizes: "The world of violence touches children so tremendously here. Barely a week goes by when some child's family member is not killed or arrested or traumatized in some manner." School staff also recognized that home and school are intimately intertwined—that supporting a child's learning requires supporting the family, as well.

Working with her staff, Moffitt prepared an inventory of the major problems that existed at the school. Statistics were gathered as support. She then met with a group of district-level administrators and members of the superintendent's staff to present her findings along with possible solutions.

On the basis of this information, district-level administrators developed a plan for presentation to the school board designed to provide assistance, not only to Sulphur Springs, but to all schools in Hillsborough County with an enrollment of free or reduced-price lunch students in excess of 90 percent. Board members, aware of the problems at Sulphur Springs and other at-risk schools in the district, supported the plan wholeheartedly.

Among the services now provided as a result of the Sulphur Springs' initiative:

- Fourth through sixth graders who are not achieving to their potential—often because of family and attendance difficulties—are placed in smaller classes with ongoing guidance services; each class has eighteen to twenty students with a teacher's aide and a teacher; the guidance counselor regularly provides whole class, small group, and individual guidance services in the classroom, consults with the teachers, and is available for children in crisis.

- Drawing on research conclusions that children who are read to frequently are better readers, Assistant Principal Cathy Valdes arranged for 75 to 100 high school students to come into the school twice a week to read to first graders; sixth graders also serve as first-grade tutors.
- Because strong self-esteem is crucial to learning, the school has instituted a daily guidance program implemented by teachers called "Positive Action" to build children's self-esteem and teach them how to make informed decisions and resolve conflicts peacefully. According to Assistant Principal Cathy Valdes, the program "teaches children how to get along with others and how to take care of themselves"; every child in every classroom begins every day with Positive Action activities; teachers at every grade level follow common units and a schoolwide assembly culminates each unit.

As the result of a separate federal grant, additional services were also made available:

- To maintain strong relationships with families, home teachers, guidance counselors, a school nurse, and a social worker make frequent home visits; classroom teachers are also encouraged to visit students' homes; according to Principal Moffitt, the school wants to convey a message to families that, "If you need help tell us—we may not be able to fix your problem, but we can find someone to help." By the 1990 to 1991 school year, services have expanded to include home teaching, parent job training, and workshops for parents to strengthen the home/school connection.
- Working with the parents in their homes, home teachers help them to integrate learning into routine home activities; for example, they may show how setting the table or helping with the laundry can be turned into a learning game for children.
- Parent workshops focus on helping parents to support their children's education at home and in school; for example, one workshop—"Video To Go"—explained the school's video learning library to parents and showed how education videos could be used to teach their children; parents can sign out the videos to use at home; equipment is also available to borrow.

In addition to the workshops, four parents receive paid training to become child care specialists. Throughout the year they provide child care for parents during the workshops. At the end of the training, they can become licensed child care specialists qualified to work at daycare centers or as teacher's aides in the public school system.

The school strives to provide comprehensive pre-school services to the community. It has three Head Start classes and one pre-kindergarten class serving approximately eighty children. The pre-kindergarten class is designed to provide daycare for working parents by operating from 7 a.m. to 5 p.m. daily, including during school vacations.

One of the first benefits the school received was the addition of a full-time nurse who visits with families in their homes to help them meet their children's health needs. The nurse also meets with families of children who have chronic health problems, who may be resistant to sending children to school because of fears for their safety. She reassures them that their children are safe and stresses the importance of regular school attendance. Because the nurse can appropriately diagnose the severity of a child's medical problem, she is often able to keep children in school who would previously have been sent home.

Freed from addressing children's health problems after the school nurse was added to the staff, the school's social worker, Pat Crosby, is now able to focus her efforts on providing other needed services to families. She works closely with families of children with poor attendance, visiting them in their homes frequently, and is available, along with the school's two guidance counselors, to deal with the children's numerous crises. She also serves as a consultant to the teachers. She meets with individual students or visits families at their request and frequently provides suggestions for helping children to cope in classroom settings. She is also involved in evaluating students for exceptional education placements.

While the school recognizes that home and school are intimately intertwined, providing a full array of services to families to support their children's education is not an easy task. Funding is a constant concern. This year, because the state is struggling financially, the school lost a day of nursing services. Principal Moffitt and other staff continue aggressively to seek grant funding to support their work. Not overextending an already stretched staff is a continual balancing act. An open-door policy, a tradition of working together collaboratively, and a willingness to share the load during crises all act to reduce stress. As social worker Pat Crosby points out: "There are a lot of pressure valves here because of the personalities. We get support from each other. We laugh and that helps us to keep things in perspective."

School staff share a commitment to serving children disadvantaged by society and a vision of quality education. They work to reconnect the home with the school by breaking the pattern of families experiencing schools as places that are uncaring and failing. They strive to work with families to provide or connect them with services and to build the skills needed to enable them to support and promote their children's learning.

Principal Moffitt concludes: "All children have a right to a quality education. If society does not take the responsibility to ensure that children—especially disadvantaged children—get above and beyond what they need to reach their potential, then society will pay a price. Our children are good and bright, but open and wounded. I believe we can help them rise above poverty. We can show them that education can make a difference. But to do so, families need to believe that the school cares. We need to give children the message: 'Listen to the people at school because they care about you.'"

For further information, please contact: Ms. Stephanie Moffitt, Sulphur Springs Elementary School, 8412 North 13th Street, Tampa, FL 33604.

Current Research Related to Topics Discussed in Chapter Five

Unmet psychological, emotional, and social needs can undermine learning and create behavior problems in the classroom **(Comer, 1985; Dweck, 1986; National Association for the Education of Young Children [NAEYC], 1988; Robinson and Mastny, 1989).** These behavior problems inevitably divert teacher and class time away from academics onto discipline issues. The American Association for Counseling and Development's Task Force on a Nation at Risk stresses that "personal and social competency must necessarily precede, as well as accompany, academic competency" ***(as summarized by* Glosoff and Koprowicz, 1990, p.1).** For students, discipline problems can lead to a cycle of suspensions, poor attendance, and further negative behaviors. Resulting academic difficulties undermine students' academic progress, leading to grade retention and increased likelihood of dropping out of school **(Hess, 1986; Lloyd, 1976; Safer, 1986).**

Students' Changing Needs

Students' development is increasingly threatened by an almost overwhelming array of challenges which are not limited to urban areas but transcend economic lines and geographical boundaries **(Shedlin, Klopf, and Zaret, 1988):** more than 60 percent of mothers with children under fourteen years of age and more than 50 percent with children under one year of age are in the labor force; more than one-third of all children under eighteen years of age are not living with both biological parents, and nearly 3,000 American children become children of divorce every day; almost one-third of all children are considered "latchkey kids" **(Children's Defense Fund, 1990).** More than two million children, with an average age of seven years, were reported abused and neglected in 1986. By 1990, this amounted to an American child being abused or neglected every forty-seven seconds **(Children's Defense Fund, 1990).**

Almost three-quarters of all children and youth have experimented with drugs in some form; since 1960, the delinquency rates of youth aged ten to seventeen has increased by 130 percent; every school day more than 100,000 children bring guns to school; a child drops out of school every eight seconds of the school day **(Children's Defense Fund, 1990);** more than nine million children in America have no health care; more than eighteen million have never seen a dentist; fewer than half of all pre-school children have been immunized against preventable diseases; each year, more than half a million teens give birth—two-thirds of these teens are White, do not live in the inner cities, and are not poor. Four hundred thousand teenagers have abortions each year ***(cited in* Shedlin, Klopf, and Zaret, 1988).** Between January 1989 and February 1990, AIDS cases among thirteen- to nineteen-year-olds increased by 40 percent **(Glosoff and Koprowicz, 1990).** Every day, six teenagers commit suicide **(Children's Defense Fund, 1990).**

Although problems such as these affect children regardless of their economic status, poverty exacerbates their impact. Lack of affordable housing, inability to provide basic food and clothing, and lack of affordable health care creates formidable barriers for poor children.

The problem of child poverty in America has reached crisis proportions. One out of five American children is raised in a family in which she or he will suffer basic deprivations as a result of poverty **(Chafel, 1990).** Twelve million American children are in poverty. Although child poverty has dropped from a peak of more than 22 percent in 1983 to about 20 percent, it still exceeds rates of the 1970s, even at the height of that decade's recession **(Sege, 1989).** Children living in families with incomes less than half the poverty rate, the poorest of the poor, have increased by 66 percent in the last ten years **(Sege, 1989).** Poverty kills an American child every fifty-three minutes ***(cited in* Shedlin, Klopf, and Zaret; 1988).**

Although poverty has surged, the "safety net" of programs to assist the poor has diminished. Congressional investigation reveals that safety-net programs do not reach the majority of families in need, are not in effect where child poverty is greatest, and reach fewer children now than in the past. The weakening impact of government programs to alleviate poverty has been a critical factor in the climbing poverty rate. One-third of the poverty increase between 1979 and 1986 has been traced to the diminished effects of cash benefit programs (Social Security, unemployment, Aid to Families with Dependent Children). Other researchers attribute 54 percent of the increase in poverty to government cuts, when non-cash benefits (food stamps, subsidized housing, Medicaid) are taken into account **(Chafel, 1990).**

Poverty extends beyond single mothers and their children. Almost 40 percent of children in poverty live in two-parent homes, many with at least one working parent **(Sege, 1989).** The working poor account for the majority of families with children living in poverty. These families include more than two million American children **(Chafel, 1990).**

Minority children are particular victims of child poverty. Half of America's African American children are poor, as are one-third of Latino children. Three-quarters of Black children in America can expect to spend at least part of their first ten years in poverty. More than half can expect to spend at least four years in poverty. Almost a third will spend at least seven of their first ten years in poverty **(Sege, 1989).**

The Role of School Staff

Elementary school classroom teachers are expected to understand issues related to the social and emotional development of their students **(Commission on Pre-college Guidance and Counseling, 1986; *Harvard Education Letter,* 1988).** The quantity and quality of child development training received by elementary teachers varies significantly.

Given this variability in the level and quality of child development training, it is not surprising that teachers' responses to counseling and support service needs differ considerably. Some teachers perceive their role as strictly limited to academic and pedagogical areas. Others recognize the impact of broader needs on academic performance, but do not feel they possess the skills or knowledge to meet those needs. Even teachers who are quite conscious of student needs and make every effort to respond may be limited by available resources and support **(Comer, 1985; Commission on Pre-college Guidance and Counseling, 1986; *Harvard Education Letter,* 1988).**

As of 1990, all states had some counselors in their elementary schools, twelve states mandated elementary school counselors, and twelve other states were considering such mandates **(Glosoff and Koprowicz, 1990).** Counselors who do work in elementary schools generally face the same problems that plague middle school or high school counselors: overwhelming caseloads that range up to several hundred students over the recommended ratios of between 50 to 1 and 300 to 1 **(Commission on Pre-college Guidance and Counseling, 1986);** vague and ill-defined roles and responsibilities with little guidance regarding goals and objectives; responsibility to fulfill a number of non-counseling administrative functions involving scheduling, attendance, test administration, supervision, discipline, and record-keeping **(*Harvard Education Letter,* 1988).**

Perhaps most relevant to elementary counseling issues, studies find that the amount of time counselors spend counseling depends largely on the affluence and education level of the community. This is true of college counseling in secondary schools, which occupied more than half the time of 40 percent of counselors in upper-income schools compared with 6 percent of the counselors in low-income communities. A similar disparity based on income occurs for career counseling and academic counseling **(*Harvard Education Letter,* 1988).**

Counselors also spend little time reaching out to parents. One survey revealed that only 10 percent of counselors had consulted with even one-third of their students' families **(*Harvard Education Letter,* 1988).** This is particularly significant in light of evidence that shows that parental expectations of students' post-graduate futures shape students' aspirations and achievement throughout their school-age years **(Commission on Pre-college Guidance and Counseling, 1986; *Harvard Education Letter,* 1988; Humes and Hohenshil, 1987; Podemski and Childers, 1987).**

School counselors are trained in a variety of skills including group counseling, family therapy, individual assessment, and placement and referral. Increasingly, researchers and advocacy groups are recognizing the importance of expanding these services in elementary schools. In 1986, the College Board recommended that comprehensive school counseling programs be established for grades K through 12. At the same time, a similar resolution was passed by the National School Board Association **(Glosoff and Koprowicz, 1990).**

In Florida, reading underachievers advanced 1.1 years in seven months a few years after counselors were hired. Children participating in special counseling groups geared for children of divorced parents showed improved school performance. Students in a group for procrastinators showed significant improvement in homework completion. And a group of fourth graders in one study showed no immediate, significant improvement over the control group after being counseled; but as high school seniors, these students showed significant differences in class rank over students not counseled. In addition, the U.S. Office of Education discovered 47 percent fewer dropouts and 50 percent fewer failures in schools where there are acceptable student/counselor ratios. Other studies further document counseling programs' positive impact on school achievement, attendance, and dropout rates **(*as cited by* Glosoff and Koprowicz, 1990).**

Evidence of academic improvement due to counseling programs is coupled with evidence of emotional and behavioral improvement. An evaluation of counseling centers in San Diego showed that the centers produced an 80 to 90 percent dropoff in suspensions and referrals to the principal. A peer facilitation program in which trained fifth graders worked with second and third graders had a positive effect on the younger students' behaviors and attitudes. Intervention also effectively lowered aggression and hostility among students identified as unusually hostile by their teachers **(*as cited by* Glosoff and Koprowicz, 1990).**

Prevention vs. Remediation

Traditionally, efforts to address elementary school guidance and support services have employed a remediation model, where needs and problems are dealt with in a reactive manner as they arise **(*Harvard Education Letter,* 1988; Melville and Blank, 1991; Podemski and Childers, 1987).** Many question the effectiveness of such a strategy, both in impact and use of resources, suggesting a more preventive approach **(American School Counselor Association [ASCA], 1981; Commission on Pre-college Guidance and Counseling, 1986; Podemski and Childers, 1987; Sheeley and Jenkins, 1985).**

A prevention model emphasizes identification of normal developmental concerns and creation of strategies to either address concerns before problems develop or detect problems in their earliest stages.

Prevention strategies focus on group rather than individual work and emphasize consultation and training activities, enhanced attention to community linkages, and efficient sharing of information **(ASCA, 1981; Commission on Pre-college Guidance and Counseling, 1986;** ***Harvard Education Letter,*** **1988; Melville and Blank, 1991; Podemski and Childers, 1987).** Group work acknowledges the intense impact of peer influence on the development of young people. Groups offer a safe place for students to receive peer and adult feedback and to practice interpersonal skills **(Glosoff and Koprowicz, 1990).** Group work may also be a more efficient use of counselor time, as it allows the counselor to interact with many students at once **(Humes and Hohenshil, 1987; Podemski and Childers, 1987; Sheeley and Jenkins, 1985).** Counselors can also maximize their resources by training children to serve as peer helpers. Since children identify strongly with their peer group, properly trained peer facilitators can effectively reach other children and assist them or refer them to adult help **(Glosoff and Koprowicz, 1990).**

Counselors in a prevention-oriented program are likely to visit classrooms to address important emotional and developmental concerns with young students through special activities. Typically, classroom guidance activities concern such issues as self-understanding, decision-making and conflict resolution skills, substance abuse prevention, appreciation of cultural and racial diversity, and divorce **(Glosoff and Koprowicz, 1990).**

Elementary school counselors or other school personnel can also create supportive learning environments for young students by initiating mentor programs in elementary schools. Partnerships between young children and adults—or even between younger and older children—may dramatically improve self-esteem and prevent dropping out and other self-destructive behaviors. A survey by Big Brothers/Big Sisters of Greater Miami indicated that mentors and their parents overwhelmingly agree that mentoring has improved the self-esteem of mentored students, increased school performance, improved family, peer, and teacher relationships, and increased involvement in cultural and educational activities. Advocates of mentoring programs suggest that matching children with mentors of similar cultural and economic backgrounds contributes to the effectiveness of the partnership **(Project PLUS and the ASPIRA Association, 1990).**

The positive effects of early intervention/prevention programs on children's academic success are clearly documented, and undoubtedly speak to the effects of these programs both on the children's acquisition of academic skills and on the development of their social/emotional well-being.

Pre-school education for "disadvantaged" children was found in the 1960s to result in a temporary (three- or four-year) elevation in test scores, and a more enduring elevation in overall school competence—only 30 percent of pre-school-enrolled children were retained in grade as opposed to 45 percent of children who were not enrolled. A study of 123 children over the course of sixteen years concluded that their enrollment in a pre-school program resulted in more of them completing high school, more going on to college or occupational education, more holding jobs, more being satisfied with their work, fewer being classified as mentally retarded, fewer being arrested, and fewer receiving public assistance **(*as cited in* Schorr, 1988).** These data suggest that support and enrichment services for young children before they enter school or in their first years of school may profoundly improve their life chances. Unfortunately, despite strong evidence of the effectiveness of early intervention, programs in this area reach only a fraction of the children who need them. Head Start, for example, reaches fewer than 20 percent of the 2.5 million children who are eligible **(Chafel, 1990).**

These prevention strategies provide several advantages over the traditional remedial approach. Because they anticipate rather than just respond to existing problems, the prevention approach is likely to be more cost-effective in both the short-run and the long-run. Researchers note that the resources and energy of remediation workers tend to be swallowed up by crisis intervention, which benefits only a small portion of the student population. Students who do not fall into extreme behaviors, and thereby do not become candidates for crisis intervention, may nonetheless be showing symptoms of distress, perhaps masked as shyness, arrogance, moodiness, or oversensitivity. All students, no matter how—or if—their troubles manifest themselves, can benefit from prevention and early intervention work **(Commission on Pre-college Guidance and Counseling, 1986; Glosoff and Koprowicz, 1990).**

School/Community Linkages

When elementary schools draw on resources of community-based organizations (CBOs), they do so primarily to serve special needs students. The potential exists to expand such partnerships, employing the resources of CBOs to address a greater range of student needs. Specifically,
staff from CBOs could be asked to provide: direct services to students to help meet counseling and support needs; education and training programs to improve and refine staff skills in identifying and responding to student counseling and support needs; and general advice and support for specific teachers **(First, *et al.*, 1988; *Harvard Education Letter,* 1988; Olsen, 1988; Orum, 1988; Podemski and Childers, 1987).** Interagency initiatives are endorsed by many student advocates, including the broad-based Education and Human Services Consortium, as a critical means of maximizing support resources for children. These collaborations maximize resources by pooling a broad range of expertise and services and by creating a shared financial base that combines the funds of several institutions **(Melville and Blank, 1991).**

The ultimate goal of school/community linkages ought to be collaboration; cooperation, as a first step in creating a more effective service-delivery system, is an important initial goal. **Atelia I. Melville and Martin J. Blank (1991),** writing for the Education and Human Services Consortium, point out that cooperation involves coordinating existing services without substantially altering those services. This creates a "neater," more effective support network for children and their families. But coordination alone does not adequately offset existing services' emphasis on remediation, nor fill gaps left by existing services. Collaborations involve defining a new set of common goals that reach beyond each agency's specific mandate to address concerns affecting all participating agencies. Collaboration means pooling resources, planning and implementing new services jointly, and sharing responsibility for outcomes **(Melville and Blank, 1991).**

Many factors can inhibit collaborations. Among these are: competitiveness; cynicism about the benefits of sharing; lack of shared leadership; inflexibility in scheduling and procedures; lack of mutual understanding between schools and community agencies; time constraints; lack of an open and inclusive participation ethic; and prescribing actions for the partnership instead of allowing players to shape their own decisions over time **(Robinson and Mastny, 1989).**

Recommendations for successful collaborations include: keep channels of communication open between schools and agencies; learn how the various partners in the collaboration operate, what their needs are, and what they perceive their roles to be; be clear on the goals of the collaboration and the role that each agency is to play in achieving these goals; follow through on commitments to hold meetings, perform tasks, or deliver services; pay attention to details such as recording and disseminating minutes of meetings; involve staff at all levels of the various agencies in joint planning and implementation **(Melville and Blank, 1991; Robinson and Mastny, 1989).**

Glosoff and Koprowicz (1990) discuss five coordination roles that a counselor must perform inside and outside the school, as suggested by the Virginia School Counselors Association:

1. Coordinate the use of school and community resources in collaboration with other team members.
2. Assist parents in gaining access to services their children need—for example, a child psychologist or a local housing agency— through a referral and follow-up process.
3. Serve as a liaison between the school, home and community agencies so that efforts to help students are successful and reinforced rather than duplicated.
4. Plan, coordinate, and evaluate the guidance program's effectiveness.
5. Coordinate the school's testing program, which usually includes interpreting test results to parents, students, and school personnel.

The burdens on schools to meet the needs of young people are overwhelming. Retired New York City Family Court Judge Nanette Dembitz points out, "There is virtually no recognition of a shared social responsibility for the well-being of our children" **(Shedlin, Klopf, and Zaret, 1988).** School/community linkages are essential. "Stretching" the current counseling staff adequately to fulfill prevention and early intervention mandates at the lower grades is not feasible. Counselors must serve as liaisons with outside agencies in order to expand the resources available to the school **(*Harvard Education Letter,* 1988).**

Multidisciplinary Teams

Effective communication and coordination between academic programs and student support services can strengthen both components. One mechanism for such communication and coordination is the creation of multidisciplinary teams made up of classroom teachers, in-school and out-of-school counselors, and other specialists **(Comer, 1985; Podemski and Childers, 1987).**

These teams can fulfill a wide variety of roles by: serving as forums for open discussions of the strengths and weaknesses of students; providing specific and detailed advice to teachers dealing with non-academic student needs; and improving staff training to identify and respond to student support service needs. By incorporating representatives familiar with both academic and social service needs, teams encourage a mix of comments and perceptions that reflect a wide variety of approaches and perspectives **(Comer, 1985; Commission on Pre-college Guidance and Counseling, 1986; Podemski and Childers, 1987).**

Additionally, inclusion of special education teachers on multidisciplinary teams can reduce premature or inappropriate referrals of students to special education programs.

Multicultural Counseling

The need for cultural sensitivity and linguistic accessibility in developing and instituting counseling and other support services often goes unmet. Neither classroom teachers nor support service personnel receive extensive schooling or training to help them understand and react to the influence of racial, cultural, and ethnic diversity on guidance and counseling efforts. Few trained bilingual support service staff with the required primary language skills are available to provide the comprehensive services needed by many language minority students, especially recently arrived immigrants. The inevitable cultural difference between a predominately White middle-class staff and low-income, minority, or immigrant students can create significant barriers to the effective identification and provision of support service needs **(Banks, 1988; First, *et al.,* 1988; Lightfoot, 1981; Olsen, 1988).** Counselors' activities can help by encouraging: student and staff acceptance of differences; school policies and behaviors that resist stereotyping; scrutinization of testing programs for bias; and outreach to parents and families of students from other cultures **(Glosoff and Koprowczi, 1990).**

Partnerships with CBOs can help schools address some of these issues, particularly for limited-English-proficient and immigrant students. These agencies often have closer ties to minority and immigrant communities, helping to resolve barriers of language, culture, and life experience. Unfortunately, schools generally have not taken advantage of assistance offered by these agencies **(First, *et al.*, 1988; Olsen, 1988; Orum, 1988).**

A Comprehensive Approach

A Special Commission on Pre-college Guidance and Counseling (1986) assembled by the College Board found counseling and guidance programs in public schools to be generally in a state of disrepair. They found counseling staff to be frequently misused and observed a particular lack of services for those most in need. They also noted that most efforts at school reform have failed to address this aspect of schooling. The commission offered the following recommendations for action by school districts:

- Establish a broad-based process in each local school district for determining the particular guidance and counseling needs of the students within each school and for planning how to meet those needs.
- Develop a program under each school principal that emphasizes the importance of the guidance counselor as a monitor and promoter of student potential, as well as coordinator of the school's guidance plan.
- Mount programs to inform and involve parents and other members of the family influential in the choices, plans, decisions, and learning activities of the student.
- Provide a program of guidance and counseling during the early and middle years of schooling, especially for students who traditionally have not been well served by schools.
- Strengthen collaboration among schools, community agencies, colleges, businesses, and other community resources to enhance services available to students.
- Establish a process in each state to determine the guidance and counseling needs of specific student populations and give support to local initiatives that address these needs.
- Revise the training of school counselors to include the specific skills and knowledge necessary to enable them to take a more central role in schools.

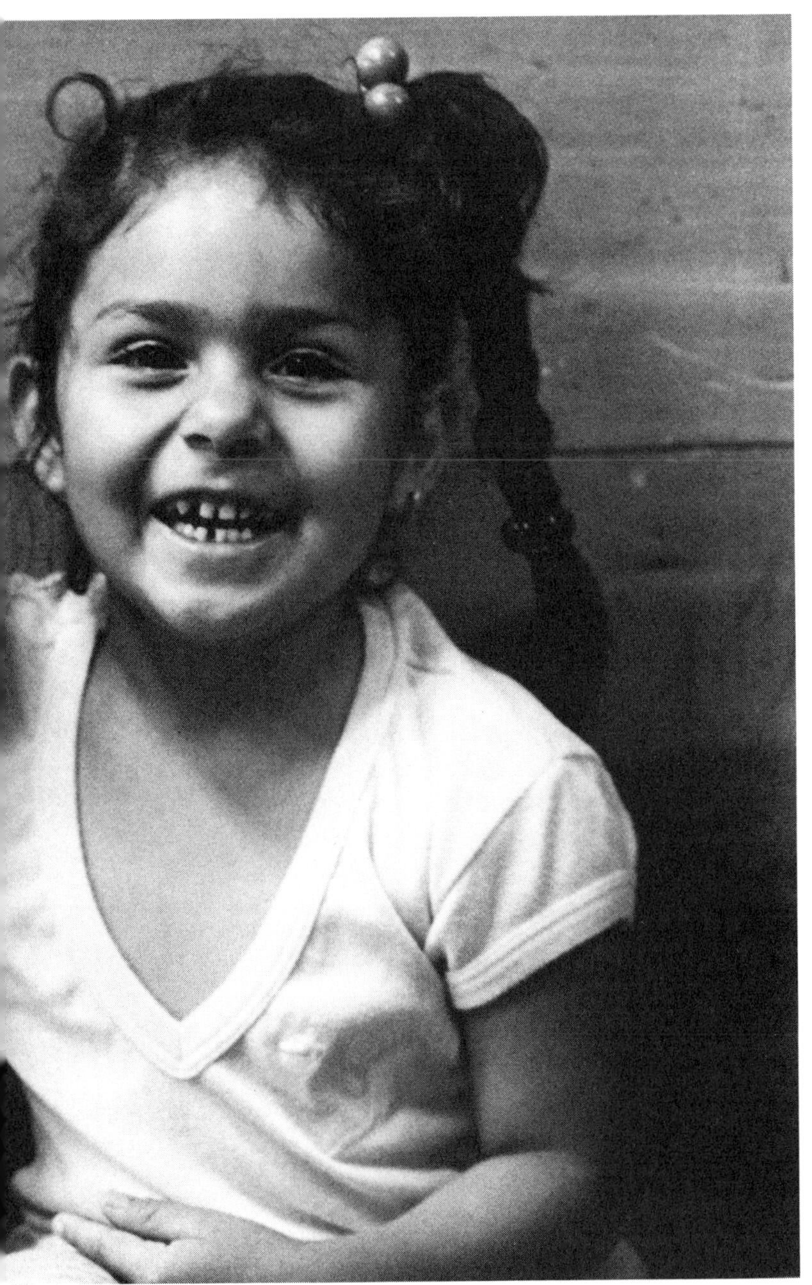

6 School Climate

Children are entitled to attend schools that are safe, attractive, and free of prejudice. Children are entitled to attend school unless they pose a danger to other children or school staff.

A Vision of School Climate at the Good Common School

Phyllis Walker, principal of the Good Common School, shows John Kramer into her office and closes the door. They maneuver past a row of open book cartons to a small sofa; a table commandeered from a kindergarten classroom holds a thermos and mugs. Phyllis sinks into the sofa, props her feet against the edge of the table, and smiles ruefully before offering the usual lament of school principals in autumn,

> "IF I EVER GET THIS SCHOOL GOING,
> I'LL NEVER CLOSE IT AGAIN!"

John, a member of a local university's education faculty, has come to the school in response to a phone call from Phyllis last evening. She had sounded weary, but quickly got to the point. "It's mid-October. The whole school should be settled down by now, but it isn't. As you know, we have about 600 students here who are taught in three separate educational units. House One, which started internal restructuring three years ago under a collaborative arrangement with the university, is in good shape. Houses Two and Three have serious problems. Will you help me think about how to work on this?"

As John and Phyllis exchange pleasantries, a secretary bursts into the room. Two fourth-grade boys just had a fight in the bathroom. Jonathan got a bloodied nose and a cut on the forehead before a teacher intervened. As the teacher escorted the boys to the principal's office, young Ramón yelled, "I'm going home!"— then dashed out the school's front door.

John waits for fifteen minutes while Phyllis phones Ramón's mother to tell her in beginner's Spanish that her son is on the way home, tends to the injured boy with help from the school nurse, escorts him to his classroom, explains the situation to the classroom teachers of both children, and returns to her office. Phyllis takes a moment, then launches into an explanation of the problem.

> *"We have a more diverse student population this year than ever before—which means the district's new admissions criteria are operating as intended. The student body is 11 percent Southeast Asian—mostly Khmer-speaking—19 percent Latino, 53 percent African American, and 17 percent Anglo. There are also a few Haitian children. These numbers reflect the makeup of the district as a whole quite accurately.*
>
> *"On the other hand, our faculty is 76 percent Anglo, 17 percent African American, and 7 percent Latino. We have some Khmer-speaking aides and one Haitian parent volunteer who helps us with translations.*

"Our next challenge is to turn ourselves into a multicultural community. Except for House One, we have a long way to go. What concerns me most is the large number of incidents that have occurred between students from different racial and language groups. I know it takes time to develop a positive social climate, but I'm worried some children are developing negative attitudes toward school. To tell the truth, I can't say I blame them. But I don't want low-grade negativity to turn into world-class alienation.

"If the current tension level lasts much longer, I worry that some youngsters will start missing school, or come in, but turn off in class. When the kids turn off, the teachers expect much less. Given a little time, that can turn into teacher pressure for grade retention. I can't allow that. You and I both know over-age kids are most likely to drop out.

"There is a lot going on because we now receive children from a much larger and more complex community. Our school's catchment area contains many small ethnic enclaves where adults with similar cultural and language backgrounds interact without conflict. But children from all of those enclaves come together here. As the result, we have greater potential for conflict.

"Some students single out individual teachers for hostility; some of it, in all honesty, is deserved. I've overheard teachers speak to students in ways that are very disrespectful.

"Then there's the "turfism" in the teacher's lounge— tensions between Anglo and African American teachers. Some of the African American teachers expect me automatically to side with them; they forget I'm responsible to the whole community. The Latino teachers have a tendency to stick together and go their own way. Again, House One is an exception. Those teachers have learned how important it is to support each other.

"You and I both know that fundamental school restructuring is the long-range solution to these problems. Under direction of the new school council, we have more changes underway in this school than I would have believed possible. But implementation takes time. Until then, we have to do something to ease the tension."

Suddenly self-conscious, Phyllis stops. Then she shakes her head and says, "John, I'm sorry to unload on you this way—." John shakes his head in amusement and responds: "I'm not surprised you need to unload. From what you've told me, it seems as though a lot of folks around here need to do the same thing. Have you thought of doing a school climate survey so everyone can get their issues on the table?" He explains how information generated by a school climate survey usually suggests ways to improve the quality of daily life in a school building.

"When people own a problem," he concludes, "they're much more likely to participate in its solution. When we do climate surveys, solutions usually get framed as recommendations that respond to the problems identified by the people interviewed. Recommendations are targeted toward the part of the school community with the power to fix a particular problem. We use staff development, parent workshops, and student leadership development activities to shore up implementation of the recommendations."

John has Phyllis's full attention, which pleases him. Some principals find the thought of a climate survey personally threatening. He thinks this is because school principals usually try to control and manage negative attitudes, while school surveys invite the expression of attitudes, negative or positive. It isn't surprising that building administrators sometimes get overwhelmed. The other day a superintendent asked him to do a school climate survey in a particular building and John declined. He was afraid the superintendent wanted to use the data to support firing the principal. He refused to be involved because he didn't want to see a good process abused.

For twenty minutes, John and Phyllis make concrete plans. Phyllis must present the proposal to the school council; she has little doubt that it will be approved. A respected chairperson must be found for a parent/teacher/student committee to identify issues to be included on survey questionnaires. The school will hire John as a consultant to manage the process. He will recruit university students to conduct interviews. He will reserve for himself the tasks of analyzing survey data, preparing recommendations, and writing a final report to be shared with everyone in the school community.

Three days in early January are identified for interviewing. John estimates it will take about a month to analyze data and prepare the survey report. As John gets up, Phyllis wishes aloud they were at the end of the process rather than the beginning. John suggests her announcement of the survey by itself will have a "cooling" effect. He reminds her to describe the process in detail to teachers during a faculty meeting and visit each homeroom to talk with students.

• • •

True to form, the Good Common School Council is enthusiastic about the proposal. Charles Williams, a seasoned parent activist widely respected for his performance on the council, will chair the project committee. Williams will identify three other parent members, the faculty will designate an equal number of teachers, and two sixth-grade members of the student council will be invited to participate.

The primary responsibility of the project committee is to identify problem areas to be probed during the structured interviews. A large sample of parents, all faculty and non-teaching staff, and a cross-section of students will be interviewed. When John meets with Charles Williams, Charles suggests John's role during the early phase of the process should include attending meetings of the committee, recording identified problems, and constructing questionnaires.

• • •

Two weeks later, John returns to the school for the first committee meeting. He can tell at a glance the committee represents most of the school community's racial and language groups. Charles explains the purpose of the survey and outlines the proposed process. He then suggests the group use a brainstorming process to identify issues. Committee members should call out issues as they come to mind; there will be no discussion or criticism at this time. John will record each issue as it is suggested.

Twenty minutes into the brainstorming session, the group is going strong. Some comments by parents have made the teachers on the committee squirm, but Charles chairs the session firmly, using humor to lighten heavy moments. The two students participate enthusiastically. Some adult members are surprised that the students identify hall and cafeteria chaos as a major problem.

At the end of a half hour, more than fifty individual issues have been identified. Charles ends the brainstorming session by suggesting John use the list of issues to draft preliminary questions for separate questionnaires to be used in interviews with parents, teachers, non-teaching staff, and students. John agrees to bring draft questionnaires to the committee's next session for discussion. The meeting is adjourned. Charles notes with satisfaction that the group met its goal of completing its business within an hour.

The next three committee meetings are spent fine-tuning questionnaires, settling on a process for selecting the sample of students to be surveyed, and developing schedules for interviewing students and teachers. The survey's design is also finalized.

Equal numbers of students from each grade will be interviewed. Different questionnaires will be used for primary and intermediate students. Although the content of questions won't change, the wording will.

Additionally, interviewers will randomly administer a "short form" of the questionnaire to as many other students as possible on the playground and in the cafeteria during lunch breaks. This will generate a larger pool of data and give more students a stake in the process, increasing the likelihood they will support needed changes during implementation.

Each teacher will be interviewed in a screened-off area of the teacher's lounge during his or her planning period, according to a schedule developed by the principal and circulated to all teachers. A similar schedule will be developed for non-teaching personnel, most of whom will be interviewed at their workstations.

At a fourth meeting in the first week of January, the committee plans how to maximize parent involvement in the survey. Ultimately, two strategies were selected. A "short form" of the parent survey instrument will be sent home with all students along with a cover letter explaining the process signed by the school principal and committee chairperson. The letter will request parents to complete the short form of the parent survey and return it to the committee, unsigned, by mail. Survey materials will be translated into all necessary languages. Additionally, parents will be encouraged to come to one of three neighborhood sites—or to the school—on a designated evening to be interviewed in greater depth. Translators will be present to help them participate.

• • •

Conducting the survey is a taxing business. John supervises a small fleet of graduate students who interview students individually in the library, during lunchtime in the cafeteria, and on the playground. Bilingual aides are assigned to the interviewing team.

During the afternoon of the second day, the interviewing team splits into two groups. One continues to talk with students; the other interviews teachers during their planning periods. During the evening, the team splits into three separate groups, fanning out to neighborhood sites where parents participate in structured interviews.

At the survey's end, John carries all of the completed questionnaires back to his office. With the help of an assistant who does data entry, he conducts a computer analysis using a statistical software package. Once all data are entered, the sorting, tabulating, and graphing are quickly completed.

The survey's findings suggest a number of recommendations. As each recommendation is drafted, John notes which individual or group in the school community has the power to implement it. Thus, some recommendations are directed to teachers, some to parents, others to students, and still others to the principal.

John knows some people will resist making changes, but he expects the power of the data to triumph over resistance. Student interviews have yielded especially strong, and sometimes poignant, information. As he works with the data collected from students, John wonders once more why schools are so reluctant to survey students—kids can be both perceptive and eloquent.

• • •

On Thursday evening, the cafeteria is nearly filled as Charles Williams moves to the podium to introduce John, who will present the survey's findings and recommendations. A group of teachers sit together in the back row; Phyllis Walker is seated alone in the front row, to the right. As he looks out over the audience, Charles is pleased to see a good mix of Anglo, Latino, African American, and Asian faces; all sectors of the community appear well represented. A sprinkling of older students is present, as well.

John uses a slide projector to display computer-generated graphics. Parent data is shared first. Among the highlights:

- Fifty-nine percent of parents worry about the safety of their children when en route to the school;
- Seventy-one percent of parents believe anti-racism training should be provided to students and faculty.

Next he presents highlights of the parent data broken out by race and ethnicity:

- Khmer-speaking parents are united in their view that the school must strengthen its linkages with immigrant community-based organizations and community-based social service providers to allow Cambodian children improved access to physical and mental health services in their own language.
- A majority of Spanish-speaking parents are worried that premature transition of their children from bilingual to monolingual English classrooms will result in academic failure and loss of the child's first language and culture; additionally, they are concerned with disrespectful treatment of some Latino students, especially those who are recent immigrants, by other students and teachers.
- African American parents urge greater efforts to ensure that students are physically safe en route to school and at school. They also want school personnel to demonstrate greater sensitivity to the complex problems young children face daily in their communities. They want their children to be treated respectfully and want the same treatment themselves.
- Anglo parents worry that changes under discussion at the school to achieve greater equity—especially detracking—might undercut the academic progress of their children.

Next, John displays staff data:

- A majority of teachers say they are frustrated by student behavior, which they describe as "out of control," especially in common areas, such as halls, corridors and the cafeteria.
- Most teachers want smaller classes and more opportunities to team teach and work with paraprofessional aides so students can receive more individualized instruction.
- Some teachers want a "tougher" stance on student discipline by the school administration; others request opportunities to improve their own classroom management skills.

John then summarizes student concerns, many of which cross racial and ethnic lines; some echo adults' concerns. For example:

- A majority of students say they sometimes feel afraid en route to school or home. A smaller number report they have felt fearful at school at least once during this school year.
- Students of all groups complain that being pushed in hallways feels unpleasant and high noise levels in the cafeteria diminish their appetites and cause headaches.
- A significant minority indicate that name calling, threats, and fights en route to school or at school have produced feelings of helplessness, humiliation, and anger that interfere with concentration at school.
- Sixty percent of African American male students report they experience discriminatory treatment from adults and/or other students one to three times a week.
- A majority of students of all ages and groups ask to be treated with greater respect by teachers and other adults.

As he speaks, John is aware of the large audience's silence. He sees relief on many student faces. Some adults look angry; others seem defensive. Because he has been through this process many times before, he is not surprised by the tension. In fact, he expects it. That's why he placed a "no-fail" tension-breaker in his briefcase last night.

At the conclusion of his presentation, John tells the audience: "I brought something to show you before we break for refreshments. When we come back, we'll talk about how to transform this school into the kind of place where folks have so much fun that they don't want to leave at the end of the day."

As he says "fun", he flashes on the screen a vacation picture of himself grinning broadly as he displays a large string of trout; a summer-blue Minnesota lake sparkles peacefully in the background. John watches the expressions rippling across the sea of faces before him. Some students giggle at the sudden change of pace. A number of teachers, most of whom have taken his class at the university, roll their eyes heavenward. There is a sprinkling of guffaws from parents. "So far, so good," he thinks.

After the break, John briefly contrasts characteristics of a school that is a truly multicultural community with characteristics of the current climate at this school. He flashes a keynote quote from researchers Gerald Pine and Asa Hilliard (1990) on the screen, then waits as the audience reads:

> *"To become moral communities that are supportive and caring, schools need to model empathy, altruism, trust, cooperation, fairness, justice, compassion, democracy, and celebration of diversity. In schools, the quality of communal caring and the sense of community conscience are largely defined by the degree of harmony and mutual respect between White and minority groups.*
>
> *"Harmony and mutual respect are measured by how well we live the values we teach and how fully we practice the ideals to which we are committed. Caring and just schools— characterized by intervention programs to counteract racism, by diverse teaching staffs, by truly multicultural curricula, by appropriate pedagogical practices, by high expectations, and by continuing emphasis on the development of self-esteem—are essential to the achievement of genuine educational equity and to the elimination of institutional racism."*

John asks for a show of hands from those who agree that creation of a more "caring and just school" is an important goal for the Good Common School. Members of the audience raises their hands. John then flashes on the screen, one by one, a series of recommended interventions intended to lessen conflict, improve community spirit at the school, and ensure fair administration of the school discipline system:

RECOMMENDATION 1: The Good Common School Council should develop and adopt a human dignity policy declaring that behavior that insults, degrades, or stereotypes any group will not be tolerated from any segment of the school community.

RECOMMENDATION 2: The Good Common School should develop and implement an anti-bias curriculum at all grade levels, using an active approach to challenging prejudice, stereotyping, bias, and racism. This curriculum will help students develop:

- a positive self-identity;
- a capacity to interact empathically with diversity;
- the ability to think critically about bias;
- the skills for defending oneself and others in the face of injustice.

(Derman-Sparks, 1989)

RECOMMENDATION 3: The principal will set in motion a three-part process to ensure fairer administration of the school discipline system:

1. The Good Common School will request district administrators to conduct a broadly-based review of the district-wide Code of Conduct. Establishment of a task force of representatives from all racial/ethnic, language, and economic sectors of the broader community will be urged to ensure the code is appropriate for use with diverse student populations. John explains that a Code of Conduct appropriate for a diverse school has several important characteristics:

- Offenses are described in behavioral terms; those of similar severity appear in the same section of the code.
- A range of consequences is described for each group of offenses, allowing administrators to choose from a limited range of punishments appropriate in severity to the disruptive behavior; these limitations on administrative discretion mean, for example, that a student may *not* be suspended from school for a trivial offense, such as tossing an orange peel upon the library floor.
- Limitations are also established on teacher discretion in making administrative referrals; teachers are prohibited from making referrals for trivial "friction" offenses, but they *must* refer to the office any student who poses a threat to the safety of individuals or property, or who breaks a law.

2. The principal will take immediate steps to lower the number of students referred by teachers to the office for disciplinary reasons by:

- Communicating a clear expectation to all teachers that mildly disruptive incidents must be handled by them in the classrooms.
- Requiring that all administrative referrals of students for disciplinary reasons be submitted in writing; written referrals must include the race/ethnicity, gender, and handicapping condition (if any) of the student, a behavioral description of the incident relating misbehavior directly to a provision of the school code, and a written description of strategies used by the teacher to solve the problem before making an administrative referral.
- Requiring that a copy of all referrals be placed in the teacher's cumulative folder, as well as that of the student.
- Requiring that classroom management skills be included in teacher evaluations.

3. Teachers whose annual evaluations disclose high rates of administrative referrals of students for disciplinary reasons will be required to undertake additional classroom management training.

The goal of this training is to help teachers understand what schools must do to support the development of self-discipline by students. Students learn self-discipline in schools where:

- Discipline policy is an extension of an overall educational focus that teaches students skills for living in a democratic community.
- Policies and procedures are applied fairly to every member of the school community, adults and students alike.
- Standards of behavior do not change according to a student's race, sex, or economic background.
- Adults responsible for implementing rules are caring and respectful of *all* students.
- Policies and practices focus on providing structures and services that teach students new behaviors rather than just on managing, punishing, or containing misbehavior.
- School-based problems at the root of student misbehavior—whether inappropriate placement or personal conflict with an undisciplined member of the school staff—are as important a focus for change as the individual student's misbehavior.
- All members of the school community accept responsibility for dealing with their share of the problem, each asking: "What can I do to contribute to a disciplined school climate?"

RECOMMENDATION 5: To prevent the downward spiral in student engagement and academic performance often caused by out-of-school suspensions, the principal will develop a high quality in-school suspension program.

RECOMMENDATION 6: Because corporal punishment is not an effective strategy for helping students develop self-discipline and permits adult behavior that would not be tolerated from students—that is, striking others—and because it tends to be administered disproportionately to students of color, it will no longer be allowed at the Good Common School.

RECOMMENDATION 7: All groups represented at school will work to make it an inclusive community that strives to end institutional racism by eliminating the racially disparate impacts of school discipline, ability grouping, and special education placement policies.

John reminds the audience that this recommendation will require preparation of a report by the principal at the end of each semester and of the school year profiling student placement in special education, substantially separate programs, and disciplinary suspensions. The data will be disaggregated by race/ethnicity, gender, and handicapping condition, and made available to all parents in their first language.

RECOMMENDATION 8: The school council's Parent Outreach Network will assume responsibility for organizing neighborhood block groups to monitor bus stops and other places where students congregate on the way to school and en route home.

RECOMMENDATION 9: The school council will set affirmative action hiring goals for the Good Common School higher than those set by the district. The principal will develop and implement a hiring plan intended to increase the number of persons of color on the school faculty, with the result that appropriate adult role models will be provided to students of all racial and language groups.

When he finishes presenting these recommendations, John asks Principal Walker and Council Chairperson Ella Davis to join him on the podium. A vigorous forty-minute question-and-answer period follows. At its conclusion, John asks the audience to provide a show-of-hands vote in support of the entire package of recommendations. For the second time this evening, a sea of hands shoots into the air.

As they turn to leave the podium, John and Phyllis exchange relieved glances. The rest won't be easy, but it will be done.

HUMAN DIGNITY POLICY

The Board of Education, recognizing that we are a multiracial, multiethnic school district, believes it is part of our mission to provide a harmonious environment in which respect for the diverse makeup of the school community is promoted. A major aim of education in the Ferndale School District is the development of a renewed commitment to the core values of a democratic society.

In accordance with this aim, the school district will not tolerate behavior by students or staff which insults, degrades, or stereotypes any race, gender, handicap, physical condition, ethnic group, or religion.

Appropriate consequences for offending this policy will be specified in the student code of conduct of each building. Staff members offending this policy will be disciplined in accordance with provisions of the appropriate employee master agreement with the School Board.

Source: Ferndale School District, Ferndale, Michigan (1988).

DOES YOUR SCHOOL PROMOTE GOOD ATTENDANCE?

Schools with high student attendance rates:

- Regularly communicate the value of good attendance to parents, students, and teachers.
- Provide frequent rewards to students with improving and sustained attendance.
- Identify students with persistent attendance problems and know the number of students at risk because of poor attendance according to each racial and language group in the school.
- Have an attendance team or staff member designated by the principal who monitors the attendance and academic progress of vulnerable students.
- Contact parents of truant students by telephone and home visits. Contacts are made in the language of the student's home.
- Form linkages with human service organizations serving students' neighborhoods.
- Interview students about their reasons for not attending to assess students' needs for services or changes in the school program.
- Assign a staff person to work with students who return to school after prolonged absence to determine their reasons for absence and to negotiate individualized agreements for improved attendance.

Source: *Steps* (NCAS, April 1987)

TEN RULES ABOUT RULES

1. Everyone affected should have a voice in determining school rules. Language barriers to full participation should be removed.
2. Rules should be clearly stated in behavioral terms.
3. Rules should be reasonable.
4. Rules should be enforceable.
5. Rules should be easily understood.
6. Rules should be taught as part of the curriculum.
7. Rules should be communicated to parents in the language spoken in the home.
8. Rules should be consistently enforced by teachers.
9. Rules should be perceived by students as being fair.
10. Rules that disproportionately impact on any group of students should be changed.

Source: First and Mizell (1980).

Problems with School Climate in U.S. Public Schools

One of the most fundamental elements of supporting school success for every student is the provision of a learning environment that welcomes and supports all children equally, regardless of their race, culture, economic class, or language.

Most school improvement efforts tend to focus on curriculum, instruction strategies, or teaching materials, paying less attention to how the school's overall climate acts to limit or expand a child's academic and social horizons. Yet few factors have a more profound effect on educational outcomes than the ways in which schools act to support some students while rejecting others. Those most likely to suffer rejection are poor, minority, or recently immigrated.

EFFECT OF SCHOOL CLIMATE ON DROPOUT RATE

The end result of experiencing persistent school rejection at many points over many years is not surprising—except for its almost incredible scale. According to educator Peter McLaren (1988), more than 25 percent of all students fail to finish high school. Among inner-city youth, dropout rates are astounding, ranging between 50 percent and 80 percent. New York City, for example, records a 66 percent rate.

Dropout rates of these magnitudes cannot be explained without placing the major responsibility within schools. Clearly, when more than half the students leave before graduation, it is the school that is failing, not the students.

Causes of Dropping Out

While there are many aspects to this failure, one study (Felice, 1981) comparing attitudes held by African American students who dropped out with those who finished high school illuminates the key role that school climate issues play in this tragedy. Among the determining reasons cited by study participants as distinguishing those who dropped out from those who finished school were: 1) perceptions of racial discrimination in school; 2) experiences of low teacher expectations; and 3) experiences of school rejection policies, such as suspension and expulsion.

Dropout Profile

An interesting profile of the dropout emerged from the data: typically, an intelligent, motivated student who has come to view school as a waste of time. In fact, the dropouts studied displayed a higher average IQ than the students who remained in school.

In her review of school dropout studies, Mary Anne Raywid (1987) notes research findings that show: 1) schools can be injurious to the mental health of students already at risk of becoming dropouts; 2) the behavior of some dropouts improves, and aggression toward others declines upon leaving school; and 3) when dropouts leave school, they acquire a greater sense of control over their lives and their self-esteem rises. One study reviewed by Raywid concludes that dropouts who return to school experience "negative effects on both psychological health and interpersonal competency." Researcher Dale Mann (1986) brings a sharp focus to the issue by revealing that 51 percent of the male dropouts he studied left school simply because they "hated it."

INSTITUTIONAL RACISM

Although the United States is certainly a multicultural society— one catalogue (Lambert, 1981) of ethnic/racial groups lists 218 in North America —it has not yet matured into a society in which all groups share equal access to its opportunities and institutions.

Growing Mismatch Between Schools and Students

U.S. public schools have historically been designed to serve a monolingual, White, Anglo, middle-class culture. But as the demographic makeup of the nation and its children becomes increasingly diverse linguistically, culturally, economically, and racially, the array of mismatches between schools and the students and communities they serve is growing rapidly.

Current minority enrollment levels range from 70 percent to 96 percent in the nation's fifteen largest school systems. A study by the Council of Great City Schools (1990) found 75 percent minority enrollment in forty-four of the nation's largest urban systems. By the mid-1980s, one study reports (First, *et. al.*, 1988), more than two million immigrant children had arrived in the U.S. from all over the world as a result of one of the largest periods of immigration in the nation's history.

By contrast, Peter McLaren (1988) notes, less than 10 percent of teachers in U.S. public schools are minorities. Even fewer are employed at administrator/principal/superintendent levels. If current trends continue, researcher Willis Hawley (1989) predicts the number of minority teachers will decrease as 40 percent of minority teachers leave their profession early and teacher training institutions fail to recruit an adequate supply of new candidates. The result will be a teaching force that is increasingly female and White, which will face the challenge of instructing a student body that is increasingly diverse. Futhermore, few schools have adequate multilingual/multicultural staff or staff assistants to serve all of their students properly.

Bias Reflected in School Reports

A compelling proof of the public schools' almost exclusive orientation to the values and needs of the White middle class is captured in an analysis of recent reports on school reform by Carl Grant and Christina Sleeter (1985), which examines their lack of focus on race, class, gender, and special needs. About half of the reports simply do not take these factors into account. The other half offer what the researchers characterize as an "irresponsible and flawed color-blind vision of society" leaving "much room for [educators] to reproduce racist, classist, and sexist practices."

Effects on Students

Educators Gerald Pine and Asa Hilliard (1990) offer an eloquent summary of the impacts of institutional racism and monocultural education:

> "The consequences...are pervasive and profound. White students tend glibly to accept the idea of equality and multiculturalism or of the superior position of their group in society without speculation or insightful analysis. They become oblivious to all but the most blatant acts of racism or ethnic discrimination and often re-label such acts as something else. They seldom give serious thought to cultural, ethnic, or racial differences or to their meaning for and influence on individuals and groups. They are subliminally socialized and oriented to believe that the western experience, culture, and world view are superior and dominant.
>
> "Students of color, by contrast, experience conceptual separation from their roots; they are compelled to examine their own experiences and history through the assumptions, paradigms, constructs, and language of other people; they lose their cultural identity; and they find it difficult to develop a sense of affiliation and connection to a school. They become 'universal strangers'—disaffected and alienated—and all too many drop out of school."

Effects on Teacher Expectations

With fewer than 10 percent minority teachers instructing a student population that is, on average, about 30 percent minority—and predominantly minority in many urban areas—it is preordained that the ethnic, cultural, class, or linguistic match between teacher and student will be poor. One of the best documented and most destructive aspects of this mismatch is the low expectation that most teachers hold for the school success of minority students.

According to Grant and Sleeter (1986), even though most low-income students or students of color come to school with optimism about their futures and the belief that schools will help them realize their visions, teachers have all too often been socialized to view the futures of their students very differently. As a result, note educators Diana Pollard (1989) and Patricia Gandara (1989), teachers may give simpler tasks to minority students, allow them to do less academic work, focus more on their social behavior than on their academic behavior, attribute poor academic performance to factors outside of the student's control, call on them less in class, and reinforce their responses less frequently.

While this issue is developed more thoroughly in Chapter 7, it is important to note here that low teacher expectations are a major contributing factor to the alienation and disconnection that many minority students experience every day in school. As young children internalize the beliefs of teachers they admire, before long they come to believe them too.

SCHOOL CRIME AND VIOLENCE

By comparison with other industrialized nations, the United States is a violent society. Not surprisingly, this violence spills over onto school grounds. The National School Safety Center (NSSC, 1990) reported almost 465,000 violent acts in or around schools during the 1987 to 1988 school year. Most disturbing is the observation that crimes "with injury" are increasing dramatically.

Weapons in Schools

NSSC has also found that students—even young children—are bringing weapons to school at an appalling rate. In California, more than 10,000 weapons were confiscated from students in a single year, including 1,131 guns. Florida witnessed a 40 percent increase in gun incidents between the 1986 to 1987 and 1987 to 1988 school years. New York City schools reported more than 1,800 weapons violations in 1989. In Birmingham, Alabama, suspensions for possession of firearms increased from 30 incidents in 1986 to 85 in 1988.

NSSC notes that one of the reasons there are more weapons in school is because there are more weapons in society. Total weaponry in private hands in the U.S. is estimated at 120 million guns; half the nation's households are estimated to possess a firearm. According to educators Richard Houston and Steven Grubaugh (1989), students carry weapons to show off a symbol of power and authority or out of fear for personal safety as increased gang rivalry and drug traffic shape the school environment. In a culture that promotes violence—by the time children reach eighteen they have seen more than 15,000 deaths on TV— weapons seem part of the natural order of things.

Hate Crime

Hate crime is also on the rise in U.S. society and, therefore, in our schools. A survey by the Los Angeles County Commission on Human Relations (1989) found that 37 percent of Los Angeles County schools surveyed had experienced incidents of hate crime during the school year. Victims spanned a broad range, including Latino, African American, White, immigrant, gay, and Jewish students. Among adults, African Americans were the primary target.

Too many adults seek to address crime and violence in schools by installing metal detectors and posting police in corridors and hallways. Without concerted attention to the underlying factors that breed crime in U.S. communities—poverty, unemployment, drug addiction, hopelessness—schools cannot be made safe. Similarly, schools will not be free from the ugliness of hate crime until it is first rooted out of the society at large.

INTERGROUP CONFLICT

Intergroup conflicts have long been a sad dimension of life in the United States. These tensions are found in the community, and because schools are a microcosm of the larger community, they are also found in schools.

According to research conducted by NCAS (First, *et al.,* 1988), sweeping demographic changes in the U.S. are resulting in classrooms of great diversity. Assumptions rooted in the dominant culture increasingly lead to misinterpretation of student behavior. Reports of physical confrontations between students are frequent as tensions flare between U.S.-born majority and minority students, between immigrant and native-born youngsters, and sometimes between immigrant groups themselves. For many students, harassment and disrespectful or culturally insensitive treatment by other students is an unavoidable part of school:

- A Filipino student in Seattle reported: "A White guy was calling us names—very derogatory names. We beat him up."
- A Haitian student in Boston declared: "I like school, but I don't like how other American students call me names. I don't like it when the Americans say: 'You dumb Haitian. Go back to Haiti.'"
- A Mexican student in San Diego noted: "Mexicans are called 'beaners.' They say we live in garbage cans."
- A Vietnamese student in Washington, DC talked of fights in school because "Black kids don't like Asian and Chinese kids. They were waiting for me in [gym] to get money from me. They think I'm Chinese. They say: 'Hey Chinese boy, give me your money...'" (First, *et al.,* 1988).

SCHOOL POLICIES AND PRACTICES

Lack of Leadership

Too often, school boards, superintendents, and principals fail to provide strong leadership by clearly articulating expectations regarding racism and respectful treatment of all students and adults in school, along with an explicit set of consequences for violations that are applied consistently and rigorously.

Educator Diane Pollard (1989) notes that some school staff give up trying to fight racism because it is hard work for which there is often no reward. In fact, there may actually be punishment when attacking racism is seen as "rocking the boat." Too often, Pollard observes, "racism is ignored or punished after the [school] administrator has been asked repeatedly to take action; and many times the administrator's attitude clearly indicates that the punishment is not to be taken seriously."

School staff are often hesitant to confront even clearly racist behavior, as in the case of a school administrator who refused to intervene when a White student called an African American teacher a "nigger," saying the student was "just having a hard day."

Daniel Abreu, a teacher at P.S. 143 in New York City, charged in public testimony (First, *et al.*, 1988) that adults in the city's schools often deliberately contribute to these tensions: "In general, the reception given to immigrant children was so negative and hostile that many of them were so turned off to their new society that they were never able to learn how to speak English. Bilingual students were called animals, jerks, garbage, idiots by many teachers ...and this unprofessional and inhumane treatment of children was condoned by the administration."

Limits of Multicultural Education Efforts

According to Sleeter and Grant (1987), those schools that make the effort to develop multicultural education programs generally set off along one of five identifiable paths, not all of which lead to the understanding and skills needed to prepare today's children as good citizens of the global village.

- **Teaching the Culturally Different.** Directed toward assimilating culturally different students into the existing social and cultural mainstream by constructing "bridges" to current school programs, the emphasis is on "doing something with students" to help them achieve competence in the dominant culture and develop a positive group identity. Little or no attention is paid to addressing the unequal distribution of goods and power among groups in the U.S.
- **Human Relations.** While the goal of this approach is to help students of different backgrounds get along better and appreciate each other more, an acceptance of the existing stratified social system is implied. While improved intergroup communications may eventually have the indirect effect of reducing inequities, issues such as poverty, institutional racism, and powerlessness are generally not addressed directly.
- **Single Group Studies.** This approach attempts to foster cultural pluralism by teaching about the experiences and contributions of distinct groups. The focus here is to develop empathy with regard to a specific group—such as Native Americans or Chicanos—but larger issues of racial oppression or the need for mobilization for social change are seldom raised. For example, an elementary teacher using this approach might construct an interesting, detailed historical unit on Native Americans without examining the plight of twentieth-century Native American communities.
- **Multicultural Education.** This approach seeks to support cultural differences and social equality by reforming the entire school program to reflect student diversity. Most proponents of this approach share certain key values: 1) cultural diversity is viewed as a strength; 2) human rights and respect for cultural diversity are considered important; 3) alternative life choices have validity; 4) social justice and equal opportunity are worthy goals; and 5) members of all ethnic groups have a right to equal distribution of power. However, even in the context of these sound values, "culture" is often examined at length at the expense of equity issues or the important role of language.
- **Multicultural and Social Reconstructionist Education.** This prepares students to promote cultural diversity and challenge social structural inequality. Unfortunately, all too often, discussion focuses on the broader society, while traditional structures within schools that promote stratification remain unquestioned.

Schools may develop and implement well-intentioned multicultural education programs while still ignoring the need to fundamentally change systemwide practices that impede school success for minority students, such as ability grouping and tracking, over- reliance on standardized achievement or intelligence tests, and the absence of adult role models for minority students.

Although some multicultural programs strive to meet the academic and social needs of culturally different students, they may do so at the cost of removing children from mainstream classrooms. NCAS has found (First, *et al.*, 1988) that few schools are engaged in comprehensive efforts to adapt basic curricula and teaching strategies. Despite the rapidly changing face of the U.S. population, most teacher training institutions pay little attention to the crucial need for professional educators with skills and knowledge to develop and implement high-quality multicultural education programs.

School Discipline

Children cannot fully benefit from school unless they attend regularly. Despite this, many schools still resort to ineffective and inequitable disciplinary policies. According to federal government surveys (NCAS, 1988), school suspension and corporal punishment continue to be the most widely practiced forms of school discipline.

In theory, school disciplinary systems have as their goal development of a classroom environment that supports learning for all children. The reality in public schools, however, can subvert that goal. When schools focus on eliminating behavioral symptoms rather than determining the underlying causes, they may actively contribute to the very behavior they are seeking to control. This cycle can result in lower student motivation and academic achievement, worsened behavior on the part of the child, or dropping out of school altogether.

Adults who are uncomfortable about examining their own behavior may also play a silent role in generating disciplinary problems. Rather than face up to these issues, some adults place responsibility for all misbehavior fully on students and raise a cry to "get rid of the troublemakers." They may justify this shift by claiming they want "good students" to have the opportunity to learn in an optimal environment. When these attitudes prevail, they jeopardize the education of many students who might be helped to learn more appropriate behavior.

School Rejection Policies

As the result of a variety of discipline policies, schools act to sever connections with children, pushing them away when efforts should be made to nurture and strengthen student involvement and interaction. When students are banned from athletics or extracurricular activities because of low grades, the lasting effect is a reduction of positive involvement with school.

Excessive and/or Destructive Punishment

Some school policies escalate punishment beyond the scale of the infractions, such as disciplinary programs that assign points for small infractions like chewing gum, then allow the points to add up over time until they result in a full suspension. The outcome for the child is serious punishment when no single serious infraction has been committed.

Equally destructive are policies that lower a student's grades for a series of infractions such as tardiness or cutting classes. Rather than hear the message of growing disengagement that poor attendance communicates, such misguided steps reinforce the child's alienation from school by devaluing academic achievement.

Suspension from school is one of the most widely practiced forms of discipline. According to the U.S. Department of Education (NCAS, 1988), during the 1985 to 1986 school year, almost two million students were suspended by U.S. public schools—approximately 5 percent of the total school population. During the same school year, suspension rates among the nation's 100 largest school systems ranged from 7 percent of enrolled students to an incredible 50 percent.

Researcher Safer (1986) has found that students who are suspended once in elementary school become significantly more likely to be suspended in middle school compared to students who are not suspended. Additionally, academic achievement of suspended students suffers and they are more likely to be held back a grade. These factors help explain why students who have experienced exclusion from school have higher dropout rates than their peers.

Use of Corporal Punishment

Despite the fact that corporal punishment is now illegal in seventeen states, it remains widely used in many schools—especially elementary schools. As noted by researcher Gordon Bauer and his colleagues (1990) and the National School Safety Center (NSSC) (1989), while corporal punishment may effectively interrupt disruptive behavior in the short run, it can harm the student by reinforcing the very behavior it seeks to alter. Students who suffer corporal punishment are likely to:

- experience anger, anxiety, and fear, none of which support learning;
- learn violent behavior from the punishment;
- experience rejection from peers;
- aim aggressive or destructive behavior at staff, students, or school property in imitation of their punishment;
- withdraw from school activities or avoid school entirely, leading to absenteeism, tardiness, truancy, and dropping out of school.

Despite these possible consequences, over one million children received corporal punishment in school at least once during the 1985 to 1986 school year (NCAS, 1988). Independent estimates place the annual number of incidents between two and three million. Bauer notes that although a wooden paddle is the most frequent instrument employed, numerous other methods are used, such as belts and sticks. Corporal punishment can also include slapping, punching, kicking, and shaking. Students can be forced to assume painful body positions, carry out excessive exercise, or be confined in small, closed spaces.

Bauer finds that the use of corporal punishment is most popular in southern and southwestern states, while often illegal in northeastern states. Despite copious research evidence of its destructive effects, a majority of parents, teachers, school boards, and state legislatures continue to support it. According to researchers, schools that employ corporal punishment are generally more punitive and have higher rates of suspension. Teachers who rely on corporal punishment tend to be authoritarian, dogmatic, and inexperienced compared to peers. They also tend to have been physically punished as children.

Perhaps the strongest rebuttal to the use of corporal punishment is offered by research that shows it simply does not work. According to Bauer and others:

- Physical punishment is associated with less development of conscience and moral development; praise and warmth are more effective.
- Children have less respect for teachers and principals who resort to physical punishment.
- Schools where corporal punishment has been abolished do not experience an increase in behavioral problems.

Bauer also observes that corporal punishment is often used as an initial disciplinary strategy rather than as a last resort, as is usually claimed by proponents—prior to referrals to school counselors, psychologists, or mental health agencies. It is practiced most often in elementary schools, where young children pose the least physical threat and are most vulnerable to damaging effects.

Inequitable Use of Discipline

One aspect of school discipline is beyond dispute. Some students are more likely to be targets of punishment than others— particularly those who are poor or children of color.

NSSC (1990) finds that boys are paddled more often than girls, that primary students receive more spankings than high school students, and that special education students are the most likely candidates to receive corporal punishment.

African American Students

According to the U.S. Department of Education (NCAS, 1988), African American students, who represent 16 percent of the U.S. public school population, received 31 percent of corporal punishment in schools during the 1985 to 1986 school year—twice the rate that would be expected from their level of enrollment. The same inequity holds true for suspensions. During that same school year, African Americans were suspended at more than twice the rate of their White peers.

As the result of their daily experiences with schools, education advocates have learned that the high punishment rates of minority students are rooted in the ways that classroom teachers refer students to the office for disciplinary reasons. In most communities, the stream of youngsters referred for disciplinary action is disproportionately male and minority. School administrators then continue this disparity as they mete out school suspensions and other punishments. This injustice undercuts student motivation and achievement and erodes efforts to maintain authority.

Lack of Accountability

Principals are rarely encouraged by superintendents to reduce suspension rates nor are they formally evaluated on their ability to narrow the racial disparities apparent in most schools. As a result, principals do not similarly evaluate teachers. This helps explain why U.S. Department of Education data on corporal punishment and suspensions display the same two-to-one level of inequity year after year without improvement.

One major source of this inequity are school codes that lack clear language about specific behavior and specific punishment. In the absence of explicitly written codes, administrators and teachers have too much latitude to subjectively define and enforce disciplinary policies. School discipline systems are also likely to have a disproportionate impact on minority students when school codes and rules are developed without input from a broad range of parents and others representing all segments of the community.

Conflict with Parents

Discussions with school personnel about disciplinary issues hold the potential for conflict and confrontation. It is not unusual for school personnel to become defensive and withhold information. Parents then become frustrated and antagonistic. In such an atmosphere, school disciplinary policies, and the schools themselves, gain little support from parents. Often, the overall result is narrowly conceived disciplinary policies implemented with little independent oversight or monitoring in an atmosphere of limited community support.

The most inequitable administration of discipline is likely to occur in schools with very diverse student populations where that racial and ethnic diversity is not reflected in the composition of the staff. Children suffer when great gaps in language, culture, and life experience between adults and students exist in schools. Left unaddressed, such gaps can lead to a variety of unfortunate results, ranging from simple misunderstanding to deeply ingrained institutional racism.

Lack of Classroom Management Skills

Understanding the Need for Training

An important determinant of school climate is the competency that teachers bring to their classrooms. As student populations have grown more diverse, many teachers have found themselves with inadequate classroom management skills. The matter is further complicated by parents and administrators who consider an effective teacher to be a person who has "a way with children," rather than a professional who has mastered certain skills that all teachers are capable of attaining.

Teachers who are long on good intentions but short on classroom management skills can behave in ways that undercut the stable, constructive learning environment they seek to establish. At cross-purposes with themselves, they send children mixed messages. An example is the teacher who urges children to be cooperative, but provides a steady diet of competitive games or classroom activities and fails to discuss the varying situations where either competitive or cooperative behavior are most appropriate.

Understanding Cultural Differences

NCAS has found (First, *et al.*, 1988) that cultural differences can also present problematic mismatches between teachers and students that can escalate into misunderstanding and conflict, particularly in the case of recently immigrated children. For example, calling someone with hand gestures is considered very rude by Cambodians, who employ such gestures to challenge another person to a fight. In many cultures, looking someone directly in the eyes is considered an act of defiance; proper deference is displayed by averting the eyes downward, a custom that many U.S.-born teachers would consider evasive.

In a paper examining cultural differences between Anglo and Latino students, author Suzanne Irujo (1989) observes a capacity on the part of Latino students for polychronic experience—the ability to consider many things at once. This can lead to classroom behavior that may appear chaotic to an Anglo teacher, such as many students talking at the same time or making multiple demands on the teacher's time and attention. Because Anglos are generally monochronic, the teacher can be overwhelmed, believing the children are out of control when they are behaving normally.

Blaming the Student

When a teacher relies too heavily on referring students to the office for disciplinary reasons, too many school administrators fail to determine if the teacher's training has prepared her to cope effectively with children who learn or behave differently. Rather than investigating the situation, administrators tend automatically to assume that the "problem" must be with the students rather than with the teacher.

ADVOCACY STRATEGIES

Parents Union for Public Schools: School Discipline Campaign

Parents Union for Public Schools (PUPS) is a grassroots, volunteer organization of parents who work to secure quality education in Philadelphia public schools by acting as mediators and advocates for the rights and responsibilities of students and parents.

PUPS handles over 400 parent advocacy requests a year, using volunteer parents to serve as advocates in schools. Parents helping other parents generates communication and trust between client and advocate because they both understand the parent perspective. Direct advocacy also helps PUPS with its other activities, affording additional sources of data and evidence to document students' needs.

For parents to be successful as change agents in schools, they must be knowledgeable of their rights and responsibilities. In response to this growing need, PUPS's workshops offer parents the training they require to be effective advocates for their children, as well as the skill to train other parents in a peer environment.

In addition to direct advocacy and training, PUPS prepares fact sheets on subjects such as parent and student rights, school discipline, and questions parents should ask schools if their children are suspended.

PUPS Suspension Report

In 1980, PUPS focused on the perpetually high suspension rate in Philadelphia public schools. Until PUPS forcefully raised the issue, the school system had not considered available suspension data when forming or evaluating its discipline policies.

To draw attention to inequities in the school system's disciplinary procedures, PUPS issued a report on suspension rates in Philadelphia schools based on data collected by the U.S. Department of Education's Office for Civil Rights. The report documented the scope and nature of the suspension problem and—drawing on information gathered by PUPS during school-site visits—provided ideas about how to reduce the public school suspension rate.

While the report paved the way for further research and action by school district officials and PUPS, its main goal was to publicize the schools' high rate of suspension and the reasons behind it. It was PUPS's belief that the collective attention of parents, students, citizens, educators, and policymakers could produce alternatives to lower the suspension rate and return suspended students to a more positive learning environment.

Recommended changes in school discipline policies contained in the PUPS report included: reporting suspensions on a monthly basis; removing attendance violations as grounds for suspension; and creation of an "in-school" suspension program that combined disciplinary action with continued academic instruction.

Media Campaign

To heighten public awareness and increase political pressure, PUPS worked with the local media to disseminate the report's findings. They hoped extensive news coverage would allow their message to reach a broad audience, encouraging popular support for the recommended changes in the school discipline system.

School discipline stories are particularly attractive to the press. Unfortunately, media attention can be superficial and fleeting, failing to address the complex issues involved. As a result, PUPS took the time to educate reporters about discipline issues by giving them generous access to the education advocacy community and providing them with thorough background information.

Meeting with School Officials

As part of its strategy to reduce suspension rates and develop disciplinary procedures and practices that resolved rather than exacerbated problems in schools, PUPS decided to work cooperatively with school district officials.

In the spring of 1982, PUPS met with the school system's associate superintendent and several district superintendents to share the report's findings and begin the process of reducing suspensions.

In an effort to establish a good relationship with parents, the superintendent agreed to meet with PUPS on a bi-monthly basis. When the superintendent left office, his successor continued the practice, believing it was a requirement. Although the incoming superintendent had a less cordial relationship with PUPS, ending these meetings would have been viewed as a slap in the face of parents.

During the meetings, PUPS continually raised the issue of high suspension rates, reviewed the shortcomings of the school system's disciplinary policies, and pushed for change.

Collaborative Work Against Corporal Punishment

Broadening its focus beyond suspensions, PUPS organized a presentation on corporal punishment for the school superintendent and the director of health.

To prepare its presentation, PUPS identified a dozen cases of student abuse in connection with corporal punishment, after obtaining parents' permission to release the records. With help from the Center for Corporal Punishment Abolition at Rutgers University, PUPS combined these cases with research criticizing the use of corporal punishment.

Changes in the Discipline Policy

Substantial changes have occurred as a result of PUPS's continuing work on school discipline issues:

- Citywide suspensions have been reduced by 2 percent; while that reduction is not large, it represents an end to annual suspension rate increases during the past decade.
- In 1985, the school superintendent issued a binding directive stating that students should not be suspended for lateness or cutting classes; however, PUPS still receives calls from parents whose children are suspended for tardiness and absenteeism.
- The 1985 directive also stated that school districts must:
  —record every suspension;
  —record the number of school days missed due to each suspension;
  —record whether a student receives an in-school or out-of-school suspension.
- As the result of collaborative efforts with other groups and organizations, corporal punishment was outlawed in Philadelphia public schools in 1988.

For further information, please contact: Parents Union for Public Schools, 311 South Juniper Street, Philadelphia, PA 19107. Telephone (215) 546-1166.

Garfield School: Revere, Massachusetts

In 1981, the Garfield School was one of six kindergarten through eighth grade elementary schools in Revere, Massachusetts. As in most Revere elementary schools in 1981, all of the 550 children enrolled in the school were White. Nine years later, approximately 350 of the 550 students enrolled—64 percent—are of color, the vast majority from Cambodia.

The number of Southeast Asian families moving into the community and enrolling their children in the Garfield School grew so rapidly that within a year the school was forced to transfer their seventh and eighth graders to another school because of overcrowding. Within four years, overcrowding became so severe that the school was again forced to transfer students—this time their fifth and sixth graders.

The challenge faced by the staff at the Garfield has been repeated across the country. But in contrast to many other schools, the staff at the Garfield, led by Principal William Waxman, embraced and welcomed their new students. As Waxman stated: "We concluded that our goal must be to offer these children the best education possible and, more importantly, to make them feel that they were wanted, that they were welcome in this land, that this school was a building full of friends, not just a place where they would learn."

Principal Waxman recognized that providing the best possible education and making the newcomers an integral part of the school community required considerable preparation on the part of both staff and students. Through his behavior and his message, he made it clear that every staff member was expected to learn about the Cambodian culture. Staff made a commitment to understand who the children were, where they came from, and why they were coming to this country. Staff who were not able to make this commitment were not welcome at the school.

The state Department of Education provided a grant to the school for staff development. Every teacher took part in workshops to learn about Cambodian culture. Teachers learned about cultural behavior that could easily be misunderstood with potentially harmful results. They learned, for example, that if Cambodian children did not look them in the eye, it was merely a sign of respect, and not to pat them on the head, because this was insulting.

The school did not stop with efforts to teach and prepare the staff. As Principal Waxman remembers: "We went on a crusade of teaching every child in school about the Cambodian children that were coming. We taught our students why these students were coming—about the suffering they had been through." Every single day, students in every classroom in the school spent half an hour or more discussing prejudice, enabling children to conquer their prejudices by helping them to recognize and understand them.

In addition to the anti-prejudice program, the school expanded its "buddy" program to encourage friendships and help new children become part of the school community. At the Garfield School, new children were always immediately paired with a buddy responsible for the new child for one week. Children were paired according to where they live so they could come to school and go home together. The staff revised this practice to pair every Cambodian child with an American buddy who introduced her to friends, sat with her at lunch, and generally showed her the ropes around the school.

The school's efforts were highly successful. Children got along well and there were very few racially motivated incidents. The school was a community of learners where each child's strengths and differences were recognized and respected. Inside the school, cultural diversity was celebrated. Outside, however, the story was different. In the community, there was great resentment of the newcomers. In response, Principal Waxman told the children that the elders would have to learn from them and he and his staff devised programs to help—team projects that involved parents and Cambodian and American students and encouraged students to go into each other's homes.

The school also attempted to address tensions between Cambodian and American teenagers. With a grant from the State Department of Education, they developed a summer program for 100 first and second graders that employed Cambodian and American teenagers as teacher aides. The children were divided into teams comprised of equal numbers of Cambodian and American children. Two teacher aides were assigned to each team, one Cambodian and one American. Teenagers were chosen because they were leaders that others would follow—often, for the Americans, the biggest troublemakers.

Principal Waxman has retired, but the Garfield School's mission has not changed. Celebration of diversity, acceptance and respect for differences, and a commitment to an integrated community of learners remain as central themes. As stated by current Principal Dorothy Foley: "I've heard other principals say to bilingual teachers, 'Those are your kids.' In this school, everyone participates in all activities. There are no 'your kids,' only 'our kids.'"

To promote this team approach and encourage collaboration and understanding among the teachers, Principal Foley started a teacher support team comprised of Cambodian and American teachers. It has a representative teacher from each grade, including kindergarten. For the first team, Foley chose teachers who were well respected by their colleagues and who were effective in teaching children of varying backgrounds and abilities—teachers who referred very few children to special education. These teachers selected additional teachers and each succeeding year, team members chose new teachers.

Principal Foley serves as a consultant to the team, but wants teachers to feel ownership of it and see each other as resources. Team members discuss children's problems, make recommendations, and provide support and follow-up to the teachers involved. Because the team includes both Cambodian and American teachers, cultural misunderstandings are dealt with quickly and effectively. Special education referrals have dropped dramatically since the team was started. The program is part of ongoing efforts at the school to create an atmosphere of innovation and risk-taking.

The school itself is structured so that children, regardless of their English language abilities, learn together as much as possible. Children report to integrated homerooms first thing in the morning that have equal numbers of American and Cambodian children. After the homeroom period, many children go in different directions because of varying language and academic needs. However, classes are coordinated so that children are covering similar content at the same time, even though the language of instruction may vary. Depending on individual needs, Cambodian children receive part of their instruction in English and part in Khmer. A bilingual Cambodian teacher works with an English as a Second Language teacher to coordinate instruction. Children return to their homeroom group for art, music, gym, lunch, and an activities period specifically designed to increase cultural understanding and promote collaboration among the children.

Diane Schwald, a second-grade teacher at the Garfield School, has a homeroom composed of an equal number of Cambodian and American students who spend part of the day in her classroom. She has developed a number of collaborative learning activities that improve self-esteem and increase cultural understanding as well as address academic goals. These activities span a range from encouraging children to help each other learn to planned, long-term collaborative projects. For example, one activity involves pairs of children writing books celebrating differences and similarities. After Cambodian children are paired with American children, the partners draw pictures of each other that depict how they are alike or different.

Similarly, one class collaborated on the making of a Big Book (oversized books several children can read together or read along with the teacher) with the theme of "Feelings" written in English and Khmer. Children were paired together—an American and a Cambodian in each group—and each partner taught the other a "feeling" word in their language. Partners then taught their word to the rest of the class. Because American children had to learn the Khmer words, they began to realize first-hand how difficult it was to learn another language. Eventually the whole class read the Big Book and taught the words to other classes in the school.

Over the years the Garfield School has strived to create a learning environment that welcomes all children. In the coming year, the school will face a unique but exciting challenge. It is to move out of its run-down, severely overcrowded building into one that is new and very modern. The new school, which includes a television studio and an advanced computer center, will be open to all children in the city. All of the children presently enrolled at the Garfield School will have a place in the new school. Eventually, the ethnic composition of the school will reflect that of the city—79 percent White, 21 percent minority.

Maintaining its supportive learning environment during this transition will require renewed effort and determination. But along with its television studio and advanced computer center, the school has a community room. Principal Foley hopes that this room will become a meeting place for parents, staff, and community people—a way for the school to remain connected and committed to all members of the community it serves.

For further information, please contact: Ms. Dorothy Foley, Principal, Garfield School, Garfield Avenue, Revere, MA 02151.

Current Research Related to Topics Discussed in Chapter Six

Importance of School Climate

The creation of school environments that are non-chaotic and are exemplified by mutual respect between school staff and students is critical to a school's success. Too often interactions between certain groups of students and school staff convey to the students that they are not welcome at the school or not expected to meet the demands of the classroom **(Dentzer and Wheelock, 1990; Maeroff, 1988; Pine and Hilliard, 1990; Wheelock, 1986).**

Students respond by developing negative attitudes and beliefs about school and their role as students. This belief system becomes part of a cycle that feeds into teachers' negative expectations, leads to continued negative school experiences, and undermines the students' engagement in and commitment to the learning process **(Fine, 1986; Fine and Rosenberg, 1983; Raywid, 1987; Schorr, 1989; Wehlage and Rutter, 1986; Wheelock, 1986).** The end result of this long developing process is complete disengagement from school when the student decides to leave the classroom permanently.

Poor students, students from ethnic minority backgrounds, and students whose primary language is other than English are most likely to suffer from rejecting school experiences **(Felice, 1981; Fine, 1986; McLaren, 1988; Pine and Hilliard, 1990).** Nationwide, over 25 percent of all students leave school before graduation, representing approximately 500,000 students each year **(McLaren, 1988; Pallas, Natriello, and McDill, 1989).** As incredible as this figure seems, it masks large differences among ethnic groups. The dropout rate for Latinos is 41 percent, for Blacks, 23 percent and for Whites, 15 percent **(McDill, Natriello, and Pallas, 1985; McLaren, 1988).**

Inner-city schools are the least successful in engaging their students. An astounding 66 percent of all public school students in New York City leave school before graduation; the rate is 80 percent for Latinos, 72 percent for Blacks, and 50 percent for Whites **(McLaren, 1988).** Likewise, in Chicago, the dropout rate is over 40 percent. At the city's non-selective schools, each with enrollment rates of over 50 percent Black and Latino, the rate rises to over 60 percent **(Designs for Change, 1985; Hess, 1986).**

Dropouts are often portrayed as low-ability, low-achieving youth who are unmotivated, alienated, suffer from low self-esteem, and come from ethnic minority families with limited educational attainment **(Fine and Rosenberg, 1983; Raywid, 1987; Rumberger, 1983; Wehlage, 1987).** In effect, leaving school early is seen as the result of personal or familial deficiencies.

Yet substanial research reveals the inaccuracies in this portrait and points to the key role that school climate plays in students' decisions to terminate their schooling early. **Felice (1981)** found that African American dropouts as compared to African American students who remained in school were much more likely to perceive racial discrimination in school. Moreover, such perceptions were strongly related to school policies of high suspensions and low teacher expectations. While many of the dropouts had low achievement in school, their IQ scores were significantly higher than their stay-in peers. Felice concludes that the dropouts were typically motivated, intelligent students who were more aware of the schools' rejecting practices, correctly attributed them to racial discrimination, and decided that the benefits to staying in school no longer outweighed the costs.

Likewise, a profile of the dropout emerged from a study by **Fine and Rosenberg (1983)** as average in achievement, relatively motivated, typical in attributions of success and failure, non-conformist, and most likely to challenge an unjust act in the classroom. In contrast, their comparable stay-in schools peers were relatively depressed, conforming, and reluctant to advocate for themselves. Fine and Rosenberg conclude that dropouts are often highly motivated, intelligent, and aware of and critical of educational institutions and labor market opportunities.

Findings from the "High School and Beyond" study **(*cited in* Wehlage, 1987)** also indicated that 50 to 60 percent of dropouts perceived teachers as low in caring and interest and believed that their school discipline code was neither fair nor effective. For most dropouts, school was a very unpleasant place long before they decided to leave. Dropouts most commonly report leaving school because they hate it, because they believe no one cares about them, and because they no longer see any reason to stay **(Mann, 1986; Raywid, 1987; Wehlage, 1987).** Not surprisingly, dropouts often experience at least a short-term increase in self-esteem and sense of control over their lives upon leaving what they perceive as an unwelcoming, unjust, and uncaring school environment **(Felice, 1981; Fine, 1986; Fine and Rosenberg, 1983; Raywid, 1987; Wehlage and Rutter, 1986).**

Racism in School

The U.S. is a multicultural society—one where members from distinct ethnic and cultural groups live, but not yet a pluralistic society—one where members from different groups share equal power and equal access to opportunities for quality lives **(Derman-Sparks, 1989; Pine and Hilliard; 1990; Suzuki, 1984).** Because this condition exists in the broader society, it is often reflected in the climate of many of our nation's classrooms.

Racism and racial bias severely disrupt the learning environment. **Derman-Sparks (1989)** defines racism and racial bias as follows: "racism is any attitude, action or institutional practice that subordinates people because of their color. This includes imposition of one ethnic group's culture in such a way as to withhold respect for, to demean, or to destroy the cultures of other races...[R]acial bias is any attitude, belief, or feeling that results in, and helps to justify, unfair treatment of an individual because of his or her identity" (p. 13).

Ample evidence exists of institutional racism in the schools **(Dentzer and Wheelock, 1990; First, *et al.*, 1988; Grant, 1990; Oakes, 1986a, 1986b; Pine and Hilliard, 1990; Pollard, 1989).** Institutional racism is revealed through its consequences. For example, although Blacks represent 16 percent of the nationwide student population, they receive 30 percent of all suspensions and account for 31 percent of the incidents of corporal punishment. Likewise, Blacks experience special education placement at more than twice their school enrollment rate, while receiving only 8 percent of placements in gifted and talented programs **(NCAS, 1988).**

In addition, minority, limited-English-proficient, and low-income students are consistently and dramatically overrepresented in low academic tracks **(Ann Arbor Task Force on Instructional Grouping, 1986; Children's Defense Fund, 1985; Dentzer and Wheelock, 1990; Slavin, 1987).** This racial and socioeconomic imbalance occurs regardless of whether student assignments are determined by placement tests, recommendations from teachers and counselors, or by student and parent choice **(Oakes, 1985; Oakes 1986a).** This same group of children are also the ones most often retained **(Illinois Fair Schools Coalition, 1985; Shepard and Smith, 1986; Smith and Shepard, 1987; Walker and Madhere, 1987).** Minority and poor children suffer disporportinately from the pernicious effects associated with all these practices.

Prejudice and bigotry blight the ambience of schools through racist acts directed at individuals or groups of students from ethnically diverse backgrounds. Documented accounts of racial slurs, threats, racist slogans, physical assaults, and ethnic conflicts in the nation's classrooms dramatically reveal how overt racism has once again come out of the closet and into the schools **(Caldwell, 1989; First, *et al.*, 1988; Los Angeles County Commission on Human Relations, 1989; Pine and Hilliard, 1990; Pollard, 1989).** Acts of violence generated by hate are no longer isolated incidents but "part of the fabric of life at schools across the country" **(Caldwell, 1989; p. 32).**

Los Angeles schools provide an example of the pervasiveness of intergroup conflict in the schools. Thirty-seven percent of the schools in Los Angeles County responding to a survey on school hate crime report incidents during the school year **(Los Angeles County Commission on Human Relations, 1989).** Two-thirds of the completed surveys came from elementary schools. Analysis by grade level reveals a high incidence of hate crime—34 percent for elementary schools, 47 percent for middle schools, and 42 percent for high schools. Moreover, the largest group of the schools reporting no incidents of hate violence had homogeneous student populations.

Of the 2,265 total incidents reported, anti-Latino acts were the greatest in number, followed by anti-Black acts. But anti-Black incidents occurred at the greatest number of schools, and Blacks were victimized at a rate more than double their representation. They represent only 14 percent of the countywide school enrollment yet were the victims of about 29 percent of the racist acts. Immigrant students were also at serious risk. About one-half of anti-Asian incidents and one-third of anti-Latino incidents were attributed to anti-immigrant bigotry **(Los Angeles County Commission on Human Relations, 1989).**

The Commission reported that racial slurs were the most common student actions, followed by physical assault, and at a much lower rate, graffiti and destruction of property.

Schools appeared to use anti-racist resources in a reactive manner. Moreover, much of what they included as resources were generic material—for example, substance abuse prevention programs and social science curriculum. Very few schools reported use of specific anti-racist materials. **(Los Angeles County Commission on Human Relations, 1989).**

The failure of schools to directly address issues of race undermines the efforts of many students of color and contributes to the development of intolerant and conflict-ridden school environments **(Caldwell, 1989; Grant, 1988, 1990; Pine and Hilliard, 1990; Pollard, 1989).** A "conspiracy of silence" surrounds issues of race relations in the policies, practices, and curricula of most schools **(Caldwell, 1989, p. 32; Pine and Hilliard, 1990).** Many White teachers have little understanding of how race, in regard to power, economics, and culture, affects the opportunities and life chances of students of color **(Grant, 1988, 1990; Suzuki, 1984).**

Teachers often fail to confront clearly racist behavior **(Caldwell, 1989; First, *et al.*, 1988).** Administrators not only often fail to provide necessary leadership by setting clear standards that are swiftly enforced, they often convey messages to teachers that they are not to "rock the boat" by confronting racism **(Caldwell, 1989; Grant, 1988; Pine and Hilliard, 1990; Pollard, 1989).** For example, in one school, White students circulated several dolls dressed in Klan costumes and one of a hanged Black person. The teacher failed to comment when she confiscated the dolls. A Black student reported that the principal "wouldn't do anything" when she went to him about the incident (*cited in* **Caldwell, 1989, p. 32).**

The failure to address issues of race is embedded in the larger issue of the Anglocentric approach that permeates school curricula and practices. Schools are solidly built on a monocultural, Anglocentric world view that tends heavily to benefit White students. School curricula are centered on western civilization to the exclusion of other perspectives and world views **(Banks, 1987; Grant, 1988; Pine and Hilliard, 1990; Ramsey, 1982).** As **Pine and Hilliard (1990)** point out, "this curriculum reinforces institutional racism by excluding from discourse and from the ethos of the school and the classroom the intellectual thought, scholarship, history, culture, contributions, and experience of minority groups" (p. 595).

When schools do attempt to address issues of race, they most often take a cultural orientation that emphasizes cultural differences and presents cultural content outside of a meaningful context. This usually results in the addition of fragmented ethnic content to the existing curriculum, such as ethnic holidays, heroes, and foods **(Banks, 1987; Grant, 1988; McLean, 1990; Ramsey, 1982).** Schools consistently fail to address the relationship of race to power and economics and how this affects students of color **(Banks, 1987; Grant, 1988; Mitchell, 1990; Suzuki, 1984).**

This failure is particularly disturbing because U.S. children are aware of racial and cultural differences by pre-school age. Moreover, children are aware that race and ethnicity are connected with privilege and power by four years of age **(Derman-Sparks, 1989; Derman-Sparks, Higa, and Sparks, 1980; Ramsey, 1982).** Unfortunately, their understanding usually reflects the prevailing societal attitudes toward ethnic and racial differences **(Derman-Sparks, Higa, and Sparks, 1980).**

These findings point to the critical need to intervene at a young age to influence children's concepts and attitudes toward race and culture. **Grant (1988)** stresses the importance of addressing issues of race, "Race needs to be dealt with from a personal and institutional perspective in school because schools have not welcomed people of color with the same zeal that people of color have demonstrated in their efforts to attend schools. In fact, schools are often guilty of destroying the passion for learning that people of color bring to school" (p. 566).

Teacher Expectations

One pernicious way schools destroy the "passion for learning" of students of color is through lower teacher expectations. Voluminous evidence exists that teachers have lower expectations for students of color **(Clark, 1990; Dentzer and Wheelock, 1990; Derman-Sparks, 1989; Gandara, 1989; Grant, 1988; Hilliard, 1990; Payne, 1984; Phillips, 1988; Pine and Hilliard, 1990; Pollard, 1989).** For example, a recent national survey of high school teachers (majority White and male) revealed that one in four agreed with the statement, "Some races of people are more intelligent than others" ***(cited in* Derman-Sparks, 1989).**

Lower teacher expectations greatly affect the atmosphere of the classroom. Teachers express their lower expectations for students of color by: giving simpler tasks to minority students than to Whites; allowing minority students to do less academic work than Whites; calling on minority children less and reinforcing their responses less, and criticizing them more for failures; paying less attention to minority students and interacting with them less frequently; focusing more on social behavior among minority students and academic behavior among Whites; and attributing poor academic achievement by minority students to factors outside their control while attributing the performance of White students to effort and other factors within their control **(Gandara, 1989; Hilliard, 1990; Pollard, 1989).**

Teachers also often hold lower expectations for poor and minority students out of what they perceive as compassion for their difficult home environment. This results in an understanding of children's problems but a failure to provide solutions to their academic concerns. While students' home environments are unlikely to change, failure to develop solutions to academic difficulties robs the children of opportunities to develop important problem-solving and coping skills to use inside and outside the school's walls. In fact, the intended acts of compassion help to ensure that the children remain in the very conditions that provoked the compassion in the first place **(Clark, 1990).**

The extent to which low expectations undermine and damage children of color is revealed by recent research that shows that Black and Latino children in the elementary grades enjoy school more and have more confidence in their own academic abilities than their White peers ***(cited in* Greenbaum, 1989).** Students of color arrive at school with optimistic visions of their future. They and their parents place great faith in the schools **(Grant, 1990).**

Issues of race in schools are further exacerbated by the shortage of teachers of color. A teacher force that is less than 10 percent minority is teaching a student population that is over 25 percent minority **(Hawley, 1989; Hodgkinson, 1988; McLaren, 1988).** The forty-four largest urban systems have 75 percent minority enrollments **(Council of Great City Schools, 1990).** Moreover, as the student population becomes increasingly more diverse the teaching forces becomes increasingly more White. The percentage of teachers of color in the work force is expected to drop to 5 percent in the coming decades as minority teachers leave the profession at twice the rate of their peers and teacher education programs fail to recruit an adequate supply of new candidates **(Hawley, 1989; Pine and Hilliard, 1990; Trent, 1990).**

Crime and Violence in Public Schools

Schools are embedded within larger communities. The conditions of schools are strongly influenced by the conditions of their neighborhoods. Violence and crime, particularly among youth, have escalated in many communities **(Lawton, 1991; Menacker, Weldon, and Hurwitz, 1990; National School Safety Center (NSSC), 1990b).**

Not surprisingly, violence spills into schools in many communities. Almost 465,000 violent crimes occurred in or around schools during 1987. While the total number of street crimes (defined as assault, rape, robbery, and theft) in and around schools did not increase from 1986, the percentage of serious crimes "with injury" rose dramatically. For example, aggravated assault increased 23 percent, but aggravated assault with injury increased 100 percent **(NSSC, 1990b).**

Children in large urban centers suffer more from student violence. In 1987, New York City reported 1,606 assaults in its schools, Chicago reported 698 violent incidents, Los Angeles, 493, and Boston, 410 **(Houston and Grubaugh, 1989).** While violent incidents tend to happen more often in junior and high schools, elementary schools do not escape. A study that surveyed teachers and sixth and eighth graders in three Chicago public elementary schools (K through 8) found the following: almost half the students (44 percent) did not feel safe in school; 8 percent reported being threatened with a gun or knife during the school year; close to one-third of the students (32 percent) reported carrying a weapon into the school during the year; almost three-fourths (73 percent) reported fistfighting with another student at least once during the year; 20 percent of the students feared for their safety on school grounds; almost half the teachers (42 percent) hesitated to confront misbehaving students out of fear for their personal safety; only 38 percent reported feeling very safe in their classrooms; only 3 percent reported feeling very safe on school grounds **(Menacker, Weldon, and Hurwitz, 1990).**

Over the years, children have brought weapons of some form into school. The difference today is that more powerful and sophiscated weaponry is easily available to children and more children are carrying weapons, greatly increasing the potential for bodily harm and death **(NSSC, 1990b).** It is estimated that on any given day more than 100,000 students carry guns to school **(NSSC, 1990a).**

Between July 1988 and June 1989, California schools confiscated 10,569 weapons. Knives were the most common weapons found (5,328), followed by explosives (2,498), weapons categorized as "other" (1,612), and guns (1,131). Likewise, Florida saw a 42 percent increase in gun incidents in schools between the 1986 to 1987 and 1987 to 1988 school years. For school years 1987–'88, 1988–'89, and 1989–'90, the number of weapon violations in New York City public schools exceeded 1,500 **(NSSC, 1990b).**

While older students are more likely to carry weapons, teachers have found weapons on children as young as kindergarten. For example, a first grader at a Manhattan elementary school brought in a loaded .25-caliber semi-automatic pistol for "show-and-tell" **(NSSC, 1990b).**

Children often carry weapons out of fear for their safety. They perceive of guns as protection **(Houston and Grubaugh, 1989; NSSC, 1990a, 1990b). Brooks (1985, *cited in* Houston and Grubaugh, 1989)** estimates that in some schools as many as 70 percent of the students carry some type of weapon. He points out that many students caught carrying a weapon claim that they had no intention of using it but were protecting themselves from the violence and disorder around them. For some children, weapons are a sign of power and status, a way to show off in front of peers **(Calhoun, 1988; NSSC, 1990b).**

The proliferation of guns in schools is a reflection of the proliferation of guns in society. Total weaponry in private hands in the U.S. is estimated at 120 million guns. Over 40 percent of these are handguns. Over half the homes in the country are estimated to contain a firearm **(NSSC, 1990b).** Children also receive constant messages that violence is an appropriate and effective way of resolving conflict. Not only are guns often pervasive in their communities, but the media often glorifies violence **(Houston and Grubaugh, 1989; NSSC, 1990b).**

Unsafe schools are often embedded in unsafe communities. **Menacker and others (1989)** hold that school crime must be viewed in the context of the community. In fact, many schools in dangerous neighborhoods have created environments that are much safer than their surrounding communities. The students and teachers surveyed by Menacker and others (1990) at the three elementary schools in Chicago had concerns about safety in school, but they also shared that they felt much safer in the school than in the surrounding neighborhood. Other students have pointed to their schools as a safe haven in the midst of violence and chaos **(Lawton, 1991).**

Schools have an obligation to provide all students with a safe and orderly environment that facilitates learning. But as schools adopt more law-and-order tactics to ensure safety, such as metal-detectors, photo ID badges, and uniformed police stationed in the corridors, the ambience becomes more like that of prison than an open place that invites inquiry and critical thinking **(Menacker, Weldon, and Hurwitz, 1990; NSSC, 1990a, 1990b).** As one architect who designed a high-security school notes, "If you start making a prison environment with eight- to ten-foot-high fences, it certainly changes the character of the school and the quality of the experience that students have while at the school" **(NSSC, 1990a, p. 5).**

Discipline in Public Schools

Most schools still seek to impose safety and order through stringent disciplinary measures, such as suspension from school and corporal punishment. These approaches are based on the premise that punishment and temporary exclusion will motivate students to change their disruptive behavior.

Despite the fact that corporal punishment has been declared illegal in many school systems and in seventeen states (California, Connecticut, Hawaii, Iowa, Maine, Massachusetts, Michigan, Minnesota, Nebraska, New Hampshire, New Jersey, New York, North Dakota, Rhode Island, Vermont, Virginia, and Wisconsin), it continues to be widely used. Recent data indicates that 1,099,861 children experienced corporal punishment at least once in a school setting during the 1985 to 1986 school year **(NCAS, 1988).**

The most recent Office for Civil Rights Survey showed that 1,993,895 students were suspended during the 1985 to 1986 school year **(NCAS, 1988).** The national suspension rate indicated that 5 of every 100 students enrolled were suspended at least once. There were wide disparities among states and among school districts within states. While the average suspension rate for the 100 largest school districts was about 7 percent, the school district with the highest rate suspended close to 50 percent of its students **(NCAS, 1988).**

Corporal punishment is most frequently used in elementary schools. Rather than serving as a last resort, corporal punishment is often the sole choice for punishment **(Bauer, *et al.*, 1990; Socoski, 1989).** Paddling with a wooden object is the most common type of corporal punishment but ear-twisting, hair-pulling, punching, shoving, and forcing children to exercise to exhaustion or assume painful positions are also used **(Bauer, *et al.*, 1990; NSSC, 1989).**

Teachers who employ corporal punishment tend to be authoritarian, dogmatic, inexperienced, and impulsive **(Bauer, *et al.*, 1990; Socoski, 1989).** They also are more likely to have been physically punished as children **(Bauer, *et al.*, 1990; NSSC, 1989).** Studies of suspension and corporal punishment show that both are often used for trivial and ambiguous offenses, and that they are used repeatedly on the same students **(*Children's Magazine*, 1987; Kaesar, 1984; Rose, 1983; Socoski, 1989; Wayson, 1984).**

Impact on Students

Suspensions during elementary school are likely to lead to further suspensions and school failure. **Safer (1986)** found that: 38 percent of suspended elementary school students received another suspension during elementary school; all suspended elementary school students were subsequently suspended at least once during middle school; elementary school students with records of repetitive classroom misconduct were twelve times as likely to be suspended in middle school; in the year following a middle school suspension, over 50 percent of suspended students experienced an average of two to three repeat suspensions.

Corporal punishment may have seriously detrimental effects on the punished child, including: withdrawing from and avoidance of school whenever possible; the experience of emotionality, anxiety, and fear; imitation of the violent punishing behavior; negative peer reactions toward the punished child; and aggressive reactions to the school, its staff, and other property or people **(Bauer, *et al.*, 1990; Rose, 1981, 1983; Socoski, 1989).** The net result of corporal punishment may be an increase in student absenteeism and a greater exhibition of aggressive, violent, and other negative student behavior **(Bauer, *et al.*, 1990; Socoski, 1989).** Despite its negative effects, many teachers, administrators, school boards, and state legislators still support corporal punishment **(Bauer, *et al.*, 1990; NSSC, 1989).**

Students who receive suspension or corporal punishment are more likely to receive failing grades, be retained in-grade, and have poor attitudes toward school. Ultimately, they are more likely to drop out of school prior to graduation **(Howell and Frese, 1982; Lloyd, 1976; Rumberger, 1983; Wehlage, 1987).** Students who drop out are twice as likely to have been suspended the previous year **(Camayd-Freixas, 1986).**

Suspensions and corporal punishment fail in their primary goal of modifying negative student behavior. It is not surprising that the same students are suspended over and over again during their school careers **(Almeida, 1988; Wheelock, 1986).** For the most part, current disciplinary policies and practices seek to address the symptoms of discipline problems, not the underlying causes **(Kaesar, 1979a, 1979b; Wayson, 1984; Wheelock, 1986).**

Inequitable Use of Discipline

Minority students, particularly males, receive suspension and corporal punishment at highly disproportionate rates compared to their White peers **(Bauer, *et al.*, 1990; *Children's Magazine*, 1987; First and Mizell, 1980).** During the 1985 to 1986 school year, the national suspension rate for Blacks was 9.1 percent, compared to 4.0 percent for Whites, 4.4 percent for Latinos, and 2.3 percent for Asians. Although Blacks represent 16 percent of the nationwide student population, they receive 30 percent of suspensions and account for 31 percent of incidents of corporal punishment **(NCAS, 1988).**

Differential treatment of minority students generally results from the nature of the disciplinary referral process, which depends on initial judgments by individual school staff members **(First and Mizell, 1980; Lufler, 1979; Wayson, 1984).** Differential suspension rates stem from violations where there is less consensus among educators regarding whether the violation is serious enough to warrant suspension (e.g., disrupting class), where there is a question of whether suspension is the appropriate response (e.g., truancy), and where the violation itself is not clearly defined (e.g., defying authority) **(First and Mizell, 1980; Kaesar, 1979b).**

Research has found dramatic differences in the use of suspension among individual schools within a school system **(Almeida, 1988; Kaesar, 1979b; Wheelock, 1986)** which do not appear to be caused by differences in student or staff characteristics **(Almeida, 1988).** Moreover, schools that suspend large numbers of students tend to do so repeatedly **(Almeida, 1988; Wheelock, 1986),** undermining the argument frequently put forth by educators that suspensions are needed to deal with the disruptive behavior of a small group of disaffected students who should be removed from the classroom to ensure that other students have the opportunity to learn.

Disciplinary problems often arise from the organizational structure and environment of the school. Disruptive behavior does not occur equally in every classroom, but tends to happen disproportionately in particular settings **(Kaesar, 1984; Wayson, 1984; Wayson, *et al.*, 1982).** School conditions that negatively affect student and staff are a much more important determinant of disruptive behavior than the circumstances of individual students. Four out of five disruptions in schools can be traced to problems in the way schools are organized and governed **(Gottfredson, 1984; Kaesar, 1979, 1984; Lasley and Wayson, 1982; Wayson, 1984).**

Alternative Strategies

Schools have instituted a variety of alternative approaches to discipline in efforts to prevent disruptive behavior from occurring. These include: conflict mediation; dispute resolution curricula; violence prevention curricula, and in-school suspensions.

In conflict mediation programs, students are formally trained as mediators to help peers resolve disputes with administrators, teachers, parents, or other students. Mediation can reduce violence, vandalism, truancy, and suspension. Conflict mediation programs enhance communication among members of the school community, improve the school climate, and provide an avenue to address common concerns **(Cheatham, 1988; Davis, 1986; Davis and Porter, 1984, 1985; Davis and Salem, 1985; Houston and Grubaugh, 1989).**

Although mediation programs are usually implemented in high schools, they have been successfully employed with children as young as eight **(Davis and Porter, 1985; Sakharov, 1987).** Principals whose schools housed such programs reported a reduction in disruption, allowing teachers to spend more time on instruction instead of classroom management. In addition, conflict managers used their abilities outside of mediation sessions, teaching their skills to parents, siblings, and peers **(Davis, 1986; Davis and Porter, 1985).**

Researchers have identified specific elements associated with the successful implementation of an in-school conflict mediation program: support and commitment from the principal; a core group of teachers interested in and knowledgeable about mediation; training as an integral and ongoing aspect of the program; a strong director who has time to devote to working with mediators, supervising hearings, and following up on dispute agreements; and collaboration with a mediation organization in the community **(Davis, 1985; Davis and Porter, 1984, 1986; Davis and Salem, 1985).**

Dispute resolution courses usually combine reading and discussion with experiential exercises, specific activities around interpersonal communication and assertiveness, one-to-one conflict mediation skills, and conflict mediation skills for third parties **(Cheatham, 1988; Wilson and Bishop, 1987).**

Violence prevention curricula focus more exclusively on alerting students through hard-hitting facts to their risk of being either a victim or perpetrator of an act of violence. These curricula encourage students to express their views on anger and to evaluate the long- and short-term consequences of fighting. They also provide more positive ways of dealing with arguments and anger, while offering students the opportunity to practice conflict resolution through role playing and other activities **(Wilson and Bishop, 1987).**

Curricula on dispute resolution and violence prevention have been developed for children as young as pre-schoolers. The curricula employ discussion of problems, role-playing, and structured experiences and are frequently integrated with conflict mediation programs **(Cheatham, 1988; Davis and Porter, 1985; NSSC, 1990b).**

Violence prevention and dispute resolution curricula have demonstrated success in changing students' attitudes toward conflict and fighting. Anecdotal evidence suggests they are also helpful in changing student behavior **(Wilson and Bishop, 1987).** In addition, these courses teach skills in active listening, oral language, problem solving, and critical thinking.

Under in-school suspension programs, students continue to be excluded from the classroom for disciplinary violations. Unlike traditional suspension programs, students are not released from school. Instead, they are assigned to an alternative program within the school during the period of their suspension. In-school suspension programs are not all equally effective. Successful programs feature: academic components to continue student learning outside of the classroom; therapeutic components aimed at behavior modifications; and widespread staff support **(Mizell, 1981; Wheelock, 1986).** Such programs can act to reduce both major and minor disruptive behavior **(Leatt, 1987; Short and Noblit, 1985; Stressman, 1985).**Unfortunately, few in-school suspension programs now in use meet these criteria **(Chobot and Garibaldi, 1982; Mizell, 1981; Short and Noblit, 1985).**

Addressing Racism in the Schools

Critical to addressing racism in the schools is the infusion of a multicultural perspective into school practices and curricula **(Caldwell, 1989; Derman-Sparks, 1989; Grant, 1988, 1990; Pine and Hilliard, 1990).** Multicultural education should provide children with a conceptual framework for understanding the experiences and perspectives of all groups. A multicultural approach to education is achieved when students can view concepts, themes, and issues from several ethnic perspectives, and the curriculum is infused with the frames of reference, history, intellectual ideas, and contributions of various ethnic groups **(Banks, 1987; Pine and Hilliard, 1990; Suzuki, 1984).** As Pine and Hilliard emphasize, "Such an approach extends students' understanding of the nature, development, complexity, and dynamics of a multicultural, pluralistic society and leads them to social action and decision-making that reduce prejudice and discrimination in their schools" (p. 598).

To combat racism effectively requires that racist acts and practices be confronted and challenged directly. School policies that clearly and unequivocally assert that racism is not acceptable, will not be tolerated, and will result in serious sanctions are imperative. Administrators not only have to execute the policies swiftly and consistently, they must also encourage and reward staff efforts to confront and reduce racism **(Mitchell, 1990; Pine and Hilliard, 1990; Pollard, 1989).**

Teachers have powerful positions in the classroom and are strong role models for students. They must make it clear through both their words and their actions that racist behavior will never be tolerated **(Caldwell, 1989; Pollard, 1989).**

Anti-racist policies must be strengthened by programs and curricula that directly confront and challenge bigotry, prejudice, and discrimination. Combating racism requires teachers to examine the relationship of race to power and economics and how these affect race relations **(Grant, 1988; Mitchell, 1990).** Anti-racist curricula and practices strive to enable children to: construct a positive, confident self-identity; interact with children of diverse backgrounds with comfort and empathy; think critically about biases and bigotry; and develop the skills required to stand up for oneself and others in the face of injustice **(Derman-Sparks, 1989).** Children learn to both respect diversity and challenge injustice.

Because discussion of racism inevitably calls forth anxiety and conflict, students and teachers need to develop listening skills, group problem-solving abilities, and conflict resolution skills **(Pine and Hilliard, 1990).** School staff must also examine how racial biases serve as filters through which they and others perceive and interpret the behavior of certain racial and ethnic groups **(Derman-Sparks, 1989; First, *et al.*, 1988; McLean, 1990).** Clearly, staff development for teachers, administrators, and others is essential.

Teachers of color have a critical role to play in addressing racism in the schools. They provide important role models for both children of color and White children **(Gandara, 1989; Graham, 1989; Hawley, 1989; Pine and Hilliard, 1990).** For White children, racism is undermined by positive interactions with effective and successful teachers of color. Integrated teaching staffs provide the potential for students to witness "cooperative and harmonious interaction between non-White and White teachers of equal status" **(Hawley, 1989, p.34).**

The Importance of Classroom Management

One of the best defenses against misbehavior is a classroom climate that engages students. Successful classroom management is critical to the creation of an environment that motivates students and facilitates their learning. The key to effective management is not so much in knowing how to respond to problems when they occur but in preventing the problems from occurring in the first place. Successful classroom management requires: thoughtful preparation of the physical environment; establishment of clear, concise rules that the students understand and agree with; swift, consistent, and fair enforcement of the rules; continual monitoring of the entire class and effective pacing of students; and clarity regarding how students can get help when they need it **(Brophy, 1986, 1987; Houston and Grubaugh, 1989).**

Successful classroom managers create a predictable and safe environment for their students by providing structure and setting clear, reasonable limits. They promote self-control by engaging in dialogue about the causes of misbehavior and helping children to find alternatives to negative behavior. Recognizing that behavioral expectations have a powerful influence on children's interactions, they provide numerous opportunities for their children to work and play together cooperatively **(Chicago Project on Teaching and Learning, 1989; Duax, 1990; National Association for the Education of Young Children, 1988).**

When children are excited about learning, when they experience success, they have much less motivation to misbehave. Successful classroom management stems in large part from teachers' understanding of their students, and their ability to provide lessons that challenge them but also allow success **(Bauer, *et al.*, 1990; Brophy, 1986; Chicago Project on Learning and Teaching, 1989).**

In diverse classrooms, this requires teachers to have a clear understanding of how easily culturally-determined behavior can be misinterpreted and lead to unnecessary conflict in the classroom. Teachers must be aware of their own cultural lens—how their backgrounds, experiences, attitudes, and values affect the way they interpret the behavior of children from differing cultural backgrounds **(Banks, 1988; First, *et al.*, 1988; Irujo, 1989).** For example, U.S. children are taught to look authority figures in the eye and downcast eyes are often interpreted as a sign of guilt; for children from some cultures, however, direct eye contact is considered disrespectful and rude **(First, *et al.*, 1988).** Likewise, **Irujo (1989)** notes that many Latino students have a polychromic orientation (the ability to consider many things at one time). Because they tend to be monochromic, many Anglo teachers fail to recognize this strength, and instead may interpret the behavior as a lack of focus and control.

Characteristics of Safe and Orderly Schools

Studies that examine safe and orderly schools find they are characterized by a fairly distinct school climate **(Kaesar, 1984; Lasley and Wayson, 1982; National Institute of Education, 1978; Wayson, 1984; Wayson, *et al.*, 1982).**

According to these studies, orderly schools possess: strong leaders who are consistently visible and available to students and staff and are strongly committed to maintaining a safe and orderly school environment; firm, fair, and consistent disciplinary rules mutually acceptable to students and staff and implemented without gender, race, or class bias; a focus on causes rather than symptoms that is broadly inclusive of all school staff and emphasizes handling routine disciplinary problems in the classroom; high expectations of all students and numerous and varied opportunities for student success; a general emphasis by staff, students, and policies on positive behavior, preventive discipline measures and student self-discipline; an emphasis on actively soliciting input, support, and critical review of all school policies and practices by parents, school staff, and the community; strong student and staff identification with and commitment to the school; and physical facilities and organizational structures that support and promote these policies **(Kaesar, 1984; Lasley and Wayson, 1982; National Institute of Education, 1978; Wayson, 1984; Wayson, *et al.*, 1982).**

7

Teacher Empowerment

Children are entitled to instruction by teachers who hold high expectations for all students and who are fully prepared to meet the challenge of diverse classrooms.

A Vision of Teacher Empowerment at the Good Common School

Julia Ortega and Margie Donelson are one cup of strong black coffee into a discussion by the time Donald Washington approaches their crowded booth at the Cafe del Rey. Six months ago, this trio of Good Common School teachers asked for time on the agenda of their favorite annual gathering of teachers to do a panel presentation entitled "Teacher Empowerment and School Reform." They were elated when the program committee accepted their proposal. Now the gathering is nearly upon them and, as Donald has joked: "It's time for the rubber to hit the road!"

The women know Donald's tardiness doesn't reflect a lack of interest. He is faculty sponsor for the Good Common School Camera Club that meets on Wednesdays after school; today is Wednesday. While Donald shakes rain from his hat and umbrella, Margie quickly recaps the ideas she and Julia have cooked up while waiting. "I think Julia should be the first speaker on the panel," she declares. "She should start by explaining why we want to make this presentation."

> Margie ticks off the reasons on her fingers:
>
> *"First, we read about school reform, and we don't like most of what we read. Second, there is a lot wrong with schools. Schools* do *fail too many kids, especially those who are considered 'different.' Lots of classrooms* are *unchallenging. Third, most schools* don't *cope well with cultural difference. Fourth, lots of schools* do *keep parents and communities at arm's length. Fifth, dropout rates* are *a national disgrace.*
>
> *"Even though these things are true, it's not all the fault of teachers. We don't control deteriorating social, economic, and physical conditions. Our resources are limited. What's more, we usually don't get to participate in important decisions about curriculum, school organization, instructional materials..."*

Julia interrupts, "Wait a minute. That's all true, but if we harp on it, we'll just sound defensive. I'd rather talk about the letters I wrote to the newspaper and what happened after that. I'd rather use examples that illustrate what happens when a teacher gets off the defensive and becomes proactive." Margie and Donald nod in agreement. The trio begins to recount a shared history. Margie takes notes.

Julia, who teaches second grade, wrote several letters to the local newspaper. She argued that all the talk about school reform would go nowhere unless teachers played a central role. Her last letter was particularly challenging:

> *Education occurs* in *classrooms as teachers and students come together around content that is mutually engaging. If teachers were more involved in decision-making about what is taught and how, what materials are used, how the school day is organized, how assessment should occur, how parents should be kept informed and involved, schools might actually begin to improve.*

Julia's letter got a swift response from several school board members. They invited her to discuss with them how she thought a school should be organized. It was surprising. Teachers in the district are seldom asked their opinions about educational matters. While nervous and not altogether confident about the details, she outlined some of the most important elements in her vision for schools: heterogeneous organization; multi-age groupings; an active pedagogy; a rich array of materials; support for non-English speakers; attention to differences; collaboration among teachers; and school-based decision-making.

Julia was further encouraged when other teachers came forward to support her ideas and express interest in starting a collaborative "new school." In fact, there were more teachers ready to help than could be accommodated in what was initially termed "the experiment."

The experiment began in the form of a school within the larger school, with Julia serving as a teacher/leader. Today, there are three individual schools-within-a-school operating within the original building. Houses One, Two, and Three each serve approximately 200 children. Many of the ideas developed by House One—the first "new school"—were eventually adopted by the other two units. Increasingly, much to Julia's surprise, the approach has taking hold in other schools throughout the district.

The teachers who began this venture quickly found they had chosen a difficult path. They had little experience with concepts such as heterogeneous student groupings, and multiculturalism wasn't much more than a slogan. Only three of the nine original teachers spoke a second language—Spanish—and collectively, the teachers had few particularly rich instructional materials to bring with them to the new school. Further, they lacked collaborative experience and were not sure how to organize a process for cooperative decision-making. They had much to learn.

Teachers who were part of the experimental group met regularly that first spring. Julia was the facilitator. They began by sharing each other's work—their teaching histories, activities they believed most successful, their greatest hopes for the new school, and what they thought they needed to know more about to reach those hopes. The teachers developed a common summer reading list that focused on topics such as multiculturalism, teacher expectations, bilingualism, school climate, cooperative learning, and integrated curriculum. They also agreed to do some journal writing and to come together two weeks before the beginning of the school year to talk and plan intensively.

Reading together proved to be a powerful experience. These teachers still do it regularly because it keeps them thinking about teaching and learning and growing intellectually. Currently, they are reading from Maxine Greene's *Landscapes of Learning*, a series of essays on education. Last year, they read together Michael Rose's *Lives on the Boundary* and Alice Walker's *The Temple of My Familiar.*

Teachers also expended considerable energy during early meetings on the matter of their expectations of students. Is it really true that all children can learn? What about the social context of many children's lives? The teachers decided they had to break through a dominant cycle of thought about "children as victims" and "teachers being expected to do too much." They came to believe much of the popular discourse surrounding schools had to be put aside—in fact, blame had to be directed away from the children and their circumstances.

Members of the group wondered, "What if we started unequivocally with the understanding and belief that all children can learn and be successful in school?" This led them naturally to other questions: "Would we organize school as we do now? Use basal materials and skill sheets? See the arts only as enrichment? Separate children by our perceptions of their ability? View different language and cultural backgrounds as barriers to learning? Keep learning activities in such short time frames? Stay with the same texts? Retain children?" In effect, teachers revisited all their practices through a different lens—the belief that all children can learn. This proved to be an important starting point.

Reminiscences come to an abrupt halt as Julie glances at her watch. "It's getting late," she notes. "We've got to get an outline for the rest of our presentation done and decide who will do what. My babysitter leaves in an hour."

Forty minutes later the task is accomplished. Julia will start the discussion, sharing favorite memories of the early days. Donald is anxious to share strategies they used to achieve a multicultural school—such as a teaching staff that reflects the diversity of the student population and sensitizing teachers to the real lives of students and their families. Margie will talk about the school's collaboration with the local university to help prepare new teachers. If each teacher speaks for twenty minutes, they calculate, another twenty will be left for questions from the audience.

On the way out of Cafe del Rey, Julia stops to apologize to Tomás Zapata for tying up one of his largest booths at the dinner hour. Tomás waves off her apology with a smile. His youngest daughter, Sara, is a student of Donald's this year and Julia is a friend of Tomás's wife. These three teachers are always welcome at Cafe del Rey.

• • •

Four weeks later to the day at 7:05 a.m., Donald pulls his car into the parking lot of Julia's apartment complex. He steps into the foyer, presses the intercom buzzer to announce his arrival, then jogs back to his car. When Julia appears bundled in parka and mittens with a thermos bottle tucked under one arm, he is busily scraping frost from the rear windshield. He and Julia will pick up Margie, who lives nearby, then share a two-hour freeway drive to the conference center. Donald is grateful for the long drive ahead. Julia's coffee will help him get fully awake and he can practice his speech.

By 9:00 a.m., the car is parked, the three Good Common School teachers have registered for the meeting, and they are busy renewing acquaintances with other teachers who regularly attend this annual gathering. Fifteen minutes later, seventy-five teachers move from the common area into the meeting room. Rows of comfortable chairs are arranged in semicircles before a blazing fire. The welcoming fireplace contrasts with sunlit snowbanks and shadowy evergreens visible through the room's broad windows. This group of "teachers who love to teach" returns here year after year to refuel their minds and refresh their spirits.

An hour is absorbed by introductions, an entertaining monologue presented by the conference convener, and meeting announcements. The first program segment is a traditional favorite called "Teacher's Voices." Four teachers representing primary, elementary, middle, and high school classrooms read from their personal journals, sharing the rhythms of their days, the struggles of their students, and the worries and hopes that characterize their professional lives. The teachers in the audience—veterans and novices alike—listen, spellbound.

The Good Common School panel is next on the program. Julia, Donald, and Margie seat themselves. Julia speaks from memory, sharing personal experiences that have ignited her own professional growth: evenings spent drafting letters to the editor; her surprise at being asked to meet with the local school board; her delight at discovering that other teachers share her vision of schooling; highlights from the early days of the House One experiment.

Donald opens his presentation on multiculturalism with anecdotes from his own experience as an African American male student in a West Coast inner-city high school. Despite the good-humored style, his message is clear: racism hurts. He explains that what he has just done—working through his own autobiography—is basic to the approach used by House One teachers as they probe their own understandings of racial, cultural, ethnic, and gender differences. He notes how this is a difficult, ongoing task that requires adults to face many of their own prejudices and stereotypes. Ultimately, he notes, it brings teachers closer together and helps them to deal more constructively with the differences in their classrooms.

He adds that working toward multicultural understanding involves learning more about students and their backgrounds, causing teachers to examine the curriculum more intensely and look both at what is taught and what materials are used. He tells the audience:

> *"We have become particularly sensitive to the materials we use. We make sure our students are represented in them and that they are free of stereotypes and biases. We find that even important, well-meaning materials portray subtle stereotypes. When we find stereotypes, we point them out to our students as a means of enlarging their sensitivities.*
>
> *"We've learned the environment we create affects the multicultural ambience of the school. What we say in class can be negated by what's on the walls or not on the walls for everyone to see. Our hallways are now full of photos and artwork that reflect this understanding. We use family histories and tie a lot of what we teach to diverse perspectives and world views as a means of honoring our multicultural commitment.*
>
> *"As teachers, we have chosen to use curriculum themes across subjects and grades—many are employed schoolwide. This creates an incentive to share ideas. During one period when 'traditions' was the theme, different teachers worked with parents and did research at the public library to develop materials we all shared. Ana Návarez, who teaches a fourth/fifth-grade grouping, took responsibility for African traditions and gave the rest of us a lot of direction on development of traditional masks. June Sorenson, who has a second/third-grade class, researched Cambodian dress and dance traditions. The 'traditions' project, which involved kindergarten through fourth/fifth grade children, turned into a wonderful multicultural celebration.*
>
> *"Over the past four years, as we've worked to gain greater mastery of multiculturalism, teachers have agreed to take several in-service courses together. African literature and Caribbean literature were particularly popular. Those of us who are not native Spanish speakers are studying Spanish. These efforts balance the European-centered academic course work that dominates U.S. colleges and universities.*
>
> *"As these activities have raised our multicultural consciousness, a lot of concern about the racial and ethnic composition of the school staff has resulted. Although 72 percent of our students are African American or Latino and 11 percent are Southeast Asian, the teaching staff is 76 percent Anglo. At that, we have more teachers of color than most schools in the district. While we don't argue that only African American or Latino teachers can effectively teach African American or Latino students, we do believe children need to see teachers who look like them and who can serve as important role models. Equally important, teachers of color provide role models for Anglo children, who too often have limited interaction with professionals from ethnically diverse groups.*

"In passing, I should note the number of teachers of color in public schools has steadily decreased since 1972. It is desperately important this decline be reversed. As a small group of teachers, we can't reverse a national trend. But we can take some responsible steps to correct the situation in our own school. One step has been the recruitment of people of color to work as teacher aides. This serves the dual purpose of helping children and bringing more people of color into the school. We hope some will decide to pursue teaching careers. Secondly, we have organized a local high school program for minority students interested in teaching, encouraging students to work in classrooms as tutors and assistant teachers. We believe this is an important teacher recruitment effort, as well as a civic contribution.

"Furthermore, we've developed a fund-raising effort to help secondary students enter teacher education programs. Finally, we have actively encouraged legislation to provide minority students with teaching grants and loan forgiveness incentives. I stress this because small local efforts aren't enough to solve this problem. Larger efforts are also essential..."

Before he finishes, Donald sees the convener flash a "time" signal. He quickly concludes his talk and introduces Margie Donelson, noting she will speak about House One's faculty participation in a partnership between several public schools and the local university to prepare new teachers.

Margie can't resist opening with a strong statement of appreciation for how the activities described by Julia and Donald have supported her own professional growth. She holds up a large yellow T-shirt with the words "KISS ME I'M IRISH" printed on the back. When the laughter dies down, she explains the shirt was a present from Julia and Donald at the end of the "traditions" project. Then she gets down to business.

"As a partnership school, we provide a variety of classroom experiences and practices for new teachers, sharing in the growth of their understanding of what it means to teach in a multicultural environment. We make it a point to support the idealism and social commitments of these prospective teachers while working to enlarge their teaching skills, their sensitivities to children and families, and their understanding of appropriate instructional strategies and materials.

"Everybody benefits as we share the work at the Good Common School with university faculty members involved in teacher education. We gain access to university libraries, assistance with development of curriculum materials, and lots of focused opportunities to reflect on classroom practice. All of us are encouraged to write, share ideas, and participate in school and classroom-based research. The result is an increase in professionalism and understanding of teaching and learning for both experienced and novice educators.

"Between participating in the school/university collaboration and welcoming community aides and secondary school tutors into our classrooms, we've been able to provide a very high level of personalization for our students. This gives us more time to step back and observe what is happening. For example, we're able to assess clearly which children need more carefully structured materials and teaching, who needs more open-endedness in the questions being posed or more opportunities to follow their own questions, who needs a larger array of concrete materials, or who can progress with fewer concrete examples. Overall, as teachers, we've come to a fuller realization of how important it is to attend to the special needs of each child. As a result, we've seen improved academic and social growth among children in our classrooms.

"One of the things I like best about the school/university collaboration is that I've become more comfortable about using writing as a means of enlarging thought and developing student self-assessment skills.

"We also engage steadily in student assessment rooted directly in classroom instruction. For example, fourth/fifth-grade teachers began a collective activity this year around writing and the assessment of writing. I want to describe it in some detail because it demonstrates the increased trust that has developed among teachers. We began by examining samples of children's writing, discussing how each of us work with writing, and agreeing to organize writing workshops in each of our classrooms. We documented our respective teaching practices, reflecting on our experiences and the children's work. This brought us much closer to children's writing.

"For the assessment study, we asked all fourth/fifth-grade students to complete a personal narrative of their own choosing—about 150, in all. We used a holistic assessment process, including criteria such as clear message, logical sequence, voice, and mechanics to try to respond descriptively and quantitatively to the question, 'How well do fourth/fifth graders in the Good Common School write?'

"We all knew it was not a perfect process. But that didn't matter. What did matter was—unlike most assessment activities—this one was embedded within classroom practice. It enlarged our discussions about writing. It provided us with more experience as readers of written discourse and broadened our insights into the teaching of writing. We became a community of writing teachers—people able to link the teaching of writing to the classroom, as well as to understand ways to connect writing and student evaluation. For us, this was empowerment of a high order.

"From these beginnings, a schoolwide program developed that includes student writing portfolios and ongoing assessment of writing. We now do student portfolios in all basic learning areas—an essential element in our desire to be more accountable to parents and children. As writing assessments have progressed, second/third-grade teachers have become deeply involved in learning more about project-centered teaching, a powerful strategy that focuses on two critical questions: 'What do we already know?' 'What do we want to find out?'

"Inspired by the work of Eliot Wigginton and the Foxfire movement, we've undertaken local projects related to the environment and television production. This connects what goes on in school with what children see every day outside of school. Further, it's a way to more fully engage the diverse interests of children. Not incidentally, new relationships with a wide variety of community resources and institutions have been developed."

Once more the "time" signal is flashed. Margie struggles to present one last large idea in her remaining minute.

"During the past two years we've had a final innovation—the 'extended school year contract.' It adds a tenth month to the school year, enabling teachers to work collaboratively on curriculum, engage in schoolwide research activities, participate in preparing schoolwide evaluations, and engage in special enrichment programs with some of the students—beyond the formal school day and during the summer. This has been a real boost.

"In a large sense, I have described to you how teachers in the Good Common School have taken considerable control over what is usually called "staff development" or "in-service education." We understand these changes require more preparation, more knowledge, and more skills. We insist the help we receive be related directly to our questions, needs, and commitments. At the Good Common School, we don't engage in externally organized generic staff development.

"We're working harder than ever before. We're also learning more. We are more professional. We are no longer paralyzed by our own isolation. And we no longer worry much about burnout, which we know to be rooted in isolation and feelings of disempowerment. By and large, we have left those feelings behind."

Late that afternoon, Donald edges his car onto the freeway. Each of the three are "coming down" from the conference differently. Donald drifts into silence. Julia's chatter slows with the passing miles. Margie, who has been deep in a paperback novel, leans forward and asks, "Can we stop for Chinese food?" Donald answers with a teasing question, "Will you wear your 'KISS ME I'M IRISH' T-shirt?"

EFFECTIVE STAFF DEVELOPMENT

Effective staff development programs have several distinguishing characteristics. Effective programs:

- Are conducted at the school during the school day with substitute teachers available for classroom coverage.
- Focus on needs and concerns as identified by teachers.
- Involve teachers, principals, and other school staff in planning, implementation, and evaluation.
- Offer a series of sessions—rather than a single session—integrated into regular school activities.
- Use both formal training sessions and informal exchanges among peers.
- Provide sufficient resources to ensure effective planning, implementation, follow-up, and evaluation.
- Provide teachers with adequate planning and group meeting time.
- Rely on support materials and outside experts as resources to be integrated into the effort, rather than elements that dictate the effort.

Source: Guerrero, *et al.* (1989); Valencia and Killion (1989).

NEW TEACHER COMPETENCIES FOR DIVERSE CLASSROOMS

California Tomorrow's Embracing Diversity *project identifies four basic areas of teacher competency required to teach effectively in classrooms that integrate foreign-born and U.S.-born students.*

Language Development

- Knowledge of second-language acquisition and classroom techniques for helping students with language acquisition—including an emphasis on concept development.
- Whole-language approaches to integrate oral language development with writing, reading, and listening.

Building and Teaching an Inclusive Curriculum

- Familiarity with a wide range of materials and literature from different cultures and periods in history to enrich the curriculum and focus on issues of culture, immigration, prejudice, and intolerance.
- Techniques for teaching "to" and "from" the experiences of the students.

Establishing a Climate of Diversity

- Ability to use the classroom as an opportunity to explore issues of personal prejudice with active discussions about tolerance and prejudice.
- Understanding the importance of never allowing incidents of intolerance to pass unaddressed, and knowledge of how to use those incidents as opportunities for learning.
- Knowledge of how to establish and uphold clear norms of acceptable behavior regarding prejudice and respect.
- Awareness of approaches to build respect, safety, trust, and responsibility within a class and a school.
- Awareness of techniques of affirmation for students and the importance of high expectations for all students.

Knowledge of Students' Cultures and Backgrounds

- Understanding the basic role of culture in shaping learning and perspectives; specific knowledge of the political, historical, economic, social, and cultural backgrounds of students in the school.

From: *Embracing Diversity,* Olsen and Mullen (1990)

Problems with Teacher Empowerment in U.S. Public Schools

CHALLENGES FACING TODAY'S TEACHERS

The challenges faced daily by classroom teachers have heightened exponentially during the past decade as intensified student needs are compounded
by increasingly diverse student cultures and languages.

From the time they enter the profession, most teachers spend much of their time behind a closed classroom door with little opportunity for collegial interactions with peers, the principal, or education leaders who might act as positive role models. Many schools offer little encouragement or recognition of professional growth. Time and resources available for experimentation or development are often severely limited. To compound matters, teachers have little or no formal voice in the formulation of school policy or practice.

After a few years, these realities tend to reduce a teacher's enthusiasm or belief in educational innovation. Many teachers eventually adopt a philosophy of self-reliance, vigorously opposing or ignoring advice or suggestions for change, regardless of the source. Others come to operate on a principle of "non-interference" with other teachers' work. As a result, although many schools have one or more "master teachers," their expertise has little influence on their less skilled peers, benefitting only those students they teach directly.

These negative forces inevitably limit a teacher's effectiveness over time. Some are driven from the classroom into administrative roles or other professions, resulting in a work force that is burned out at one end and inexperienced at the other. The growing shortage of highly motivated and well-qualified teachers is a major barrier to meaningful school improvement.

TEACHER EFFICACY AND TEACHER EXPECTATIONS

Researchers have noted that teacher efficacy—a teacher's belief in his or her ability to instruct their students effectively—predicts a capacity to hold high expectations for all students. Educator Thomas Good (1987) observes that teachers with a strong sense of efficacy are more confident and at ease, exhibiting less negative behavior in the classroom. They tend to hold high expectations for their students and, consequently, they produce achievement gains.

On the other hand, teachers with a low sense of efficacy are more likely to hold low expectations for their students. Because they concentrate on rule enforcement and classroom management, less time is available for positive interaction and academic content. The result is less academic gain.

Impact of Teacher Expectations

Classroom teachers play a profound role in shaping the course of a student's schooling. As a result of their classroom experiences, students can be urged toward maximum achievement or condemned to poor academic performance and disciplinary problems—indicators that they may be among those who will leave school before graduation. One of the most enduring impacts teachers have are the expectations they express to individual students concerning the child's chances for school success or failure.

Good (1987) defines teacher expectations as "inferences that teachers make about the future behavior or academic achievement of their students based on what they know about these students now." During the last twenty years, it has become increasingly clear that expectations teachers communicate to their students act to shape academic achievement in substantial ways.

Effects of Teacher Expectations

In his comprehensive review of the research, Good notes two principal prevailing effects:

1. **The self-fulfilling prophecy effect,** in which a teacher's erroneous expectation leads to behavior that causes the expectation to become true.
2. **The sustaining expectation effect,** in which a teacher expects previously observed student behavior patterns to continue and is therefore unable to appreciate or benefit from improvements that occur.

Good and his colleagues suggest the following process to describe how teacher expectations operate in the classroom:

- Teachers form different expectations for individual student behavior and achievement early in the school year based on what they already know about the individual student.
- Teachers behave differently toward individual students on the basis of these different expectations.
- This differential treatment tells individual students how they are expected to behave in class and perform academically.
- If the teacher's treatment is consistent over time and not resisted or changed by the student, it is likely to affect the child's self-confidence, motivation, aspirations, classroom conduct, and interactions with the teacher.
- The student's behavior resulting from the teacher's treatment reinforces the teacher's original expectations, causing the student to conform further to these expectations.
- Over time, high-expectation students will be led to achieve their potential; low-expectation students will not gain their potential.

According to Good, variables that have a strong impact on how a teacher forms expectations include a student's track or group placement, classroom conduct, physical appearance, race, socioeconomic status, ethnicity, sex, speech characteristics, previous academic performance, and special education labels. As noted by educator Charles Payne (1984), the variables of race and ethnicity—particularly as expressed by language—seem most powerful in shaping teachers' initial low expectations.

How Low Expectations Are Communicated

When teachers hold low expectations for certain students, these are communicated to children in a variety of ways. Among those noted by Good and Payne:

- Giving those perceived as low achievers ("lows") less time to answer a question; interrupting "lows" more often during their answers.
- Giving "lows" the answer to questions rather than offering clues or rephrasing the question to encourage them to work toward an answer.
- Criticizing "lows" more often for failure.
- Praising "lows" less often for their success.
- Failing to give "lows" feedback on their classroom answers; when feedback is offered, it is brief and less informative.
- Calling on "lows" less often in class; paying less attention to "lows" in general and interacting with them less frequently.
- Seating "lows" farther away from the teacher.
- Exhibiting less friendly interaction with "lows," including less smiling, eye contact, and nonverbal indicators of support.
- Offering "lows" less exciting instruction, less emphasis on meaning, and more rote and drill practice.
- Demanding less work and effort from "lows."

Although this differential treatment may seem subtle, children both observe and internalize the messages teachers give them about their potential. In a study of children's perceptions of teacher expectations (Weinstein, *et al.*, 1987), elementary school students were fully aware their teachers offered more opportunity to those viewed as high achievers, and that those viewed as "lows" received more rigid instruction and more negative feedback about school work and classroom behavior.

In his summary of the research, Charles Payne concludes teacher expectations vary with a student's social status, affecting both the quantity and quality of teaching the child receives. These effects are greatest for students who are younger, of lower socioeconomic status, or members of minority groups.

FACTORS CONTRIBUTING TO LOW TEACHER EFFECTIVENESS

Poor-Quality Training

Teachers' abilities to respond effectively to the academic and social needs of all students are strongly influenced by the quality of their training and the range of their experience both before and after entering the profession. Many teachers— especially those who teach students from different cultural and language backgrounds—find their training has left them ill equipped for the classroom of the 1990s.

Teacher education generally involves concentration on a major field of study along with a mandatory curriculum of education courses that purport to prepare an individual to instruct a classroom. This is followed by a period of student teaching during which a new teacher is observed in a school setting by more experienced teachers. After certification, periodic "in-service" training is offered with the claim of keeping teachers current with their profession. Most observers are highly critical of every phase of this process.

An Array of Negative Conditions

After five years of studying the education of teachers, educator John Goodlad (1990) has concluded "...the necessary condition for vigorous, coherent, and self-renewing programs for teacher preparation are not in place. In seeking to renew teacher education, we must reckon with an array of vexing conditions." Among them, he finds:

- **Low prestige and status of the teaching profession.** Teacher colleges around the country have shed their images as "teachers' schools" following in the footsteps of major public and private universities that grant low status to teacher education, even when they claim it as their main mission. This lowered status results in a temporary, part-time faculty largely concerned with seeing that students meet state certification requirements—there is little incentive to consider the state of the art.
- **Unclear mission and identity at teacher education institutions.** Only two university presidents in Goodlad's study viewed teacher education as a central mission; in most cases, researchers could not easily identify an institution's locus of authority, responsibility, or philosophy concerning teacher preparation. Teacher education program budgets were rarely protected from being raided to meet other priorities.
- **Shifting reward system.** Across the country, colleges and universities are placing increased value on research and publications and decreased value on teaching students. Goodlad notes that rewards are greater for those who study teachers than for those who educate them.
- **An ill-defined profession.** In contrast to many other professions, there is no clear beginning or ending point to teacher education. Goodlad describes "casual entry and passage of students through the programs" in teacher education institutions; he also observes a lack of both interaction among peers and informal professional socialization, resulting in a weak sense of professional identity.

- **Misguided regulatory intrusions.** Because the goal of many teacher education institutions is merely to prepare students for state certification, they design their curriculum around state regulations. Such regulations are often the product of a political system concerned more with public opinion and bureaucratic control than with quality teaching. When student teachers are confronted with conflicting demands between what they have learned in college and what the system prescribes, they generally opt to conform to the system.
- **Poor training of student teachers.** Starting with a lack of coordination between teacher education institutions and collaborating schools, oversight of student teachers tends to become the sole responsibility of the local school principal. Student teaching programs generally suffer from a short supply of qualified cooperating teachers and the assignment of student teachers on the basis of murky criteria.

Influence of Student Teacher/Cooperating Teacher Relationship

In her review of the research on teacher training, Pauline Grippen (1989) highlights the influence of the relationship between the student teacher and the cooperating teacher. Typically, a student teacher is paired with a single cooperating teacher for the duration of the training period. The usual result of this collaboration is an undue concentration on classroom management at the expense of learning about student instruction strategies, a discounting of pedagogy learned during formal training at college, the stressing of "survival" skills, and an emphasis on the personal rather than professional relationship between the two parties.

Grippen notes the outcome of this approach to teacher training is that teachers—regardless of their preparation—tend to fall back on the same teaching strategies they experienced as students. The result is a cycle of teacher behavior passed largely intact from one generation to the other—a behavior characterized by teacher-dominated instruction, low level questioning, an emphasis on the acquisition of basic skills, and neglect of the wide range of variables that impact student instruction.

After considering the current state of teacher education, Goodlad concludes, "Few of the future teachers in our sample would begin their important work with a comprehensive grasp of the role of schools, with the ability to transcend subject matter and make it readily accessible to large numbers of their students, with the range and depth of instructional knowledge and skills requisite to promoting some significant learning in all children and youth, and with the traits and abilities essential to working with colleagues on school renewal."

Limited Professional Growth

Staff Development Programs

Staff development programs, as defined by Guerrero and his colleagues (1989), seek to train new teachers, inform teachers of new curriculum and teaching strategies, instruct in the use of new technology, reinforce previously learned skills, develop new skills, and provide a forum for teachers to share their ideas and strategies.

Too often, however, professional development programs contribute more to staff frustration and resentment than to school improvement. When teachers regard in-service training as "an ordeal to be endured," it can increase their resistance to change.

The typical staff development program encompasses a series of training sessions designed to address a specific "deficiency" in teacher skills, abilities, or knowledge as identified by a school administrator or the central office. Workshops are frequently conducted by an outside "expert" who has little contact with staff prior to or after the session. Evaluation may be minimal and monitoring of skills development perfunctory. Too many schools do not offer teachers the personal support or technical assistance to help them internalize new knowledge and put it into practice.

Obstacles to Change

In their examination of staff development case studies, Sheila Valencia and Joellen Killion (1989) identify five major obstacles to achieving teacher change:

1. **Short-term in-service training.** Most attempts at in-service training take the form of brief, infrequent workshops mandated by central office or building administrators; these workshops lack opportunities for follow-up, practice, or feedback, offering superficial approaches to complex problems. In a given year, the average teacher participates in about three days of in-service training, rarely more than one day at a time.
2. **Teacher isolation.** Most teachers experience the balance of the school day alone in their classroom with minimal professional contact with other adults—there is little opportunity for interaction with peers to share strategies or observe others in action. In most schools, there is little or no time for professional collaboration; when teachers do find time for brief interaction in the halls or the teachers' lounge, conversation is most likely to focus on non-professional subjects.
3. **Comfort with the status quo.** The introduction of new concepts and techniques can disrupt the classroom, causing problems where none existed before and making both students and teachers uncomfortable. During a period of change, teachers can feel less competent as they struggle with novel strategies. The threat of change is often met with defensive behavior and resistance to learning.
4. **Failure to appreciate the learning needs of teachers.** Central office or building administrators often fail to understand that teachers should be viewed as learners when confronted with new concepts. Like children, adults experience stages of learning that must be acknowledged and addressed.
5. **Strict fidelity to instructional procedures.** Curricula are often designed by "experts" with the notion that they should be "teacher-proof." A strict adherence to the prescribed teaching plan denies the teacher's role as an active agent of change in the classroom. Effective development cannot occur when teachers are viewed as incompetent to make effective instructional decisions.

Increased Work Loads

Educators Thomas Popkewitz and Kathryn Lind (1989) find school reform efforts often result in increased work for teachers without increased compensation or even recognition. An ironic outcome can be further bureaucratization as school administrators seek to track results. Already faced with an overwhelming work load, teachers can find their time scheduled even more strictly to fit in the added burden of school improvement. While often presented to teachers in the context of greater autonomy and decision-making power, the results of school reform efforts can be exactly the opposite.

Reliance on Teacher Testing

As an analogy to increased dependency on standardized tests for students, school reform efforts across the country have also increased use of standardized competency tests to make critical career decisions about teachers. As of 1987, researchers Stephanie Salzman and Patricia Whitfield (1989) found forty-four states that require prospective teachers to pass a performance test prior to certification; every state but Alaska and Iowa was in the process of adopting some form of teacher testing. Although some tests involve writing samples, critics George Madaus and Diana Pullin (1987) warn that the majority are multiple-choice tests of uneven quality and dubious validity.

Salzman and Whitfield note that while "virtually all the states have made some form of commitment to teacher testing, the diversity of philosophies and attitudes toward the issue is substantial. The states differ in terms of when they test prospective teachers, what their tests cover, the difficulty of their instruments, and which test are used. Virtually every aspect of teacher testing has been subject to considerable debate."

Faulty Assumptions and Unfounded Claims

As argued by Madaus and Pullin, teacher competency tests rest on the faulty assumptions that: 1) the skills and abilities measured by standardized competency tests are necessary for effective classroom teaching; and 2) tests are actually capable of measuring these skills and competencies.

Their review of previous research and examination of sample tests lead them to conclude that the subject matter tested is largely unrelated to successful teaching, and claims of test validity—that the test actually measures what it claims to measure—are unfounded and, perhaps worse, unchallenged.

Cultural Bias of Standardized Tests

Many observers are also concerned that standardized teacher competency tests—like standardized tests for students—are biased against certain groups. An examination of pass/fail rates in a given year reported by Salzman and Whitfield supports this charge. In California, 74 percent of African Americans, 61 percent of Latinos, and 50 percent of Asians failed the state's Basic Educational Skills Test. The rate of failure among Whites was 24 percent. In Florida, only 35 percent of African Americans, 51 percent of Latinos, and 63 percent of Asians passed while 90 percent of Whites achieved passing scores. In Georgia, the failure rate among African Americans was 66 percent, with 52 percent for Latinos, and only 11 percent for Whites. In Texas, testing kept 84 percent of African Americans and 65 percent of Latinos from becoming teachers.

Hidden Motive Ignores Dangers

Madaus and Pullin conclude, "If we require prospective teachers to take these...tests because we want to improve the public image of teaching, then let's admit that is our motive. But let's also admit that this public relations gambit ignores many serious psychometric, scientific, and ethical concerns having to do with the correctness of the inferences or decisions made about test-takers on the basis of their scores."

While the need to stress professional competency and accountability is certainly an important component of effective school improvement, strategies that rely on current standardized teacher competency tests as career gateways are, at best, misinformed and misguided. At worst, they may be a punitive, low-cost device embraced by policymakers to diffuse public concern and anger about the dismal quality of the nation's schools.

SHORTAGE OF TEACHERS

Recent studies of the teaching profession predict a shortage of teachers during the 1990s due to rising student enrollment, increased retirement from an aging work force, inability to retain personnel, and—most importantly—the profession's failure to attract new teachers.

When teaching is viewed largely as a low-status, low-pay profession with long hours and limited career advancement, it's not surprising that young people heading to college are preparing for more rewarding futures.

Lack of Teachers of Color

As noted by Patricia Graham (1987), former dean of the Harvard University Graduate School of Education, lack of teachers of color when student enrollment is increasingly diverse is of particular concern. In all but two of the nation's twenty-five largest cities, children of color make up the majority of public school enrollment. By the end of this decade, it is estimated that between 30 and 40 percent of U.S. school children will be non-White. At the same time, the number of teachers of color will continue to decline. The result will be an increasingly White teaching force instructing an increasingly diverse student population.

In her review of the problem, Graham finds fewer African Americans now attending college and graduate school, and—among those who do—fewer who are choosing the teaching profession. With African American public school enrollment at about 16 percent nationwide, African American teachers constitute less than 7 percent of the work force, down from 8 percent in recent years.

Graham underscores the urgency of having African American teachers as role models for the benefit of all students. For students of color and for White students as well, African American teachers present successful adults who are making a valuable contribution to society. She finds the roots of the minority teacher shortage lie in the fact that almost half of African American children begin life in poverty, then receive an education that is simply not as good as that received by Whites. These factors combine with the low status of the teaching profession—only 1 percent of high-achieving African Americans express interest in teaching—and obstacles such as teacher competency testing to further narrow the field of potential candidates.

High Teacher Dropout Rate

As observed by researchers Martin Haberman and William Rickards (1990), the teacher shortage is exacerbated by the alarming rate at which teachers leave their profession. After six years of service, about half of all new teachers stop teaching. In urban schools, the average term of service drops to five years. Expert opinion suggests that it take about three years for the urban teacher to become competent in the classroom, presenting the irony of teachers leaving just when they are fully ready to teach.

Reasons for Leaving

Haberman and Rickards's survey of teachers leaving the Milwaukee school system ranked their top reasons for leaving as: 1) student discipline; 2) inadequate support from administrators and supervisors; 3) heavy work load; 4) lack of parental support; 5) underachieving students; 6) clerical burdens; and 7) dealing with students' cultural backgrounds.

The study contrasts teachers' concerns when they first entered the school system with their reasons for leaving. While student discipline and lack of parental support remained relatively constant, concern about under-achieving students fell from first place for new teachers to fifth place for teachers who were leaving. Concern about dealing with differing cultural backgrounds dropped from third place for new teachers to seventh place for departing teachers.

New teachers were less concerned about working conditions, ranking heavy work load and clerical burdens toward the bottom. By the time they left, however, heavy work load had advanced to third place and clerical burdens climbed to number six. Inadequate support from administrators moved up from fifth place to second place. Clearly, working conditions that could have been improved came to the forefront by the time these teachers departed.

TEACHER EMPOWERMENT: VISION AND REALITY

According to a recent survey (Ashby, *et al.*, 1989), teachers tend to view their empowerment as becoming able to make a difference, gaining a sense of impact, and having some control over their professional destiny. Considering the variables that would support such outcomes, teachers offered the following ranking: 1) administrative support; 2) responsibility for meaningful tasks; 3) decision-making related to curriculum; 4) decisions on teaching assignments; 5) input on school policies and procedures; 6) choice in determining staff development programs.

The reality for most teachers in elementary public schools presents a very different picture. Schools tend to enforce teacher isolation both from their peers and their superiors. Central office control and excessive bureaucracy deny meaningful teacher input into curricula, instructional strategies, or school policies and procedures. Staff development is conducted from the top down in a piecemeal fashion. Financial resources are often grossly inadequate. The status of the profession has fallen to an all-time low.

Teachers stand at the heart of every child's school experience. They have the potential to be central actors in the task of school improvement. Unfortunately, the gap between vision and reality is as gaping here as in any facet of school life. Effective reform will have to consider the entire teaching experience from undergraduate training to student teaching to in-service staff development. As with perhaps no other element of school improvement, the results of a determined, large-scale effort can be truly profound.

Project EXCEL: The Teacher Support Network

The Teacher Support Network is one of five components of Project EXCEL (Excellence in Community Educational Leadership), an effort by the **National Council of La Raza** to demonstrate and evaluate effective models by which Latino community-based organizations (CBOs) can improve educational outcomes for Latino students.

Project EXCEL utilizes staff, resources, services, and facilities of Latino CBOs to address: persistent under-education in the Latino community; lack of bilingual personnel in schools; lack of coordinated family-wide learning programs; and lack of school resources to address the non-academic needs of students and families.

La Raza's Role

The National Council of La Raza participates in Project EXCEL as an advisor, providing expertise in research and acting as a resource facilitator.

La Raza provides CBOs with training, assistance, and research data to help them conduct local community/education needs assessments. La Raza also conducted surveys and interviews of CBOs to determine available services. While most CBOs have little experience with the education of school-aged students, many have expertise in pre-school and recovery programs, offsetting the traditional view that education services are exclusively the domain of schools.

After considering the particular needs of the community and the services and the resources available through local CBOs, La Raza then designs model programs for each community in collaboration with CBOs. Model programs include components for staff training and instruments for data collection and program evaluation.

Participation of Community-Based Organizations

Programs within Project EXCEL are all operated by Latino CBOs, reflecting La Raza's belief that schools should utilize resources available in the community. Each program is geared toward a service needed at schools.

Project EXCEL is based on the concept that CBOs can form partnerships with schools to enable schools to take advantage of their unique abilities to combine social services with educational programming for students and families that schools fail to serve well. Cooperative relationships between CBOs and schools encourage teachers and administrators to raise their expectations for Latino students and improve educators' ability to work with Latino communities.

To help foster early success, CBOs initially involved in Project EXCEL were organized with close ties to La Raza. However, requests by funders for program activities in specific geographic areas forced La Raza to select some CBOs that had no previous relationship with La Raza. These organizations were selected on the basis of their ability to provide a well-organized staff and a strong reputation in the local community.

The Teacher Support Network

Project EXCEL's Teacher Support Network is designed to organize community resources to offer training and assistance to Latino teachers and others working with Latino children. The goal is to raise expectations for Latino students and increase teacher effectiveness, in part by creating positive linkages between educators and the community.

After working with parents, community leaders, and school staff to assess perceptions of teacher needs and attitudes, La Raza developed workshop topics and parent/teacher activities to help bridge communication gaps and dispel misconceptions. These motivational and educational activities often take place in the Latino community, enabling teachers to gain a better understanding of the home environment of Latino students.

The Teacher Support Network offers participating teachers the opportunity to form cooperative relationships with other teachers and community members and the chance to share successful strategies and programs.

CBOs make a unique contribution to the Teacher Support Network by identifying people with the time and desire to help teachers as school aides. Because they are in direct contact with the community, CBOs are often in a position to encourage participation by individuals who might otherwise remain outside the school environment. These recruiting efforts assist teachers in understanding Latino youth and give Latino children the chance to see role models in their classrooms.

Other components of the programs include: mini-grants for teacher-generated enrichment programs; ceremonies recognizing teachers who make outstanding contributions to the education of Latino students; and a project advisory committee of principals, bilingual supervisors, staff development specialists, and community leaders.

Other EXCEL Programs

Other programs in Project EXCEL:

- **Academia del Pueblo** has established after-school and summer "academies" to offer education assistance to help children meet or exceed grade promotion requirements in elementary school. The Academia utilizes CBO resources and employs public and private school staff who use exemplary teaching practices, including team teaching, cross-age tutors, and cooperative learning.

- **Project Success** is designed to increase high school completion and college entrance rates by providing Latino youth in middle or junior high school with academic enrichment, career and academic counseling, and other special services. The project equips young people with the skills and interests to enroll and succeed in college-preparatory curriculum when they reach high school.
- **Project Second Chance** recognizes that a large proportion of Latino youth leave school without diplomas. The basic aim of the project is to provide educational services and counseling to allow young people to gain a high school equivalency certificate or diploma and continue some form of education—either traditional post-secondary schooling or specialized training.
- **Parents as Partners** is based on the concept that Latino parents are their children's most important teachers, but often lack the skills to help their children progress through school. The program offers a variety of educational seminars to parents, ranging from how to create a home environment that reinforces and expands children's learning to teaching parents about school structures and policies.

For further information, please contact: National Council of La Raza, 810 1st Street, N.E., Washington, DC 20002-4205. Telephone (202) 289-1380.

Rethinking Schools: Milwaukee, Wisconsin

In 1985, a small group of committed educators in Milwaukee formed a study group called Rethinking Schools to discuss pertinent educational issues. All had been active for many years in various education struggles. They were particularly concerned about the reactive position teachers all too often take in response to education policy they have little voice in creating. As Bob Peterson, a member of the original group, recalls: "We wanted to stop being on the defensive all the time. We were tired of constantly trooping down to the school board meetings to stave off yet another attack on teachers and decent education programs."

After considerable debate, the group decided that a newspaper written by those on the front line of education that combined theory and practice would give teachers a stronger voice in the formation of education policy. This newspaper, also called *Rethinking Schools,* was born.

Rethinking Schools was designed to allow teachers to respond in a proactive manner to education policy and practice they believed harmful to children—a forum for people working in schools to exchange ideas and analyses. While the paper would specifically addresses the politics of educational reform in the Milwaukee school system, it would place these concerns in the context of the national educational reform efforts.

As Peterson remembers: "Timing could not have been more opportune for us to start our organizing project with the newspaper at its core. Throughout the city, criticism of the public school system was mounting. Several commissions had exposed the schools' failure to provide the majority of students with an equal and quality education. The business community was concerned about poorly trained workers and run-down schools that could not attract middle-level management people. The Latino and African American communities were angry over the miseducation of their children and the lack of power they had over the schools."

Members of the study group sent out letters to university and public school educators and community people with similar perspectives on education reform. As they worked to clarify and define the goals and purposes of the paper and the philosophy it would espouse, they discovered considerable differences of opinion among themselves. They struggled through heated debates and long discussion, determined to elucidate their goals and vision. In the process, people joined and left the group. At times, members departed because of differences in perspectives, but more often because of the time commitment required for many who were already overextended. The core group that remained was composed of six to eight people, mostly public school teachers. While several others have played important roles over the years, and the circles of collaborators and supporters have grown steadily, this group has remained the stable core of the Rethinking Schools organization.

Educational equity is the driving force behind the Rethinking Schools study group. Achieving it requires that all children, regardless of race or class, have qualitatively similar educational experiences that result in similar outcomes, including graduation rates, employment options, and college placement and completion. According to the group, social power structures are biased toward class and race; because schools reflect this bias, they strongly favor White middle-class children; thus, a strong anti-racist position, including critical evaluation of curriculum and teaching practices, is required to promote educational equity.

Rethinking Schools builds ties between various communities and groups working for educational change. It works to educate teachers, parents, and others about a pro-equality, progressive perspective on education. The founders of the newspaper realize that many people find their ideas and positions radical, but they hope to challenge teachers—particularly those not open to new ideas—to think critically about what they do by providing them with a critical analysis of flawed policies along with examples of ones that work.

Rooted in both theory and practice, *Rethinking Schools* seeks to bridge the gap between academic research, policy formation, and practice. As Cynthia Ellwood, one of the founders, explains: "Policy discussion is impoverished by a lack of understanding about what goes on in schools. We hope to enrich this discussion by bringing to bear information about what goes on in schools and classrooms. Likewise, practitioners in schools have a lot to learn from academic research."

Rethinking Schools is also an organizing tool. Distributing the newspaper required building a network of activists and supporters willing to pass it out in Milwaukee's many neighborhoods and 150 schools. Because the group wanted to reach as many teachers and administrators as possible, they decided to distribute the paper free of charge. Most importantly, concludes Bob Peterson: "It lets the voices of those people most excluded from policy debates—teachers, parents, and students—be heard."

From the beginning, the founders knew they did not want just to criticize policies they saw as flawed. They realized they needed to combine sound critical analysis based on current theory and practice with concrete alternatives for teachers to try. Along with a critical analysis of school issues, the paper regularly includes bibliographies of relevant material for teaching, straightforward suggestions for teaching practice, and a page of student writing generally submitted by Milwaukee public school teachers. The paper clearly delineates the consequences of specific policies, places them in the context of larger educational and social concerns, and poses practical alternatives.

Rethinking Schools has used a combination of analysis and action with marked success to address a number of critical school issues. The first issue, published in April of 1986, took on the staple of daily school life—the basal reader. The lead article, "Confessions of a Kindergarten Teacher: Surviving Scott Foresman" by Rita Tenorio, one of the founders of *Rethinking Schools*, provided a firsthand account of the problems and negative consequences of basal reader use. As an alternative to the workbook exercises and fragmented skill drills of the basal, she offered a range of teaching options that encouraged children and teachers to communicate with each other, exchange ideas, and use language skills to purposefully explore the world around them. An accompanying editorial placed the basal reader issue within larger reform concerns. The paper also urged teachers to organize around classroom issues to regain the independence required to teach well.

A loose network of teachers organized around the issue of basal readers, including members of the Milwaukee Kindergarten Association, Teachers Applying Whole Language, the Milwaukee chapter of the National Association for the Education of Young Children, the Ad Hoc Committee for Whole Language, and the reading committee of the Milwaukee Teachers' Education Association. Eventually, members of the study group were awarded places on the Reading Textbook Evaluation Committee that made citywide decisions about the materials and programs available to Milwaukee's 5,500 teachers.

As the organization continued to raise the issue, it became a vehicle through which teachers and policymakers became educated about alternatives to the basal system. School board members were personally lobbied on the matter and meetings were organized where teachers testified against basal reader adoption. By 1988, the campaign forced the Milwaukee public schools to reject adoption of a single citywide basal program in favor of a system that allowed teachers three reading approaches—a basal approach, a literature-based approach, and a whole-language approach.

The Rethinking Schools organization has reproduced this blend of strategies to address a number of pressing educational issues with similar results. It thwarted the school department's intention to institute a program to standardize curricula across the system and took on the issue of standardized testing. As with other campaigns, they used information to organize and to actively contest policy decisions.

Through activities of its core members and others involved with the newspapers, the Rethinking Schools organization remains connected to a number of overlapping campaigns working to make schools better for all children. Members of Rethinking Schools knew that support of the teacher's union was essential for the success of any long-term strategy for school reform. They recognized that teachers could move their proposals forward by pushing the administration to institute change and by providing a network for coalition-building throughout the city. Activists allied with Rethinking Schools challenged union leadership, won one-third of the seats on the union executive board, and elected a new vice president.

In a few short years, *Rethinking Schools* has grown from the brainchild of a small discussion circle of educators to an influential force in education reform. From its initial printing of 6,000 copies in November of 1986, the paper has grown to a distribution of over 30,000. *Rethinking Schools* survives on a shoestring budget funded largely by foundation grants that have allowed its development from a cut-and-paste operation to a computerized desktop system housed in a office.

The Milwaukee community now looks to *Rethinking Schools* for well-reasoned positions on controversial educational issues. Yet success brings new concerns. The newspaper staff struggles to sustain the exhausting effort required to produce the paper and organize around issues, in addition to holding down demanding jobs as teachers.

Recognizing that they are a small, closely-knit group, they question how to bring others into the core. They struggle with how best to organize supporters to sustain the local effort while simultaneously influencing national reform work. Funding remains a constant concern. The group realizes that foundations are unlikely to sustain the effort indefinitely and they debate the merits of paid subscriptions and advertising.

Rethinking Schools has succeeded to a remarkable degree in influencing educational reform in Milwaukee and across the nation by offering an analysis of education issues informed by those with the most inside knowledge of classrooms—teachers. At the same time, the founders have given a voice to those too long silenced in the debate about the future of schooling—parents, teachers, and students.

For further information, please contact: Rethinking Schools, 1001 East Keefe Avenue, Milwaukee, WI 53212.

Current Research Related to Topics Discussed in Chapter Seven

Inadequate Teacher Preparation

Teachers, regardless of their preparation, tend to teach as they were taught **(Goodlad, 1990; Grippen, 1989; Loper, 1989; Olsen and Mullen, 1990; Valencia and Killion, 1989).** Teachers from one generation to the next continue to believe that "teaching is telling" **(Wilson, 1990, p. 206).** Teacher behavior remains characterized by teacher-dominated instruction, low-level questioning, limited teacher/student and student/student interaction, and an emphasis on the acquisition of basic skills. Teachers too seldom challenge their students intellectually by demanding they defend their ideas, justify their answers, and explain their reasons **(Chicago Project on Teaching and Learning, 1989; Goodlad, 1984; Schmidt, 1991; Suzuki, 1984; Wilson, 1990).**

Both past and present research shows that the education of educators is woefully inadequate in preparing prospective teachers **(Cheney, 1990; Conant, 1963; Sarason, Davidson, and Blatt, 1962, *cited in* Goodlad, 1990; Payne, 1984; McLaren, 1988).** Among researchers and educators, there is almost unanimous agreement that the system that prepares educators is so fundamentally flawed that a major overhaul is required if prospective teachers are to be prepared to meet the myriad demands of the students they will find in the classrooms of the twenty-first century **(Cheney, 1990; Carnegie Forum on Education and Economy, 1986; Dill, 1990; Eubanks and Parish, 1990; Goodlad, 1990; Grippen, 1989; Payne, 1984; Sirotnik, 1990; Wise, 1990).**

After completing an intensive five-year study of twenty-nine representative teacher preparation programs in eight states that gathered 1,800 hours of individual and group interviews and classroom observations, as well as extensive survey data, programmatic documentation, and historical reviews, **Goodlad and his colleagues (1990)** concluded that teacher education is a "neglected enterprise" (p. 188). As Goodlad points out, "it takes enormous strength of imagination and extraordinary faith to believe that by the year 2000 we can have the best schools in the world, while we continue to neglect the education of those who will teach in them" (p. 187).

The low prestige and status suffered by the vast majority of teacher preparation programs and the accompanying low priority given to teacher education in the schools and colleges of education in the major universities is one of the most damaging conditions acting as a barrier to effective teacher preparation **(Cheney, 1990; Goodlad, 1990; Wise, 1990; Wisniewski, 1990).** Only two of the university presidents in Goodlad's study spontaneously identified the preparation of teachers as central to their institution's mission. Moreover, even with the current flurry of activity around school reform, most of the presidents, provosts, and many others interviewed perceived teacher education to have dropped in importance in recent years. Reflective of their status, teacher education programs seldom had protected budgets that could not be siphoned off by others with competing interests.

Goodlad (1990) found few faculty members engaged in renewing their programs of teacher education, and many future teachers felt they and their goals were little valued by the universities they attended. The heavy teaching, curriculum development, and service demands required of exemplary teaching programs received very limited recognition in the reward structures of most institutions **(Goodlad, 1990).** This resulted in part from the move of universities from predominately teaching to largely knowledge-producing entities with the concurrent increased emphasis on research and publication **(Cheney, 1990; Goodlad, 1990; Olson, 1990). Cheney (1990)** reports that at research universities 64 percent of the faculty spend five hours or less per week on classroom instruction but 86 percent spend six hours or more per week on research.

Perhaps the most damaging finding of **Goodlad's team (1990)** is the degree of disjuncture between teacher education and the realities of schooling. Prospective teachers often complained of the lack of connection between the theory they learned at the university and the policies and practices they encountered in the classroom. Other researchers echo this concern **(Cheney, 1990; Grippen, 1989; Olsen and Mullen, 1990; Payne, 1984; Trent, 1990).** The teachers interviewed by **Olsen and Mullen (1990)** were largely critical of the failure of teacher preparation programs to address adequately the challenges and issues of diverse classrooms. They pointed out that all too often their university courses were taught by faculty that had not been inside a classroom for years. As the student population has grown increasingly diverse, the gap between the classrooms new teachers are prepared to teach in and the classrooms they actually face has grown increasingly large.

Goodlad found that when student teachers were confronted by discrepancies between what they were taught and what the school districts expected of them, they were generally advised to conform to school demands. Instead of support to take risks, try out new ideas, and challenge the traditional ways of doing things, new teachers were encouraged to maintain current practice, to "fit in" **(Goodlad, *cited in* Olson, 1990).**

Trent (1990) also points to the importance of opportunities for future teachers to practice their emerging skills in a wide range of contexts. He reports on a survey that revealed that teachers believed that their limited competency with African Americans and other ethnic minorities resulted from inadequate curriculum content covering the experiences of ethnic minorities, and limited multicultural experiences in or outside of schools. Trent contends that curricula explicitly designed to address the issues of race and ethnicity, combined with opportunities for future teachers to practice their emerging skills in a wide range of contexts, would increase their sense of competency and thereby reduce the stress they experience teaching in racially diverse classrooms.

Likewise, **Olsen and Mullen (1990)** hold that teacher preparation programs should model the classroom diversity, climate, and multicultural content their students need to emulate. The teachers in their study strongly recommended that the faculty of teacher preparation programs gain the required expertise and knowledge in the backgrounds and cultures of diverse populations, in second-language acquisition, and in the implications for K through 12 classrooms of recent widespread immigration.

The disjointed path of future teachers is unlikely to change as long as teacher preparation programs and cooperating schools continue to follow separate routes. Regular and systematic collaboration between university staff and cooperating school teachers in the planning and implementation of the teacher education curriculum was the rare exception in **Goodlad's (1990)** sample.

Likewise, university personnel had limited authority over the student teaching placements and the subsequent supervision of student teachers. Cooperating teachers were often chosen by principals. Availability and proximity rather than recognition of teaching competence were frequently the prevailing criteria for selection. This problem was exacerbated by the fact that student teaching was dominated by a single teacher in a singe classroom rather than teams of teachers or the whole school's faculty **(Goodlad, 1990).**

Grippen's (1989) analysis of the student teacher/cooperating teacher relationship confirms this finding and points to a dyad characterized by: undue concentration on classroom management at the expense of teaching strategies; disregard for the pedagogy learned in university courses; stress on "survival" skills; and an emphasis on the personal rather than the professional relationship between the two parties.

In addition to isolation in a single classroom with a single teacher, discrepancies between theory and actual school practice, and the lack of collaboration between university personnel and cooperating school staff, future teachers suffered from a lack of opportunities to benefit from their shared experience. Because teacher preparation programs generally lacked clearly defined beginning and ending points, students tended to progress through them haphazardly. Institutional efforts to foster peer identification and socialization within teaching as a profession were generally sporadic or nonexistent **(Goodlad, 1990).**

Lacking a base for professional socialization, prospective teachers are more dependent on the curriculum and teaching practices found in their programs. Yet **Goodlad (1990)** found that curricula in teacher education programs are severely constrained by state certification requirements that can change with political whim. Educators who struggled to work creatively within state requirements found their efforts repeatedly undermined by changes in state regulations **(Goodlad, 1990).**

Goodlad and his colleagues (1990) propose a series of nineteen presuppositions or postulates that they consider essential for the successful renewal of teacher education programs. Their recommendations for restructuring teacher preparation programs are anchored in these postulates. The nineteen postulates address such themes as commitment, autonomy, responsible parties, mission, inquiry-oriented and reflective practice, equitable access for all children, dilemmas and tensions inherent in teaching, an adequate supply of exemplary settings, and freedom from the vagaries of state regulation.

The centerpiece of **Goodlad and his colleagues' (1990)** recommendations is the creation of "centers of pedagogy" committed to the preparation of future teachers and the advancement of effective teaching policies and practices. The centers would be autonomous in regard to their faculty and budget. The centers would be clear in their mission and have control over the selection and guidance of their students, who as a group would share a common educational purpose and vision.

Drawing on exemplary teaching practices, numerous opportunities to observe and practice in a variety of classrooms and schools, and relevant coursework found at the center, future teachers would progress from students to reflective practitioners. Staff at the centers would introduce early, and encourage throughout a prospective teacher's course of study, discussion of the dilemmas and tensions inherent in teaching—including the teacher's responsibilities in a political democracy, the rights of parents, the moral obligation to meet the twin goals of equity and excellence for all children, and the incongruities between what research says works for children and what occurs in practice in classrooms **(Goodlad, 1990; Olson, 1990).**

Goodlad's team (1990) strongly supports and endorses the development of school/university partnerships to provide the infrastructure required to carry out the work of the proposed centers. Other researchers and educators have also pointed to the promise of school/university partnerships **(Grippen, 1989; *Harvard Education Letter,* 1988; Holmes Group, 1990; Maloy and Jones, 1987; Porter, 1987).**

With partnerships, classroom teachers and school administrators play a prominent role in planning and conducting education theory courses for undergraduate and graduate education students. Their involvement is intended to provide a greater grounding in the real world of the schools. At the same time, college faculty and public school staff design an extensive clinical experience component. Rather than acting as generally passive student teachers, education students are expected to serve as assistant teachers, accepting significant responsibility for planning, organizing, and conducting instruction. Collaboration between college faculty and school staff ensures a greater link between the clinical experience and education theory **(Goodlad, 1990; Grippen, 1989; Maloy and Jones, 1987; Olsen and Mullen, 1990; Porter, 1987).** Partnerships also provide the necessary structure required for the simultaneous renewal of schools and the preparation of the future teachers who will work in them.

Shortage of Teachers

High-quality teacher education programs to attract well-qualified students are essential to meet the demand for new teachers in the next century. Because at least one-third of the nation's current teachers are forty-five or older, the impending retirements in the coming decades will lead to a need for a large number of qualified teachers **(Bradley, 1990a).** Researchers place the total demand for new public and private school teachers during the next decade at two to two-and-a-half million teachers. This translates to at least 200,000 new teachers a year **(Bradley, 1990a; Darling-Hammond, 1987).**

While recent statistics suggest that the crisis in teacher supply is not as drastic as predicted in the 1980s, national data mask the significant problems experienced in certain areas of the country and in certain certification categories **(Bradley, 1990a; Graham, 1987; Middle School Task Force, 1988).**

Moreover, the trends that appear responsible for the respite in the shortage could easily reverse. For example, it appears that teachers eligible for retirement are choosing to remain on the job longer to reap the benefits of the substantial salary gains most received during the 1980s, although their eventual retirement is inevitable **(Bradley, 1990a).** In addition, the number of students entering teacher education programs has increased, and teacher ranks have been swelled both by a large number of teachers returning to the classroom after time away and by a smaller number of teachers entering the profession through alternative certification routes **(Bradley, 1990a).**

The question of teacher supply is complicated by the fact that while some states and school districts report a surplus of teachers, others are actively recruiting them **(Bradley, 1990a).** This is due in part to the uneven distribution of population growth across the U.S. **(Hodgkinson, 1988).** For example, from 1980 to 1984, the number of children under the age of five increased by 9 percent nationally, but this represented an increase of 17 percent in the west, 11 percent in the south, 5 percent in the northeast, and only 2 percent in the midwest **(Hodgkinson, 1988).** This uneven distribution combines with the tendency for immigrants to flock to urban centers **(First, *et al.*, 1988).** The result is that some school districts are reporting dropping enrollments while others, most often urban centers, are flooded with new enrollees and suffer from severe teacher shortages **(Bradley, 1990a; Council of Great City Schools, 1990).** For example, in 1987, New York City reported teacher shortages of 2,500 to 4,200 **(Middle School Task Force, 1988)**.

Moreover, **Darling-Hammond (*cited in* Bradley, 1990a)** holds that the extent of the teacher shortage is underestimated because districts hire approximately 20,000 teachers each year under procedures that allow the "emergency" credentialing of unlicensed teachers.

Lack of Teachers of Color

In addition to severe shortages in certain localities, bilingual teachers, special education teachers, teachers of mathematics and sciences, and teachers of color in all areas remain in short supply **(Bradley, 1990a; First, *et al.*, 1988; Graham, 1987).** The lack of teachers of color is particularly disturbing in light of the increasing diversity found in many of the nation's classrooms. Half the states have public school populations that are more than 25 percent non-White, and estimates are that between 30 and 40 percent of U.S. schoolchildren will be non-White by the end of the century **(Graham, 1987; Hodgkinson, 1985).** In all but two of the nation's twenty-five largest cities, the majority of the students are of color **(Graham, 1987).**

In contrast to this diversity, the nation's teaching force is overwhelmingly White and will become increasingly so over the next few decades **(Graham, 1987; Pine and Hilliard, 1990; Trent, 1990).** Non-White groups comprise 20 percent of the U.S. population **(Armstrong, 1991),** but children of color comprise on average 30 percent of the school-age population; in many urban centers, they are the overwhelming majority **(Council of Great City Schools, 1990).** The percentage of teachers of color has recently dropped from 12 to 9 percent **(Hodgkinson, 1988)** and is expected to drop further to 5 percent **(Pine and Hilliard, 1990).** The disparities at the administrative level are even more severe. Ninety-seven percent of all superintendents and 90 percent of all principals in U.S. public schools are White **(Feistritzer, 1988).** This reality points to the critical need to prepare all new teachers to meet the challenges of diverse classrooms. Equally important, staff development programs must address the issues and concerns teachers face in diverse classrooms, including cultural sensitivity and prejudice reduction training.

Graham (1987) and others **(Grant, 1990; Pine and Hilliard, 1990)** point to the critical need for teachers of color to provide important role models for both children of color and White children. Teachers of color can also help children from ethnically different backgrounds bridge the gap between home and school cultures. Equally important, they provide valuable resources to White teachers who are struggling to meet myriad needs in their ethnically diverse classrooms **(Bradley, 1990b; First, *et al.*, 1988; Olsen and Dowell, 1989; Trent, 1990).**

Graham (1987) traces the problem of the dearth of African American teachers to a decline in college enrollments. In 1976, 33.5 percent of African American high school graduates between the ages of eighteen and twenty-four were enrolled in college; by 1983 this number had decreased to 27 percent **(Graham, 1987).** Moreover, the number of African Americans in college who choose education as a career has dropped sharply, at twice the rate of decline for Whites. Less than 1 percent of top-scoring Black students express an interest in teaching **(Graham, 1987).** But the roots of the problem go deeper. Graham points to the devastating poverty that close to half of all Black children grow up in and the inequitable education they experience in school.

In the long run, increasing the pool of talented, compassionate teachers of color requires improving the teaching in the schools they attend as children. In the meantime, increased efforts in recruiting both young students and older individuals of color to teaching is essential to begin to address the problem **(Bradley, 1990b, 1991; First, *et al.*, 1988; Graham, 1987; Olsen and Mullen, 1990).**

A recent survey of respondents to *Recruiting New Teachers*, a national advertising campaign that promotes teaching as a career, suggests that there is an untapped pool of talented individuals of ethnic minority background who are interested in teaching **(Bradley, 1991).** One-quarter of the respondents were members of minority groups, a surprisingly high figure given that minority groups comprise only 20 percent of the total population and less than 10 percent of the current teaching force **(Armstrong, 1991; Bradley, 1991).** A high number of the respondents were older and many were college-educated. Minority respondents perceived the system to be racially biased—less than 35 percent felt that they would be openly welcomed by principals and White teachers **(Bradley, 1991).**

The nation's pool of 500,000 paraprofessionals also provides a promising source of language-rich and ethnically diverse teachers **(Bradley, 1990b; Council of Great City Schools, 1990; First, *et al.*, 1988; Olsen, 1988).** Paraprofessionals not only have extensive experience working with children; many of them are very well-connected within their communities. A number of states and universities are planning or have implemented alternative certification programs to enable paraprofessionals to become licensed teachers.

However, conflicting evidence leaves questions about the effectiveness of alternative programs in preparing well-qualified teachers. Part of the problem results from the considerable disparity in the quality of the various programs **(Bradley, 1990a). Goodlad (1990)** reports that the data from his extensive study of teacher preparation programs do not support alternative certification routes, at least as most commonly designed.

Other researchers have pointed to their success **(Bradley, 1990b; Cheney, 1990; Dill, 1990). Cheney (1990)** reports that more than 22 percent of the teachers hired under New Jersey's alternative certification program have been of color—double the percentage in the teaching force. Moreover, the teachers scored higher on the National Teacher Examination than teacher education graduates and have remained in the profession longer.

Not only do schools need to devise ways to attract new teachers, they also need to take steps to retain the ones already in their classrooms. Fully half of all new teachers leave the profession within the first six years—in urban settings, within the first five **(Haberman and Rickards, 1990; Tifft, 1988).** Teachers of color leave the profession at nearly twice the rate of White teachers. A recent Louis Harris Poll found that 41 percent of the Black and Latino teachers surveyed planned on leaving teaching in the next five years, compared to 25 percent of their White peers **(*cited in Harvard Education Letter*, 1989).** Moreover, research suggests that the best and the brightest leave teaching earlier and at higher rates than their peers **(*cited in* Cheney, 1990; Trent, 1990).** The teachers left behind in the classrooms may be those most resistant to change and least prepared to meet the challenges of the current student population.

A recent survey **(Haberman and Rickards, 1990)** of teachers leaving Milwaukee public schools provides insight into the causes of teacher flight. At the time of their departure, working conditions had come to the forefront of the most critical problems they faced. For example, the teachers had ranked inadequate support from administrators and supervisors as fifth out of twelve on their list of concerns before they began teaching. At the time of their departure it had moved to third. Likewise, a heavy work load had moved from ninth to fifth.

Poor-Quality Staff Development

Ideally, staff development provides school personnel with the opportunity and the means to improve professional skills, increase knowledge and understanding of education, and experiment with new ideas. Staff development programs should build on a solid theoretical and practical foundation laid during the staff's pre-service educational experience. In fact, there is increasing evidence that in-service staff development fails to provide staff with the education, training, and support they need to meet students' needs **(Corcoran, Walker, and White, 1988; Darling-Hammond, 1987; Lieberman, 1988; Middle School Task Force, 1988; Sizer, 1987; Valencia and Killion, 1989).**

Once individuals enter the teaching profession, they are seldom provided with opportunities to acquire and integrate knowledge and experience, to expand their skills, or to experiment with innovative approaches **(Corcoran, Walker, and White, 1988; Frymier, 1987; Rosenholtz, 1985; Valencia and Killion, 1989).** Typical staff development programs are aimed at addressing a specific "deficiency" in the skills, abilities, or knowledge of teachers as identified by a central office administrator or an outside expert **(McLaughlin and Marsh, 1978; Middle School Task Force, 1988; Valencia and Killion, 1989).**

These programs generally encompass a single session for a few hours or, at most, a single school day. Often they are mandated by district- or building-level administrators. They are usually conducted by outside consultants who have minimal contact with teachers participating in the program and little knowledge about their perceived concerns and needs. There is little, if any, recognition of the needs of teachers as learners who progress through identifiable stages of concern and change with respect to innovation. After the session, there is little, if any, follow-up, monitoring, or evaluation. The expectation is that teachers will and should implement the innovation through a strict, rigid adherence to the plan **(Corcoran, Walker, and White, 1988; Hord and Huling-Austin, 1986; Lambert, 1988; Middle School Task Force, 1988; Rosenholtz, 1985; Valencia and Killion, 1989).**

As **Valencia and Killion (1989)** point out, "such [staff development] efforts tend to provide superficial, quick fixes to long-term, complex problems" (p. 5). Not surprisingly, teachers frequently report dissatisfaction with in-service activities **(Cheney, 1990; Corcoran, Walker, and White, 1988)** and many consider them useless and "little more than an ordeal to be endured" **(Middle School Task Force, 1988, p. 46).**

Teacher Evaluation

Teacher evaluation can play an important role in ensuring that appropriate staff development activities are available to respond to specific needs and concerns of teachers. Too often, however, the roles of evaluator and supervisor are intertwined. An evaluation, which provides feedback to teachers on improving their performance, is combined with an assessment for tenure or promotion. Not surprisingly, teachers are more concerned about negative evaluations for career advancement than in seeking assistance for improvement **(Corcoran, Walker, and White, 1988; Darling-Hammond, 1986; Rosenholtz, 1985; Valencia and Killion, 1989).**

Teacher evaluation is used too frequently to assure compliance with policy and minimum standards of performance, with a focus on the elimination of poor teachers rather than on professional growth. This results in large part because evaluation is guided by a bureaucratic conception of teaching. The bureaucratic conception of teaching implies that teachers implement curriculum and use strategies planned and developed by administrators and specialists. Teachers are seen more as technicians than professionals—they do not plan or critically review their work but rather merely perform it **(Darling-Hammond, 1986; Popkewitz and Lind, 1989).** As currently conducted, many teachers do not find evaluations useful **(Bacharach, Bauer, and Shedd, 1986; Corcoran, Walker, and White, 1988; *Harvard Education Letter*, 1989; Valencia and Killion, 1989).**

Teacher skepticism toward evaluations is further exacerbated by recent state mandates requiring teachers to pass standardized competency tests. Many policymakers, reformers, and educators see teacher examinations as a key to revitalizing schools, improving the quality of teaching, and restoring the public's faith in the public education system **(Madaus and Pullin, 1987; Salzman and Whitfield, 1989; Shepard and Kreitzer, 1987).** As of 1987, forty-four states required prospective teachers to pass a competency examination for certification and every state except Alaska and Iowa had adopted or was in the process of adopting teacher testing requirements **(Salzman and Whitfield, 1989).**

Scores on teacher competency tests are used to make career decisions about prospective and practicing teachers. The legitimacy of these decisions is based on the assumption that the tests are valid. That is, that 1) the objectives, skills, and competencies purportedly measured by the test are necessary for minimal success in the classroom, and 2) the test items actually measure those objectives, skills, and competencies **(Madaus and Pullin, 1987, p. 32).**

The validity of teacher competency tests is currently based solely on the judgment of a panel of experts, usually classroom teachers, school administrators, and other professional educators. The "experts" judge the match between the objectives of the test and the items used to measure those objectives. More importantly, the panel judges whether the test objectives and test items are relevant to classroom practice **(Madaus and Pullin, 1987; Salzman and Whitfield, 1989).**

The opinions and beliefs of practitioners are important, but they are not sufficient basis for decisions on the competency of teachers. They must be tested against actual performance in the classroom. To date, this critical component of test validation has not occurred. In spite of the absence of such evidence, standardized teacher tests are widely accepted by policymakers as legitimate indicators of teacher effectiveness **(Madaus and Pullin, 1987; Salzman and Whitfield, 1989).** The irony is that "[p]olicymakers defend mandated teacher certification tests as a means of improving the quality of what they suspect is a less-than-adequate teacher corps. Yet the validity of the tests on which policymakers pin their hopes for improving teacher quality rests exclusively on the judgments of a tiny fraction of the members of that very teacher corps" **(Madaus and Pullin, 1987, p. 35).**

Considerable evidence shows that current teacher competency tests are not equally valid or fair for all examinees **(Graham, 1987; Salzman and Whitfield, 1989; Shepard and Kreitzer, 1987).** The failure rates for candidates taking the California teacher competency test was 74 percent for Blacks, 61 percent for Latinos, 50 percent for Asians, and only 24 percent for Whites. Likewise, on Florida's teacher competency test, only 10 percent of the White candidates failed, but the failure rate for Blacks was 65 percent, Latinos 49 percent, and Asians 37 percent **(Salzman and Whitfield, 1989).** Georgia's exam had a pass rate of 87 percent for Whites but only 34 percent for Blacks; Louisiana had a pass rate of 78 percent for Whites and 15 percent for Blacks **(Graham, 1987).**

Darling-Hammond (1986) argues that the way to address competency concerns in the teaching force is not through testing but by the implementation of a rigorous process of peer review, similar to that of the medical and legal professions. She recommends that this process include: rigorous and peer-dominated selection and induction into teaching; periodic reviews of individual teachers' performances conducted by expert peers and administrators using a wide range of indicators that deal with both the substance and process of teaching; use of reviews and self-evaluation to guide professional development; special forums and support systems for the referral and redress of apparent cases of malpractice, incompetence, or unprofessional performance; ongoing peer review of all teachers' practices so that standards of practice can be continually developed and improved; and collective control by teachers of decisions about the structure, form, and content of their work (p. 544).

The Need for Effective Staff Development

Individuals entering the teaching profession face a paradox. Their pre-service training and education is often inadequate to prepare them fully to teach. At the same time, new teachers generally find themselves teaching in the schools with the least attractive working conditions, most limited resources, poorest leadership, and fewest well-trained teachers. These schools also tend to serve less-advantaged children who require more time, effort, and innovation from the teaching staff. Even the best schools provide little staff development aimed specifically at the new teacher, who is often left to "sink or swim" **(Bradley, 1990a; Corcoran, Walker, and White, 1988; Moran, 1990; Middle School Task Force, 1988; Rosenholtz, 1985).**

Research suggests that teachers "peak" after five to seven years in the classroom and either maintain their level of effectiveness or actually become less effective **(McLaughlin and Marsh, 1978; Rosenholtz, *cited in* Smith and Scott, 1989).** Their years in the classroom reduce desire for change and enthusiasm for, and belief in, educational innovations. This "calcifying effect" is not inherent in the teaching role. To a great degree, it stems from the conditions of teaching **(Corcoran, Walker, and White, 1988; Maloy and Jones, 1987; McLaughlin and Marsh, 1978; Rosenholtz, 1985).** The work of teachers is dominated by isolation, a lack of recognition and reward for professional self-improvement, a lack of administrative support and collegiality, little or no input into the decisions that critically affect their work, severe time constraints, limited resources, vague and often conflicting educational goals, and an absence of public recognition and respect. Given these conditions, teachers seldom have the opportunity to interact with or observe their colleagues **(Corcoran, Walker, and White, 1988; Frymier, 1987; Lieberman, 1988; Rosenholtz, 1985; Smith and Scott, 1989; Valencia and Killion, 1989).**

Isolated in classrooms, many teachers come to believe that they are solely responsible for the success of their students. As a result, teachers resist seeking advice and support from their peers or offering it to less experienced or struggling colleagues. Many work on the belief that "you do not interfere with another teacher's teaching" **(Little, 1984, p. 99; Rosenholtz, 1985; Smith and Scott, 1989; Valencia and Killion, 1989).**

As a result of their isolation, teachers often vacillate between a belief that what they are doing is working fairly well and therefore should not be tampered with, and a sense of futility about their profession and their ability to help students learn **(Moran, 1990; Valencia and Killion, 1989).** Both attitudes lead to a resistance to experimentation, particularly since change unsettles the classroom and fosters temporary feelings of inadequacy in even the most competent teachers **(Little, 1984; Valencia and Killion, 1989).**

Staff development activities can offer an escape from these limiting conditions. But in many cases, they reinforce conditions that "calcify" teachers' professional growth. Teachers frequently lack exemplary models to emulate, and are too often deprived of the benefits of the advice, experience, and expertise of their colleagues **(Corcoran, Walker, and White, 1988; Lieberman, 1988; Little, 1984; Rosenholtz, 1985).**

In addition, reform efforts that purport to improve teachers' working conditions can, in fact, lead to reduced teacher responsibility and control through increased bureaucracy and greater monitoring **(Giroux, 1987; Popkewitz and Lind, 1989). Popkewitz and Lind** examined the implementation of the Wisconsin Teaching Incentives Program in three districts. At all three sites, they found that the concerns about the quality of teachers' working conditions including issues of responsibility and autonomy were translated into problems of teacher motivation and incentives and the need to manage, evaluate, and reorganize the work of teachers to increase efficiency. Instead of redefining the conditions of work, the reforms increased the demands on teachers and resulted in a reduction of their autonomy and creativity.

Characteristics of Effective Staff Development

Effective staff development programs are characterized by: efforts focused on the needs and concerns as identified by teachers; collaboration between teachers and administrators in planning, implementation, and evaluation; a continuous, long-term process that is integrated into the regular activities of the school; formal training sessions conducted by teachers on site and followed by informal exchange among colleagues about the usefulness of what was taught; supporting materials and technical assistance, including guided practice and coaching; expectations that teachers will adapt what they learn to their particular classrooms; a school staff committed to change; and support of the effort by district-level administrators, including provision of the necessary resources **(Berlin and Jensen, 1989; Guerrero, *et al.*, 1989; Hord and Huling-Austin, 1986; Little, 1984; Maloy and Jones, 1987; McLaughlin and Marsh, 1978; Olsen and Mullen, 1990; Rosenholtz, 1985; Valencia and Killion, 1989).**

Leadership at both building and district levels plays a pivotal role in the implementation of successful staff development efforts. Teachers are not usually willing to take the risks required for change without the support and recognition of their principals. In the most successful programs, principals are actively involved in all phases **(Berlin and Jensen, 1989; Corcoran, Walker, and White, 1988; McLaughlin and Marsh, 1978; Rosenholtz, 1985).** District-level leadership helps provide required resources and ensure consistency in expressed values, priorities, and goals at the building and district levels. Because teachers may resist change when they experience conflict between implementation of new practice and requirements of central-office mandates, district-imposed regulations about curricular text coverage and pressures to raise student achievement test scores can undermine staff development efforts **(Corcoran, Walker, and White, 1988; Duffy and Roeler, 1986; Lambert, 1988; Little, 1984).**

Because it incorporates many of the elements of successful staff development in its structure, peer coaching is one of the most promising avenues for professional growth for teachers. Peer coaching involves the modeling of new teaching methods by expert teachers, followed by guided practice and feedback in protected situations, and coaching of teachers in actual classroom situations **(Joyce and Showers, 1982; Neubert and Bratton, 1987).** In peer coaching efforts, participating teachers jointly attend training sessions, collaborate on planning and implementation, and observe each other in the classroom. More knowledgeable and experienced teachers serve as coaches to their peers, providing suggestions for improvement, demonstration, and reteaching when necessary **(Joyce and Showers, 1982; Showers, 1985).**

Alternative Professional Roles

Alternative professional roles provide avenues for teachers to increase their voice in decision-making, and to plan, conduct, and evaluate their work.

Providing optional roles for teachers is a powerful way to enhance their sense of efficacy and professional development. Alternative professional roles create different career options for classroom teachers who traditionally have had only two: stay in the classroom and focus on teaching, or leave the classroom and leave teaching as well. **(*Harvard Education Letter*, 1988; Lambert, 1988).**

Teachers are released from classroom duties to experiment with alternative professional roles. These roles might involve serving as researchers or curriculum or staff developers, as mentors or master teachers, as project administrators, or as evaluators. The alternative roles enable teachers to expand and diversify the resources and skills available within the public school and the school system. Because teachers retain their classroom perspective, they are likely to bring new ideas and approaches to the conduct of the various alternative professional roles that have traditionally been handled only by specialists **(Goswami and Stillman, 1987; *Harvard Education Letter*, 1988; Porter, 1987; Schwartz, 1984).**

Teacher Empowerment

A sense of efficacy, a meaningful voice in the decisions that structure the conditions under which they work, and the responsibility and authority to plan, conduct, and evaluate their work are essential components of teacher empowerment **(Ashby, *et al.*, 1989; Darling-Hammond, 1986; Giroux, 1987; Lambert, 1988).** Teacher empowerment is critical for enduring teacher change.

In a recent survey **(*cited in* Ashby, *et al.*, 1989),** teachers indicated that administrative support, responsibility for meaningful tasks, control and decision-making related to curriculum, decisions on teaching assignments, input on policies and procedures, and choice in and determination of staff development result in a sense of empowerment. They identified ongoing communication, higher teacher salaries, professional support, decision-making power at the classroom level, and recognition of teacher accomplishment as elements of a school climate conducive to empowerment.

8

School Finance

Children are entitled to equal educational opportunity supported by the provision of greater resources to schools serving students most vulnerable to school failure.

A Vision of School Finance at the Good Common School

School Superintendent Jesse "Doc" Holloran glances over the large cluttered top of his walnut desk, then to the old-fashioned schoolhouse clock on the wall. It reads 11 p.m. He turns back to the financial spreadsheet displayed on his desk-side computer monitor screen. Numbers composed of green light blur, clear momentarily as he rubs his eyes, then blur again. For tonight, he has "hit the wall." Besides, he has a 7 a.m. breakfast meeting with a school board member.

His weariness is generated by the annual budget process, a beast that devours time and energy in huge proportions. As he pads across the carpeted outer office in stocking feet to retrieve his loafers from a spot near the water cooler, he hears the distant click of a computer keyboard coming from the school controller's office. It is a reassuring sound. Skip Jamison is one of the best school business managers Doc has known.

During most of the year, their working relationship is fairly simple. Skip prepares expense reports; Doc reads them. However, this month is different. The district operating budget for the coming school year is under preparation. It will be considered by the school board next week. Once the board approves the budget proposal, lump sum allocations for each school site will be determined. Then the district's various school councils will develop spending plans to reflect school improvement goals for each school.

Each year at this time, Doc compares last year's expenditures for his district with the national averages. Here, as elsewhere, educational expenditures turn on two key variables: average teacher salaries and the school's pupil/teacher ratio. The average salary of a teacher employed by ISD #4 is at the national average, around $28,000. But the pupil/teacher ratio is twenty to one, compared to the national average of about eighteen to one.

At ISD #4, as nationally, teacher salaries, benefits, and extra duty pay account for half of total school expenditures; the other 50 percent is made up of non-teaching salaries, benefits, and operating expenses. Non-teaching staff include administrators, counselors, librarians, social workers, psychologists, teacher aides, secretaries, custodians, maintenance workers, cafeteria workers, bus drivers, security personnel, and others.

The operating budget Doc will submit contains one controversial proposal intended to lower the cost of central administration and turn the money saved over to local schools. He will propose that more than a dozen central office positions be eliminated. Affected certified personnel covered by the master union contract will be reassigned to classrooms in schools that have especially high pupil/teacher ratios. Four secretaries will be laid off.

On the morning he shares this proposal with the Administrative Council, there is the devil to pay. Within an hour, rumors sweep the administration building that "massive" layoffs are in the works. For a couple of days, he uses his private entrance and rest room to avoid the big chill in the corridors.

He manages the flap by describing the proposal with great specificity to the education writer of the daily paper. This helps to quiet the rumor mill. Still, the episode reminds him of a simple truth about his role as school superintendent—every decision has a political cost, either on the inside or the outside. This particular decision is well received by the community, but the staff is upset. The next tough decision might make the staff happy, but start parents snapping at his heels.

"Not much like the old days," he thinks as he locks the door to the darkened building behind him. "I just did line-item budgets, explained them to the board, and sent them out to the schools. I didn't spend hours writing budget notes. I carried them all in my head. Now, with parents, teachers, and principals involved, it's a very different situation."

Naturally, there are still last-minute questions to answer. How many teacher aides are the financial equivalent of a full-time guidance counselor? How much would it cost to set up a parent panel and hire consultants to revise the District Code of Conduct? What does it cost to conduct a climate survey and implement the recommendations at an elementary school?

At a practical level, the process is a nuisance for superintendents. But at a deeper level, he is proud of the district's school councils. They have worked hard to develop school improvement goals, some of which will soon be well achieved. How well will partially depend on how adequately they are funded.

Fortunately, during his three years in this district he has made some progress in persuading school board members that it really does cost more to educate poor children and others who are disadvantaged by society. The district budget that he will present to the board reflects that commitment, and he expects it to be approved without much debate.

In the "old days," some schools had expansive budgets; others were hard pressed for basic supplies. Doc learned about this the hard way on the first day of his first superintendency in a small North Carolina school district over twenty-five years ago. That morning an African American assistant principal had sternly looked him over and asked in a tone laden with sarcasm, "Now that you're here, does that mean we're going to have toilet tissue at this school?" He smiled at the memory. Her school *never* ran out of toilet tissue during his three-year tenure in the district. He saw to it personally.

As he drives home, he thinks: "Times have changed, but power is still power. Those who have it use it." Last-minute pitches for favored projects will land on his desk before the budget process ends. But with various council chairpersons watching every board action like hawks, sweetheart deals are pretty much a thing of the past.

When the school board meeting arrives and budget discussions rise to the top of the agenda, Doc seizes the teachable moment to make some brief remarks about lump sum budgeting. He borrows most of his comments from *The How-To Guide to Lump Sum Budgeting* prepared by Leadership for Quality Education in Chicago. After explaining how the purpose of the new budgeting process is to allow parents and staff to shape a spending plan that fits student needs, he shares a quote from the how-to guide: "Some organizations, like prisons, marching bands, or the military may need a rigid centralized administration. Schools need something different. They need budgets that are customized by the people at the local school who best know the needs of their students."

He concludes by explaining that the local school councils will devise spending plans for next year by taking into consideration the lump sum allocated by the school board, the goals of local school improvement plans, expected enrollment, and this year's budget, which serves as a starting point.

The budget discussion goes smoothly, in no small part due to Doc Holloran's review of budget materials with individual board members at breakfast meetings during the preceding two weeks. Several people in the audience speak against central office changes, but the board holds firm. When the motion to approve the budget passes four to one a burst of applause comes from the school council chairpersons in the room.

The next morning, budgetary action at ISD #4 has shifted from the central administration building to individual schools across the district. A new set of players moves quickly. All district principals receive information about their lump sum allocations at an 8:30 a.m. meeting.

By 1 p.m., Phyllis Walker and Good Common School Council Chair Ella Davis sit in the principal's office. Phyllis hands Ella three copies of the district's operating budget and a variety of backup materials—including the school improvement plan, a copy of this year's school budget, enrollment projections for next year, and the "how-to" guide produced by Doc Holloran and Skip Jamison. Now the council's Budget Committee has everything that it needs to begin.

As they talk, Phyllis makes a series of notes about additional information to request from Skip Jamison. She will drop the list off to him on her way to school tomorrow morning. On a second sheet of notepaper, she writes a reminder to order extra refreshments for the council meeting next week; attendance will be large. In the meantime, the Budget Committee has its work cut out. And work for the committee means work for her. Her job will be to answer questions when she can and get answers from the central office when she can't. The list of questions on her yellow legal pad lengthens as the week wears on.

Council Chair Davis opens the first meeting of the Budget Committee with a broad overview of lump sum budgeting. She notes four major factors that determine the amount of money a school receives.

- **The number of students**. This determines the number of teachers and other school staff, and money for books, equipment and supplies.
- **Special needs of students.** Funds over and above the basic distribution are available to schools if the students have special needs arising from handicapping conditions, limited-English-proficiency, poverty, etc.
- **Square footage of the building.** Funding for repairs, custodial supplies, and maintenance staff are determined, to a degree, by building square footage.
- **Special programs.** Some special school programs are based on outside considerations, such as desegregation or overcrowding.

Ella explains that the school council can decide how best to use these dollars, so long as their decisions comply with the law, employee contracts, and school board policy. She give examples: textbook funds cannot be used to pay teachers—it is against the law; class size cannot be fifty students because that would violate the teachers' contract. But within these limits there is a great deal of leeway. Special funds, such as state and federal Chapter I money, have considerable flexibility. As long as the council stays within the legal boundaries, it is constrained only by the imagination of its members.

Further elaborating policy on desegregation money, Principal Walker explains that local funds should first be used to help promote integration. Where this is not possible, they can be used to help improve student achievement. The council can allocate special program funds to help meet the goals of each school's improvement plan and desegregation plan without violating these plans.

Discussion then turns to staffing formulas and formulas for non-personnel expenditures, utilities, postage, equipment, and plant operation. After these are concluded, someone notes the late hour. The group agrees to reconvene the following evening to tackle issues about special federal and state program funds for special education, bilingual education, Chapter I, and Vocational Education. They also agree to reconvene on Saturday, if necessary. The meeting is adjourned.

The next week, Phyllis Walker watches people stream into the school cafeteria to attend the evening meeting of the Good Common School Council. Two council members, a parent and a teacher, are seated behind a long table distributing legal pads, pencils, inexpensive calculators, and copies of both the district operating budget and the proposed school budget as drafted by the council's Budget Committee.

Suddenly, Principal Walker gives a sigh of relief. Doc Holloran walks in a side door and drops his coat and scarf on a chair. She had hoped he might turn up at the meeting, but didn't want to ask him to come. As professionals, they have their tough moments, but tonight she would like to give him a big hug. A lot of questions are bound to be asked. Between them, she and Doc will have all of the answers.

As the council chair gavels the meeting to order, Phyllis sits down beside two fifth-grade girls who came with their parents. She knows her presence will discourage their giggles. She does a quick head count of the teachers and parents in the room. About seventy-five in all—the largest attendance yet for a council meeting.

She leans over and whispers in eleven-year-old Gena's ear, "Will you and Cheryl go out very quietly to my car and bring in the extra boxes of donuts on the front seat? Here's the key. Be sure to lock it again." Then she sits back and listens.

Problems with School Finance in U.S. Public Schools

During the last two decades, spending on public schools has significantly increased. In 1987, as reported by the U.S. Department of Education (1988), U.S. citizens expended more than $160 billion a year to educate almost 40 million public school students—a per-pupil expenditure of about $4,000.

But this figure masks large differences in per-pupil expenditures. Wealthy districts with predominately White student populations spend considerably more money on each child then poor urban districts with large enrollments of low-income, minority, or limited-English-proficient students.

VARIATIONS IN EDUCATION SPENDING

Tracking educational expenditures in the public schools can be an enormously complex and confusing task for parents and interested citizens unless school systems and/or advocacy organizations help to interpret information and processes to the public.

Line-Item vs. Program-Based Budgets

Many school districts use line-item budgets, which allocate funds to a variety of budgetary categories, such as staff, equipment, materials, transportation, and construction. While these categories indicate the nature of the expenditure, they do not indicate its programmatic purpose or geographic destination. Given information in line-item form, parents will have a very difficult time determining expenditures for specific activities—such as fifth-grade mathematics or sixth-grade science—or for a specific school. School-based and program budget processes are required in order to ensure public accountability.

State Variations in Per-Pupil Expenditure

Large differences in funding exist among states, between districts within states, and between schools within school districts. For example, according to researcher Robert Jewell (1990), during the 1987 to 1988 school year, Alaskan schools had the highest per-pupil expenditure, an average of $6,473 per student. Arkansas schools appeared at the other end of the scale, reporting average per-pupil expenditures of $2,452. Wide variations for average teacher salaries were also found, with a high in Alaska of $40,424 and a low in South Dakota of $19,758.

Spending variations among states—which vary by a factor of more than 2.5:1—can largely be explained by: 1) the ability to pay for public education as reflected by a state's per capita income; 2) the commitment to support public education as displayed by the percentage of per capita income devoted to education spending; and 3) the percentage of the state's population enrolled in public schools.

Per capita income, the variable that exerts the strongest effect on education spending levels, differs significantly by state. Jewell notes that citizens of Connecticut enjoy the highest per capita income at $21,266, along with the most favorable teacher/student ratio in the country. Mississippi has the lowest per capita income of $10,292, while ranking forty-ninth in the nation in both per-pupil expenditure and average teachers' salaries. Stated simply, the greater the level of personal income, the greater the level of per-pupil expenditure.

Links Between Per-Pupil Spending, Teacher Salaries, and Teacher/Student Ratios

Examining expenditures within schools, Jewell found a strong connection between per-pupil spending levels and both average teachers' salaries and teacher/student ratios. Schools with greater resources tend to expend these resources on higher teacher salaries and more teachers, allowing them to attract more capable staff and offer more favorable teacher/student ratios.

Yet schools in many urban areas show high teacher salaries along with unfavorable teacher/student ratios. Higher metropolitan labor costs and the need to offer "combat pay" to attract staff to inner-city schools require many urban schools to expend a greater percentage of their resources on personnel, limiting the size of their staff and siphoning funds from other areas of operation.

Variations within States

Spending differences between some school districts within the same state are as striking as differences among states. According to education analyst Carol Ascher (1989), in New York City the average per-pupil expenditure for the 1988 to 1989 school year was about $4,300. In nearby suburban counties, spending was significantly higher: $6,605 in Westchester; $6,539 in Nassau; $6,189 in Rockland; and $5,852 in Suffolk.

Reliance on Property Taxes

Such variations exist because local property taxes continue to be a substantial source for education funding. In the 1950s and 1960s, schools were almost entirely funded by local property taxes. Federal funds were largely limited to supporting special programs. During the 1970s, state aid increasingly supplemented local funding, acting in many areas to reduce financial inequities. By the mid-1980s, states generally funded more than 50 percent of non-federal costs. But state aid to local schools has not kept up with inflation, has not replaced missing federal dollars, and generally has not resulted in extra money for poor urban districts.

The common focus of various school finance reform efforts challenges continued reliance on local property taxes as a primary source of school funding. Because local property taxes are added to state education funding to make up the total school budget for a local community, poorer districts with low property values or little taxable property have considerably less funds than more wealthy districts.

Legal Action Redresses Inequity

Researcher JoAnna Natale (1990) reports that large differences in school spending between districts have resulted in recent successful legal action in four states—Texas, Kentucky, Montana, and New Jersey—where the courts have ordered state legislatures to move away from reliance on local property taxes toward more equitable systems of school funding. Similar lawsuits are pending in Alaska, Connecticut, Indiana, Minnesota, North Dakota, Oregon, and Tennessee. At the federal level, legislation has recently been proposed to require states to submit funding equalization plans in order to qualify for federal education money.

Issues Raised by Reform Efforts

Observers of school finance reform have noted some tough issues raised by these efforts, as expressed by Natale.

- **Does more money really mean better education?** Although research findings on this point are mixed, this is largely the result of poor-quality research. Logic clearly suggests the positive value of funding: a school can't provide an effective science curriculum without a proper laboratory or teach a foreign language without a teacher fluent in that language.
- **What exactly does equity mean?** Achieving educational equity requires more than a simple allocation of equal dollars for each student. Equal spending will not produce equity where vast differences exist between schools or between communities. To achieve a level playing field, children disadvantaged by society require greater resources.
- **Tensions exist between local control and state-mandated equalization formulas.** State-imposed school spending caps designed to equalize funding can seem to a wealthy school district like a punishment for their hard work and success.
- **Implementing a new plan takes time.** Changing schools requires a sustained, long-term effort. Advocates in Texas, for example, feel their funding reforms will take ten years to realize. One activist notes, "It will be harder to keep it than to get it."

EFFECTS OF FUNDING INEQUITIES ON CHILDREN

Funding disparities have documentable impacts on the education, growth and development of children. Poor school districts are characterized by:

- higher ratios of students to teachers and administrators;
- program limitations that inhibit the capacity to address individual student needs;
- limited supplies and teaching materials;
- an inferior capacity to monitor and evaluate educational programs.

Students in poor urban districts have lower academic achievement levels and are more likely to drop out of school, regardless of their race or ethnicity.

Comparing three Maryland elementary schools in different districts, *Baltimore Sun* reporter Kathy Lally (1989) discovered "dramatic variations in time spent with teachers, quality of environment, equipment and supplies, and sophistication of instruction, all of which shape the way [children] are taught and learn, and all of which are related to how much money their schools have." Among her findings:

- **Baltimore's Holabird Elementary School.** In this inner-city school, the average per-pupil expenditure is $2,100. In a depressing, dingy building, children are faced with an undertone of hostility and stress. The school has one borrowed computer but no software to run on it. A teacher with more than thirty years of experience is paid just over $27,000. The school spends $2.67 per pupil on library books and supplies; a randomly selected library book was published in 1926 and last checked out in 1969. The school employs twenty-three staff members to serve 302 children.
- **Caroline County's Preston Elementary School.** In this more rural area, per-pupil spending is the lowest in the state at $1,858, but the school displays brightly painted cinder block walls and is carefully tended. The first-grade class has a new television, a new world globe, and a new map of the U.S. As the result of special county bond issuance, Preston has purchased thirty-one computers, allowing students access three days a week for twenty minutes. A teacher with eleven years of experience makes $28,745. The school spends $10.07 per pupil on library books and supplies. A staff of thirty-two serves 388 children.
- **Longfellow Elementary School in Howard County.** In this prosperous suburban community, per-pupil spending is $2,647. Teachers have assistants, allowing them to spend more time with individual students. Seventeen computers are spread around the building at various sites. A teacher with eight years of experience earns $30,998. The school spends $17.95 per pupil on library books and supplies. A staff of forty-three serves 380 children.

Even though the Maryland state aid formula is designed to equalize funding, this clearly has not been achieved. As Caroline County Commissioner William Ecker notes, "The children who need the most are given the least."

FINANCE PROBLEMS FOR URBAN SCHOOLS

For a variety of reasons, urban schools face the toughest finance problems. Researcher Carol Ascher (1989) offers a compilation of contributing factors.

- **State aid systems work against urban schools.** As state governments have increasingly provided funding for local schools: 1) state aid has not kept pace with inflation, replaced missing federal dollars, or provided extra money to poor urban districts; 2) "hold harmless" provisions in many state funding allocation plans ensure that wealthy districts will not receive less revenue; thus, in order to provide extra help for urban districts, the whole budget must be expanded; 3) financial support does not always keep pace with increased enrollment and other expenses; 4) state aid is generally calculated on the basis of Average Daily Attendance (ADA), tending to discriminate against urban schools with high absentee rates; for example, the New York City Board of Education claims reliance on ADA excludes 15 percent of students from state support; 5) the current mood of the country is tilted toward "excellence" away from "equity," encouraging states to allocate extra money for "excellence" projects rather than to support disadvantaged urban students.
- **State control over local budgets has increased.** Growth of state funding has been accompanied by an increase in state control, weakening local power to raise money or determine how to spend it.
- **Federal money has both declined and shifted from categorical to block grants.** Categorical grants are dedicated for a specific use (bilingual, handicapped, etc.), whereas block grants can be used for broader purposes. The needs of urban schools are better met by categorical grants, which covered 16 percent of costs as compared to 8 percent under block grants.
- **The capacity for school support in urban areas has declined. Raising revenue in many urban areas is difficult.** With minimal development of new housing, there are fewer opportunities to raise property-based school taxes. In many areas, city councils try to attract new business with abatements and exemptions. Elderly and less affluent citizens can contribute little to the tax base while drawing on publicly funded social services.
- **It costs more to educate urban students.** Urban teachers are often more experienced and, therefore, more expensive. The cost of land and materials and labor for construction and maintenance is higher in urban areas. Vandalism is more costly. For example, the Los Angeles School District paid $25 million for its security force in 1987 to 1988, adding to local district expenses for burglar alarms, fire alarms, security fences, and insurance.
- **Urban students have special needs.** By the mid-1980s, 30 percent of urban school-aged children were poor; 70 percent were minority. In New York City, 63 percent of the city's school children live in poverty. With 35 percent of the state's school enrollment, New York City educates 54 percent of all the state's special education children and 80 percent of all limited-English-proficient students. Many city school districts must take on extra programs and services to address desegregation, addicted or pregnant students, disciplinary problems, irregular or poor attendance, transportation, and hungry children.

NEED FOR CAPITAL IMPROVEMENT

Recent school finance reform efforts have focused largely on issues of resource levels and funding mechanisms. Capital improvements have not been considered as carefully. Researcher Kathleen Westbrook (1989) has found the average age of school buildings in the United States is more than fifty years old.

Westbrook estimates the cost of deferred maintenance to the nation's schools is in excess of $30 billion. The American Association of School Administrators, the Council of Great City Schools, and the National School Boards Association (1983) concur, setting the figure at $25 billion.

In the absence of a national effort to repair and maintain the educational infrastructure, Westbrook notes there has never been a systematic collection of data for policy analysis concerning public school capital needs. Each school district is left to make the case for physical improvements on its own.

Without a systematic national effort to raise this urgent need for massive capital investment, schools are likely to continue to deteriorate. Surveys of state legislative personnel find that issues concerning physical facilities rank last among education priorities (Westbrook, 1989).

INVESTING IN RESTRUCTURED SCHOOLS

Efforts to increase parent participation, to employ more realistic and comprehensive student assessment systems, to offer students more appropriate instruction and curriculum, to provide teachers with greater training and support, and to address students' guidance and support service needs will require significant financial investment.

Poor urban districts must repair their educational "base" as they seek to become Good Common Schools. This will require repairing and rebuilding physical facilities, purchasing basic instructional equipment and materials, and hiring additional staff.

Money alone cannot guarantee a better education for children. If the public continues to spend money on schools that are structured to sort out children and educate them for different futures, and that fail to prepare students for the realities of a diverse society, the "one best system" will remain deeply troubled in spite of massive financial investment.

The Abbott Case: Litigation and Community Support

Since 1975, the **Education Law Center (ELC),** a non-profit, public-interest law firm specializing in public school reform in New Jersey, tracked the effects of the Public School Education Act of 1975—reform legislation governing the financing of New Jersey public schools.

The legislation was passed in response to a 1973 New Jersey Supreme Court decision that found the state's education funding statute unconstitutional. Although the 1973 legislation gave poorer districts taxing power to raise money for schools, it required low-income, urban districts to impose high tax rates to meet their educational needs. It also linked supplemental state "equalization aid" to the amount raised by local property taxes. While raising serious doubts about the newly established funding scheme, the Court found it constitutional in 1976.

It soon became clear to ELC that inherent flaws in the new system were causing great disparities in funding and educational services. Annual per-pupil funding in poor urban districts averaged $1,250 less than funding in property-rich districts. More than 45 percent of urban district students never graduated. For those who remained in the school system, schools were over-crowded, poorly equipped buildings with inadequate staff and rudimentary curricula. Since the 1975 reform act was passed, it was fully funded only twice, further limiting its equalizing effect.

The Abbott Case

In February 1981, ELC filed a class-action suit contending that New Jersey's education finance system caused significant educational expenditure and program disparities between poor and wealthy school districts. Plaintiff students in the case were selected from among children living in school districts with the lowest property values who demonstrated the greatest educational needs.

In addition to a decision finding the educational funding system unconstitutional, ELC sought a ruling to guarantee a tax-based standard that assured availability of similar resources for children with similar needs wherever they attended school. Futhermore, such a standard should not unreasonably burden or impact economic and social conditions in poor, urban communities.

Linking Litigation With Grassroots Advocacy

Although litigation is their primary strategy, ELC recognizes that legal advocacy has its limitations. Lawsuits require a high level of understanding of legal rules and procedures and encourage participation of only the legal advocate.

ELC believes collaboration between legal and lay persons provides the most comprehensive advocacy for systemic change. By working with a community-based, non-legal organizations, ELC can coordinate legal strategies with community organizing strategies to allow parents, students, and concerned members of the community to participate actively in the process of change.

ELC was aware the citizens of New Jersey needed a better understanding of the school funding system. To achieve this, ELC staff worked to build organizational and financial support networks to broaden public understanding of education funding reform and to gather and analyze evidence necessary to prove its case.

The Abbott Advisory Panel

To develop a community support network to work in tandem with the litigation strategy, ELC sought to coordinate its activities with various organizations and individuals concerned about education inequities in New Jersey by forming an advisory panel.

The main functions of the panel were to keep people informed about the litigation's progress, to allow concerned citizens to help to define the educational needs incorporated in the litigation, and to educate others about how to become involved. Some panel members provided new plaintiffs, participated as witnesses, submitted *amicus* briefs, and discovered additional witnesses and facts to support the claims in the case. Through this process, panel members became more knowledgeable about funding issues and were able to inform others in their various organizations.

This network maintained itself by means of strong relationships which developed over years of working together. Since informal lines of communication already existed between many of the groups and individuals serving on the advisory panel, few formal meetings were required to circulate information.

School Finance Video

ELC helped to produce a school finance video to bring a visual and human element to a highly technical issue. Resources for the video were provided in part by Essex College and the Urban School Superintendents of New Jersey. Mixing newly produced materials with clips from television reports, ELC used the video as an educational/support tool during speeches and conference presentations, and as background material for media interviews.

Alternative School Financing Workshop

In July of 1985, ELC and the Urban School Superintendents of New Jersey sponsored a week-long workshop on alternative methods of financing public school education. Workshop participants included urban school administrators, representatives of statewide advocacy organizations, and the Abbott Advisory Panel. National and state experts in school finance and ELC staff served as consultants.

Workshop participants studied the existing statutory financing formula, examined characteristics of effective formulas, and analyzed statistical simulations of allocations under various funding approaches. The week culminated with a day devoted to the discussion of alternative funding options with a bipartisan group of state legislators.

Speaking Engagements

Public speaking engagements were an important forum to educate the public about inequities in the state education finance system. The more recognition the Abbott case received, the more people wanted to hear about it. Unfortunately, ELC lacked the funding and staff time to formally develop knowledgeable speakers on funding issues. Most of the burden to deliver speeches fell on ELC's executive director, Attorney Marilyn Morheuser.

Speaking engagements generated funds and support. When ELC spoke to urban city councils to discuss reasons why cities should be in favor of funding changes, they received a grant from one city council to support the organization's work. After an ELC presentation, The Committee to Save the Children offered support by organizing its members to attend the trial and by releasing a summary of the case and related issues. A New Jersey anti-apartheid group pledged and collected $1,000, seeing Abbott as a case against an apartheid-like system in the United States.

Coalition for Urban Advocates

The Coalition for Urban Advocates included many who also served on the Abbott advisory panel, but focused more specifically on education in relationship to other urban concerns. ELC joined with the coalition and with the Institute for Citizen Involvement in Education and Project School to sponsor a joint meeting of advocacy, parent, and youth service organizations.

The meeting's agenda included presentations on the Abbott case, how the Department of Education could respond to the problem, and a discussion of urban school problems by the school superintendent of Jersey City. The meeting produced a volunteer system to support the Abbott fight in the Supreme Court and generated political support for funding and policy changes in the legislature.

The Slow Wheels of Justice

After ten years of exhaustive and expensive litigation, the New Jersey Supreme Court handed down its decision in the Abbott case in the summer of 1990, finding the Public School Education Act of 1975 unconstitutional.

The Court mandated amendments to ensure education funding for poorer districts at the same level as property-rich districts. According to the ruling, funding could not depend on the ability of local school districts to tax and had to be guaranteed by the state at a level adequate to provide for the special educational needs of poor urban districts.

For further information, please contact: The Education Law Center, 155 Washington Street, Room 209, Newark, NJ 07102-3016. Telephone (201) 624-1815.

PROMISING PRACTICES

Montlake School: Seattle, Washington

When Principal Levaun Dennett arrived at the Montlake Elementary School in 1982, she was anxious to work with the staff there to improve learning for the approximately 250 students, half of whom were from single-parent homes and more than one-third of whom qualified for the federally-funded school lunch program. Enthusiastic and determined to initiate change, she and the staff met to identify what they saw as the crucial issues facing them as educators. Over and over again, class size came up as a stumbling block to effective teaching in the classroom.

The staff spent time looking for ways to reduce class size without additional resources. During her second year, Principal Dennett proposed creation of a daily one-hour reading period taught by the entire teaching staff. The librarian, science teacher, special education teacher, and Chapter I teacher all agreed, reducing class size to an average of fifteen students. For this reading period, children were grouped according to their skills in reading rather than their grade. All the children in the school, including those designated special education students, were integrated into the reading groups.

Building on the success of the reading group, the staff expanded the plan for all language arts and mathematics instruction. The following year, all children were grouped according to their skills rather than their grade for all their language arts and mathematics instruction. Again, the librarian, science teacher, special education teacher, and Chapter I teacher were all assigned to teach these groups. Class size ranged from twelve to twenty-two students. Students requiring the most one-to-one instruction were in the smallest classes and the most independent students were in the largest.

Teachers sharing children in their skill groups were also provided mutual planning time. They shared struggles and ideas and collaboratively began to develop new approaches to try in their classrooms. A team emerged and flourished.

The school had succeeded in achieving smaller classes by using their resources in a different way. This restructuring effort involved no extra money and no additional staff time. Moreover, because school staff were involved in all decisions every step of the way, the local union was very supportive of the changes. In fact, the school was held up by the union as an example of what could be accomplished when administrators and teachers work together.

Under the restructured plan, children receiving special education and Chapter I services were not pulled out of the classroom for services, but were taught language arts and mathematics in integrated classrooms with other children working on similar objectives. Because this was not the usual procedure, Principal Dennett was very concerned that the school might not conform to the regulations governing Chapter I and special education services. She spent considerable time and energy negotiating with school-district and state-level officials to address these concerns.

Fortunately, at the time, achieving greater integration among Chapter I, special education, and regular education services was a major education goal for the state of Washington. Special education staff from the state and from Seattle's central school office were very supportive of Montlake's efforts to reduce class size and integrate all children for instruction. They developed a plan to ensure that Montlake would meet the requirements of the special education regulations. Specifically, in addition to clarifying with parents exactly how the plan worked, the special education teacher taught children receiving special education services during at least one group time. The special education teacher also served as an ongoing consultant to the regular education teachers.

Negotiating Chapter I regulations proved more difficult. All potential avenues seemed to end in roadblocks. In the end, Seattle's superintendent agreed to pay Montlake's Chapter I teacher from local funds because of concerns over the regulations.

After one full year of implementation of what had now become known as the "Montlake Plan," the school found itself in a dilemma. Children and teachers were thriving under the new structure. Children were much more successful, and behavior problems had decreased. Consequently, there were less referrals to special education and the school lost half the funding needed for the special education teacher. A resulting increase in test scores, one of the factors used to allocate Chapter I funds, moved the school to the bottom of the list for Chapter I placement where no money was available. In addition, Seattle provided "intervention teachers" to schools on the basis of many factors—including the number of children receiving free lunches, the number from single-parent families, the number of bilingual and special education students, and test score results. Because of improvements in some of these areas at Montlake, the school also lost half of its funding for an intervention teacher.

As Principal Dennett recalls: "We struggled with how to make the program stable enough to last. We did not want to keep getting punished for doing a good job." Not one to be defeated, Dennett swung back into action. When she explained what had happened to state Department of Education officials, they agreed to provide one year of funding under a special education grant for efforts at integration. The school district provided matching funds. The Montlake Plan was saved for another year.

Energized at their success with the skills groups and reaping the benefits of collaboration, teachers decided to expand their efforts. Children were still grouped by skill level for language arts and mathematics, but beginning in 1985, children were grouped in mixed-aged clusters, identified as the child's "core" group, for their remaining subjects. Children of varying abilities and different ages were grouped together, with each group comprised of children from more than one grade. Core groups included Kindergarten/first, second/third, and fourth/fifth grade clusters. Teachers were also grouped into teams of three or four, with each team sharing a common planning time.

Although the school continued to expand its innovation in grouping and teaching approaches and achieved further success, their struggle to maintain funding did not end. The more successful the school became, the more funding it seemed to lose. As Principal Dennett only half-jokingly lamented: "I was such a successful leader I defunded the school."

After two full years of the Montlake Plan, the school lost funding for four positions, including special education, Chapter I, and intervention teachers. This time, due to the innovative efforts of a parent, the school applied for and received a federal discretionary grant from the Department of Education, allowing them to replace all four lost positions. In addition, the school was able to develop a computer laboratory open to all students.

The federal grant, however, only provided one year of funding. At the end of the year, the staff found themselves in the same frustrating position—no funding for the four positions required to maintain the program at its present level. Fresh out of new ideas but determined to take a stance, the staff decided to continue the work without the four positions.

Montlake was now the only school in the district not receiving additional resources outside of the minimum guaranteed by union contract. The school was no longer eligible for any categorical or discretionary funds. The staff hoped that once central office staff became aware that their students were not receiving an equitable share of the funding, they would receive additional money. When the state department of special education gave Seattle additional money to target resources for Montlake, the school system was able to release enough money to replace one of the four teaching positions. But the Montlake Plan began its fourth year of implementation three teaching positions short.

The loss of three teaching positions required an increase in class size. The staff agreed to continue mixed-aged grouping and team teaching. The years of smaller class size had allowed the teachers to experiment with innovative practices and new approaches. Smaller class size had allowed for more physical space for children and reduced discipline problems. Grouping children in ways that provided many opportunities for success had resulted in motivated, engaged learners and also contributed significantly to the decrease in discipline problems. The smaller classes had provided time for teachers to organize curriculum around integrated themes that were more relevant and interesting for students and that encouraged more creative teaching. Because teachers worked in teams, they were no longer isolated and had support for trying out new ideas. Class size itself had become less crucial.

In the fifth year of the Montlake Plan, children remain grouped by skill rather than grade level for their language arts and mathematics instruction and are in mixed-age and ability groups for their remaining subjects. A grant awarded to the school under Washington State's "Schools for the Twenty-first Century" program provides ten extra paid days for every staff member for staff development—time the staff has used for team planning, developing curriculum innovations, and trying out new ideas. In addition, because revisions of Chapter I regulations make a whole-school approach to service delivery easier, the school again receives Chapter I money.

But funding problems remain. For the current year, the team structure designed by the staff required nine teachers for implementation—three teams of three teachers each. Because the school department continues to assign teachers to schools based on the number of children enrolled and on a single teacher in a self-contained classroom, the school was assigned only eight teachers. After extensive lobbying efforts by present principal Christi Clark, along with teachers and parents, the school department agreed to provide a ninth teacher.

While the staff at the Montlake School remains committed to the Montlake Plan, the time and energy required to fight for funding drains valuable resources that could be better used to develop teaching and curriculum innovations.

For further information, please contact: Ms. Christi Clark, Principal, Montlake Elementary School, 2409 22nd East Street, Seattle, WA 98112.

Current Research Related to Topics Discussed in Chapter Eight

Spending Differentials

In the past decade, spending on education has increased significantly, nearly 25 percent in real terms **(Colvin, 1989).** In 1987, U.S. expenditures on public schools averaged $4000 per student **(U.S. Department of Education, 1988).** However, this figure masks large differences in per-pupil expenditures among school districts. These differences exist among states, among school districts within states, and even among schools inside a single school district **(Ascher, 1989; Cardenas, 1988; Jewell, 1990; Hollifield, 1990; Natale, 1990; U.S. Department of Education, 1988).**

For the 1987 to 1988 school year, average per-pupil expenditures varied by a factor of more than 2.5 to 1 among the fifty states and the District of Columbia. Alaska had the highest average expenditure at $6,473 per pupil; Arkansas has the lowest at $2,452 **(Jewell, 1990).**

Jewell (1990) explored causes for the wide disparities in the level of funding among the states. His analysis revealed that a large part of the variations (over 90 percent) were a function of: a) ability to pay—the per capita income or total personal income earned annually in a state divided by the population of the state; b) effort—the proportion of all personal income earned in a state allocated to public education through state and local sources; and c) pupil burden—the proportion of a state's total population enrolled in public school. Ability to pay alone accounted for over 60 percent of the variations in per-pupil expenditures among the fifty-one systems.

Jewell (1990) found that lower-income states allocated a greater proportion of income to public education but still had lower per-pupil expenditures than high-income states. Not surprisingly, an inverse relationship between student burden and expenditures was found. States with higher burdens also tended to put forth greater effort. That is, states with higher proportions of their populations enrolled in public schools spend greater proportions of their income on public education. These states generally also had lower per capita incomes. Thus, even with their greater effort, they still had lower per pupil expenditures than states with higher per capita incomes and lower student burdens.

Jewell (1990) also looked at school-related factors that explained variations in expenditures. He found more than 63 percent of the variations in average expenditures accounted for by variations in average teachers' salaries. Pupil/teacher ratio was a second school-based factor strongly related to expenditures. When the effects of pupil/teacher ratios were added to those of teachers' salaries, the two variables accounted for almost 88 percent of the variations in average per-pupil expenditure. Jewell concludes that school districts within states with greater resources appear to use those resources to hire more teachers and pay them higher salaries. Other researchers have drawn similar conclusions ***(see, for example,* Hanushek's (1989) review).**

Similar funding disparities to those at the state level are found among districts within states **(Ascher, 1989; U.S. Department of Education, 1988).** The disparity between property wealth in the wealthiest and poorest districts in Texas reflects a 700 to 1 ratio. The wealthiest district has over $14,000,000 of property wealth per student while the poorest has approximately $20,000. Less than 3 percent of the state's property wealth supports the 300,000 students enrolled in the lowest-wealth schools, while the 300,000 students enrolled in the highest-wealth schools have over 25 percent of the state's property wealth to support their education **("Excerpts from Unanimous *Edgewood* Ruling," 1989).** Likewise in New York, the suburban counties surrounding New York City spend $1,000 to $2,000 more per pupil than the city **(Ascher, 1989).** Congruent with **Jewell's (1990)** state-level findings, lower student expenditures in property-poor schools districts are not due to a lack of tax effort. Generally property-rich districts can tax low and still spend high but property-poor districts must tax high just to spend low **("Clerk's Summary," 1990; Natale, 1990; Newman, 1990b).**

Poor Districts vs. Wealthier Districts

The impact of spending differentials is further magnified by the varying nature of school districts. Funding disparities that already exist between poor urban districts and wealthier districts are increased by greater student needs. Poor districts tend to be in urban areas with high concentrations of low-income, minority, limited-English-proficient, or immigrant children. Because state funding allocations do not accurately reflect the costs of bilingual, compensatory, and other special programs, districts often bear much of the expense **(Ascher, 1989).** For example, New York City enrolls 35 percent of the state's school population but has 63 percent of all those living in poverty, 54 percent of all full-time special education students, and 80 percent of all students with limited English proficiency **(Ascher, 1989).**

Urban districts bear substantial costs for programs designed to address the complex needs of their student population. These may include programs for pregnant and addicted teens, dropout prevention programs, as well as transportation and food programs **(Ascher, 1989).**

In addition, urban districts often have to offer "combat pay" to attract qualified teachers. For example, teachers' salaries in several large urban areas including Houston and Philadelphia average over $6,000 more than statewide teacher salaries **(Ascher, 1989). Jewell (1990)** found that while states with high teacher salaries generally had favorable pupil/teacher ratios, a number of states had high salaries with unfavorable ratios. Analysis of these states revealed a tendency toward high concentrations of population in metropolitan areas. He suggests that states with high metropolitan concentrations must pay high teacher salaries to remain competitive in the labor market.

The conditions of the physical plants in poor urban districts are much worse than in wealthier districts. School buildings need major repairs and renovations. Laboratory equipment is seriously outmoded or nonexistent **(Corcoran, Walker, and White, 1988; Education Law Center, 1985; "Clerk's Summary," 1990).** Moreover, the cost of land for schools and materials and labor for their construction and maintenance are higher in cities as well **(Ascher, 1989).**

Capital needs have mounted significantly in the last decade. Nationally, 75 percent of all public school capital programs are financed through taxes on real or personal property **(Westbrook, 1989).** Amounts allocated for capital improvement in states with state loan programs are generally small, fixed, and have little relationship to the actual needs of the local schools **(Westbrook, 1989). Westbrook (1989)** estimates the deferred maintenance and capital needs for the country are in excess of 28 to 30 billion dollars. An undue proportion of that burden falls on poor urban school districts.

Urban areas have greater difficulty raising money to support their schools. The limited development of new housing reduces the options for raising property-based school taxes. Adding to this, city councils frequently hold out abatements and exemptions as incentives to attract commercial real estate interests **(Ascher, 1989).** As Ascher emphasizes, "schools must compete with a variety of other urgently needed services for the small and declining urban tax dollar" (p. 4).

Diversity of educational programs, quality of physical facilities, materials, and equipment, and qualifications of school staff are all lower in poor districts than in wealthier districts. Poor districts also have less capacity to monitor and evaluate programs to allow schools to maintain successful efforts and modify or discard unsuccessful ones **(Ascher, 1989; Colvin, 1989; Congressional Budget Office, 1986; Dossey, *et al.*, 1988; Morheuser, 1984; Natale, 1990; National Assessment of Educational Progress, 1985; National Coalition of Advocates for Students, 1985).**

Efforts to track educational expenditures in the public schools are complicated by the way financial data is collected. Financial data is rarely recorded or collected by function at the school or classroom level. Moreover, present data does not reveal how much U.S. schools spend on elementary as opposed to secondary education, or on teaching specific subjects—reading, for instance, or science. Nor is it known what the relative spending is on students with various characteristics **(Colvin, 1989).**

Equalization of Resources

Advocates for poor or minority students have long argued that disparity in school resources guarantees some students a poor-quality education. Their arguments have not been helped by research that has failed to find a consistent relationship between funding and student performance **(Ascher, 1989; Colvin, 1989; Hanushek, 1989; Murname, 1981).** Much of this research uses an input/output or production/function approach. This model assumes that the "output" of the educational process, student achievement, is directly related to a series of inputs **(Hanushek, 1979, 1989).** While inputs may vary, instructional expenditures are usually measured by teacher experience and education level (as determinants of teacher salary) and class size or pupil/teacher ratio. Standardized test score results are the basic determinant of output **(Hanushek, 1989).**

The failure to find a consistent relationship between expenditures and student achievement as measured by this approach does not mean that money does not matter. Aside from citing the numerous methodological concerns, not the least of which is determining and measuring appropriate "inputs" and "outputs," others have argued that the input/output model is totally inappropriate for the study of the educational process because of its static, non-interactive nature **(Clauset and Gaynor, 1982; Goodlad, Sirotnik, and Overman, 1979; Natale, 1990; Sirotnik and Oakes, 1981).** Moreover, research has clearly and repeatedly demonstrated that teachers and schools differ dramatically in their effectiveness **(Edmonds, 1981, 1982; Glen, 1981; Hanushek, 1989; Purkey and Smith, 1982, 1985; Sizemore, 1985).** As **Hanushek (1989)** points out, "there seems little question that money could count—it just does not consistently do so within the current organization of schools" (p. 49). As one lawyer astutely pointed out, if school wealth makes little difference, then the wealthy districts should not mind transferring some of their money to the poorer districts **(*cited in* Ascher, 1989).**

The fact remains that students attending poor districts demonstrate lower achievement rates and have higher dropout rates than their counterparts in wealthier districts, regardless of race or ethnicity. **(ASPIRA, 1983; Designs for Change, 1985; "Clerk's Summary," 1990; Hess, 1986; Wehlage, 1987; Wetzel, 1987).** There is little argument that wealthier districts offer additional learning opportunities that are denied to students in poorer districts. Wealthier districts are able to provide their students with a broader educational experience including more advanced and diversified curricula, more up-to-date technological equipment, better facilities, better libraries, lower student/teacher ratios, and more parent involvement and dropout prevention programs **(Ascher, 1989; Cardenas, 1987; "Clerk's Summary," 1990; Education Law Center, 1985; "Excerpts from Unanimous *Edgewood* Ruling," 1989; Natale, 1990).**

During the 1950s and 1960s, education was largely funded at the local level through property taxes with federal funds generally used for special programs. Since 1970, partly in an effort to reduce disparities between property-rich and property-poor districts, state funding has increasingly supplanted local dollars. By 1984, states generally funded more than 50 percent of non-federal school costs **(Ascher, 1989).**

While the move toward increased state funding through equalization formulas offered hope in reducing the inequities between districts, several factors have diminished the effectiveness of this strategy. State funding depends heavily on the condition of the state economy. Economic downturns during the last few years in some states have dried up state funding sources, eroding recent progress in equalizing education spending **(Shanker, 1990; U.S. Department of Education, 1988).** States simply have not had the money to replace lost federal dollars, give extra money to poor school districts, or to keep up with the costs of increasing student enrollments and other expenses, such as capital repairs **(Ascher, 1989; Hollifield, 1990).** Additionally, state aid to school districts is generally calculated by Average Daily Attendance data (ADA), which acts to discriminate against urban districts with high absentee rates **(Ascher, 1989).**

Lally (1989) provides vivid descriptions of three elementary schools in Maryland that provide vastly different educational experiences for the children enrolled in them, even though Maryland has a state aid formula that purports to equalize funding. The schools vary dramatically in terms of the time teachers are able to spend directly with students, the quality of the learning environment, equipment and supplies, and sophistication of instruction.

Hollifield (1990), in his review of research completed by Kern Alexander for the Appalachia Educational Laboratory, provides evidence on the state level for the failure of equalization formulas to achieve their promise. According to Hollifield, four states—Kentucky, Tennessee, Virginia, and West Virginia—did not have equitable education funding, even though all four had enacted state equalization formulas. Several reasons were presented to account for the failure of the equalization formulas to achieve equitable funding, including: failure of the legislation to provide adequate funding; depressed economic conditions; and failure of complex formulas to adequately assess the fiscal needs of the local districts.

The failure or lack of state efforts to achieve equitable funding among their school districts has led to a number of lawsuits. Four states—Texas, Kentucky, Montana, and New Jersey—have successfully mounted legal challenges against large differences in school spending between districts. Courts in these states have ordered their legislatures to move away from reliance on local property taxes toward more equitable systems of school funding **(Cardenas, 1988; Colvin, 1989; Natale, 1990).** Similar lawsuits are pending in Alaska, Connecticut, Indiana, Minnesota, North Dakota, Oregon, and Tennessee **(Natale, 1990).** In all, lawsuits are under consideration or have been filed in at least seventeen states **(Newman, 1990a).**

The federal government has also begun to take action. Recently, federal legislation has been proposed to require states to submit funding equalization plans or lose control of federal education monies beginning in 1996. Under the plan, the U.S. Department of Education would distribute the recovered funds to poor school districts **(Natale, 1990).**

Many see renewed concern about disparities in funding and resurgence of court involvement as a much-needed change **(Cardenas, 1988; Hollifield, 1990; Natale, 1990; Newman, 1989; Newman, 1990a).** Education systems are dynamic and affected by myriad factors. Devising solutions to equalize funding that can withstand the test of time is a daunting task. State equalization efforts require continual re-evaluation and monitoring. As C. Kent McGuire, an education professor at the University of Colorado points out, "You wouldn't expect a system to hold up in perpetuity. Changes in the economy, in student enrollment, and in emphases in education (such as the recent push to raise teacher salaries) could all affect a future round of solutions, just as those changes affected solutions reached in the 1970s" ***(cited in*** **Natale, 1990, p. 42).**

State equalization formulas rightfully attempt to address large disparities in funding but they also inevitably create tensions between local control and state mandates. Wealthy districts resist state-imposed caps on spending and believe that they are an unfair penalty **(Natale, 1990; Walker, 1990).** Districts also argue that state efforts at equalizing funding are not always responsive to local needs, yet often tie local administrators' hands when it comes to funding decisions. District administrators point out that each year state dollars come with different stipulations. Districts that depend heavily on state funds do not know each year which programs will be refunded or how much money will be available for discretionary spending **(Ascher, 1989; Wise and Gendler, 1989).**

While equal spending appears to be a prerequisite for an equal education, it does not guarantee one. A recent analysis of studies examining the relationship between educational expenditures and student achievement found that only certain types of expenditures are likely to produce increases in student achievement: money spent on programs, materials, and activities that have demonstrated effectiveness at promoting achievement will affect achievement; money spent on mediocre new textbooks to replace mediocre old textbooks is not likely to improve student achievement—no matter how much is spent **(Childs and Shakeshaft, 1986).**

An increasing number of educators, researchers, and advocates hold that equity work should focus on the classroom and not the school district. They argue that equity must be defined as access to high-level curricula, effective teaching practices, adequate equipment, and other educational resources rather than as a financial measure **("Clerk's Summary," 1990; Colvin, 1989; Natale, 1990).** According to Julie Underwood, an assistant professor of education at the University of Wisconsin, "Equal dollars for equal children is not...an answer to equity. Equity isn't always equal. Equity is giving children what they need to start out so they have a level playing field" **(Natale, 1990, p.25).** Along these lines, the relationship between school finance and student outcomes is not simply measured by standardized test scores but more accurately by such variables as: student enrollment in college placement classes; availability of honors programs; variety of advanced math, science, and foreign-language classes offered; and student graduation college enrollment and employment figures **(Ascher, 1989; "Clerk's Summary," 1990; Cardenas, 1987).**

Researchers and educators have pointed to the urgent need to use additional monies more effectively. Additional funding without subsequent changes in the ways schools are structured and operated may accomplish little in terms of student achievement **(Colvin, 1989; Hanushek, 1989; Levin, 1989; Newman, 1990a).**

Programs for Students with Special Needs

Beginning in the mid-1960s, the federal government created a series of categorical grant programs designed to address the special needs of specific students. The two most prominent programs are Chapter I (formerly Title I), which targets students disadvantaged by society, and P.L. 94-142 (Education for Handicapped Children Act), which targets physically, psychologically, and emotionally disabled children. The programs were first established because in many schools the needs of handicapped and disadvantaged children were not even recognized.

Funds are distributed to school systems under these programs on the basis of the number of eligible children enrolled. Funds must be used in support of projects that serve eligible children exclusively. These programs are designed to "supplement, not supplant" local services, that is, to expand services provided to eligible children by the schools rather than replace services provided with local resources **(Medina, 1989).**

Currently, these two programs account for two-thirds of all federal funds distributed to elementary and secondary schools **(Sumberg, 1989),** but fall far short of funding either program adequately. P.L. 94-142, for example, promised that the federal government would pay 40 percent of the excess cost of educating disabled students. In fact, the federal government pays only about 10 percent **(Ballard and Farrar, 1989).** Similarly, a recent analysis by **Levin (1989)** concludes that federal and state programs for students disadvantaged by society assist only one-third of those requiring services and, even then, provide only 40 percent of the per-student allocation required to meet academic needs. Based on these figures, Levin calls for a fourfold increase of spending on at-risk students.

It is likely that the directive nature of these grants and their accompanying financial and administrative requirements are necessary to ensure that funds will, in fact, be used to benefit targeted students. The financial pressures faced by most school districts combined with the political influence of more affluent families make it unlikely that such funds would be used exclusively on children disadvantaged by society in the absence of binding legislative and administrative requirements.

The effectiveness of these two federal programs has led to the creation of similar programs by various states, with funding generally distributed in the same manner as the federal programs. Programs operated by schools as the result of state funding are usually intended to build upon, and operate in conjunction with, the federal programs **(Kutner, *et al.*, 1983; Moore, *et al.*, 1983).**

Federal and state funds targeted to at-risk children have allowed school systems to create and implement many effective programs to address special needs. But the same rules ensuring that funds will be used exclusively for students with differing needs also act to undermine efforts to implement innovative changes in problem areas such as grouping practices, grade structure, instructional practices, and discipline **(Kutner, *et al.*, 1983; Moore, *et al.*, 1983).** For example, the Montlake Elementary School in Seattle, Washington established small class sizes, cross-age groupings, and team teaching in mathematics and reading, resulting in the elimination of special education labels for many students. As a consequence of these valuable structural changes, the school district lost funding that was predicated on clear identification—that is, labeling—of disadvantaged students. Without the labels, there was no funding (see the description of the Montlake School in this chapter).

This reflects a long-standing dispute in the educational community between those who advocate for relatively unrestricted local discretion in the use of federal grants and those who support restrictions to ensure that the goals of the grant program are realized. Although the situation with the Montlake Elementary School may suggest the need for legislative or administrative changes in specific provisions of the program, innovative programming should not be developed at the expense of serving the target population of students. Rather, programs should strive to balance and promote both goals.

Monitoring and Evaluation

A major difficulty in assessing the effectiveness of federal and state grant programs stems from a lack of effective monitoring and evaluation. For many programs, monitoring and evaluation emphasize compliance with accounting, financial, and administrative rules. While these requirements are certainly important, they should not be the exclusive focus of monitoring and evaluation efforts.

Contemporaneous information is rarely gathered regarding the project's development process and implementation and its immediate and long-term impacts. Outcome data tend to be limited and superficial. Federal or state governments rarely provide sufficient funding and time to identify operational goals and objectives, develop specific project plans, and conduct detailed project evaluations **(Medina, 1989).**

Yet better and more creative accountability systems are needed to make the best use of incentive monies. These systems could involve using year-to-year change rather than absolute levels of student achievement. They should also require finance methods that do not punish success by removing resources once goals have been achieved.

Sources for Promising Practices

CHAPTER ONE

Literatura Infantil

Dr. Paul Nava, director, Watsonville Migrant Education Program (personal interview, September 25, 1990).

Lupe Soltero, teacher, Literatura Infantil (personal interview, October 24, 1990).

Olsen, L., and Dowell, C. (1989). "Literatura Infantil: Binding Families Together." In L. Olsen and C. Dowell, *BRIDGES: Promising Programs for the Education of Immigrant Children*, pp. 118–22. San Francisco, CA: California Tomorrow.

Watsonville Migrant Education Program (1989). *Literatura Infantil.* Watsonville, CA: Author.

Sterne Brunson School Development Program

Delores Gavin, coordinator, School Development Program, Benton Harbor (personal interview, September 25, 1990).

Joyce Johnson, principal, Sterne Brunson School (personal interview, October 10 and 16, 1990).

Rita Broadway, parent, Sterne Brunson School (personal interview, December 17, 1990).

Haynes, N. M.; Comer, J. P.; and Hamilton-Lee, M. (1988). "The School Development Program: A Model for School Improvement." *Journal of Negro Education* 57(1):11–21.

CHAPTER TWO

Lacoste Elementary School

Joy Connor, assistant principal, Lacoste Elementary School (personal interview, November 13, 1990).

Beverly Gordon, teacher, Lacoste Elementary School (personal interview, November 13, 1990).

Kathleen Warner, teacher, Lacoste Elementary School (personal interview, November 26, 1990).

Dawson, M. M. (1987). "Beyond Ability Grouping: A Review of the Effectiveness of Ability Grouping and Its Alternatives." *School Psychology Review* 16(3):348–69.

Brooklyn New School

Mary Ellen Bosch, director, Brooklyn New School (personal interview, September 26, 1990).

Linda Ellman, parent, Brooklyn New School (personal interview, September 18, 1990).

CHAPTER THREE

La Escuela Fratney

Bob Peterson, program implementor, La Escuela Fratney (personal interview, December 11, 1990).

Becky Trayser, teacher, La Escuela Fratney (personal interview, December 12, 1990).

Bietila, S., and Levine, D. (1988). "Riverwest Neighbors Win New Fratney School." *Rethinking Schools* 2(3):1, 7.

Peterson, B. (1990). "The Struggles for Decent Schools." *Democracy and Education* 4(3):3–12.

Staff, Parents, and Students of La Escuela Fratney (1989). *La Escuela Fratney: Year One.* Milwaukee, WS: Milwaukee Public Schools.

CHAPTER FOUR

North Carolina Elementary Schools: Grades 1 and 2

Cindi Heuts, elementary consultant, Communication Skills Section, North Carolina Department of Public Instruction (personal interview, October 4, 1990).

Jeanne Joyner, elementary consultant, Mathematics Section, North Carolina Department of Public Instruction (personal interview, September 13, 1990).

Laura Mask, consultant, grades 1 and 2, North Carolina Department of Public Instruction (personal interview, October 17, 1990).

Carol Midget, teacher, Southport Elementary School (personal interview, September 17, 1990).

North Carolina Department of Public Instruction. (1990). *North Carolina's Grades 1 and 2 Assesment in Communication Skills and Mathematics.* Raleigh, NC: Author.

Graham Parks School

Linda Fobes, teacher, Graham Parks School (personal interview, December 1, 1990).

Judy Richards, teacher, Graham Parks School (presentation at Lowell Leadership Academy, November 8, 1990).

Len Solo, principal, Graham Parks School (presentation at Lowell Leadership Academy, November 8, 1990, and personal interview, November 26, 1990).

CHAPTER FIVE

Sulphur Springs Elementary School

Pat Crosby, social worker, Sulphur Springs Elementary School (personal interview, December 13, 1990).

Stephanie Moffitt, principal, Sulphur Springs Elementary School (personal interview, December 12, 1990).

Cathy Valdes, assistant principal, Sulphur Springs Elementary School (personal interview, December 12, 1990).

CHAPTER SIX

Garfield School

Dorothy Foley, principal, Garfield School (personal interview, October 24, 1990).

Diane Schwald, teacher, Garfield School (personal interview, October 30 and November 1, 1990).

First, J.; Kellogg, J. B.; Willshire Carrera, J.; Lewis, A., and Almeida, C. A. (1988). *New Voices: Immigrant Students in U.S. Public Schools,* pp. 84–87. Boston, MA: National Coalition of Advocates for Students.

CHAPTER SEVEN

Rethinking Schools

Cynthia Ellwood, editor and writer, *Rethinking Schools* (personal interview, October 17, 1990).

Bob Peterson, editor and writer, *Rethinking Schools* (personal interview, September 20, 1990).

Rita Tenorio, editor and writer, *Rethinking Schools* (personal interview, October 24, 1990).

Karp, S. (1990, June)."Rethinking Schools." *Z Magazine,* pp. 6–11.

Peterson, B. (1990). "The Struggles for Decent Schools." *Democracy and Education* 4(3):3–12.

CHAPTER EIGHT

Montlake School

Christi Clark, principal, Montlake School (personal interview, September 18, 1990).

Levaun Dennett, former principal, Montlake School (personal interview, October 15, 1990).

Dentzer, E., and Wheelock, A. (1990). *Locked In/Locked Out: Tracking and Placement Practices in Boston Public Schools,* pp. 127–28. Boston, MA: Massachusetts Advocacy Center.

Bibliography

CHAPTER ONE

Becher, R. M. (1984, January). *Parent Involvment: A Review of Research and Principles of Successful Practice.* Washington, D.C.: National Institute of Education.

Berman, P. (1984, January). *Improving School Improvement: A Policy Evaluation of the California School Improvement Program. Vol. 1. Executive Summary and Recommendations.* Berkeley, CA: Berman, Weiler Associates.

Brandt, R. (1989, October). "On Parents and Schools: A Conversation with Joyce Epstein." *Educational Leadership,* pp. 24–27.

Brooks, G., and Sussman, R. (1990, spring). "Involving Parents in the Schools: How Can 'Third-Party' Interventions Make a Difference?" *Equity and Choice,* pp. 44–55.

Chan, Y. (1987, November). *Parents: The Missing Link in Education Reform.* Prepared Statement before the House Select Committee Hearing on Children, Youth, and Families, Indianapolis, IN.

Chavkin, N. F. (1989, summer). "Debunking the Myth about Minority Parents." *Educational Horizons,* pp. 119–23.

Chavkin, N. F., and Williams, D. L., Jr. (1988, winter). "Critical Issues in Teacher Training for Parent Involvement." *Educational Horizons,* pp. 87–89.

Cistone, P. J.; Fernandez, J. A.; and Tornillo, P. L. (1989, August). "School-Based Management/Shared Decision Making in Dade County." *Education and Urban Society* 21(4):393–402.

Clark, R. M. (1983). *Family Life and School Achievement: Why Poor Black Children Succeed or Fail.* Chicago, IL: University of Chicago Press.

Comer, J. P. (1984, May). "Home/School Relationships As They Affect the Academic Success of Children." *Education and Urban Society* 16(3):323–37.

Cummins, J. (1986). "Empowering Minority Students: A Framework for Intervention." *Harvard Educational Review* 56(1):18–36.

Davies, D. (1988). "Benefits and Barriers to Parent Involvement." Unpublished manuscript, Boston University, Institute for Responsive Education, Boston, MA.

Epstein, J. L. (1984a, April). *Effects of Teacher Practices of Parent Involvement: Change in Student Achievement in Reading and Math.* Baltimore, MD: Johns Hopkins University, Center for the Social Organization of Schools.

Epstein, J. L. (1984b, November). *Home and School Connections in Schools of the Future: Implications of Research on Parent Involvement.* Baltimore, MD: Johns Hopkins University, Center for the Social Organization of Schools.

Epstein, J. L. (1984c, winter). "School Policy and Parent Involvement: Research Results." *Educational Horizons,* pp. 70–72.

Epstein, J. L. (1984d, March). *Single Parents and the Schools: The Effect of Marital Status on Parent and Teacher Evaluations.* Baltimore, MD: Johns Hopkins University, Center for the Social Organization of Schools.

First, J.; Kellogg, J.; Willshire Carrera, J.; Lewis, A.; and Almeida, C. (1988). *New Voices: Immigrant Students in U.S. Public Schools.* Boston, MA: National Coalition of Advocates for Students.

Foster, K. (1984, March). "Parent Advisory Councils: School Partners or Handy Puppets?" *Principal,* pp. 26–31.

Fruchter, N. (1984, fall). "The Role of Parent Participation." *Social Policy,* pp. 32–36.

Greenberg, P. (1989, May). "Parents as Partners in Young Children's Development and Education: A New American Fad? Why Does It Matter?" *Young Children* 44(4):61–75.

Haynes, N. M.; Comer, J. P.; and Hamilton-Lee, M. (1989). "School Climate Enhancement through Parental Involvement." *Journal of School Psychology* 27:87–90.

Heller, R. W.; Woodworth, B. E.; Jacobson, S. L.; and Conway, J.A. (1989, November). "You Like School-Based Power, but You Wonder If Others Do." *The Executive Educator,* pp. 15–18.

Henderson, A. T. (1981). *Parent Participation—Student Achievement. The Evidence Grows.* Columbia, MD: National Committee for Citizens in Education.

Henderson, A. T. (1987). *The Evidence Continues to Grow. Parent Involvement Improves Student Achievement.* Columbia, MD: National Committee for Citizens in Education.

Henderson, A. T.; Marburger, C. L.; and Ooms, T. (1986). *Beyond the Bake Sale. An Educator's Guide to Working with Parents.* Columbia, MD: Committee for Citizens in Education.

Hoover-Dempsey, K. V.; Bassler, O. C.; and Brissie, J. S. (1987). "Parent Involvement: Contributions of Teacher Efficacy, School Socioeconomic Status, and Other School Characteristics." *American Educational Research Journal* 24(3):417–35.

Jennings, W. B. (1989). "How to Organize Successful Parent Advisory Committees." *Educational Leadership* 47(2):42–45.

Jensen/Miller School Council (1990). *Jensen and Miller School Improvement Plan.* Chicago, IL: Author.

Johnston, M., and Slotnik, J. (1985, February). "Parent Participation in the Schools: Are the Benefits Worth the Burdens?" *Phi Delta Kappan,* pp. 430–33.

Leler, H. (1983). "Parent Education and Involvement in Relation to the Schools and to Parents of School-Aged Children." In R. Haskins and D. Addams, eds., *Parent Education and Public Policy.* Norwood, NJ: ABLEX.

Lieberman, A. (1988, May). "Teachers and Principals: Turf, Tension, and New Tasks." *Phi Delta Kappan,* pp. 648–53.

Lightfoot, S. L. (1981). "Toward Conflict and Resolution: Relationships between Families and Schools." *Theory into Practice* 20(2):97–104.

Lindle, J.C. (1989a). "Take Parents Seriously, and They'll Get Seriously Involved." *The Executive Educator,* pp. 24–25.

Lindle, J.C. (1989b). "What Do Parents Want from Principals and Teachers?" *The Executive Educator,* pp. 12–14.

Lindquist, K. M., and Mauriel, J.L. (1989, August). "School-Based Management: Doomed to Failure?" *Education and Urban Society* 21(4):402–16.

Lipsky, M. (1980). *Street-Level Bureaucracy. Dilemmas of the Individual in Public Services.* New York, NY: Russell Sage Foundation.

Little, J. W. (1984). "Seductive Images and Organizational Realities in Professional Development." *Teachers College Record* 86(1):84–102.

Lomotey, K., and Swanson, A. D. (1989 August). "Urban and Rural Schools Research: Implications for School Governance." *Education and Urban Society* 21(4):436–54.

Lueder D. C. (1989, October). "Tennessee Parents Were Invited to Participate—and They Did: A Statewide Effort to Strengthen Parent/School Partnerships Has Generated an Enthusiastic Response." *Educational Leadership,* pp. 14–17.

McLaughlin, M. W., and Shields, P. M. (1987, October). "Involving Low-Income Parents in the Schools: A Role for Policy?" *Phi Delta Kappan,* pp. 156–60.

Malen, B.; Ogawa, R.T.; and Kranz, J. (1990, February). "Site-Based Management: Unfilled Promise. Evidence Says Site-Based Management Hindered by Many Factors." *The School Administer,* pp. 32–59.

Maloy, R. W., and Jones, B. L. (1987). "Teachers, Partnerships, and School Improvement." *Journal of Research and Development in Education* 20(2):19–24.

Marburger, C. L. (1985). *One School at a Time: School-Based Management, A Process for Change.* Columbia, MD: National Committee for Citizens in Education.

Marockie, H., and Jones, H. L. (1987). "Reducing Dropout Rates through Home/School Communication." *Education and Urban Society* 19(2):200-205.

Mitchell, J. E. (1990, February). "Coaxing Staff from Cages for Site-Based Decisions to Fly." *The School Administrator,* pp. 23–26.

Noblit, G. W. (1986). "What's Missing from the National Agenda for School Reform? Teacher Professionalism and Local Initiative." *The Urban Review* 18(1):40–51.

Ogbu, J. U. (1981, February). "Schooling in the Ghetto: An Ecological Perspective on Community and Home Influences." Paper presented at the National Institute of Education Follow-Through Planning Conference, Philadelphia, PA.

Olsen, L. (1988). *Crossing the Schoolhouse Border. Immigrant Students and the California Public Schools.* San Francisco, CA: California Tomorrow.

Rasinski, T. V. (1989, December). "Reading and the Empowerment of Parents." *The Reading Teacher,* pp. 226–31.

Rasinski, T. V., and Fredericks, A. D. (1989). "Dimensions of Parent Involvement." *Reading Teacher* 43(2):180–82.

Schiamberg, L. B., and Chun, C. (1986). "The Influence of Family on Educational and Occupational Achievement." Paper presented at the Annual Meeting of the American Association for the Advancement of Science, Philadelphia, PA.

Seeley, D. S. (1989, October). "A New Paradigm for Parent Involvement." *Educational Leadership,* pp. 46–48.

Tizard, J.; Schofield, W. N.; and Hewison, J. (1982). "Collaboration between Teachers and Parents in Assisting Children's Reading." *British Journal of Educational Psychology* 52:1–15.

Wayson, W. W. (1984, January). Prepared Statement before the House Subcommitte on Elementary, Secondary, and Vocational Education, Hearing on School Discipline, Washington, D.C.

Williams, D. L. (1981). *Final Interim Report: Southwest Parent Resource Center.* Austin, TX: Southwest Educational Development Laboratory.

Williams, D. L., and Chavkin, N. F. (1989, October). "Essential Elements of Strong Parent Involvement Programs." *Educational Leadership,* pp. 18–20.

Zeldin, S. (1990, spring). "The Implementation of Home/School/Community Partnerships: Policy from the Perspective of Principals and Teachers." *Equity and Choice,* pp. 56–63.

CHAPTER TWO

Advocates for Children of New York. (1985). *Public High School, Private Admission.* New York, NY: Author.

Anderson, R. C.; Hiebert, E. H.; Scott, J. A.; and Wilkinson, I. A. (1985). *Becoming a Nation of Readers: The Report of the Commission on Reading.* Washington, D.C.: U.S. Department of Education, National Institute of Education.

Anderson, S. (1989, fall). "Drawn Off Course." *California Tomorrow* 4(4):6–13.

Ann Arbor Task Force on Instructional Grouping (1986, July). *Report of the Task Force on Instructional Grouping.* Ann Arbor, MI: Ann Arbor Public Schools.

Bamber, C. (1989). "Public School Choice Is Coming: Who Will Be Ready and Who Will Be Left Behind?" *Network for Public School* 14(6):1.

Bastian, A. (1989). "Response to Nathan: Choice Is a Double-Edged Tool." *Educational Leadership,* pp. 56–57.

Bastian, A.; Fruchter, N.; Gittell, M.; Gree, C.; and Haskins, K. (1985). *Choosing Equality: The Case for Democratic Schooling.* A Report of the New World Foundation. San Francisco, CA: Public Media Center.

Blank, R. K. (1984, December). "The Effects of Magnet Schools on the Quality of Education in Urban School Districts." *Phi Delta Kappan,* p. 270.

Chang, H. N. (1990). *Newcomer Programs. Innovative Efforts to Meet the Educational Challenges of Immigrant Students.* San Francisco, CA: California Tomorrow.

Children's Defense Fund (1985). *Black and White Children in America: Key Facts.* Washington, D.C.: Author.

Dawson, M. M. (1987). "Beyond Ability Grouping: A Review of the Effectiveness of Ability Grouping and Its Alternatives." *School Psychology Review* 16(3):348–69.

Dentzer, E., and Wheelock, A. (1990, March). *Locked In/Locked Out: Tracking and Placement Practices in Boston Public Schools.* Boston, MA: Massachusetts Advocacy Center.

Education Commission of the States (1989, February). *A State Policy-Maker's Guide to Public School Choice.* Denver, CO: Author. (ERIC Document Reproduction Service No. ED 306 702)

Finch, L. (1989, July). "The Claims for School Choice and Snake Oil Have a Lot in Common." *The American School Board Journal,* pp. 31–32.

Finley, M. K. (1984). "Teachers and Tracking in a Comprehensive High School." *Sociology of Education* 57:233–43.

First, J.; Kellogg, J. B.; Willshire Carrera, J.; Lewis, A.; and Almeida, C. A. (1988). *New Voices: Immigrant Students in U.S. Public Schools.* Boston, MA: National Coalition of Advocates for Students.

Gartner, A., and Lipsky, D. K. (1987, November). "Beyond Special Education: Toward a Quality System for All Students." *Harvard Educational Review* 57(4):367–95.

Goodlad, J. I. (1984). *A Place Called School: Prospects for the Future.* New York, NY: McGraw-Hill Book Co.

Green, R. L., and Griffore, R. J. (1978). "School Desegregation, Testing, and the Urgent Need for Equity in Education." *Education* 99(1):16–19.

Haney, W. (1984, winter). "Test Reasoning and Reasoning about Testing." *Review of Educational Research,* p. 628.

Harvard Education Letter (1989, March/April). "The Mainstreaming Debate." *HEL* 5(2):1–5.

Johnson, D. W., and Johnson, R. T. (1982). "The Effects of Cooperative and Individualistic Instruction on Handicapped and Non-handicapped Students." *Journal of Social Psychology* 118:257–68.

Johnson, R. T.; Johnson, D. W.; and Stanne, M. B. (1986). "Comparison of Computer-Assisted Cooperative, Competitive, and Individualistic Learning." *American Educational Research Journal* 23(3):382–92.

Kaufman, N. L. (1985). Review of Gesell Preschool Test. In J. V. Mitchell, ed., *Ninth Mental Measurement Yearbook.* Lincoln, NE: University of Nebraska, Buros Institute of Mental Measurement.

Landau, J. (1987, May). *Out of the Mainstream: Education of Disabled Youth in Massachusetts.* Boston, MA: Massachusetts Advocacy Center.

Levin, H. (1987). "Accelerated Schools for Disadvantaged Students." *Educational Leadership* 44(6):19–21.

Lezotte, L., and Taylor, B. (1989, February). "How Closely Can Magnet Schools Be Aligned with the Effective Schools Model?" *Equity and Choice,* pp. 25–29.

McClellan, M. C. (1988, June). "Testing and Reform." *Phi Delta Kappan,* p. 769.

Madaus, G., and Pullin, D. (1987, June). *Questions to Ask When Evaluating a High-Stakes Testing Program.* NCAS Backgrounder. Boston, MA: National Coalition of Advocates for Students.

Medina, N., and Neill, M. (1988). *Fallout from the Testing Explosion.* Cambridge, MA: FairTest.

Medina, N., and Neill, M. (1990). *Fallout from the Testing Explosion.* 3rd ed. Cambridge, MA: FairTest.

Mitchell, R., with Haycock, K., and Navarro, M. S. (1989, summer). "Off the Tracks." *Perspective* 1(3).

Moore, D. R., and Davenport, S. (1988). *The New Improved Sorting Machine.* Chicago, IL: Designs for Change.

Moore, D. R., and Davenport, S. (1989a, February). "High School Choice and Students at Risk." *Equity and Choice,* pp. 5–10.

Moore, D. R., and Davenport, S. (1989b, August). "Cheated Again: School Choice and Students at Risk." *The School Administrator,* pp. 12–15.

Nathan, J. (1989, July). "Before Adopting School Choice, Review What Works and What Fails." *The American School Board Journal,* pp. 28–30.

Nathan, J., ed. (1989). *Public Schools by Choice: Expanding Opportunities for Parents, Students, and Teachers.* St. Paul, MN: Institute for Learning and Teaching.

National Association for the Education of Young Children (NAEYC) (1988, January). "NAEYC Position Statement on Developmentally Appropriate Practice in the Primary Grades Serving Five- through Eight-Year-Olds." *Young Children,* pp. 64–84.

National Coalition of Advocates for Students (1985, September). "Misclassification: A Barrier to Excellence in Schools." *Steps* 2(2).

National Coalition of Advocates for Students (1988). *A Special Analysis of the 1986 Elementary and Secondary Civil Rights Survey Data.* Boston, MA: Author.

National Coalition of Advocates for Students, and National Association of School Psychologists (1986). *Advocacy for Appropriate Educational Services for All Children.* Boston, MA: Authors.

National Coalition of Advocates for Students, National Association of School Pyschologists, and National Association of Social Workers (1987, May 27). "Rights Without Labels." *Education Week,* p. 22.

Oakes, J. (1985). *Keeping Track: How Schools Structure Inequality.* New Haven, CT: Yale University Press.

Oakes, J. (1986a). "Keeping Track, Part 1: The Policy and Practice of Curriculum Inequality." *Phi Delta Kappan* 68(1):12–17.

Oakes, J. (1986b). "Keeping Track, Part 2: Curriculum Inequality and School Reform." *Phi Delta Kappan* 68(2):148–54.

Oakes, J. (1986c). "Tracking, Inequality, and the Rhetoric of Reform: Why Schools Don't Change." *Journal of Education* 168(1):60–80.

Oakes, J., and Lipton, M. (1990). *Making the Best of Schools. A Handbook for Parents, Teachers, and Policymakers.* New Haven, CT: Yale University Press.

Orum, L. S. (1988). *Making Education Work for Hispanic Americans: Some Promising Community-Based Practices.* Los Angeles, CA: National Council of LA RAZA.

Pink, W. (1984). "Creating Effective Schools." *Educational Forum* 49(1):91–107.

Price, J. R., and Stern, J. R. (1987, spring/summer). "Magnet Schools as a Strategy for Integration and School Reform." *Yale Law and Policy Review,* p. 312.

Randall, R., and Geiger, K. (1991). *School Choice: Issues and Answers.* Bloomington, IN: National Educational Service.

Riddle, W., and Stedman, J. B. (1989, April 5). *Public School Choice: Recent Developments and Analysis of Issues.* Congressional Research Service Report for Congress No. 89-219 EPW. Washington, D.C. (ERIC Document Reproduction Service No. ED 305 747)

Rosenbaum, J. E. (1978). "The Structure of Opportunity in School." *Social Forces* 57(1):236–56.

Shepard, L. A., and Smith M. L. (1988, summer). "Flunking Kindergarten: Escalating Curriculum Leaves Many Behind." *American Educator,* p. 36.

Slavin, R. E. (1987a, summer). "Ability Grouping and Its Alternatives: Must We Track?" *American Educator,* pp. 32–48.

Slavin, R. E. (1987b). "Cooperative Learning: Where Behavioral and Humanistic Approaches to Classroom Motivation Meet." *The Elementary School Journal* 88(1):29–37.

Slavin, R. E. (1987c). "Developmental and Motivational Perspectives on Cooperative Learning: A Reconciliation." *Child Development* 58:1161–67.

Sorensen, A. B., and Hallinan, M. T. (1986). "Effects of Ability Grouping on Growth in Academic Achievement." *American Educational Research Journal* 23(4):519–48.

Willshire Carrera, J. (1989). *Immigrant Students: Their Legal Right of Access to Public Schools. A Guide for Advocates and Educators.* Boston, MA: National Coalition of Advocates for Students.

Wuthrick, M. (1990, March). "Blue Jays Win! Crows Go Down in Defeat!" *Phi Delta Kappan,* pp. 553–56.

Ysseldyke, J. E.; Algozzine, B.; Richey, L.; and Graden, J. (1982). "Declaring Students Eligible for Learning Disability Services: Why Bother With the Data?" *Learning Disabilities Quarterly* 5:37–44.

CHAPTER THREE

Anderson, C. W., and Smith, E. L. (1987). "Teaching Science." In V. Koehler, ed., *The Educator's Handbook: A Research Perspective.* New York, NY: Longman.

Anderson, R. C.; Hiebert, E. H.; Scott, J. A.; and Wilkinson, I. A. (1985). *Becoming a Nation of Readers: The Report of the Commission on Reading.* Washington, D.C.: U.S. Department of Education, National Institute of Education.

Arvizu, S. F., and Saravia-Shore, M. (1990). "Cross-Cultural Literacy. An Anthropological Approach to Dealing with Diversity." *Education and Urban Society* 22(4):364–76.

Bain, H., *et al.* (1989, March). "A Study of Fifty Effective Teachers Whose Class Average Gain Scores Ranked in the Top 15 Percent of Each of Four School Types in Project STAR." Paper presented at the Annual Meeting of the American Educational Research Association. San Francisco, CA. (ERIC Document Reproduction Service No. ED 307 246)

Banks, F. F. (1988). "Factors Which Affect the Academic Achievement of Black Students." In C. Glenn, ed., *Equity in Secondary Schools: New Perspectives, A Report to the Massachusetts Board of Education.* Quincy, MA: Massachusetts Department of Education.

Banks, J. A. (1987, May). "The Social Studies, Ethnic Diversity, and Social Change." *The Elementary School Journal* 87(5):531–43.

Baptiste, H. P., Jr. (1986). "Multicultural Education and Urban Schools from a Sociohistorical Perspective: Internalizing Multiculturalism." *Journal of Educational Equity and Leadership* 6(4):295–312.

Bennett, W. J. (1986). *First Lessons. A Report on Elementary Education in America.* Washington, D.C.: United States Government Printing Office.

Bonnstetter, R. J. (1989, November). "Teacher Behaviors That Facilitate New Goals." *Education and Urban Society* 22(1):30–39.

Brophy, J. (1986). "Teacher Influences on Student Achievement." *American Psychologist* 41(10):1069–77.

Brophy, J. (1987). "Teacher Effects Research and Teacher Quality." *Journal of Classroom Interaction* 22(1):14–23.

Brophy, J., and Good, T. (1986). "Teacher Behavior and Student Achievement." In M. C. Wittrock, ed., *Handbook of Research on Teaching.* 3rd ed. New York, NY: Macmillan Co.

Brown, A. L., and Palincsar, A. S. (1985). *Reciprocal Teaching of Comprehension Strategies: A Natural History of One Program for Enhancing Learning.* Technical Report No. 334. Urbana, IL: University of Illinois, Center for the Study of Reading.

Carbo, M. (1987, November). "Deprogramming Reading Failure: Giving Unequal Learners an Equal Chance." *Phi Delta Kappan,* pp. 197–202.

Chall, J. S., and Snow, C. E. (1988). "School Influences on the Reading Development of Low-Income Children." *Harvard Education Letter* 4(1):1–4.

Cheney, L. V. (1990). *Tyrannical Machines. A Report on Educational Practices Gone Wrong and Our Best Hopes for Setting Them Right.* Washington, D.C.: National Endowment for the Humanities.

Chicago Project on Learning and Teaching (1989). *Best Practice: Teaching and Learning in Chicago.* Chicago, IL: Author.

Cicchetti, D., and Hesse, P., eds. (1982). *Emotional Development.* Washington, D.C.: Jossey-Bass, Inc..

Clary, L. M. (1989). *How Well Do I Adjust to Differences in Learning Styles When I Teach Reading?* (ERIC Document Reproduction Service No. ED 310 360)

Comer, J. P. (1984, May). "Home/School Relationships as They Affect the Academic Success of Children." *Education and Urban Society* 16(3):323–37.

Corcoran, T. B.; Walker, L. J.; and White, J. L. (1988). *Working in Urban Schools.* Washington, D.C.: Institute for Educational Leadership.

Cummins, J. (1984). *Bilingualism and Special Education: Issues in Assessment and Pedagogy.* San Diego, CA: College-Hill Press.

Cummins, J. (1986). "Empowering Minority Students: A Framework for Intervention." *Harvard Educational Review* 56(1):18–36.

Cushner, K., and Trifonovitch, G. (1989, September). "Understanding Misunderstanding: Barriers to Dealing with Diversity." *Social Education,* pp. 319–21.

Damon, W. (1983). *Social and Personality Development, Infancy through Adolescence.* New York, NY: W. W. Norton and Co.

Dentzer, E., and Wheelock, A. (1990, March). *Locked In/Locked Out: Tracking and Placement Practices in Boston Public Schools.* Boston, MA: Massachusetts Advocacy Center.

DeSilva, B. (1986, June). "Schoolbooks: A Question of Quality." Hartford, CT: A *Hartford Courant* Special Report.

Dunn, R. (1987). "Research on Instructional Environments: Implications for Student Achievement and Attitudes." *Professional School Psychology* 2:43–52.

Dunn, R., *et al.* (1989, March). "Survey of Research on Learning Styles." *Educational Leadership* 46(6):50–58.

Dweck, C. S. (1986). "Motivational Processes Affecting Learning." *American Psychologist* 41(10):1040–48.

Dweck, C. S., and Elliott, E. S. (1983). "Achievement Motivation." In E. M. Hetherington, ed. *Socialization, Personality, and Social Development.* New York, NY: Wiley.

Everston, C.; Emmer, E.; Sanford, J.; and Clements, B. (1983). "Improving Classroom Management: An Experiment in Elementary Classrooms." *The Elementary School Journal* 84:173–88.

First, J.; Kellogg, J. B.; Willshire Carrera, J.; Lewis, A.; and Almeida, C. A. (1988). *New Voices: Immigrant Students in U.S. Public Schools.* Boston, MA: National Coalition of Advocates for Students.

Fordham, S. (1988). "Racelessness as a Factor in Black Students' School Success: Pragmatic Strategy or Pyrrhic Victory?" *Harvard Educational Review* 58(1):54–84.

Fordham, S., and Ogbu, J. U. (1986). "Black Students' School Success: Coping with the 'Burden of "Acting White."'" *The Urban Review* 18(3):176–206.

Good, T., and Brophy, J. (1987). *Looking in Classrooms.* 4th ed. New York, NY: Harper and Row.

Good, T. L. (1987, July/August). "Two Decades of Research on Teacher Expectations: Findings and Future Directions." *Journal of Teacher Education,* pp. 32–47.

Goodlad, J. I. (1984). *A Place Called School: Prospects for the Future.* New York, NY: McGraw-Hill Book Co.

Goodman, K. S., *et al.* (1988). *Report Card on Basal Readers.* New York, NY: Richard C. Owen.

Harvard Education Letter (1988, March). "Cultural Differences in the Classroom." *HEL* 4(2):1–4.

Hilgersom-Volk, K. (1987, May). "Celebrating Students' Diversity Through Learning Styles." *OSSC Bulletin* 30(9):1–27.

Hodgkinson, H. L. (1985). *All One System: Demographics of Education Kindergarten Through Graduate School.* Washington, D.C.: Institute for Educational Leadership.

Hoover-Dempsey, K. V.; Bassler, O. C.; and Brissie, J. S. (1987). "Parent Involvement: Contributions of Teacher Efficacy, School Socioeconomic Status, and Other School Characteristics." *American Educational Research Journal* 24(3):417–35.

Howard, J., and Hammonds, R. (1986). "Doing What's Expected of You: The Roots and Rise of the Dropout Culture." *Metropolitan Education,* pp. 53–71.

Hunt, D. (1979). "Learning Style and Student Needs: An Introduction to Conceptual Level." In J. W. Keefe, ed., *Student Learning Styles: Diagnosing and Prescribing Programs.* Reston, VA: National Association of Secondary School Principals.

Kamii, C. (1985, September). "Leading Primary Education Toward Excellence, Beyond Worksheets and Drill." *Young Children,* pp. 3–9.

Knight, S. L.; Waxman, H. C.; and Padron, Y. N. (1989, May/June). "Students' Perceptions of Relationships Between Social Studies Instruction and Cognitive Stategies." *Journal of Educational Research* 82(5):270–76.

LaFontaine, H. (1987). "At Risk Children and Youth—The Extra Educational Challenges of Limited-English-Proficient Students." Paper prepared for the 1987 Summer Institute of the Council of Chief State School Officers, Washington D.C.

Loper, (1989, March). "Learning Styles and Student Diversity." *Educational Leadership,* p. 53.

McLean, S. V. (1990, winter). "Early Childhood Teachers in Multicultural Settings." *The Educational Forum* 54(2):197–204.

McPike, L. (1987, spring). "Shared Decision-Making at the School Site: Moving Toward a Professional Model." *American Educator* 46:10–17.

McTighe, J., and Lyman, F. T. (1988, April). "Cueing Thinking in the Classroom: The Promise of Theory-Embedded Tools." *Educational Leadership,* pp. 17–25.

Medina, N., and Neill, M. (1988). *Fallout from the Testing Explosion: How 100 Million Standardized Exams Undermine Equity and Excellence in America's Public Schools.* Cambridge, MA: FairTest.

Montero-Sieburth, M. (1989). "Restructuring Teachers' Knowledge for Urban Settings." *Journal of Negro Education* 58(3):332–44.

Murphy, J.; Weil, M.; and McGreal, T. L. (1986). "The Basic Practice Model of Instruction." *The Elementary School Journal* 87(1):83–95.

National Assessment of Educational Progress (1985). *The Reading Report Card.* Princeton, NJ: Educational Testing Service.

National Association for Education of Young Children (NAEYC) (1988, January). "NAEYC Position Statement on Developmentally Appropriate Practice in the Primary Grades Serving Five- Through Eight-Year-Olds." *Young Children,* pp. 64–84.

National Coalition of Advocates for Students (NCAS). (1988). *Criteria for Evaluating an AIDS Curriculum.* Boston, MA: Author.

National Coalition of Advocates for Students (NCAS), *et al.* (1990). *Guidelines to HIV and AIDS Student Support Services.* Boston, MA: Author.

National Council of Teachers of English Commission on Reading (1987). *Report Card on Basal Reader.* Urbana, IL: Author.

National Research Council (1989). *Everybody Counts: A Report to the Nation on the Future of Mathematics Education.* Washington, D.C.: National Academy Press.

Neisser, U., ed. (1986). *The School Achievement of Minority Children: New Perspectives.* Hillsdale, NJ: Lawrence Erlbaum Associates.

Noblit, G. W. (1986). "What's Missing from the National Agenda for School Reform? Teacher Professionalism and Local Initiative." *The Urban Review* 18(1):40–51.

Olsen, L. (1988). *Crossing the Schoolhouse Border, Immigrant Students and the California Public Schools.* San Francisco, CA: California Tomorrow.

Pearson, P. D., and Dole, J. A. (1987). "Explicit Comprehension Instruction: A Review of Research and a New Conceptualization of Instruction." *The Elementary School Journal* 88(2):151–65.

Peterson, B. (1988, March/April). "NCTE Issues 'Basal Report Card.'" *Rethinking Schools,* pp. 8–10.

Phillips, C. B. (1988, January). "Nurturing Diversity for Today's Children and Tomorrow's Leaders." *Young Children,* pp. 42–47.

Piaget, J., and Inhelder, B. (1969). *The Psychology of the Child.* New York, NY: Basic Books.

Porter, A. (1989, June/July). "A Curriculum Out of Balance: The Case of Elementary School Mathematics." *Educational Researcher,* pp. 9–15.

Porter, A. C., and Brophy, J. (1988, May). "Synthesis of Research on Good Teaching: Insights from the Work of the Institute for Research on Teaching." *Educational Leadership,* pp. 74–85.

Ramsey, P. G. (1982, January). "Multicultural Education in Early Childhood." *Young Children* 37(2):13–24.

Reyhner, J., and Garcia, R. L. (1989). "Helping Minorities Read Better: Problems and Promises." *Reading Research and Instruction* 28(3):84–91.

Schmidt, P. (1991, February). "Three Types of Bilingual Education Effective, E.D. Study Concludes." *Education Week* 10(22):1, 23.

Schwille, J.; Porter, A.; Alford, L; Freeman, D.; Irwin, S.; and Schmidt, W. (1986). *State Policy and the Control of Curriculum Decisions: Zones of Tolerance for Teachers in Elementary School Mathematics.* Research Series No. 173. East Lansing, MI: Michigan State University, Institute for Research on Teaching.

Sizer, T. (1984). *Horace's Compromise: The Dilemma of the American High School.* Boston, MA: Houghton Mifflin Co.

Sleeter, C. E., and Grant, C. A. (1987). "An Analysis of Multicultural Education in the United States." *Harvard Educational Review* 57(4):421–44.

Snow, C., and Hakuta, K. (1987). "The Cost of Monolingualism." Unpublished monograph. Cambridge, MA.

Stice, C. F., and Dunn, M. B. (1985, November). "Learner Styles and Strategy Lessons: A Little Something for Everyone." Paper presented at the Annual Meeting of Southeastern Regional Conference of the International Reading Association, Nashville, TN.

Strother, D. B. (1985). "Classroom Management." *Phi Delta Kappan* 66(10):725–28.

Suzuki, B. H. (1984, May). "Curriculum Transformation for Multicultural Education." *Education and Urban Society* 16(3):294–322.

Teddlie, C.; Kirby, P.C; and Stringfield, S. (1989, May). "Effective versus Ineffective Schools: Observable Differences in the Classroom." *American Journal of Education,* pp. 221–36.

Twentieth-Century Fund Task Force on Federal Elementary and Secondary Education Policy (1983). *Making the Grade.* New York, N.Y.: Author.

U. S. Government Accounting Office (1987). *Bilingual Education: Research and Evaluation Contracts.* Washington, D.C: Author.

Viadero, D. (1990, November 28). "Battle Over Multicultural Education Rises in Intensity." *Education Week* 10(13):1, 11, 13.

Weinstein, R. S.; Marshall, H. H.; Sharp, L.; and Botkin, M. (1987). "Pygmalion and the Student: Age and Classroom Differences in Children's Awareness of Teacher Expectations." *Child Development* 58:1079–93.

Wong-Fillmore, L., *et al.* (1985). *Learning English Through Bilingual Education.* Washington, D.C.: National Institute of Education.

Wurzel, J. S. (1989). *Toward Multiculturalalism. A Reader in Multicultural Education.* Yarmouth, ME: Intercultural Press, Inc.

CHAPTER FOUR

American Educational Research Association, American Psychological Association, and National Council on Measurement in Education (1985). *Standards for Educational and Psychological Testing.* Washington, D.C.: American Psychological Association.

Anastasi, A. (1988). *Psychological Testing.* 6th ed. New York, NY: Macmillan Co.

Baenen, N. (1988, April). "Perspectives After Five Years: Has Grade Retention Passed or Failed?" Paper presented at the Annual Meeting of the American Educational Research Association, New Orleans, LA.

Bastian, A.; Fruchter, N.; Gittell, M.; Gree, C.; and Haskins, K. (1985). *Choosing Equality: The Case for Democratic Schooling.* A Report to the New World Foundation. San Francisco, CA: Public Media Center.

Brandt, R. (1989, April). "On Misuse of Testing: A Conversation with George Madaus." *Educational Leadership,* pp. 26–29.

Brown, R. (1989, April). "Testing and Thoughtfulness." *Educational Leadership*, pp. 31–33.

Byrnes, D., and Yamamoto, K. (1986). "Views on Grade Repetition." *Journal of Research and Development in Education* 20(1):14–20.

Cannell, J. (1987). *Nationally Normed Elementary Achievement Testing in America's Public Schools: How All Fifty States Are Above the National Average*. Daniels, WV: Friends for Education.

Cummins, J. (1984). *Bilingualism and Special Education: Issues in Assessment and Pedagogy*. San Diego, CA: College-Hill Press.

Dentzer, E., and Wheelock, A. (1990, March). *Locked In/Locked Out: Tracking and Placement Practices in Boston Public Schools*. Boston, MA: Massachusetts Advocacy Center.

FairTest. (1990, winter). *Standardized Tests and Our Children: A Guide to Testing Reform*. Cambridge, MA: Author.

Fiske, E. B. (1988, April 10). "America's Test Mania." *The New York Times*, section 12, p. 20.

French, D.; Wass, G.; Stright, A.; and Baker, J. (1986). "Leadership Asymmetries in Mixed-Age Children's Groups." *Child Development*, p. 57.

Gallup, A. M. (1986, September). "The Eighteenth Annual Gallup Poll of the Public's Attitudes Toward the Public Schools." *Phi Delta Kappan*, pp. 43–59.

Gampert, R., and Opperman, P. (1988, April). "Longitudinal Study of the 1982–83 Promotional Gates Students." Paper presented at the Annual Meeting of the American Educational Research Association, New Orleans, LA.

Gardner, H. (1985). *Frames of Mind: The Theory of Multiple Intelligences*. New York, NY: Basic Books.

Gastright, J. F. (1989, March). "The Nation Reacts: A Survey of Promotion/Retention Rates in Forty Urban School Districts." Paper presented at the Annual Meeting of the American Educational Research Association. San Francisco, CA. (ERIC Document Reproduction Service No. ED 307 714)

Gill, D., and Levidow, L., eds. (1987). *Anti-Rascist Science Teaching*. London, England: Free Association Books.

Gnezda, M. T., and Bolig, R. (1989). "A National Survey of Public School Testing of Pre-kindergarten and Kindergarten Children." Paper commissioned by the National Forum on the Future of Children and Their Families and the National Association of State Boards of Education.

Goodman, K. S., *et al.* (1988). *Report Card on Basal Readers*. Katonah, NY: Richard C. Owen.

Gould, S. J. (1981). *The Mismeasurement of Man*. New York, NY: W. W. Norton and Co.

Gurthrie, J. T. (1988). *Indicators of Reading Education*. Brunswick, NJ: Center of Policy Research in Education.

Haney, W. (1984, winter). "Test Reasoning and Reasoning about Testing." *Review of Education Research*, p. 628.

Haney, W., and Madaus, G. (1989, May). "Searching for Alternatives to Standardized Tests: Whys, Whats, and Whithers." *Phi Delta Kappan* 70(9):683–87.

Hess, G. A. (1986). "Educational Triage in an Urban School Setting." *Metropolitan Education* 2:39–52.

Hess, G. A.; Wells, E.; Prindle, C.; Liffman, P.; and Kaplan, B. (1987). "Where's Room 185? How Schools Can Reduce Their Dropout Problem." *Education and Urban Society* 19(3):330–55.

Holmes, T., and Matthews, K. (1984). "The Effects of Nonpromotion on Elementary and Junior High School Pupils: A Meta-Analysis." *Review of Educational Research* 54:232–42.

Hoover, M. B.; Politzer, R. L.; and Taylor, O. (1987, April/July). "Bias in Reading Tests for Black Language Speakers: A Sociolinguistic Perspective." *Negro Educational Review* 81.

Illinois Fair Schools Coalition (1985, June). *Holding Students Back: An Expensive Reform that Doesn't Work*. Chicago, IL: Author.

Kaufman, N. L. (1985). "Review of Gesell Preschool Test." In J. V. Mitchel, ed. *The Ninth Mental Measurement Yearbook*. Lincoln, NE: University of Nebraska, Buros Institute of Mental Measurement.

Koretz, D. (1988, summer). "Arriving at Lake Woebegone." *American Educator* 8:8–15, 46–52.

Labaree, D. F. (1984). "Setting the Standard: Alternative Policies for Student Promotion." *Harvard Educational Review* 54(1):67–87.

Levin, H. (1987, March). "Accelerated Schools for Disadvantaged Students." *Educational Leadership* 44(6):19–21.

Lewis, A. C. (1990, May/June). "Trend Away from Standardized Testing Gaining Momentum." *Education Reporter* 24(2):1, 2.

Loewen, J. (1980). "Possible Causes of Lower Black Scores on Aptitude Tests." Unpublished manuscript. Burlington, VT: University of Vermont.

McClellan, M. C. (1988, June). "Testing and Reform." *Phi Delta Kappan*, p. 769.

Madaus, G. (1985, May). "Test Scores as Administrative Mechanisms in Educational Policy." *Phi Delta Kappan*, pp. 611–18.

Madaus, G. (1986). *Testing and the Curriculum: From Compliant Servant to Dictatorial Master.* Boston, MA: Center for the Study of Testing, Evaluation, and Educational Policy.

Madaus, G., and Pullin, D. (1987, June). *Questions to Ask When Evaluating a High-Stakes Testing Program*. NCAS Backgrounder. Boston, MA: National Coalition of Advocates for Students.

Mann, D. (1986). "Can We Help Drop-Outs: Thinking about the Undoable." *Teachers College Record* 87.

Massachusetts Advocacy Center (1988). *Status Report: Nonpromotions in Boston Public Schools*. Boston, MA: Author.

Medina, N., and Neill, M. (1988). *Fallout from the Testing Explosion*. Cambridge, MA: FairTest.

Medina, N., and Neill, M. (1990). *Fallout from the Testing Explosion*. 3rd. edition. Cambridge, MA: FairTest.

Medway, F. (1985). "To Promote or Not Promote?" *Principal* 64(3):22–25.

Meier, D. (1982–83, winter). "Why Reading Tests Don't Test Reading." *Dissent.*

Meisels, S. J. (1989, April). "High-Stakes Testing." *Educational Leadership,* pp. 16–22.

Mitchell, J. V., ed. (1985). *The Ninth Mental Measurement Yearbook.* Lincoln, NE: University of Nebraska, Buros Institute of Mental Measurement.

National Association for the Education of Young Children (NAEYC) (1988, January). "NAEYC Position Statement on Developmentally Appropriate Practice in the Primary Grades Serving Five- Through Eight-Year-Olds." *Young Children,* pp. 64–84.

National Association for the Education of Young Children (NAEYC) (1988, March). "NAEYC Position Statement on Standardized Testing of Young Children Three Through Eight Years of Age." *Young Children,* pp. 42–47.

National Coalition of Advocates for Students (1986). *Advocacy for Appropriate Educational Services for All Children.* Boston, MA: Author.

National Coalition of Advocates for Students (1986). *Student Grade Retention.* Boston, MA: Author.

National Coalition of Advocates for Students (1986, March). "Misuse of Standardized Testing: A Barrier to Excellence." *Steps* 1(4):1–6.

National Commission on Testing and Public Policy (1990). *From Gatekeeper to Gateway: Transforming Testing in America.* Boston, MA: Author.

National Forum on Assessment (1991, May). *Criteria for Evaluation of Student Assessment Systems.* Washington, D.C.: The Council for Basic Education; Cambridge, MA: FairTest.

Neill, M., and Medina, N. (1989). "Standardized Testing: Harmful to Educational Health." *Phi Delta Kappan* 70(9):688.

North Carolina Department of Public Instruction (1990). *North Carolina's Grades 1 and 2 Assessment in Communication Skills and Mathematics.* Raleigh, NC: Author.

Oakes, J., and Lipton, M. (1990). *Making the Best of Schools. A Handbook for Parents, Teachers, and Policymakers.* New Haven, CT: Yale University Press.

Overman, M. (1989, April). "Practical Applications of Research: Student Promotion and Research." *Phi Delta Kappan* 67(8):609–13.

Palmer, J. R. (1987, December 14). Letter to the Editor, *New York Times.*

Pratt, D. (1986). "On the Merits of Multi-Age Classrooms." *Research in Rural Education* 3(3):111–15.

Pullin, D. (1985, December). *Educational Testing: Impact on Children at Risk.* NCAS Backgrounder. Boston, MA: National Coalition of Advocates for Students.

Safer, D. (1986a). "Nonpromotion Correlates and Outcomes at Different Grade Levels." *Journal of Learning Disabilities* 19(8):500.

Safer, D. (1986b). "The Stress of Secondary School for Vulnerable Students." *Journal of Youth and Adolescence* 15(5):405–17.

Schultz, T. (1989, October). "Testing and Retention of Young Children: Moving From Controversy to Reform." *Phi Delta Kappan,* pp. 125–29.

Shepard, L. A. (1989, April). "Why We Need Better Assessments. Educators Should Use a Variety of Measures, Make Substantive Improvements to Standardized Tests, and Remove Incentives to Teach to the Test." *Educational Leadership,* pp. 4–9.

Shepard, L. A., and Smith, M. L. (1985). *Boulder Valley Kindergarten Study: Retention Practices and Retention Effects.* Boulder, CO: Boulder Valley Public Schools.

Shepard, L. A., and Smith, M. L. (1986). "Synthesis of Research on School Readiness and Kindergarten Retention." *Educational Leadership* 44(3):78.

Shepard, L. A., and Smith, M. L. (1988, summer). "Flunking Kindergarten: Escalating Curriculum Leaves Many Behind." *American Educator* 36:34–38.

Smith, M. L., and Shepard, L. A. (1987, October). "What Doesn't Work: Explaining Policies of Retention in the Early Grades." *Phi Delta Kappan,* pp. 123–34.

Soo Hoo, S. (1989, March). "Teacher Researcher: Emerging Change Agent." Paper presented at the Annual Meeting of the American Educational Research Association. San Francisco, CA. (ERIC Document Reproduction Service No. ED 307 255)

Taylor, O., and Lee, D. L. (1987, April/July). "Standardized Tests and African-American Children: Communication and Language Issues." *Negro Educational Review,* p. 67.

Tittle, C. K. (1978). Review of WISC-R. In O. Buros, ed., *Eighth Mental Measurement Yearbook.* Lincoln, NE: University of Nebraska, Buros Institute of Mental Measurement.

Tyson-Bernstein, H. (1988). *A Conspiracy of Good Intentions: America's Textbook Fiasco.* Washington, D.C.: Council for Basic Education.

Veenman, S.; Lem, P.; and Winkelmolen, B. (1985). "Active Learning Time in Mixed-Age Classes." *Educational Studies* 11(3):171–80.

Walker, E., and Madhere, S. (1987). "Multiple Retentions: Some Consequences for the Cognitive and Affective Maturation of Minority Elementary Students." *Urban Education* 22(1):85–95.

Willer, B., and Bredekamp, S. (1990, July). "Redefining Readiness: An Essential Requisite for Educational Reform." *Young Children,* pp. 22–24.

Williams, D. (1979). "Black English and the Standford-Binet Test of Intelligence." Unpublished doctoral dissertation, Stanford University, Stanford, California.

Wodtke, K.; Harper, F.; Schommer, M.; and Brunelli, P. (1985). *Social Context Effects in Early School Testing: An Observational Study of the Testing Process.* Baltimore, MD: Johns Hopkins University.

Wolf, D. P. (1989, April). "Portfolio Assessment: Sampling Student Work." *Educational Leadership* 46(7):35–39.

CHAPTER FIVE

American School Counselor Association (ASCA). (1981). *The Practice of Guidance and Counseling by School Counselors.* Alexandria, VA: Author.

American School Counselor Association (ASCA). (1983). *Cross/Multi-Cultural Counseling.* Alexandria, VA: Author.

Banks, F. F. (1988). "Factors Which Affect the Academic Achievement of Black Students." In C. Glenn, ed., *Equity in Secondary Schools: New Perspectives, A Report to the Massachusetts Board of Education.* Quincy, MA: Massachusetts Department of Education.

Chafel, J. A. (1990, July). "Children in Poverty: Policy Perspectives on a National Crisis." *Young Children,* pp. 31–37.

Children's Defense Fund (1987). *A Children's Defense Budget, 1988.* Washington, D.C.: Author.

Children's Defense Fund (1988). *A Children's Defense Budget, 1989.* Washington, D.C.: Author.

Children's Defense Fund (1990). *Children 1990: A Report Card, Briefing Book, and Action Primer.* Washington, D.C.: Author.

Comer, J. P. (1985). "Yale Child Study Center School Development Program." Unpublished manuscript, Yale University Child Study Center, New Haven, CT.

Commission on Pre-college Guidance and Counseling (1986, October). *Keeping the Options Open.* New York, NY: College Entrance Examination Board.

Dweck, C. (1986). "Motivational Processes Affecting Learning." *American Psychologist* 41:1040–48.

First, J.; Kellogg, J. B.; Willshire Carrera, J.; Lewis, A.; and Almeida, C. A. (1988). *New Voices: Immigrant Students in U.S. Public Schools.* Boston, MA: National Coalition of Advocates for Students.

Glosoff, H. L., and Koprowicz, C. L. (1990). *Children Achieving Potential: An Introduction to Elementary School Counseling and State-Level Policies.* Washington, D.C.: National Conference of State Legislatures, and Alexandria, VA: American Association for Counseling and Development.

Harvard Education Letter (1988, June). "Guidance and Counseling: Too Little, Too Late?" *HEL* 4(3):1–5.

Hess, G. A. (1986). "Educational Triage in an Urban Setting." *Metropolitan Education* 2:39–52.

Hodgkinson, H. L. (1985). *All One System: Demographics of Education, Kindergarten through Graduate School.* Washington, D.C.: Institute for Educational Leadership.

Humes, C., and Hohensill, T. (1987). "Elementary Counselors, School Psychologists, School Social Workers: Who Does What?" *Elementary School Guidance and Counseling* 22(1):37–45.

Lightfoot, S. L. (1981). "Toward Conflict and Resolution: Relationships between Families and Schools." *Theory into Practice* 20(2):97–104.

Lloyd, D. N. (1976). "Concurrent Prediction of Dropout and Grade of Withdrawal." *Educational and Psychological Measurement* 36:983–91.

Melville, A. A., and Blank, M. J., (1991). *What It Takes: Structuring Interagency Partnerships to Connect Children and Families with Comprehensive Services.* Washington, DC: Education and Human Services Consortium.

National Association for the Education of Young Children (NAEYC) (1988, January). "NAEYC Position Statement on Developmentally Appropriate Practice in the Primary Grades Serving Five- Through Eight-Year-Olds." *Young Children,* pp. 64–84.

National Coalition of Advocates for Students, *et al.* (1990). *Guidelines for HIV and AIDS Student Support Services.* Boston, MA: Author.

Olsen, L. (1988). *Crossing the Schoolhouse Border, Immigrant Students and the California Public Schools.* San Francisco, CA: California Tomorrow.

Orum, L. S. (1988). *Making Education Work for Hispanic Americans: Some Promising Community-Based Practices.* Los Angeles, CA: National Council of LA RAZA.

Podemski, R., and Childers, J. (1987). "The School Counselor's Role: Reexamination and Revitalization." *Planning and Changing* 18(1):17–22.

Project PLUS, and ASPIRA Association (1990). *A Special Resport on Mentoring.* Washington, D.C.: Author.

Robinson, E. R., and Mastny, A. Y. (1989). *Linking Schools and Community Services. A Practical Guide.* New Brunswick, NJ: Rutgers School of Social Work, Center for Community Education.

Safer, D. (1986). "The Stress of Secondary School for Vulnerable Students." *Journal of Youth and Adolescence* 15(5):405–17.

Schorr, L. B., with Schorr, D. (1988). *Within Our Reach Breaking the Cycle of Disadvantage.* New York, NY: Doubleday.

Sege, I. (1989, March 12). "Poverty's Grip on Children Widens." *Boston Sunday Globe,* pp. 1, 20, 21.

Shedlin, A.; Klopf, G. J.; and Zaret, E. S. (1988). *The School as Locus of Advocacy for All Children.* New York, NY: Elementary School Center.

Sheeley, V. L. and Jenkins, D. (1985). *Tomorrow's School Counselors: Directions Revealed for Their Education.* Bowling Green, KY: Western Kentucky University.

Solomon, H.; Chaikin, M.; and Miller, D. (1988, July). *Study of Exemplary Guidance Programs in the Elementary Schools.* Brooklyn, NY: New York City Public Schools Office of Educational Assessment.

CHAPTER SIX

Almeida, C. A. (1988). "Identifying Effective Middle Schools in an Urban School System Through Statistical Profiles of Nonpromotion, Suspension, and Attendance Rates." Unpublished master's thesis, Tufts University, Medford, MA.

Ann Arbor Task Force on Instructional Grouping (1986, July). *Report of the Task Force on Instructional Grouping.* Ann Arbor, MI: Ann Arbor Public Schools.

Armstrong, L. (1991, March). "Census Confirms Remarkable Shifts in Ethnic Make-up." *Education Week* 10(26):1, 16.

Banks, F. F. (1988). "Factors Which Affect the Academic Achievement of Black Students." In C. Glenn, ed., *Equity in Secondary Schools: New Perspectives, A Report to the Massachusetts Board of Education.* Quincy, MA: Massachusetts Department of Education.

Banks, J. A. (1987). "The Social Studies, Ethnic Diversity, and Social Change." *The Elementary School Journal* 87(5):531–43.

Bauer, G. B.; Dubanoski, R.; Yamauchi, L. A.; and Honbo, K. A. M. (1990, May). "Corporal Punishment and the Schools." *Education and Urban Society* 22(3):285–90.

Brophy, J. (1986). "Teacher Influences on Student Achievement." *American Psychologist* 41(10):1069–77.

Brophy, J. (1987). "Teacher Effects Research and Teacher Quality." *Journal of Quality Classroom Interaction* 22(1):14–23.

Caldwell, J. (1989, January 20). "The Need for 'Anti-Racism' Education." *Education Week* 9(3):32.

Calhoun, J. A. (1988, April/May). "Violence, Youth, and a Way Out." *Youth Policy* 10(4):8–11.

Camayd-Freixas, Y. (1986, February). *Preliminary Report on Dropout Data.* Boston, MA: Boston Public Schools, Office of Research and Development.

Cheatham, A. (1988). *Directory of School Mediation and Conflict Resolution Programs.* Amherst, MA: National Association for Mediation in Education.

Chicago Project on Learning and Teaching (1989). *Best Practice: Teaching and Learning in Chicago.* Chicago, IL: Author.

Children's Defense Fund (1985). *Black and White Children in America: Key Facts.* Washington, D.C.: Author.

Children's Magazine (1987). *Report Card for Parents: Corporal Punishment in America's Schools.* New York, NY: Rodale Press.

Chobot, R. B. and Garibaldi, A. (1982). "In-School Alternatives to Suspension: A Description of Ten School District Programs." *The Urban Review* 14(4):317–36.

Clark, L. C. (1989, December/1990, January). "Expectations and 'At-Risk' Children." *Rethinking Schools,* p. 5.

Council of Great City Schools (1990, November). *Strategies for Success: Achieving the National Urban Education Goals.* Washington, D.C.: Author.

Davis, A. M. (1986, July). "Dispute Resolution at an Early Age." *Negotiation Journal.*

Davis, A. M., and Porter, K. (1984). "Dispute Resolution: The Fourth 'R.'" *Journal of Dispute Resolution* 31:1–19.

Davis, A. M., and Porter, K. (1985, winter). "Tales of Schoolyard Mediation." *UPDATE on Law-Related Education* 9(1):20–28.

Davis, A. M., and Salem, R. A. (1985, spring). "Resolving Disputes. The Choice is Ours." *UPDATE on Law-Related Education* 9(2):20–36.

Dentzer, E., and Wheelock, A. (1990, March). *Locked In/Locked Out: Tracking and Placement Practices in Boston Public Schools.* Boston, MA: Massachusetts Advocacy Center.

Derman-Sparks, L. (1989, winter). "Challenging Diversity With Anti-Bias Curriculum." *School Safety,* pp. 10–13.

Derman-Sparks, L.; Higa, C. T.; and Sparks, B. (1980). "Children, Race and Racism: How Race Awareness Develops." *Interracial Books for Children Bulletin* 11(3 and 4):3–15.

Designs for Change (1985, January). *The Bottom Line: Chicago's Failing Schools and How to Save Them.* (Chicago School Watch, Report No. 1). Chicago, IL: Designs for Change.

Duax, T. (1990, March/April). "Fostering Self-Discipline." *Rethinking Schools,* pp. 5, 6.

Felice, L. (1981). "Black Student Dropout Behavior: Disengagement From School Rejection and Racial Discrimination." *The Journal of Negro Education* 50:415–424.

Ferndale School District (1988). *Human Dignity Policy.* Ferndale, MI: Author.

Fine, M. (1986). "Why Urban Adolescents Drop Into and Out of Public High School." *Teachers College Record* 87(3).

Fine, M., and Rosenberg, P. (1983, summer). "Dropping Out of High School: The Ideology of School and Work." *Journal of Education* 163(3):257–72.

First, J.; Kellogg, J. B.; Willshire Carrera, J.; Lewis, A.; and Almeida, C. A. (1988). *New Voices: Immigrant Students in U.S. Public Schools.* Boston, MA: National Coalition of Advocates for Students.

First, J., and Mizell, M. H. (1980). *Everybody's Business: A Book about School Discipline.* Columbia, SC: Southeastern Public Education Program.

Gandara, P. (1989, March). "'Those' Children Are Ours: Moving Toward Community." *Equity and Choice,* pp. 5–12.

Gottfredson, D. C. (1984). *Environmental Change Strategies to Prevent School Disruption.* Baltimore, MD: Johns Hopkins University, Center for the Social Organization of Schools.

Graham, P. A. (1987, April). "Black Teachers: A Drastically Scarce Resource." *Phi Delta Kappan,* pp. 598–605.

Grant, C. A. (1988, May). "The Persistent Significance of Race in Schooling." *The Elementary School Journal* 88(5):561–69.

Grant, C. A. (1990, September). "Desegregation, Racial Attitudes, and Intergroup Contact: A Discussion of Change." *Phi Delta Kappan* 72(1):25–32.

Grant, C. A., and Sleeter, C. (1985). "Equality, Equity, and Excellence: A Critique." In P. Altbach; G. Kelley; and L. Weis, eds., *Excellence in Education* (pp. 139–60). Buffalo, NY: Prometheus.

Grant, C. A., and Sleeter, C. (1986). *After the School Bell Rings.* Lewis, England: Falmer.

Greenbaum, S. (1989, winter). "Minority Education: Quality/Equality." *School Safety,* p. 33.

Hawley, W. D. (1989, March). "The Importance of Minority Teachers to the Racial and Ethnic Integration of American Society." *Equity and Choice,* pp. 31–36.

Hess, G. A. (1986). "Educational Triage in Urban School Setting." *Metropolitan Education* 2:39–52.

Hilliard, A.G. (1989, December/1990, January). "Teachers and Cultural Styles in a Pluralist Society." *Rethinking Schools,* p. 3.

Hodgkinson, H. L. (1988). "The Right Schools for the Right Kids." *Educational Leadership,* pp. 10–14.

Houston, R., and Gruaugh, S. (1989, April). "Language for Preventing and Defusing Violence in the Classroom." *Urban Education* 24(1):25–37.

Howell, F. M., and Frese, W. (1982). "Early Transition into Adult Roles: Some Antecedents and Outcomes." *American Educational Research Journal* 19:51–73.

Illinois Fair Schools Coalition (1985, June). *Holding Students Back: An Expensive Reform That Doesn't Work.* Chicago, IL: Author.

Irujo, S. (1989, May). "Do You Know Why They All Talk at Once? Thoughts on Cultural Differences Between Hispanics and Anglos." *Equity and Choice,* pp. 14–18.

Kaesar, S. (1979a). *Orderly Schools That Serve All Children: A Review of Successful Schools in Ohio.* Cleveland, OH: Citizens' Council for Ohio Schools.

Kaesar, S. (1979b). "Suspensions in School Discipline." *Education and Urban Society* 11(4):465–84.

Kaesar, S. (1984, September). *Citizen's Guide to Children Out of School: Issues, Data, Explanations, and Solutions to Absenteeism, Dropouts, and Disciplinary Exclusion.* Cleveland, OH: Citizen's Council for Ohio Schools.

Lambert, R. D. (1981, March). "Ethnic/Racial Relations in the United States in Comparative Perspective." *The Annals of the American Academy,* pp. 189–205.

Lasley, T. J., and Wayson, W. W. (1982, December). "Characteristics of Schools with Good Discipline." *Educational Leadership,* pp. 28–31.

Lawton, M. (1991, March). "California Educators Take Stock of Efforts to Ensure Schools Are Safe, Secure." *Education Week* 10(27):1–19.

Leatt, D. J. (1987, March). "In-School Suspension Programs for At-Risk Students." *OSSC Bulletin* 30(7):1–28.

Lightfoot, S. L. (1981). "Toward Conflict and Resolution: Relationships between Families and Schools." *Theory into Practice* 20(2):97–104.

Lloyd, D. N. (1976). "Concurrent Prediction of Dropout and Grade of Withdrawal." *Educational and Psychological Measurement* 36:983–91.

Los Angeles County Commission on Human Relations (1989,October). *Intergroup Conflict in Los Angeles County Schools.* Los Angeles, CA: Author. (ERIC Document Reproduction Service No. ED 312 362)

Lufler, H. S. (1979). "Debating with Untested Assumptions: The Need to Understand School Discipline." *Education and Urban Society* 11(4):450–64.

McDill, E. L.; Natriello, G.; and Phallas, A. (1985). "Raising the Standards and Retaining Students: The Impact of the Reform Recommendations on Potential Dropouts." *Review of Educational Research* 55(4):415–33.

McLaren, P. (1988). "Broken Dreams, False Promises, and the Decline of Public Schooling." *Journal of Education* 170(1):41–65.

McLean, S. V. (1990, winter). "Early Childhood Teachers in Multicultural Settings." *The Educational Forum* 54(2):197–204.

Maeroff, G. L. (1988, May). "Withered Hopes, Stillborn Dreams: The Dismal Panorama of Urban Schools." *Phi Delta Kappan,* pp. 632–38.

Mann, D. (1986). "Can We Help Drop-Outs: Thinking about the Undoable." *Teachers College Record* 87(30).

Menacker, J.; Weldon, W.; and Hurwitz, E. (1990, April). "Community Influences on School Crime and Violence." *Urban Education* 25(1):68–80.

Mitchell, V. (1990, April). "Curriculum and Instruction to Reduce Racial Conflict." ERIC Clearinghouse on Urban Education. *DIGEST* 64.

Mizell, M. H. (1981, June 11). Prepared Statement before the Georgia State Senate Study Committee on Suspension and Discipline in the Schools and the Study Committee on Juvenile Justice. Atlanta, Georgia.

National Association for the Education of Young Children (NAEYC) (1988, January). "NAEYC Position Statement on Developmentally Appropriate Practice in the Primary Grades Serving Five- through Eight-Year-Olds." *Young Children,* pp. 64–84.

National Coalition of Advocates for Students (1987). "School Attendance: Are Your District's Practices Hurting Students At Risk?" *Steps* 1(7):1–10.

National Coalition of Advocates for Students (1988). *A Special Analysis of the 1986 Elementary and Secondary Civil Rights Survey Data.* Boston, MA: Author.

National Institute of Education (1978, January). *Violent Schools—Safe Schools: The Safe School Study Report to the U.S. Congress.* Washington, D.C.: U.S. Government Printing Office.

National School Safety Center (1989, May) *Corporal Punishment in Schools.* Malibu, CA: Author.

National School Safety Center (1990a, March). *School Crisis Prevention and Response.* Malibu, CA: Author.

National School Safety Center (1990b, June). *Weapons in Schools.* Malibu, CA: Author.

Oakes, J. (1985). Keeping Track: *How Schools Structure Inequality.* New Haven, CT: Yale University Press.

Oakes, J. (1986a). "Keeping Track: The Policy and Price of Curriculum Inequality." *Phi Delta Kappan* 68:12–15.

Oakes, J. (1986b). "Tracking, Inequality, and the Rhetoric of Reform: Why Schools Don't Change." *The Journal of Education* 168:60–80.

Olsen, L., and Mullen N. A. (1990). *Embracing Diversity: Teachers' Voices from California's Classrooms.* San Francisco, CA: California Tomorrow.

Pallas, M.; Natriello, G.; and McDill, E. L. (1989, June/July). "The Changing Nature of the Disadvantaged Population Current Dimensions and Future Trends." *Educational Researcher* 18(5):16–22.

Payne, C. M. (1984). *Getting What We Ask for. The Ambiguity of Success and Failure in Urban Education.* Westport, CT/ London, England: Greenwood Press.

Phillips, C. B. (1988, January). "Nurturing Diversity for Today's Children and Tomorrow's Leaders." *Young Children,* pp. 42–47.

Pine, G. J., and Hilliard, A. G. (1990, April). "Rx for Racism: Imperatives for America's Schools." *Phi Delta Kappan,* pp. 593–600.

Pollard, D. S. (1989, October). "The Resurgence of Racism. Reducing the Impact of Racism on Students." *Educational Leadership,* pp. 73–75.

Ramsey, P. G. (1982, January). "Multicultural Education in Early Childhood." *Young Children* 37(2):13–24.

Raywid, M. A. (1987). "Making School Work for the New Majority." *Journal of Negro Education* 56(2):221–28.

Rose, T. L. (1981). "The Corporal Punishment Cycle: A Behavioral Analysis of the Maintenance of Corporal Punishment in the Schools." *Education and Treatment of Children* 4(2):157–69.

Rose, T. L. (1983). "Current Uses of Corporal Punishment in American Public Schools." *Journal of Educational Psychology.*

Rumberger, R. W. (1983). "Dropping Out of High School: The Influence of Race, Sex, and Family Background." *American Educational Research Journal* 20(2):199–220.

Safer, D. (1986). "The Stress of Secondary School for Vulnerable Students." *Journal of Youth and Adolescence* 15(5):405–17.

Sakharov, M. (1987, May). "Children's Creative Response to Conflict." Paper presented at the Massachusetts Conference on Violence and Public Health, Boston, MA.

Schorr, L. B. (1989, winter). "Breaking the Cycle of Disadvantage." *School Safety,* pp. 4–7.

Shepard, L. A., and Smith, M. L. (1986). "Synthesis of Research on School Readiness and Kindergarten Retention." *Educational Leadership* 44(3):78.

Short, P. M., and Noblit, G. W. (1985, November). "Missing the Mark in In-School Suspension: An Explanation and Proposal." *NASSP Bulletin,* pp. 112–15.

Slavin, R. E. (1987, summer). "Ability Grouping and Its Alternatives: Must We Track?" *American Educator,* pp. 32–48.

Sleeter, C. E., and Grant C. A. (1987, November). "An Analysis of Multicultural Education in the United States." *Harvard Education Review* 57(4):421–44.

Smith, M. L., and Shepard, L. A. (1987, October). "What Doesn't Work: Explaining Policies of Retention in the Early Grades." *Phi Delta Kappan,* pp. 129–34.

Socoski, P. K. (1989, June 23). "A Call for the End of Corporal Punishment in Schools." Paper presented at the Annual Meeting of the Institute for Democracy in Education, Athens, OH. (ERIC Document Reproduction Service No. ED 310 522)

Stessman, C. W. (1985, February). "In-School Suspension—Making It a Place to Grow." *NASSP Bulletin,* pp. 86–88.

Suzuki, B. H. (1984, May). "Curriculum Transformation for Multicultural Education." *Education and Urban Society* 16(3):294–322.

Trent, W. (1990, spring). "Race and Ethnicity in the Teacher Education Curriculum." *Teachers College Record* 91(3):361–69.

Walker, E., and Madhere, S. (1987). "Multiple Retentions: Some Consequences for the Cognitive and Effective Maturation of Minority Elementary School Students." *Urban Education* 22(1):85.

Wayson, W. W. (1984, January). Prepared Statement before the House Subcommittee on Elementary, Secondary, and Vocational Education, Hearing on School Discipline, Washington, D.C.

Wayson, W. W.; DeVoss, G.; Kaesar, S.; Lasley, T.; and Pinnell, G. S. (1982). *Handbook for Developing Schools with Good Discipline.* Bloomington, IN: Phi Delta Kappan.

Wehlage, G. (1987). "At-Risk Students and the Need for High School Reform." *Education* 107:18–28.

Wehlage, G., and Rutter, R. (1986). "Dropping Out: How Much Do Schools Contribute to the Problem." *Teachers College Record* 87(3).

Wheelock, A. (1986). *The Way Out: Student Exclusion Practices in Boston Middle Schools.* Boston, MA: Massachusetts Advocacy Center.

Wilson, R., and Bishop, A. (1987). "Peer Violence Prevention Curriculum." Paper presented at the Massachusetts Conference on Violence and Public Health, Boston, MA.

CHAPTER SEVEN

Ashby, S.; Larson, R.; and Munroe, M. J. (1989, February). "Empowering Teachers: The Key to School-Based Reform." Paper presented at the Annual Meeting of the Association of Teacher Educators, St. Louis, MO. (ERIC Document Reproduction Service No. ED311 004)

Bacharach, S. M.; Bauer, S. C.; and Shedd, J. B. (1986). *The Learning Workplace: The Conditions and Resources of Teaching.* Ithaca, NY: Organizational Analysis and Practice.

Bain, H., *et al.* (1989, March). "A Study of Fifty Effective Teachers Whose Class Average Gain Scores Ranked in the Top 15 Percent of Each of Four School Types in Project STAR." Paper presented at the Annual Meeting of the American Educational Research Association. San Francisco, CA. (ERIC Document Reproduction Service No. ED 307 246)

Berlin, B. and Jenson, K. (1989, November). "Changing Teachers." *Education and Urban Society* 22(1):115–21.

Bradley, A. (1990a, September). "Even As Gaps in Data Are Fillled, Teacher-Supply Debate Lingers." *Education Week* 10(3):1–15.

Bradley, A. (1990b, June 20). "States Are Looking to Paraprofessionals as Promising Source of Minority Teachers." *Education Week* 9(39):1, 17.

Bradley, A. (1991, March 13). "Recruitment Ads Said to Uncover Teacher Source. Survey Reveals Interest among Minorities." *Education Week* 10(25):1–25.

Carnegie Forum on Education and the Economy (1986). *A Nation Prepared: Teachers for the Twenty-first Century.* New York, NY: Author.

Cheney, L. (1990). *Tyrannical Machines. A Report on Educational Practices Gone Wrong and Our Best Hopes for Setting Them Right.* Washington, D.C.: National Endowment for the Humanities.

Chicago Project on Learning and Teaching (1989). *Best Practice: Teaching and Learning in Chicago.* Chicago, IL: Author.

Conant, J. B. (1963). *The Education of American Teachers.* New York, NY: McGraw-Hill Book Co.

Corcoran, T. B.; Walker, L. J.; and White, J. L. (1988). *Working in Urban Schools.* Washington, D. C.: Institute for Educational Leadership.

Council of Great City Schools (1990, November). *Strategies for Success: Achieving the National Urban Education Goals.* Washington, D.C.: Author.

Darling-Hammond, L. (1986). "Proposal for Evaluation in the Teaching Profession." *The Elementary School Journal* 86(4):531–51.

Darling-Hammond, L. (1987). "Schools for Tomorrow's Teachers." *Teachers College Record* 88(3):354–58.

Dill, V. S. (1990, November). "Support for the 'Unsupportable.'" *Phi Delta Kappan* 72(3):198, 199.

Duffy, G., and Roehler, L. (1986, January/February). "Constraints on Teacher Change." *Journal of Teacher Education,* pp. 55–58.

Eubanks, E. E., and Parish, R. L. (1990, November). "Why Does the Status Quo Persist?" *Phi Delta Kappan* 72(3):196–97.

Feistritzer, E. (1988, May). "Point: 'A Good Ole Boy Mentality Rules Your Schools.'" *The Executive Educator,* pp. 25–37.

First, J.; Kellogg, J. B.; Willshire Carrera, J.; Lewis, A.; and Almeida, C. A. (1988). *New Voices: Immigrant Students in U.S. Public Schools.* Boston, MA: National Coalition of Advocates for Students.

Frymier, J. (1987, September). "Bureaucracy and the Neutering of Teachers." *Phi Delta Kappan,* pp. 9–14.

Giroux, H. A. (1987). "Educational Reform and the Politics of Teacher Empowerment." *New Education* 9(1 and 2):3–12.

Good, T. L. (1987, July/August). "Two Decades of Research on Teacher Expectations: Findings and Future Directions." *Journal of Teacher Education,* pp. 32–47.

Goodlad, J. I. (1984). *A Place Called School: Prospects for the Future.* New York, NY: McGraw-Hill Book Co.

Goodlad, J. I. (1990, November). "Better Teachers for Our Nation's Schools." *Phi Delta Kappan* 72(3):184–94.

Goswami, D., and Stillman, P. R. (1987). *Reclaiming the Classroom: Teacher Research as an Agency for Change.* Upper Montclair, NJ: Boynton Cook Publishers.

Graham, P. A. (1987, April). "Black Teachers: A Drastically Scarce Resource." *Phi Delta Kappan,* pp. 598–605.

Grant, C. A. (1990, September). "Desegregation, Racial Attitudes, and Intergroup Contact: A Discussion of Change." *Phi Delta Kappan* 72(1):25–32.

Grippen, P. C. (1989, February). "Using Research on Teaching Excellence to Re-model Teacher Education." Paper presented at the Annual Meeting of the Eastern Educational Research Association. Savannah, GA. (ERIC Document Reproduction Service No. ED 304 425)

Guerrero, F., *et al.* (1989, March). "A Potpourri of Staff Development Practices: What Works, What Doesn't." Paper presented at the Annual Meeting of the American Educational Research Association. San Francisco, CA. (ERIC Document Reproduction Service No. ED 311 564)

Haberman , M., and Rickards, W. H. (1990, October). "Urban Teachers Who Quit. Why They Leave and What They Do." *Urban Education* 25(3):297–303.

Harvard Education Letter (1988). "Learning from Children: Teachers Do Research." *HEL* 4(4):1–5.

Harvard Education Letter (1989, May/June). "Good Teaching: Do You Know It When You See It?" *HEL* 5(3):1–4.

Hodgkinson, H. L. (1985). *All One System: Demographics of Education, Kindergarten through Graduate School.* Washington, D.C: Institute for Educational Leadership.

Hodgkinson, H. L. (1988). "The Right Schools for the Right Kids." *Educational Leadership,* pp. 10–14.

Holmes Group, Inc. (1980). *Tomorrow's Teachers: A Report of the Holmes Group.* East Lansing, MI: Author.

Hord, S. M., and Huling-Austin, L. (1986). "Effective Curriculum Implementation: Some Promising New Insights." *The Elementary School Journal* 87(1):97–115.

Joyce, B., and Showers, B. (1982). "The Coaching of Teaching." *Educational Leadership* 40(1):4–10.

Lambert, L. (1988, May). "Staff Development Redesigned." *Phi Delta Kappan,* pp. 665–68.

Lieberman, A. (1988, May). "Teachers and Principals: Turf, Tension, and New Tasks." *Phi Delta Kappan,* pp. 648–53.

Little, J. W. (1984). "Seductive Images and Organizational Realities in Professional Development." *Teachers College Record* 86(1):86–102.

Lober, S. (1989, March). "Learning Styles and Student Diversity." *Educational Leadership,* p. 53.

McLaren, P. (1988). "Broken Dreams, False Promises, and the Decline of Public Schooling." *Journal of Education* 170(1):41–65.

McLaughlin, M. W., and Marsh, D. D. (1978). "Staff Development and School Change." *Teachers College Record* 80(1):69–94.

Madaus, G. F., and Pullin, D. (1987, September). "Teacher Certification Tests: Do They Really Measure What We Need to Know?" *Phi Delta Kappan,* pp. 31–37.

Maloy, R. W., and Jones, B. L. (1987). "Teachers, Partnerships, and School Improvement." *Journal of Research and Development in Education* 20(2):19–24.

Middle School Task Force (1988). *The Middle School Task Force Report.* New York, NY: New York City Board of Education.

Moran, S. W. (1990, November). "Schools and the Beginning Teacher." *Phi Delta Kappan* 72(3):210–13.

Neubert, G. A., and Bratton, E. C. (1987, February). "Team Coaching: Staff Development Side by Side." *Educational Leadership,* pp. 29–32.

Olsen, L. (1988). *Crossing the Schoolhouse Border: Immigrant Students and the California Public Schools.* San Francisco, CA: California Tomorrow.

Olsen, L., and Dowell, C. (1989). *Bridges. Promising Programs in the Education of Immigrant Children.* San Francisco, CA: California Tomorrow.

Olsen, L., and Mullen, N. A. (1990). *Embracing Diversity: Teachers' Voices from California's Classrooms.* San Francisco, CA: California Tomorrow.

Olson, L. (1990, October). "Goodlad's Teacher Education Study Urges College 'Centers of Pedagogy.'" *Education Week* 10(8):1, 12.

Payne, C. M. (1984). *Getting What We Ask for. The Ambiguity of Success and Failure in Urban Education.* Westport, CT: Greenwood Press.

Pine, G. J., and Hilliard, A. G. (1990, April). "Rx for Racism: Imperatives for America's Schools." *Phi Delta Kappan,* pp. 593–600.

Popkewitz, T. S., and Lind, K. (1989, summer). "Teacher Incentives as Reforms: Teachers' Work and the Control Mechanism in Education." *Teachers College Record* 90(4):575–94.

Porter, A. C. (1987, October). "Teacher Collaboration: New Partnerships to Attack Old Problems." *Phi Delta Kappan,* pp. 147–52.

Rosenholtz, S. J. (1985, January). "Political Myths about Education Reform: Lessons from Research on Teaching." *Phi Delta Kappan,* pp. 349–55.

Salzman, S., and Whitfield, P. T. (1989, August). "Teacher Competency Testing: Panacea or Pandora's Box?" Paper presented at the Meeting of the Northwest Association of Teacher Educators, Tacoma, WA. (ERIC Document Reproduction Service No. ED 311 028)

Sarason, S. B.; Davidson, K. S.; and Blatt, B. (1962). *The Preparation of Teachers.* New York: Wiley.

Schmidt, P. (1991, February). "Three Types of Bilingual Education Effective, E. D. Study Concludes." *Education Week* 10(22).

Schwartz, J. (1984). "Teacher Directed In-Service: A Model That Works." *Teachers College Record* 86(1):223–37.

Shepard, L. A., and Kreitzer, A. E. (1987, August/September). "The Texas Teacher Test." *Educational Researcher,* pp. 22–31.

Showers, B. (1985). "Teachers Coaching Teachers." *Educational Leadership* 42(7):438.

Sirotnik, K. A. (1988, November). "Studying the Education of Educators: Methodology." *Phi Delta Kappan,* pp. 241–46.

Sirotnik, K. A. (1990, May). "On the Eroding Foundation of Teacher Education." *Phi Delta Kappan.*

Sizer, T. R. (1987, January/February). "High School Reform and the Reform of Teacher Education." *Journal of Teacher Education,* pp. 28–34.

Smith, S. C., and Scott, J. J. (1989, September). *Encouraging School Staff to Collaborate for Instructional Effectiveness.* Eugene, OR: Oregon School Study Council. (ERIC Document Reproduction Service No. ED 310 557)

Suzuki, B. H. (1984, May). "Curriculum Transformation for Multicultural Education." *Education and Urban Society* 16(3):294–322.

Teddlie, C.; Kirby, P. C.; and Stringfield, S. (1989, May). "Effective versus Ineffective Schools: Observable Differences in the Classroom." *American Journal of Education,* pp. 221–36.

Tifft, S. (1988). "Who's Teaching Our Children?" *Time* 132(2):58–64.

Trent, W. (1990, spring). "Race and Ethnicity in the Teacher Education Curriculum." *Teachers College Record* 91(3):361–69.

Valencia, S. W., and Killion, J. P. (1989, February). *Implementing Research-Based Reading and Writing Programs Overcoming Obstacles to Teacher Change: Three Case Studies.* (ERIC Document Reproduction Service No. ED 305 595)

Weinstein, R. S.; Marshall, H. H.; Sharp, L.; and Botkin, M. (1987). "Pygmalion and the Student: Age and Classroom Differences in Children's Awareness of Teacher Expectations." *Child Development* 58:1079–93.

Wilson, S. M. (1990, November). "The Secret Garden of Teacher Education." *Phi Delta Kappan* 72(3):204–209.

Wise, A. E. (1990, November). "Policies for Reforming Teacher Education." *Phi Delta Kappan* 72(3):200-201.

Wisniewski, R. (1990, November). "Let's Get On with It." *Phi Delta Kappan* 72(3):195.

CHAPTER EIGHT

American Association of School Administrators; Council of Great City Schools; and National School Boards Association (1983). *The Maintenance Gap: Deferred Repair and Renovation in the Nation's Elementary and Secondary Schools.* Washington, DC: Council of Great City Schools.

ASPIRA (1983, June). *Racial and Ethnic High School Dropout Rates in New York City: A Summary Report.* New York: Author.

Ascher, C. (1989). *Urban School Finance: The Quest for Equal Educational Opportunity.* Washington, D.C. (ERIC Document Reproduction Service No. ED 311 147)

Ballard, B. J., and Farrar, D. (1989). "Education of the Handicapped." In A. Sumberg, ed., *Education Budget Impact Alert.* Washington, D.C.: Committee for Education Funding.

Cardenas, J. A. (1987). "Financial Resources and Educational Outcomes: Does Money Make a Difference?" *Intercultural Development Research Association Newsletter* 14(9).

Cardenas, J. A. (1988, February). "Is School Consolidation the Solution to Achieving School Finance Equity?" *Intercultural Development Research Newsletter* 15(2):1–4.

Childs, T. S., and Shakeshaft, C. (1986, fall). "A Meta-Analysis of Research on the Relationship between Educational Expenditures and Student Achievement." *Journal of Educational Finance* 12:249.

Clauset, K. H., and Gaynor, A. K. (1982, December). "A Systems' Perspective on Effective Schools." *Educational Leadership* 40:54–59.

"Clerk's Summary of Key Provisions in N.J.'s High Court Ruling in *Abbott.*" (1990, June 13). *Education Week* 9(38):19.

Colvin, R. L. (1989, January/February). "School Finance: Equity Concerns in an Age of Reforms." *Educational Resarcher* 18(1):11–15.

Congressional Budget Office (1986). *Trends in Educational Achievement.* Washington, D.C.: U.S. Government Printing Office.

Corcoran, T. B.; Walker, L. J.; and White, J. L. (1988). *Working in Urban Schools.* Washington, D. C.: Institute for Educational Leadership.

Designs for Change (1985, January). *The Bottom Line: Chicago's Failing Schools and How to Save Them.* (Chicago School Watch, Report No. 1). Chicago, IL: Designs for Change.

Dossey, J. A.; Mullis, I. S.; Lindquist, M. M.; and Chambers, D. L. (1988). *The Mathematics Report Card: Are We Measuring Up?* Princeton, NJ: Educational Testing Service.

Edmonds, R. (1981). "Making Schools Effective." *Social Policy* 17:56–59.

Edmonds, R. (1982, December). "Programs of School Improvement: An Overview." *Educational Leadership* 40:4–11.

Education Law Center (1985). *Background of Abbott vs. Burke: A Challenge to School Financing in New Jersey.* Newark, NJ: Author.

"Excerpts from Unanimous *Edgewood* Ruling." (1989, October 11). *Education Week* 9(6):20.

Gallup, A. M., and Elam, S. M. (1988). "The Twentieth Annual Gallup Poll of the Public's Attitude toward the Public Schools." *Phi Delta Kappan* 70(1):33.

Glen, B. C. (1981). *What Works? An Examination of Effective Schools for Poor Black Children.* Cambridge, MA: Harvard University, Center for Law and Education.

Goodlad, J. I.; Sirontnik, K. A.; and Overman, B. C. (1979). "An Overview of the Study of Schooling." *Phi Delta Kappan* 61:174–78.

Hanushek, E. A. (1979). "Conceptual and Empirical Issues in the Estimation of Educational Production Functions." *Journal of Resources* 14(3):351–88.

Hanushek, E. A. (1989). "The Impact of Differential Expenditures on School Performance." *Educational Researcher* 18(4):45–51.

Hess, G. A. (1986). "Educational Triage in an Urban School Setting." *Metropolitan Education* 2:39–52.

Hollifield, J. (1990, August). "State Education Finance Systems: Inequitable, Immoral, and Illegal." *R and D Preview* 8(5):2–3.

Jewell, R. W. (1990). "State Comparisons in Public School Spending." *The Administrator's Notebook* 34(2).

Kutner, M. A.; Addison, L.; Hutner, A.; and Sherman, J. D. (1984). *Federal Education Policies and Programs: Intergovernmental Issues in Their Design, Operation, and Effects.* Washington, D.C.: Department of Education.

Lally, K. (1989, February 12). "A Tale of Three Classrooms: Effect of School Spending Disparities Starkly Apparent." *The Baltimore Sun,* section A1.

Leadership for Quality Education (1990, March). *The How-to Guide to Lump Sum Budgeting.* Chicago, IL: Author.

Levin, H. M. (1989). "Mapping the Economics of Education." *Educational Researcher* 18(4):13–16.

Medina, N. J. (1989). *Grantwriter's Guide to Federal Elementary and Secondary Education Programs.* Boston, MA: Education Policy Research.

Moore, M. T., *et al.* (1983). *The Interaction of Federal and Related State Education Programs, Volume 1.* Princeton, NJ: Educational Testing Service.

Morheuser, M. J. (1984, January). "Crisis in Public Education: A New Jersey Perspective." *Association for Children of New Jersey Newsletter* 7(1):1.

Murname, R. J. (1981). "Interpreting the Evidence on School Effectiveness." *Teachers College Record* 83(1):19–35.

Natale, J. A. (1990, March). "Just Deserts: When It Comes to Equalizing School Finances, the Courts Aren't Swallowing What Society and the Schools Dish Out." *The American School Board Journal,* pp. 20–42.

National Advisory Council on the Education of Disadvantaged Children (1981). *Title I Today: A Factbook.* Washington, D.C.: U.S. Department of Education.

National Assessment of Educational Progress (1985). *The Reading Report Card: Progress Toward Excellence in Our Schools.* Princeton, NJ: Educational Testing Service.

National Coalition of Advocates for Students (1985). *Barriers to Excellence: Our Children at Risk.* Boston, MA: Author.

Newman, M. (1989, September 27). "Financial Awards for High-Performing Schools Are Gaining Favor." *Education Week* 9(4):1, 13.

Newman, M. (1990a, June). "Finance System for New Jersey Schools Is Struck Down." *Education Week* 9(38).

Newman, M. (1990b, March 7). "Texas Lawmakers Weigh Seven Plans on School Finance." *Education Week* 9(24):1, 23.

Purkey, S. C., and Smith, M. S. (1982, December). "Too Soon to Cheer? Synthesis of Research on Effective Schools." *Educational Leadership* 40:64–69.

Purkey, S. C., and Smith, M. S. (1985). "School Reform: District Policy Implications of the Effective Schools Literature." *Elementary School Journal* 85(3):353–89.

Shanker, A. (1990, June 13). "Where We Stand." *Education Week* 9(38):19.

Sirotnik, K. A., and Oakes, J. (1981). "A Contextual Appraisal System for Schools: Medicine or Madness?" *Educational Leadership* 34:164–73.

Sizemore, B. A. (1985). "Pitfalls and Promises of Effective Schools Research." *Journal of Negro Education* 54(3):269–88.

Stonehill, R. M., and Anderson, J. I. (1982). *An Evaluation of ESEA Title I.* Washington, D.C.: U.S. Department of Education.

Sumberg, A., ed. (1989). *Education Budget Impact Alert.* Washington, D.C.: Committee for Education Funding.

U.S. Department of Education (1988). *The Condition of Education.* Washington, D.C.: U.S. Government Printing Office.

Walker, R. (1990, March 7). "Blueprint for State's New School System Advances in Kentucky." *Education Week* 9(24):1, 21.

Wehlage, G. G. (1987). "At-Risk Students and the Need for High School Reform." *Education* 107:18–28.

Westbrook, K. (1989, March 9–12). "K–12 Capital Outlay: The Need for a National Investigation." Paper presented at the Annual Meeting of the American Education Finance Association, San Antonio, TX. (ERIC Document Reproduction Service No ED 305 715)

Wetzel, J. R. (1987, June). *American Youth: A Statistical Snapshot.* Washington, D.C.: William T. Grant Foundation, Commission on Youth and America's Future.

Wise, A. E., and Gendler, T. (1989). "Rich Schools, Poor Schools: The Persistence of Unequal Education." *The College Board Review* 151:12–37.

NCAS Member Organizations

The National Coalition of Advocates for Students (NCAS) is a network of experienced child advocacy organizations that work to improve access to quality education for the most vulnerable students. It is the only national coalition working full time on these issues. NCAS is a nonprofit, tax exempt, independent public interest organization.

NCAS member organizations have developed a common perspective about children and schools. They share a commitment to public education, to maximum student access to quality education, and to state and local advocacy as a constructive approach to school improvement.

NCAS Executive Committee

Chairperson
Lola Glover
Coalition for Quality Education

Second Vice Chairperson
Paul Weckstein
Center for Law and Education

Secretary
Denise De La Rosa
The National Council of La Raza

Treasurer
Janet Stotland
The Education Law Center

Immediate Past Chair
Laurie Olsen
California Tomorrow

NCAS Executive Co-Directors

Joan First
Richard Gray, Jr.

Member Organizations

Advocates for Children of New York
24–16 Bridge Plaza South
Long Island City, NY 11101

Arkansas Advocates for Children and Families
931 Donaghey Building
Little Rock, AR 72201

ASPIRA Association, Inc.
1112 16th Street, NW, Suite 340
Washington, DC 20036

Atlantic Center for Research in Education
P.O. Box 1068
Durham, NC 27702

California Tomorrow
Fort Mason Center, Building B
San Francisco, CA 94123

Center for Law and Education
236 Massachusetts Avenue, NE, Room 504
Washington, DC 20002

Children's Defense Fund
122 C Street, NW
Washington, DC 20001

Mississippi Human Services Coalition
P.O. Box 1684
Jackson, MS 39205

Citizens Education Center Northwest
310 1st Avenue, South, Suite 330
Seattle, WA 98104

Coalition for Quality Education
1702 Uptown Avenue
Toledo, OH 43620

Designs for Change
220 S. State Street, Suite 1900
Chicago, IL 60604

The Education Law Center
155 Washington Street, Room 209
Newark, NJ 07102

The Education Law Center
801 Arch Street, Suite 610
Philadelphia, PA 19107

Institute for Citizen Involvement in Education
10 Seminary Place, Room 229C
New Brunswick, NJ 08903

Intercultural Development Research Association
5835 Callaghan Road, #350
San Antonio, TX 78228

Kentucky Youth Advocates
2034 Frankfort Avenue
Louisville, KY 40206z

Massachusetts Advocacy Center
95 Berkeley Street, Suite 302
Boston, MA 02116

National Black Child Development Institute
1463 Rhode Island Avenue, NW
Washington, DC 20005

National Council of La Raza
810 1st Street, NE, 3rd Floor
Washington, DC 20002-4205

Parents Union for Public Schools
311 South Juniper Street, Suite 602
Philadelphia, PA 19107

Statewide Youth Advocacy, Inc.
410 Alexander Street
Rochester, NY 14607-1028

Student Advocacy Center
617 East University, #226
Ann Arbor, MI 48104